IEE PROFESSIONAL APPLICATIONS OF COMPUTING SERIES 6

Series Editors: Professor P. Thomas
Dr R. Macredie
J. Smith

Trusted Computing

Other volumes in this series:

Trusted Computing

Edited by
Chris Mitchell

The Institution of Electrical Engineers

Published by: The Institution of Electrical Engineers, London,
United Kingdom

©2005: The Institution of Electrical Engineers

The Institution of Electrical Engineers,
Michael Faraday House,
Six Hills Way, Stevenage,
Herts., SG1 2AY, United Kingdom

British Library Cataloguing in Publication Data

Mitchell, Chris
  Trusted computing. – (Professional applications of computing ; PC006)
  1. Computer security 2. Computer networks – Security measures
  I. Title II. Institution of Electrical Engineers
  005.8

ISBN-10: 0 86341 525 3
ISBN-13: 978 086341 525 8

Typeset in India by Newgen Imaging Systems (P) Ltd., Chennai, India
Printed in the UK by MPG Books Ltd., Bodmin, Cornwall

Preface

This book is designed to provide an introduction to trusted computing technology and its applications. It is intended to be as up to date as possible at the time of writing (early 2005). It is divided into four main parts, as follows:

1. Introduction to trusted computing,
2. Trusted computing technologies,
3. Applications of trusted computing, and
4. The future of trusted computing.

The first part consists of three chapters, each approaching trusted computing from a somewhat different perspective. In the second part, made up of Chapters 4 and 5, two technologies fundamental to the future application of trusted computing are discussed. The discussion of applications of trusted computing in Part 3 contains five chapters, each looking at a different possible application of this technology. Finally, Part 4 contains a single chapter giving thoughts on the future of this potentially revolutionary technology.

This book has been a collaborative effort by all the authors, and I would like to thank them all for the efforts they have made to help provide an integrated whole. I would also like to thank the production staff at the IEE for their help during the writing of this book – in particular I must thank Sarah Kramer for her patience and invaluable support.

Chris Mitchell
April 2005

Contents

Chapter 1

What is trusted computing?

Chris J. Mitchell

1.1 Introduction

The word trust means many different things to different people and in different contexts. Like the word security, it has become so overused that it is almost meaningless unless a definition is provided. This is certainly the case for the term 'trusted computing', and so one thing that we try to do in this chapter is define what trust means in this particular context. This theme is returned to in many of the other chapters in this book.

So what does trust mean for the purposes of this book? Well, perhaps the simplest definition would be that trusted computing refers to a computer system for which an entity has some level of assurance that (part or all of) the computer system is behaving as expected. The entity may be any one of various things, including the human user of the PC or a program running on a remote machine. The degree of coverage of this assurance, that is, whether it covers all aspects of the system or just some part, and the nature of the entity to which assurance is provided, vary depending on the system and the environment within which it is used.

Bodies such as the Trusted Computing Group standardise specific functionality to be incorporated into end systems which are known as 'trusted platforms'. Depending on how the specified functionality is implemented, such a platform is then able to provide a degree of assurance about some aspect of its operation.

Section 1.2 and Chapters 2 and 3 of this book, expand on the notion of trusted computing, and present definitions from a variety of perspectives. The definitions given are thus different although not, we believe, contradictory. The differences can be summarised in the following way:

- In this chapter we are concerned with the what of trusted computing, that is, what the technology is at a relatively high level of abstraction.

- Chapter 2 is concerned with the why of trusted computing, that is, what is the technology for, and why it is designed the way it is. This explains why the discussion in that chapter is couched in terms of computers that are optimised to safeguard the processing of private and secret data. Chapter 2 also considers how separated environments can be used to support the desired goals of protecting secret and private data.
- Chapter 3 provides the how of trusted computing, that is, it describes in some detail how trusted computing technology works. Of course, this should be read in the context of the discussion in Chapter 2, which should help provide the motivation for this design.

1.2   Computer security and trusted computing

Computer security is a long-established subject, with a considerable literature dating back to the 1960s. There are many books on the subject of secure computing (see, e.g. Gollmann [1] and Pfleeger [2]). Trusted computing, with the meaning applied in this book, is a much more recent phenomenon, and is essentially one specialised part of the larger subject of computer security. One reason that the notion has emerged is because of the changing nature of computer systems, and their increasing ubiquity.

Historically, computer security has provided a theory to understand and reason about fundamentally important security functionality within operating systems. This functionality covers a number of issues such as access control to resources within the context of multi-user operation. Most of computer security is thus concerned with security aspects of software, and pays relatively little attention to hardware security issues.

The reason for this is clear. Until the advent of the PC, computers were relatively large and expensive devices, typically with a number of users. The hardware was often kept in a physically secure location, to which access was only granted to authorised staff. Hence the main security issue was to design the file system software such that one user could not access data and resources to which he or she was not entitled, including other users' data. The security of the hardware was not something directly addressed – it was essentially a prerequisite for the correct operation of the software.

This resulted in a large and well-developed theory of computer security, covering such topics as multi-level system security and a host of models for access control systems. This theory remains very important; however, despite overlapping terminology, this is not the main subject of this book. Terminological confusion is a particular problem, not just because of the overuse of the word trust, but because the term Trusted Computing Base (TCB) has become widely used to mean something somewhat different to the recent use of trusted computing.

As defined in the Orange Book [3] (see also Gollmann [1]) the TCB is the totality of protection mechanisms within a computer system, including hardware, firmware and software. Whilst this is by no means unrelated to trusted computing, as discussed here, the meaning is definitely not the same.

Of course, it is true that physically secure subsystems have always had a place in the spectrum of secure computing, but they have mainly been used in specialist applications. For example, many secure subsystems have been designed and used in applications requiring physical security for stored keying material – examples of such systems include the IBM 4758 [4] (see also Chapter 15 of Reference 5 for a discussion of interfaces to such subsystems).

The traditional assumptions regarding the physical security of important computer systems are clearly completely inappropriate for the vast majority of PCs in use today. Most such PCs have only a single user, and no physical security is provided for the PC hardware. Short-term access to the PC can easily result in unauthorised copying of information and/or modifications to software and data; this is easy to achieve regardless of what software protections exist, simply by temporarily removing a hard disk and attaching it to a different system. That is, regardless of how 'secure' the operating system is in the traditional sense, the lack of guarantees about physical security means that the correctness of software or information stored on the PC cannot be trusted; neither can the confidentiality of any such information. The situation is made worse by the fact that modern PC operating systems and application software are enormously complex, and removing all software vulnerabilities is almost an impossible task. Hence for a combination of reasons today's systems are very vulnerable to a range of attacks.

Trusted computing as we mean it in this book is an idea which has arisen from the need to address these problems. Trusted computing refers to the addition of hardware functionality to a computer system to enable entities with which the computer interacts to have some level of trust in what the system is doing. Pearson [6] defines a related notion, namely that of a trusted platform, as follows: 'A Trusted Platform is a computing platform that has a trusted component, probably in the form of built-in hardware, which it uses to create a foundation of trust for software processes'.

The exact nature of a trusted platform is an issue that is explored in later chapters in this book (see, in particular, Chapters 2 and 3). An interesting discussion of trust and trusted computing can be found in Varadharajan's recent article [7]. A useful high-level introduction to trusted computing has also been given by Felten [8]. Finally note that an exploration of the implications of trusted computing for future distributed computing is explored in Chapter 2.

1.3 Trusted computing – a very brief history

Use of the term trusted computing as we mean it in this book is surprisingly recent, although some of the key ideas have been around for much longer. Two of the earliest papers to discuss trusted computing in the sense used here were published as recently as 2000 [9,10]. As discussed by Pearson [6], the Trusted Computing Platform Alliance (TCPA), an industry alliance created to develop and standardise trusted platform technology, was formed in October 1999. The TCPA released the first specifications in early 2001, defining a fundamental component of a trusted platform, namely a Trusted Platform Module (TPM). A TPM would typically be implemented as a chip mounted on a PC motherboard, and would provide a 'root' for all trusted functionality on the PC (in combination with the BIOS).

The work of the TCPA was inherited by its successor the TCG (Trusted Computing Group), which is continuing to develop these specifications. The TCPA specifications are described in some detail in a book published in 2002 [11] (and summarised in Reference 6). An analysis of certain privacy issues relating to the TCG has been provided by Reid *et al.* [12]. Further information about the more recent TCG specifications and their contents is provided in Chapter 3.

The TCPA and TCG have not been the only source of developments relating to trusted computing. We briefly mention some of the key developments here; again, Chapter 3 provides considerably more information.

Probably the best-known development in this area is the proposals from Microsoft, initially under the name Palladium, and subsequently under the title of Next Generation Secure Computing Base (NGSCB). NGSCB is a secure operating system architecture, which requires the underlying platform to possess certain trusted features. This includes the features that are provided by a TCG TPM, together with certain other processor enhancements. The architecture of NGSCB would appear to have changed significantly since the first announcements of Palladium, and an overview of some of the current work in this area is provided in Chapter 4. Useful background on the evolution of NGSCB is provided in References 13–15.

The AEGIS architecture dates back to a paper by Arbaugh, Farber and Smith published in 1997 [16] – a more recent paper on AEGIS was published by Suh *et al.* [17]. This architecture does not correspond precisely to the notion of trusted computing as discussed in this book, but like TCG relies on hardware security features to provide trust functions for computer systems, including a trusted boot process and measures to allow applications to securely store their data. A related scheme has been described by Itoi *et al.* [18].

The Terra system architecture [19,20] has a number of similarities to the current version of NGSCB (see Chapter 4). Terra is based on the notion of a Trusted Virtual Machine Monitor (TVMM) that partitions a computing platform into multiple, isolated virtual machines. The system requires the underlying hardware to have certain support functions, similar to those required by NGSCB. This would include functionality such as that which is provided by a TCG-conformant TPM.

Finally, we note that trusted computing has been the subject of a considerable amount of criticism. Suggestions have been made that trusted computing is both a potential threat to user privacy and a threat to the ability of the owner of a PC to use it as they see fit. It is outside the scope of this introductory chapter to describe all the issues raised; we simply note that some of the most outspoken criticism can be found in the papers of Anderson [21] and Arbaugh [22].

1.4   Trusted computing – current status

The TCG is continuing to develop both its fundamental specifications, including those for the TPM, and also profiles for use of the specifications in different types of platform. One particularly noteworthy aspect of the latest version of the TPM specifications (version 1.2), is that it incorporates a new way of providing privacy protection for trusted platforms. The previous version of the specifications relied on a trusted third party to provide pseudonyms for trusted platforms, so that a user could deploy unlinkable multiple pseudonyms to prevent linking of transactions.

This approach attracted a certain amount of criticism, since this put the third party in a powerful position. As a result, a new system has been devised which allows for trusted platform anonymity/pseudonymity without relying on a trusted third party to keep the links between pseudonyms secret. This new technique, known as Direct Anonymous Attestation (DAA), is due to Brickell, Camenisch and Chen [23,24]. A historical perspective on the development of DAA is provided in Chapter 5. It is interesting to note that Camenisch, one of the authors of DAA, has also recently proposed further ways of improving privacy for trusted platforms [25].

Meanwhile, as discussed in Chapter 4, Microsoft is continuing to develop NGCSB as an operating systems platform that will exploit the features provided by TCG hardware. As mentioned above, NGSCB (and parallel initiatives, such as Terra) rely on both a hardware 'root of trust' (i.e., something analogous to a TPM) and certain other processor enhancements. As discussed in Chapter 3, chipsets to provide all the necessary hardware functions are being developed by both Intel (as part of the LaGrande Technology initiative) and ARM.

Finally, in addition to Terra (and again as mentioned in Chapter 3), a number of efforts are under way to provide public domain trusted operating systems making use of TCG and other hardware security functionality. In particular, a number of versions of Linux providing similar trusted functionality to that provided by NGSCB are being developed. One example of such work is described by Sadeghi and Stüble [26].

1.5 Applications of trusted computing

There are many potential applications of trusted computing technology, and although we consider a number of them in this book (in Chapters 6–10), it seems likely that this is just scratching the surface. We briefly mention some of the applications proposed so far (see also Reference 11).

- Balacheff *et al.* [27] and Spalka, Cremers and Langweg [28] have independently proposed using trusted computing functionality to enhance the security of the digital signature process. These proposals build upon the TCPA specifications, but would almost certainly apply equally to more recent TCG specifications.
- Schechter *et al.* [29] discuss the use of trusted computing functionality to provide greater security for end nodes in peer-to-peer (P2P) computing networks. Independently, Kinateder and Pearson [30] have considered the use of trusted computing functionality to support a distributed reputation system designed for use in P2P. The application of trusted computing to security in P2P systems is discussed in considerably greater detail in Chapter 10 of this book.

- The use of trusted computing functionality to support single sign-on solutions was introduced in Reference 31. A more general discussion of this topic can be found in Chapter 6.
- Chen *et al.* [32] propose the use of trusted computing functionality to improve the security and privacy of a biometric user authentication process.
- Possible beneficial interactions between a trusted platform and a physically secure module, such as a smart card, are discussed by Balacheff *et al.* [33].
- The use of trusted computing functionality to support an identity management solution has been discussed by Mont *et al.* [34,35].
- Currently, the protection of broadcast video content is typically provided by proprietary 'set-top boxes'. This is clearly not a solution appropriate for future scenarios where broadcast content will be available to mobile users on a variety of personal devices. The transfer of content protection techniques to mobile platforms using trusted computing functionality is discussed in Chapter 7.
- For some time we have seen a trend towards the personalisation of Internet services. This personalisation typically requires the use of potentially sensitive personal information, raising end user privacy concerns. In Chapter 8 an approach is described to control the dissemination of such personal information using trusted computing technology.
- Finally, the possible use of secure execution environments, as supported by trusted platforms, to enable secure distribution of TTP services is considered in Chapter 9. One particular example of a TTP service which might fit well into this scenario is examined in detail, namely, that provided by a Certification Authority.

A number of other possible applications of trusted platforms are outlined in References 11, 20 and 36. Interactions with Digital Rights Management (DRM) technologies are explored by Erickson [37]. Finally, a somewhat different application angle has been considered by Marchesini *et al.* [38]. They describe experiments using a Linux operating system running on a TPM-equipped hardware platform to yield a 'virtual' secure coprocessor.

1.6   The future of trusted computing

Finally, we briefly consider the possible future of trusted computing. Some thoughts on what sorts of security functions will be enabled in future networks of trusted computing devices are provided in Chapter 2. A summary of possible future developments is given in Chapter 11.

1.7   Further information

The finalised TCG specifications are available for free download from the TCG website at:

```
http://www.trustedcomputinggroup.org
```

The latest information about Microsoft's NGSCB can be found at:

```
http://www.microsoft.com/resources/ngscb/default.mspx
```

Intel provide information on LaGrande Technology at:

```
http://www.intel.com/technology/security/
```

IBM trusted computing resources are available at the following site. This site includes downloadable Linux drivers for a TCPA-conformant TPM chip:

```
http://www.research.ibm.com/gsal/tcpa/
```

Enforcer is a Linux Security Module designed to protect the integrity of a Linux file system; it can interact with TCPA hardware to provide higher levels of assurance for software and sensitive data. For further details see:

```
http://enforcer.sourceforge.net/
```

References

1 D. Gollmann. *Computer Security*. John Wiley and Sons, Chichester, UK, 1999.
2 C. P. Pfleeger. *Security in Computing*. Prentice Hall PTR, Upper Saddle River, NJ, 2nd edn, 1997.
3 Department of Defense. *Department of Defense Trusted Computer System Evaluation Criteria*. DoD 5200.28-STD, 1985.
4 IBM. *PCI Cryptographic Processor: CCA Basic Services Reference and Guide, Release 2.41*, September 2003.
5 A. W. Dent and C. J. Mitchell. *User's Guide to Cryptography and Standards*. Artech House, Boston, MA, 2005.
6 S. Pearson. Trusted computing platforms, the next security solution. Technical Report HPL-2002-221, Hewlett-Packard Laboratories, November 2002. Available at `http://www.hpl.hp.com/techreports/`
7 V. Varadharajan. Trustworthy computing. In X. Zhou, S. Su, M. Papazoglou, M. E. Orlowska, and K. G. Jeffery, eds, *Proceedings of the 5th International Conference on Web Information Systems Engineering (WISE 2004)*, November 22–24, Brisbane, Australia, volume 3306 of Lecture Notes in Computer Science, pp. 13–16, Springer-Verlag, Berlin, 2004.
8 E. W. Felten. Understanding trusted computing: will its benefits outweigh its drawbacks? *IEEE Security & Privacy*, 1(3):60–62, 2003.
9 B. Balacheff, L. Chen, S. Pearson, G. Proudler, and D. Chan. Computing platform security in cyberspace. *Information Security Technical Report*, 5(1):54–63, 2000.
10 L. Chen, S. Pearson, G. Proudler, D. Chan, and B. Balacheff. How can you trust a computing platform? In *Proceedings of Information Security Solutions Europe (ISSE 2000)*, 2000.
11 S. Pearson, ed. *Trusted Computing Platforms: TCPA Technology in Context*. Prentice Hall PTR, New York, 2002.

12 J. Reid, J. M. Gonzalez Nieto, and E. Dawson. Privacy and trusted computing. In *Proceedings of the 14th International Workshop on Database and Expert Systems Applications (DEXA '03)*, September 1–5, Prague, Czech Republic, pp. 383–388, IEEE Computer Society, Los Alamitos, CA, 2003.

13 P. England, B. Lampson, J. Manferdelli, M. Peinado, and B. Willman. A trusted open platform. *IEEE Computer*, 36(7):55–62, 2003.

14 P. England and M. Peinado. Authenticated operation of open computing devices. In L. Batten and J. Seberry, eds, *Proceedings of the 7th Australasian Conference on Information Security and Privacy (ACISP 2002)*. Melbourne, Australia, July 3–5, *volume 2384 of Lecture Notes in Computer Science*, pp. 346–361, Springer-Verlag, Berlin, 2002.

15 M. Peinado, Y. Chen, P. England, and J. Manferdelli. NGSCB: A trusted open system. In H. Wang, J. Pieprzyk, and V. Varadharajan, eds, *Proceedings of the 9th Australasian Conference on Information Security and Privacy, (ACISP 2004)*, July 13–15, Sydney, Australia, *volume 3108 of Lecture Notes in Computer Science*, pp. 86–97, Springer-Verlag, Berlin, 2004.

16 A. W. Arbaugh, D. J. Farber, and J. M. Smith. A secure and reliable bootstrap architecture. In *Proceedings of the 1997 IEEE Symposium on Security and Privacy*, May 4–7, Oakland, CA, pp. 65–71, IEEE Computer Society Press, Los Alamitos, CA, 1997.

17 G. E. Suh, D. Clarke, B. Gassend, M. van Dijk, and S. Devadas. AEGIS: architecture for tamper-evident and tamper-resistant processing. In *Proceedings of ICS'03*, pp. 160–171, ACM Press, New York, 2003.

18 N. Itoi, W. A. Arbaugh, S. J. Pollack, and D. M. Reeves. Personal secure booting. In V. Varadharajan and Y. Mu, eds, *Proceedings of the 6th Australasian Conference on Information Security and Privacy (ACISP 2001)* July 11–13, Sydney, Australia, *volume 2119 of Lecture Notes in Computer Science*, pp. 130–144, Springer-Verlag, Berlin, 2001.

19 T. Garfinkel, B. Pfaff, J. Chow, M. Rosenblum, and D. Boneh. Terra: a virtual machine-based platform for trusted computing. In *Proceedings of SOSP'03*, October 19–22, Bolton Landing, New York, pp. 193–206, ACM Press, New York, 2003.

20 T. Garfinkel, M. Rosenblum, and D. Boneh. Flexible OS support and applications for trusted computing. In *Proceedings of HotOS IX: The 9th Workshop on Hot Topics in Operating Systems*, May 18–21, Lihue, Hawaii, pp. 145–150, USENIX Association, Berkeley, CA, 2003.

21 R. Anderson. Cryptography and competition policy – issues with 'trusted computing'. In *Proceedings of PODC'03,* July 13–16, Boston, MA, pp. 3–10. ACM Press, New York, 2003.

22 B. Arbaugh. Improving the TCPA specification. *IEEE Computer*, 35(8):77–79, 2002.

23 E. Brickell, J. Camenisch, and L. Chen. Direct anonymous attestation. Technical Report HPL-2004-93, Hewlett-Packard Laboratories, June 2004. Available at http://www.hpl.hp.com/techreports/

24 E. Brickell, J. Camenisch, and L. Chen. Direct anonymous attestation. In B. Pfitzmann and P. Liu, eds, *Proceedings of CCS'04*, pp. 132–145, ACM Press, New York, 2004.

25 J. Camenisch. Better privacy for trusted computing platforms (extended abstract). In P. Samarati, D. Gollmann, and R. Molva, eds, *Proceeding of the 9th European Symposium on Research in Computer Security (ESORICS 2004)*, Sophia Antipolis, France, September 13–15, *volume 3193 of Lecture Notes in Computer Science*, pp. 73–88, Springer-Verlag, Berlin, 2004.

26 A.-R. Sadeghi and C. Stüble. Taming 'trusted platforms' by operating system design. In K. Chae and M. Yung, eds, *Proceedings of the 4th International Workshop on Information Security Applications, (WISA 2003)*, August 25–27, Jeju Island, Korea, Revised Papers, *volume 2908 of Lecture Notes in Computer Science*, pp. 286–302, Springer-Verlag, Berlin, 2004.

27 B. Balacheff, L. Chen, D. Plaquin, and G. Proudler. A trusted process to digitally sign a document. In V. Raskin and C. F. Hempelmann, eds, *Proceedings of the 2001 New Security Paradigms Workshop*, pp. 79–86, ACM Press, New York, 2001.

28 A. Spalka, A. B. Cremers, and H. Langweg. Protecting the creation of digital signatures with trusted computing platform technology against attacks by Trojan Horse programs. In M. Dupuy and P. Paradinas, eds, *Trusted Information: The New Decade Challenge, Proceedings of the IFIP TC11 Sixteenth Annual Working Conference on Information Security (IFIP/Sec'01)*, June 11–13, Paris, France, *volume 193 of IFIP Conference Proceedings*, pp. 403–419, Kluwer Academic Publishers, Boston, 2001.

29 S. E. Schechter, R. A. Greenstadt, and M. D. Smith. Trusted computing, peer-to-peer distribution, and the economics of pirated entertainment. In *Proceedings of The Second Annual Workshop on Economics and Information Security*, May 29–30, College Park, MD, 2003.

30 M. Kinateder and S. Pearson. A privacy-enhanced peer-to-peer reputation system. In K. Bauknecht, A. Min Tjoa, and G. Quirchmayr, eds, *Proceedings of the 4th International Conference on E-Commerce and Web Technologies*, September 2–5, EC-Web, Prague, Czech Republic, *volume 2738 of Lecture Notes in Computer Science*, pp. 206–216, Springer-Verlag, Berlin, 2003.

31 A. Pashalidis and C. J. Mitchell. Single sign-on using trusted platforms. In C. Boyd and W. Mao, eds, *Proceedings of the 6th International Conference on Information Security, (ISC 2003)*, October 1–3, Bristol, UK, *volume 2851 of Lecture Notes in Computer Science*, pp. 54–68, Springer-Verlag, Berlin, 2003.

32 L. Chen, S. Pearson, and A. Vamvakas. On enhancing biometric authentication with data protection. In R. J. Howlett and L. C. Jain, eds, *Proceedings of the Fourth International Conference on Knowledge-Based Intelligent Engineering Systems and Allied Technologies*, Vol. 1, pp. 249–252, IEEE Press, Los Alamitos, CA, 2000.

33 B. Balacheff, D. Chan, L. Chen, S. Pearson, and G. Proudler. Securing intelligent adjuncts using trusted computing platform technology. In J. Domingo-Ferrer, D. Chan, and A. Watson, eds, *Proceedings of the Fourth Working Conference*

on *Smart Card Research and Advanced Applications (CARDIS)*, pp. 177–195, Kluwer Academic Publishers, 2000.

34 M. C. Mont, S. Pearson, and P. Bramhall. Towards accountable management of identity and privacy: sticky policies and enforceable tracing services. In *Proceedings of 14th International Workshop on Database and Expert Systems Applications (DEXA '03)*, September 1–5, Prague, Czech Republic, pp. 377–382, IEEE Computer Society, Los Alamitos, CA, 2003.

35 M. C. Mont, S. Pearson, and P. Bramhall. Towards accountable management of privacy and identity information. In E. Snekkenes and D. Gollmann, eds, *Proceedings of the 8th European Symposium on Research in Computer Security ESORICS 2003*, October 13–15, Gjøvik, Norway, *volume 2808 of Lecture Notes in Computer Science*, pp. 146–161, Springer-Verlag, Berlin, 2003.

36 Z. Yan and Z. Cofta. A method for trust sustainability among trusted computing platforms. In S. Katsikas, J. Lopez, and G. Pernul, eds, *Proceedings of the First International Conference on Trust and Privacy in Digital Business (TrustBus 2004)*, August 30–September 1, Zaragoza, Spain, *volume 3184 of Lecture Notes in Computer Science*, pp. 11–19, Springer-Verlag, Berlin, 2004.

37 J. S. Erickson. Fair use, DRM and trusted computing. *Communications of the ACM*, 46:34–39, 2003.

38 J. Marchesini, S. Smith, O. Wild, and R. MacDonald. Experimenting with TCPA/TCG hardware, or: how I learned to stop worrying and love the bear. Technical Report TR2003-476, Department of Computer Science, Dartmouth College, Hanover, NH, December 2003. Available at http://www.cs.dartmouth.edu/reports/

Chapter 2

Concepts of trusted computing

G. J. Proudler

2.1 Introduction

Maintaining a sufficient level of security is a challenge that businesses and society face as they increase their reliance on IT infrastructures. Increasing numbers of threats, less time to react to new threats and a vast array of computing power available to hackers to develop and launch new attacks mean that we cannot relax. Increasing client mobility and new applications pose new questions for security designers and challenge the old concept of the network perimeter, especially in the complex heterogeneous highly connected world that we live in. New approaches to the problem are needed to protect the infrastructures that are currently deployed and those needed to serve business in the future. Innovation and breakthrough thinking are needed to redesign the way that we construct and connect the different components within an IT infrastructure. Workstations, laptops, Personal Digital Assistants (PDAs), servers, appliances, storage, routers, printers and other components must all connect together seamlessly, securely and robustly and be able to change and adapt to new security issues as they arise.

> We are proud of HP's leadership in the Trusted Computing Group because we realize the immense value of bringing the industry together to build a new foundation for trustworthy computing. It's a long term play, but one that's essential for the security of IT infrastructures. Without new trusted platforms, operating systems and applications, we face the prospect of being overwhelmed by threat. That's a prospect that HP is working hard to avoid, so we treat the work of TCG as being essential to the future of computing.
>
> Tony Redmond, Vice President and CTO for HP Services, HP Security Lead.

2.2   Overview

Q: What are trusted platforms?
A: Trusted platforms are computers that are optimised to safeguard the processing of private and secret data.

In this chapter we describe (at a very high level) what trusted computing is, how it affects the architecture of a computer, what you can actually do (now – at the time of writing) with first-generation trusted platforms and what (we anticipate) you will be able to do with future generations of trusted platforms. Trusted computing is a 'work in progress', and this book will probably be out-of-date by the time you read it. Nevertheless, readers of this chapter should be able to grasp the concepts behind trusted computing, without being introduced to intricate details.

We increasingly fear for the safety of resources represented by digital data. The availability of a huge variety of software and the ability to communicate have led to the explosive growth of computer software, home computing, corporate computer networks and the Internet. Unfortunately current systems are often vulnerable to software attack launched from the network, or via simple physical access to platforms. The potential for network attack is increasing as more and more computers connect to networks and are 'always on'. The most publicised network attacks are by viruses, worms and the like. These can cause enormous disruption and expense, but the damage is nothing compared to what could be done by a sophisticated attacker intent on discovering secret and/or private information, and misusing it. Such an attacker could obtain sensitive information and misuse it or partially corrupt it before its owner was even aware that the attack had occurred. Less publicised forms of software attack concern the misuse of data by those who have legitimate access to that data. (It is often alleged that 'insider' attacks, where the holder of data behaves in bad faith, cause significant damage but are concealed for reasons of commercial confidence.) The owner of data may (of course) do anything he wishes with his data, but often the holder of data is not the owner, and has a duty not to misuse that data. An employee of a company has a duty to protect company information, for example. An employee of a hospital or financial institution has a duty to protect records and not use them for purposes other than those granted by the patient or account holder, for example.

Traditional security models in computing could be compared to that of a fortress with a heavily guarded perimeter. But, in today's world of remote work-ers, wireless users, trading partners and connected customers, we must re-examine our expectations of perimeter defences. Protecting the perimeter or point of contact with the Internet is still important, but insufficient to provide end-to-end security. An effective security strategy must be far more flexible and sophisticated – simply posting a guard at the gate to the network is not enough. Infrastructure security requirements have evolved from 'keeping the bad guys out' to 'letting the right people in'.

Trusted computing is an industry initiative intended to protect data in computer platforms from software attack – and that includes protecting servers, desktops, laptops, PDAs, mobile phones and computer peripherals. It should be normal for soft-ware to operate the way it was implemented, without fear of meddling, even when a computer is connected to a network and interacting with that network. Trusted computing tries to satisfy that expectation, and gives us ways to reason about the information security mechanisms in a computer platform, making it explicit how and why, and to what degree, we can trust a platform to process information.

Trusted computing is a means to mitigate the dangers faced by digital data. We know of no way to protect information from harm apart from providing separated environments in which to operate on data. Trusted platforms provide such environments, and enable definition of the applications that are permitted by a platform to operate on selected data in such environments. Thus a user can protect financial information by stating the applications that his or her platform will permit to operate on financial data, for example. This requires new (trusted) computer architectures. Different architectures will provide safe environments of differing strength and cost (depending on their design and construction). Data will be manipulated on its owner's computer (and potentially anyone else's computer, for that matter), without interference or hindrance, even though that computer is a communicating device, dynamically executing arbitrary programs loaded from the network.

'Trust' means different things to different people. In trusted computing we use it in the sense of behavioural reputation: something is trusted if it behaves in the expected manner for a particular purpose. We do not mean to imply that all platforms will provide strong security functions (they might not) or even that all platform behaviour will be desirable (it may not), but strong security functions and desirable behaviour are certainly the goal, and are the reasons why the computer industry is pursuing trusted computing. Trusted platforms are so-called because they provide a technological implementation and interpretation of the factors that permit us, in everyday life, to trust others. All trust is (still) derived from people (and hence organisations), and normal reasons for trust still apply – it is safe to trust something when:

- (it can be unambiguously identified)
- (it operates unhindered)
- (the user has first-hand experience of consistent, good, behaviour) OR (the user trusts someone who vouches for consistent, good, behaviour).

Trusting a person, for example, requires identification of the person, a belief that his behaviour will be normal (he does not have a gun to his head, for example), and personal experience of his normal behaviour or references describing his normal behaviour. Trusted platforms express all of these factors by technological means. They provide multiple unambiguous (real-name or anonymous or pseudonymous) identities for platforms. They provide evidence why a particular platform can claim to permit unhindered execution of selected applications on data. They provide means to report a platform's environment, so a respondent can build experience of a particular environment. They enable others to provide references for platform environments.

As mentioned previously, we do not know how to ensure that software operates as implemented, unless it is isolated from possible interference from other software processes. So trusted platforms provide collections of separated processing environments for Operating Systems (OSs), applications and applets (and other things, which we mention later). We will put sets of application(s) and data into a separated environment and let them interact. In doing so, we limit the scope of that processing, hopefully to a set of desirable effects. We must permit separated applications to communicate, of course, but we can request the platform to place restrictions on the communications between environments. A platform could, for example, permit only encrypted traffic between environments (by insisting on encrypting and decrypting all traffic) using keys provided by the applications and/or data. The platform could, for example, permit only traffic that was tagged and directed to other parts of the platform or to other separated environments in the same platform. The platform could even direct traffic flow based on policies.

Most types of computers already have separated environments, albeit of varying strength. In this sense, trusted platforms are an extension of current platforms, with an additional minimal set of isolated immutable functions that are an essential characteristic of trusted platforms, plus improved separation properties for applications in more advanced platforms. Current (first generation) trusted platforms are conventional platforms with some new immutable functions isolated in a separate chip (think 'embedded enhanced smartcard'). Some future generation trusted platforms will include other new chips that provide a curtained separated environment for a hypervisor [1], which in turn provides separated environments for OSs and applications and applets. Other future generation trusted platforms may support nothing but a Virtual Machine (VM) that provides separated environments for OSs. Future generation platforms may also exploit parallel processors, which naturally provide another dimension of isolated execution environments.

Note that virtualisation is useful in trusted computing primarily because it is the most promising method to achieve separation without extensive hardware support, not because it is a method of creating virtual hardware. The means of virtualisation, where some sort of VM hosts separated applications or where a hypervisor hosts separated OSs, is outside the current scope of the TCG specifications. Of course, ordinary virtualisation is most probably insufficient for high security separated environments – these will require (at least): improved memory management to separate kernel space and process space; restricted access via Direct Memory Access (DMA) and so on.

As well as protecting applications, trusted platforms use separated environments to protect some immutable functions (which we call 'Roots of Trust'). These Roots of Trust are functions that must operate as expected, irrespective of any other process in a platform, because without them there is no way to believe anything reported by a platform. Trusted platforms enforce and report the properties of separated processing environments, and recognise software, so secrets and private data can be manipulated by the proper software. We know of no practical way for a machine to unambiguously distinguish arbitrary software other than to measure it (create a digest of the software using a hash algorithm), and hence we associate secrets and private data with software measurements. As a result, trusted platforms must protect secrets and private data, since there is no point in associating particular data with particular applications if arbitrary applications can easily access those secrets and private data.

In the crude trusted platform architecture shown in Figure 2.1, the bottom (hardware layer) provides the means to recognise a VM or hypervisor, and the

Layer number	Layer function	Evidence for layer
2	Execution spaces	Statements by layer 1
1	VM/hypervisor	Measurements by layer 0
0	Hardware	Identity key and credential

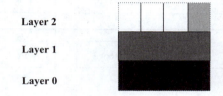

Layer 2

Layer 1

Layer 0

Figure 2.1   Layered model of a trusted platform

VM/hypervisor provides means to isolate OSs, applications and applets. We have evidence that the hardware contains Roots of Trust by virtue of an identity key and associated credential, which states that the entity with access to that key is a platform with the appropriate Roots of Trust and the means to make measurements of software. The hardware layer uses the identity key to sign a measurement of the VM/hypervisor, providing evidence of a VM/hypervisor in a platform with immutable functions. Once we know the VM/hypervisor, we can look up its quality of application–isolation–environment using some database, and decide whether those isolation properties are good enough for our purposes. Then we use the VM/hypervisor to instantiate and enforce and report statements about the isolated execution spaces in which we execute our OSs, applications and applets.

It follows that a VM/hypervisor is a critical component in (most) trusted platforms. It must be well designed, as small as possible to engender a high degree of confidence in its operation and be open to (or submitted for) independent examination by the security community.

The more general trusted platform architecture given in Figure 2.2 (where TOS denotes a Trusted Operating System) illustrates the possibility of a hierarchy of trusted platforms and hence layers of virtualisation. Each parent platform acts as the bottom layer of each child platform. Thus the application isolation environments of the bottom platform provide isolation for the first-level virtual platform (plus its immutable functions). The application isolation environments of the first-level platform provide isolation for the second-level virtual platform (plus its immutable functions), and so on. The vertical lines in the diagram indicate a VM/hypervisor separation boundary, and the horizontal lines indicate a privilege-hierarchy separation boundary (such as that enforced by processor 'rings'). In the diagram, the bottom layer contains three different sets of Roots of Trust, which are separated by some platform mechanism.

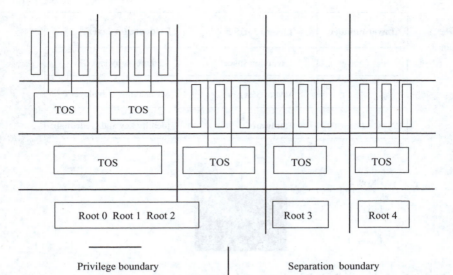

Figure 2.2   Virtual trusted platforms

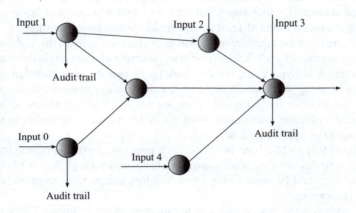

Figure 2.3   A connected graph of separated environments

Roots 0–2 contain a mechanism that separates two child VMs/Hypervisors, while Root 3 and Root 4 have only one child VM/hypervisor. The VM/hypervisors then create further separated environments by use of conventional privilege mechanisms.

Trusted platform architectures enable the composition of services in which individual elements can operate in the way they have been implemented. (There is no guarantee, of course, that they will do what their designers intended, only that they will do what their implementation permits and constrains them to do.) In the generalised model of service decomposition on trusted platforms shown in Figure 2.3, the circles represent separated execution environments. A VM or hypervisor maintains the environments and enforces properties: what is allowed in the environment, the form of the I/O traffic (encrypted, tagged, etc.), and gathers audit data about the processing that occurs in each environment. Any service can be composed using this service, giving greater confidence in the execution of that service. An arbitrary service can be decomposed into primitives, and individual primitives can be allocated to different trusted platforms depending on their separation environment properties. Some environments might be just ordinary threads and processes, and suitable to host less-sensitive primitives. Others could be curtained environments, suitable for hosting more sensitive primitives, for example. The diagram illustrates that the VM or hypervisor must enable those environments to communicate, in order to compose a service. In the diagram, individual separated environments are shown accepting inputs (controlled by the host infrastructure) and producing outputs (delivered by the host infrastructure).

Note that this composition model enables description of services that can execute on today's ordinary platforms, will execute on today's first-generation trusted platforms and will execute on next generation trusted platforms. It therefore opens the possibility for the design of services that can operate on mixed infrastructures, with different types of platform (varying hardware and/or software). This is critical, since we cannot switch to a trusted infrastructure in one go, and require a migration path from an infrastructure of today's platforms to an infrastructure of next generation trusted platforms.

2.3   Trusted Computing Group

Much of the platform technology described in this book is specified by the Trusted Computing Group (TCG) [2]. TCG technology enables platform owners to turn-on strong data protection mechanisms, so that data owners can use them to protect data. Crucially, if a platform owner has permitted a data owner to protect data but later turns off these protection mechanisms, the protected data remains protected – it simply becomes unavailable until the protection mechanisms are re-enabled.

The distinctive feature of TCG technology is that it permits a platform to execute any software, but still protects the information in that platform. Nothing in the TCG specifications stops anyone from accessing their information. Anyone who creates information can decide which applications can access their information. But anyone using applications to access someone else's information needs to convince someone that it is safe for those applications to access someone's information.

The TCG is committed to privacy. One unfortunate side effect of this is that the TCG protection mechanisms require complex controls:

- TCG protection mechanisms are powerful and could be misused, so they need to be controlled by the platform's owner;
- but different owners all want platforms to 'work out of the box', on delivery;
- but different owners want their platforms to work differently;

- so the controls must permit platforms to be in any of several mutually incompatible states, which has the consequence that the controls are complex.

At the same time, control must be easy so that trusted platforms can be used with minimal training. This conundrum has been addressed by a delegation mechanism, whereby any subset of a bewildering choice of owner controls can be delegated to other people, to trusted software and to trusted services. Owners can use the controls themselves, or (for example) choose to delegate their privilege to any combination of a person, a software wizard on CDROM, a trusted OS or a service provided by their Internet provider.

Another effect of the TCG's commitment to privacy is a complex choice of mechanisms to provide platform identities. TCG protection mechanisms need to be uniquely tagged, to permit identification, so someone knows when they are 'talking' to a genuine trusted platform. This would enable tracking and correlation of activities whenever the computer is used to access the Internet. To counteract this, the TCG provided methods to blind the unique tagging information embedded in a platform, so it can be used just to recognise a platform, and not to identify it. By that, we mean that the embedded information itself cannot be used as an identity (it cannot be used directly to distinguish information that is exported by a platform). The TCG provides two protocols to obtain actual identities, and they can be used separately or together. The protocols make different assumptions about what should be trusted to prevent correlation of identities, and hence provide identities with different properties. Some identities can be correlated, if that is what is required, and other identities cannot be correlated, if that is what is required. An organisation might want to correlate the identities in its platforms, whereas some consumers might prefer their identities to be anonymous, for example. On the other hand, a consumer might need an identity to be pseudonymous, meaning that the identity is not a real name but can be recognised again after being seen once, to create an audit trail (for example). TCG technology enables all of these options.

It cannot be over emphasised that TCG technology does not stop the execution of software, does not prevent access to data (and consequently does not prevent denial of service attacks), but does prevent access to information (the meaning of data). TCG designers do not sit at their desks with a white cat on their laps, plotting to take over the world! The TCG is committed to open computing, and TCG technology can be used on any type of computing platform and by any type of OS. TCG trusted computing technology does not require software to be sourced or signed by the TCG – there is nothing fundamental in trusted computing that would stop any software executing on a trusted platform. Any software that runs on today's platforms should run on TCG trusted platforms. The technology does prevent access to information, in the sense that while any program could execute and access any data, the program can be prevented from interpreting the data in a meaningful way. What TCG technology does is to enable the owner of data (with the permission of the platform owner) to attach a policy to encrypted data, to control what particular software is able to access the information represented by the plain text (decrypted) version of that encrypted data. Data owners decide what software meets the security requirements that are necessary to protect their information, and include that software in their policy. If software is mentioned in a policy, the platform will permit the data to be decrypted in the presence of that software (and hence the information interpreted). Otherwise it will not.

Certification in trusted platforms is simply evidence that someone vouches for the trust properties of a device (such as a Trusted Platform Module (TPM) or a Hard Disk Drive (HDD)) or the platform itself, or some firmware or software. Certification is used by a data owner when deciding what to put in a policy, and what not to put in it. Clearly, certification has to be done by an entity that has some credibility with the data owner. Otherwise the data owner has no idea whether he or she can trust a certified 'something' to be part of the platform configuration that is permitted to access his or her information. Anyone can provide certification, as long as that 'anyone' is trusted by the data owner.

The TPM specification is criticised for being confusing, and there is no doubt that it is complex. It has been said [3] that trusted computing does not have a learning curve – it has a learning cliff. And it is certainly true that it is new technology, and there is a lot of confusion and misinformation surrounding trusted computing, what it is, what it does, and what it might do. There are actually several reasons why the TCG specifications are the way they are:

- TCG specifications are partitioned and written to simplify the development of particular pieces of TCG technology. Thus the TPM specifications are an attempt to gather in one place everything that is necessary for chip vendors to develop TPMs, and other specifications are written to make it easy for software writers and so on. Even the TPM specifications are subdivided to make it more convenient for TPM developers: design principles in part I of the TPM specification; all the data structures in part II; all the commands in part III; all the test vectors in part IV.
- The TCG is writing specifications for different types of platform. So the TPM specifications are generic (for all platforms) and the platform-specific specifications customise the TPM specifications for particular platforms, by describing the way that a TPM fits into particular platform architectures.
- The specifications were developed and adapted as the technology was designed and developed. It is not the case that the original trusted platform designers had a fully developed vision of trusted platforms and brought a fully formed architecture to the organisation. The reality is that the architecture (and hence the specification) evolved over time as designers created additional and better methods of improving the protection of data in platforms.

It is probable that the TCG specifications would be easier to understand if they were completely rewritten. Unfortunately this is unlikely to happen (at least in the short term). A complete rewrite would require a huge investment to ensure that the rewritten documents had the same meaning as the original documents, and most TCG participants are already very busy creating new specifications and creating products that use those specifications. It is expected, however, that the current specifications will be revised to improve their clarity.

The TCG defined trusted computing also satisfies other constraints that are all too obvious to manufacturers, yet often invisible to customers. These additional constraints include:

- (cost) the technology must be low cost in order to be included in common forms of computing platform;
- (backwards compatibility) existing applications must still be able to execute on trusted platforms;
- (government import/export regulations) cryptographic hardware should not do bulk encryption, because some sovereign states control the export of bulk encryption hardware equipment, others control its import, and want different methods of bulk encryption;
- (maintain performance) make as much use of the main platform CPU as possible, because people will not use a service that is slow. (The main CPU typically has access to far more resources than the TPM);
- (provide incremental advantages) the full benefits of trusted computing cannot be delivered all at once because too many changes are required, so a staged evolution is necessary, yet each stage must deliver its own value or customers will not purchase it.

2.4   Trusted platforms

Trusted platforms are well suited to the processing of private and secret data.

Those familiar with computer architectures will know that computer systems need to know the *type* of data that will be processed, because different operations are done on different types of data, and operations that are possible on one type of data might be impossible on another type of data. Integers, Boolean data, strings, floating point numbers, for example, are all types of data in computer systems. Certain operations are possible on floating point numbers that are meaningless on integer numbers, and operations that can be done on strings may produce nonsense if applied to integers. In this vein, trusted platforms may be considered to introduce three new types of data, and will perform different operations on each one of these:

- Public data is data whose distribution is uncontrolled. A telephone number in a public directory is an example of public data. It is (or can be) widely known.
- Private data is data whose distribution is controlled under the terms of policies set by the owner of that data. An ex-directory telephone number or credit-card number is an example of private data.
- Secret data is data that is never disclosed. Some secrets are knowledge that is never used (such as having committed an unobserved indiscretion!), and are of no practical use as long as they remain secret. Other secrets are used without revealing the secret itself. One example of such a secret is a secret food recipe. Another example is a cryptographic key: cryptographic signature algorithms are deliberately designed to prove that one has a secret key without revealing the key itself.

The classification of some data is ambiguous – a name could be public data or could be private data, for example. And the above definition conflicts with some common usages of the terms public, private and secret. It is common to say that a group of people have a secret, for example, but we would say that they have private data, because that 'secret' has been distributed in a controlled manner. One component of an asymmetric key pair is called a public key and the other is called a private key. But the 'public key' may well be private data if its distribution is controlled, and the 'private key' is typically a secret because it is typically used without being revealed.

Trusted platform mechanisms provide privacy (in the common sense of the word) for private and secret data because trusted platforms can protect data, and there can be no privacy unless data can be protected. The mechanisms maintain privacy in spite of their associated overheads by (1) giving control of protection mechanisms to the platform's owner, and (2) providing methods that enable recognition of a trusted platform without identifying a particular trusted platform.

First-generation platforms (1) enhance existing methods of controlling access to data and (2) add a new dimension to existing methods of controlling access to data.

● The enhancement is the provision of low-cost ubiquitous hardware that provides existing cryptographic services. This enables existing applications to use conventional information security mechanisms in trusted platforms without themselves being modified.

● The new dimension is the provable enforcement of policies attached to data. Challengers can interrogate trusted platforms and select targets according to their trust properties, for safe processing of information. Data can be sent to a trusted platform only when it is in an acceptable state, and/or installed in a trusted platform such that it can be used only when the platform is in a defined state.

Normal cryptographic services use keys to encrypt data, decrypt data and sign data. In typical ordinary (non-trusted) platforms, at least one master key must be stored in the platform (often on the HDD). If you can locate the master key, you can read it and hence read all the user data. It might be argued that an OS can control access to master keys, but an OS's protection is irrelevant if a storage medium (the HDD, for example) is removed and put into another platform that does not enforce access controls. Trusted platforms improve existing typical cryptographic services by keeping and using the master key in a protected processing engine, and by protecting passwords with the same techniques used to protect user data. In a trusted platform, the master key is stored by a trusted subsystem (typically a security-hardened chip) and all user data are (directly or indirectly) encrypted by that master key. Since the master key never leaves the subsystem and all decryption operations using the master key occur within the subsystem, the master key cannot be discovered by snooping on the platform or by moving the HDD to another platform, for example.

Conventional OS access controls introduce an additional vulnerability, namely the proof-of-privilege (typically a password) that must be stored on the platform. Most platforms actually store a one-way-derivative of the proof-of-privilege, such that it is possible to use the derivative to check a presented proof-of-privilege but impossible to deduce the proof-of-privilege from the derivative. This is typically vulnerable, however, to a so-called 'dictionary attack': many users choose a password that is derived from normal language or contains just a few characters, so attackers can read the plain-text derivative of the password, copy it to another platform, and then guess likely passwords ad infinitum until they find one that corresponds to the derivative. Once the attacker has found the password, he can simply masquerade as a legitimate user. Trusted platforms prevent dictionary attacks on passwords by encrypting the proof-of-privilege along with user data, and performing all access control operations within the trusted subsystem.

Software processes on a platform cannot use passwords (or the like) to prove privilege to the host platform. (If software processes could safely store a password, they would not need to prove privilege to the host platform in order to access secrets protected by the host platform!) Trusted platforms therefore break new ground by adding a new dimension to access control: incorporating into encrypted data the platform state that must exist when the data is decrypted. To be precise, when user data is encrypted, a trusted subsystem incorporates a measurement of a future platform state into the encrypted data. When the subsystem is asked to decrypt user data, the subsystem internally decrypts the data and inspects the indication of 'future platform state'. If the indication matches the current platform state, the subsystem exports the decrypted data to the caller. Otherwise, the subsystem refuses to return the decrypted data to the caller. (Actually, when data is encrypted, a trusted platform also incorporates a measurement of current platform state into the encrypted data, and returns that measurement when and if data is successfully decrypted. This is discussed further in the next paragraph.)

The difficulty with this new dimension of access control is the need to define platform state. Software states are represented as digests computed over software that is active in the platform, but what software should be measured? Too coarse, and the state may not be sufficiently restrictive; too fine and the state may not represent all circumstances of interest. And what happens when a state changes (because of a software upgrade, for example)? Luckily it is not as bad as it seems. If the OS cannot separate an application from other applications, there is no point in knowing what application is being used, because the data is potentially available to other (rogue) applications on the platform. It follows that what really needs to be measured is the OS. The problem then simplifies to that of dealing with upgrades in the OS. If the OS is being upgraded, the existing OS needs to re-encrypt data so that the data will be revealed to just the upgraded OS. Upgraded software therefore needs to check that data purporting to come from a previous version of the software actually does come from the previous version of software. This is the reason for storing 'current platform state' along with 'future platform state' when encrypting data: when the upgraded software obtains user data from the trusted subsystem, it checks previous platform state (the 'current platform state' when the data was encrypted) to verify that it indicates the previous version of software.

Next-generation trusted platforms should be able to enforce policies. The platform's immutable functions enforce a policy on the OS (checking software measurements of the OS), and the OS enforces a policy on the applications (using a richer language, enforcing the contents, I/O and audit of isolated application environments).

Trusted platforms can (of course) in principle execute any conventional policy that can execute on an ordinary platform, because trusted platforms can execute ordinary software. The difference is that trusted platforms report and enforce hard policies, and enable enforcement of soft policies.

- Hard policies are those where verification is deterministic, and are implemented by dictating the platform state that must exist when information is revealed. An example of a hard policy is 'only if a program with digest ABC is the only software currently executing in the same software compartment as target data'.
- Soft policies are those where verification is subjective, cannot be verified by the platform, or is dependent upon some future event. They are implemented with the assistance of third parties (combinations of other trusted platforms and trusted people). An example of a soft policy is 'only if the user is the medical practitioner currently on duty who has responsibility for the medical treatment of Mr Smith'.

2.5 Limitations of trusted platforms

It is important to emphasise that trusted platforms are intended to protect against software attack, and offer a limited degree of protection against physical attack. While the degree of physical protection in trusted platforms can be expected to increase over time, the reality is that any physical protection can be broken by someone with enough skill, time and money – there is a continual 'arms race' between designers and attackers. TCG trusted platforms are in fact designed with the assumption that some platforms will be compromised. As a result, if a particular trusted platform is 'broken', only the information held by that platform is revealed to the attacker.

If a particular trusted platform is broken and impostors are created, the ease of detection of those impostors depends on the methods used to provide identities for those platforms. Some identity methods [4] provide genuine anonymity, so it is very difficult (if not impossible) to spot an impostor. Other (pseudonymous) identity methods enable correspondents to recognise a repeat contact with a platform without being able to attach a name to that platform, and impostors can be spotted simply by too-frequent use of a platform identity. (This point illustrates a fundamental conflict between anonymity and audit – if a task is important enough to warrant an audit trail, it probably should not be done by an anonymous platform.)

2.6 Using trusted computing

As a result of trusted computing, a data owner can have improved confidence that a policy is enforceable and will be enforced. The mechanisms that trusted platforms use for policy enforcement are derived from: (1) being able to measure platform state and use such measurements for access control, and (2) being able to migrate keys from one platform to another under control of a (third party) migration authority [5]. The first feature enables policies to be enforced after committal. The second feature enables enforcement of soft policies and also defers policy enforcement until the very last moment before committal. It is, of course, essential that a target platform has proven that it is a trusted platform and that acceptable policy enforcement mechanisms are executing on the target platform, in order to execute the policy. Such enforcement mechanisms might be a trusted platform subsystem, or might be trusted software executing on the platform.

To enforce a hard policy, data is encrypted and the encrypting key is stored via the trusted subsystem along with an indication of the OS and service that is intended to operate on the data. In the future, if a service wishes to operate on the data, the service must ask the trusted subsystem for the decryption key. If the current platform state is the platform state stored with the encrypted data, the subsystem releases the decryption key to the software, and the software can access the data. Crucially, note that this system enables a platform to execute any software it wishes. Software can access data only if it was intended that this particular software should access the data, but any software can execute. This property distinguishes trusted computing from previous security technologies, which required a platform to boot into a predefined state if it was necessary to release data into a predefined state.

To enforce a soft policy, data is doubly encrypted. One (inner wrapping) key is given to the destination, presumed to have certain soft properties. The second (outer wrapping) key is given to a third party with the instructions to reveal the second key to the destination if the destination has those soft properties (in the judgement of the third party). Trusted platforms achieve this by having the third party undo the outer wrapping and rewrap with a third key belonging to the destination. The destination then uses the third key followed by the first key to obtain the data. This is part of TCG's so-called 'migration' processes.

Of course, data can be protected both by hard and soft policies. By way of an example, consider a policy to protect personal medical records belonging to a Mr Smith. First, a health-service representative encrypts Smith's personal medical records using a symmetric key, and encrypts the symmetric key using a trusted platform key with the hard policy that medical-policy-enforcement software must control the key, and the soft policy that only a medical practitioner who has responsibility for the medical treatment of Fred Smith can access the data. The health-service representative then uses TCG's key-copying functions to copy it to a trusted health-service server. Later, Smith is injured and goes to hospital. The physician on duty requests Smith's medical records from the health-service's server. The trusted server verifies (by some out-of-band process) the physician's credentials and that he or she is the practitioner currently on duty, and copies Smith's trusted platform key and encrypted symmetric key to the trusted-client-platform being used by the physician. The trusted-client verifies that the client is executing medical-policy-enforcement software, and uses the trusted platform key to decrypt Smith's symmetric key. The medical-policy-enforcement software verifies that all executing software is certified as confirming to medical ethics and uses Smith's symmetric key to decrypt Smith's medical records. The physician then inspects Smith's medical records. (We note in passing that trusted platforms also provide other ways to achieve the same result.)

We assert that this ability to attach policies to data is essential in the Internet age, and hence that trusted platforms are essential to the Internet age. Otherwise, how can anyone protect their data in an open platform? In the long term, we might envisage a global distributed computing infrastructure, where only the required processes, separated in the required manner and connected in the required manner, are able to access data that is controlled by policies. This enables sensitive data to be processed and used in any node of that future computing infrastructure. In the short term, consumers need to be able to say 'only my banking application can access my bank account details', and have confidence that this will be enforced (for example).

It is primarily this ability to attach enforceable policies to data that caused hostile reactions to trusted computing, to the TCG and to the TCG's predecessor, the Trusted Computing Platform Alliance (TCPA). The other hostile reaction is to a side effect of trusted computing, whereby each platform acquires cryptographic identities that can unambiguously identify data generated by trusted platforms. When awareness of trusted computing first became widespread, it was immediately recognised as a powerful technology and conspiracy theories thrived in an information vacuum. The reality was that the technology was (and still is, in many ways) in its infancy, and that its designers understood how to employ it in organisations but not in the consumer environment. Manufacturers planned to roll-out the technology for critical information infrastructures (government, companies and the like) but did not know how to roll-out the technology for consumers. Consequently nothing was said about the introduction of the technology to ordinary consumers, and that silence was interpreted as secrecy surrounding a master plan to take control of computer platforms away from their owners.

The supposed intent of the enforceable-policy mechanisms was to prevent development of alternatives to programs belonging to dominant market players, and to prevent the easy exchange of data (particularly the exchange of copyrighted material). The supposed intent of the cryptographic identities was to enable tracking of all transactions done with trusted platforms. The reality is that enforceable-policy mechanisms are necessary to protect data in a communicating open platform, and that cryptographic identities are necessary to prove that platforms have enforceable-policy mechanisms. Enforceable-policy mechanisms enable users to protect their information on their platforms, and enable users to protect their information on other platforms, such as those provided by commercial service providers, or by the next generation of the Internet (expected to be a GRID-like environment), and even by government databases.

Should third parties be able to use enforceable-policy mechanisms to protect their (third party) data on consumer platforms? It seems reasonable to suggest that the answer is 'yes', provided the platform's owner agrees. After all, TCG has designed data protection mechanisms that are under the full control of the platform's owner (albeit that there are additional mechanisms whereby the platform's owner can delegate his privileges), and the mechanisms cannot be used without permission from the platform owner. The concern, of course, is that platform owners might not be able to participate in a given ecosystem unless they agree to provide access to an enforceable-policy mechanism. It is axiomatic, however, that if information genuinely requires protection, some mechanism or process must provide confidence that the information will be protected. That confidence can take many forms: enforceable-policy mechanisms in a trusted platform; the attributes and qualities of the platform owner; or the context in which a platform exists, for example. The degree of confidence almost certainly varies with the method, and it could well be that trusted platforms provide a more convenient and/or higher level of confidence than many existing methods. It may therefore be appropriate to insist on enforceable-policy mechanisms if specific information requires a level of confidence or convenience that only trusted platforms can provide. But a concern does arise if third parties refuse to consider other methods that can provide sufficient confidence and convenience. This would disenfranchise consumers who did not have trusted platforms.

As regards development of alternatives to popular programs, it can be argued that trusted computing can both hinder and improve matters. On the one hand, it can be argued that preventing manipulation of information except in controlled environments (and keeping information encrypted except in those environments) makes it impossible to reverse engineer data structures. On the other hand, it can be argued that these strong protection mechanisms remove the justification that secret proprietary data formats are necessary for protection of data.

It is true that trusted computing technology could be part of a Digital Rights Management system, to restrict use of copyrighted material, but that was not the impetus for trusted computing. It is also true that a trusted platform's data protection mechanisms could be used inappropriately, merely to restrict choice, in circumstances where no data protection is really required. But this is not the raison d'etre of trusted computing, just inappropriate use.

It still remains the case that data owners must be convinced that alternative programs will protect information as well as 'OEM programs'. Otherwise the policies specified by data owners will not include the alternative programs. This social issue cannot be addressed by technology alone.

Once policies can be enforced, it becomes possible to reinvent the way we use computers and build computer infrastructures. We previously introduced the concepts of secret, private and public data and said that trusted platforms are ideal for manipulating secret and private data. In fact, it may be the case that trusted platforms will blur the distinction between private and secret data to the extent that private data can be used in situations where only secret data is acceptable today. Thus in a future world where trusted computing is a ubiquitous utility, one's credit card information (private data) might be used instead of an authentication secret: the use of a credit card number according to its owner's policy in an environment that reliably enforces policy is equivalent to the user using an authorisation secret in a traditional manner. It also has the added advantage of enabling access for a service without previously registering.

Trusted platforms can also enable 'agent technology'. Agents propagate through an arbitrary computer network doing the will of their owner but, despite enthusiastic study, agent technology has had limited commercial success. This is largely because of security concerns and limits on what they can usefully achieve without access to sensitive (private) data. With ubiquitous trusted computing, however, software agents can carry private data and secret keys (symmetric keys and/or private asymmetric keys) with them, and use them to create data authorised by the agent, on behalf of the agent's owner.

Ultimately, trusted platforms may enable a global ubiquitous computing and communication infrastructure, where users neither know nor care where their data is stored or processed, because they know that use of their information is controlled by enforceable policies.

References

1 A hypervisor may be defined as 'a software layer that implements VMs having the same instruction-set architecture as the hardware upon which the hypervisor executes': See Bressoud and Schneider. Hypervisor-based fault tolerance. *ACM Transactions on Computer Systems*, 14 (1): 80–107, February 1996.
2 The TCG's specifications (and other material) are available at www.trustedcomputinggroup.org.
3 Commented by Mr Nate Bohlmann of the Atmel Corporation.
4 One TCG protocol for obtaining platform identities is a zero-knowledge proof called 'Direct Anonymous Attestation' (DAA). The technical details of DAA are described in HP's Technical Report HPL-2004-93, available from www.hpl.hp.com/techreports/2004/HPL-2004-93.html.
5 Some aspects of key migration are described in 'Migration and maintenance mechanisms' in S. Pearson ed.: *Trusted Computing Platforms – TCPA Technology in Context*. Prentice Hall, New York, 2003, ISBN 0-13-009220-7, Chapter 8.

Chapter 3

An overview of trusted computing technology

Eimear Gallery

3.1 Introduction

3.1.1 Overview

'Computer security is undeniably important, and as new vulnerabilities are discovered and exploited, the perceived need for security solutions grows' [1]. As things stand today, neither the computer user nor a communicating party can trust much about a personal computer, despite numerous attempts made to enhance security.

If computer hardware is accessible, then there are a variety of ways to modify the operating system (OS) and installed applications. Even if the physical security of the hardware is guaranteed, many means of compromising system integrity remain. Current OSs and applications are highly complex, thereby making it almost impossible to remove all vulnerabilities. In conjunction with this, users can easily run malicious software capable of damaging the system's integrity.

As the use of personal computing devices, be they PCs, PDAs, mobile phones or broadcast receivers, becomes increasingly widespread, they may be used for administering bank accounts, performing e-commerce transactions or managing personal information, all of which require the user to trust the personal device. In combination with this, there are a variety of reasons why a communicating party may need to trust a remote device; for example, the third party may be a bank where the remote device is being used for e-commerce, the third party may be a content provider where the remote device is performing digital rights management (DRM) or the remote device may be performing other security functions, such as authentication or key management, on behalf of third party.

Various approaches to improving computer security exist, for example, redesigning the OS, changing programming methodologies or altering the PC hardware [1].

More recently, however, the shift towards 'trusted computing platforms', has been identified as a potentially valuable approach.

3.1.2   Purpose and scope

This chapter provides an introduction to various trusted computing initiatives currently under development, and is composed of four main sections:

1. The concept of trusted computing is initially examined.
2. An overview of the most recent trusted computing industry specifications is presented, in conjunction with a synopsis of current industry developments.
3. Information is also presented on research and development work being conducted in this area by both the academic and open source communities.
4. Finally, a subset of the projects being completed in parallel to the trusted computing initiatives are explored. The main aim of these initiatives is also to develop a more secure and trustworthy platform via the deployment of alternative mechanisms.

More specifically, Section 3.2 of this chapter introduces the concept of trusted computing. The meaning of trust is briefly examined, in conjunction with the functionality required of a trusted computing platform.

Section 3.3 describes work completed by the Trusted Computing Platform Alliance (TCPA); this is work which has been continued and extended by the Trusted Computing Group (TCG).

In Section 3.4, Microsoft's Next Generation Secure Computing Base (NGSCB), formerly known as Palladium, is investigated. In contrast to the TCG specification set, however, little technical information on NGSCB has yet been published.

Section 3.5 explores Intel's LaGrande Technology (LT) initiative, which has led to the production of a set of enhanced hardware components designed to evolve the Intel Architecture-32-bit platform into a trusted platform (TP).

ARM's Trustzone technology is briefly examined in Section 3.6. Like Intel's LT initiative, ARM's TrustZone provides a set of hardware security extensions to the current ARM processor architecture in order to facilitate the implementation of a more trustworthy platform.

Despite the fact that the commercial initiatives outlined above have received the majority of publicity with respect to the emergence of trusted computing technologies, the open source and academic communities have also begun to investigate the world of trusted computing. Section 3.7 briefly examines PERSEUS, an example of one such open source proposal.

Sections 3.8 and 3.9 briefly cover alternative architectures, whose aim is also to enable more secure and more trustworthy platform development, via the deployment of mechanisms other than those described in the exploration of trusted computing technologies. The technologies examined include the IBM 4758, AEGIS and Executable Only Memory (XOM).

3.2   What is trusted computing?

3.2.1   Trust

Recent interest in the area of trusted computing has led to a great deal of discourse regarding the precise meaning of 'trust' in the context of trusted computing. 'Trusted computing' has become a term defined by many.

As highlighted by Anderson [2], there are subtle differences between a system which is considered trusted, and a trustworthy system. That is:

- a trusted system or component is defined as one whose failure can break the security policy [3]; and
- a trustworthy system or component is defined as one that will not fail [3].

From examination of work undertaken by a variety of trusted computing projects, it becomes apparent, however, that the term trusted computing is usually used in a sense consistent with the following definition, as given by the TCG:

- a trusted system or component is one that behaves in the expected manner for a particular purpose.

The concept of trust has been explored in greater depth by Balacheff *et al.* [4], who chose to classify TP components into two groups, those that satisfy the behavioural definition of trust and those that fulfil the social definition of trust.

1. Behavioural trust is dynamic:
   - it provides a means of knowing whether a platform can be trusted; and
   - it results from the dynamic collection of behavioural evidence.
2. Conversely, social trust is static:
   - it provides a means of knowing whether a platform should be trusted; and also
   - provides evidence as to whether a platform is capable of behaving properly.

3.2.2   Trusted computing functionality

The functionality that a TP should provide has also become an issue of debate in the trusted computing community.

The TCG requires that a TP possesses the following features as a minimum requirement [5]:

- Protected capabilities and shielded locations, encompassing all Trusted Platform Module (TPM) capabilities and data areas which must be protected from interference and prying. Protected capabilities and shielded locations must be trusted if the platform is to be trusted. Protected capabilities include functionality, such as integrity metric reporting, key management, random number generation, sealing of data, all of which are described in greater detail throughout the chapter. Shielded locations include areas in which integrity metrics and keys are stored.

- Platform attestation mechanisms, where attestation is defined as the process by which the accuracy of information may be guaranteed. The TCG describes the various forms of attestation that must be completed with respect to a TP:

  attestation by the TPM, which provides proof of data known only to the TPM;

  attestation to the platform, which provides proof that the platform can be trusted to report integrity metrics. This is performed using platform credentials;

  attestation of the platform, which provides proof of a set of the platform's integrity measurements; and

  authentication of the platform, which provides evidence of a platform's claimed identity.

- Integrity measurement, storage and reporting functionality, such that the state of the platform, or platform characteristics affecting the trustworthiness of the platform, can be recorded, stored and accurately reported when required.

The functionality provided by a TP, as defined by Microsoft [6,7], encompasses the integrity and confidentiality protection of particular commands and data locations, platform attestation and integrity measurement, storage and reporting functionality as described above. It additionally incorporates:

- process isolation, whereby an integrated isolation kernel facilitates the execution of several OSs in parallel on the same machine, and controls the access of these OSs to system resources; and
- a secure path to and from the user, through the hardware extension of user input and output devices.

Sadeghi and Stüble [8] express the opinion that if the concept of the TP is to be truly accepted, the assimilation of both consumer and software provider requirements is necessary. A TP, as defined in their paper, should include the following functionality:

- platform attestation to external entities;
- integrity protection of the OS and underlying hardware;
- confidentiality and integrity protection of application code and data during execution;
- confidentiality and integrity protection of application code and data during storage;
- a trusted path to the user such that confidentiality of user input can be assured;
- secure channels to devices and between applications to ensure the confidentiality, integrity and authenticity of communicated data; and
- reliability assurance, necessitating size restrictions on trusted critical components.

We will now move on to examine more closely the most prominent research and development initiatives in the area of trusted computing.

3.3   The TCG specification set

3.3.1   Introduction

Trusted computing platform specifications were first developed by the TCPA,[1] which was founded in January 1999. After the release of the initial draft specification in October 1999, the original alliance, which included HP, IBM, Intel and Microsoft, invited other companies to become involved. By 2002, over 150 companies had joined and the specifications had become an open industry standard [4]. In April 2003, however, it was announced that the TCPA was to be superseded by the TCG[2] who adopted the TCPA specifications with the intention of expanding and developing them.

3.3.2   The TCG

The TCG is made up of six fundamental organisational components: the board, the market working group, the best practices group, the advisory council, administration and the technical committee, who oversee the operation of technical working groups. There are currently 13 active working groups, whose primary responsibilities are described as follows by the TCG [9].

- The TPM work group is accountable for specifying how the TPM architecture, as described by the technical committee, can be implemented;
- The trusted TCG software stack work group is responsible for the provision of a set of APIs for application vendors wishing to utilise TPM functionality;
- The mobile phone work group is currently adopting the TCG concepts to mobile devices;
- The peripheral work group is examining the trust-related properties of peripherals, where the trustworthiness of a computing platform may be affected by the trustworthiness of peripheral devices connected to the platform;
- The server-specific work group is responsible for the provision of definitions, specifications, guidelines and technical requirements essential for the implementation of TCG technology in servers;
- The storage systems work group focuses on standards for security services on dedicated storage systems;
- The conformance work group is generating the necessary specifications and documents for the definition of protection profiles and other evaluation criteria;
- The PC client work group is accountable for the provision of common functionality, interfaces and a minimum set of security and privacy requirements for a PC client which uses TCG components to establish its root of trust;
- The infrastructure work group is responsible for the integration of the TCG platform-specific specifications into Internet and infrastructure technologies;
- The PDA work group is responsible for adapting the TCG concepts for the PDA;

---

[1] www.trustedcomputing.org
[2] www.trustedcomputinggroup.org

- The user authentication work group aims to comprehensively define the role of user authentication in the trusted computing infrastructure to examine how this feature impinges upon the trustworthiness of the platform;
- The hard copy work group is accountable for the definition of a minimum set of functional, interface and privacy requirements for hard copy components that use TCG components to establish their root of trust; and, finally,
- The marketing work group is responsible for creating awareness of the TCG.

3.3.3   The TP

We begin our investigation of the TCG TP with the definition of two basic terms:

- a platform, as defined by Balacheff *et al.* [4], is any computing device, for example, PC, server, mobile phone or appliance, capable of computing and communicating electronically with other platforms; while
- a TP is defined as a computing platform that has a trusted component, which is used to create a foundation of trust for software processes.

The functioning of a TP is outlined in Figure 3.1.

In order to convert a generic platform into a TP offering the three fundamental services outlined in Section 3.2.2, three rudimentary roots of trust must be embedded within it, namely, the Root of Trust for Measurement (RTM), the Root of Trust for

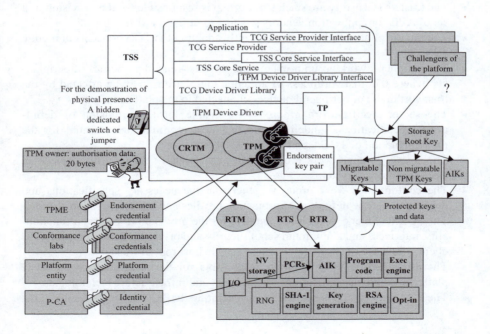

Figure 3.1   A trusted platform

Storage (RTS) and the Root of Trust for Reporting (RTR). A root of trust is defined as a component that must be trusted [5]. 'A complete set of roots of trust has at least the minimum functionality necessary to describe the platform characteristics that affect the platform's trustworthiness' [5].

The RTM is a computing engine capable of making reliable integrity measurements, and is typically implemented as the normal platform engine controlled by a particular instruction set: the Core Root of Trust for Measurement (CRTM). On a PC, the CRTM may be contained within the BIOS or BIOS boot block (BBB) and executed by the platform when it is acting as the RTM. Ideally, however, this program code, the CRTM, would be located in the TPM [4].

The RTS is a computing engine capable of maintaining an accurate summary of integrity measurements made by the RTM. The RTR is a computing engine capable of reporting data held by the RTS. The RTR and the RTS together constitute the minimum functionality that should be offered by a TPM.

In order to support RTS and RTR functionality, the TPM incorporates various functional components, such as: I/O; Non-Volatile (NV) storage; Platform Configuration Registers (PCRs), used to store integrity measurements; a Random Number Generator (RNG); a SHA-1 engine; key generation capabilities; an RSA engine; an execution engine; and an opt-in component.

Every TPM also has a basic set of keys associated with it. The most significant of these is a unique Endorsement Key (EK) pair, used only for encryption/decryption purposes. The private decryption EK is known only to the TPM and never revealed outside the TPM. An EK is embedded in a TPM in order to enable a small number of critical encrypted messages to be sent to the TPM [4].

All other TPM keys are protected in a separate key hierarchy, where only one key, the Storage Root Key (SRK), is stored permanently inside the TPM. All TPM-protected objects, be they key objects or indeed arbitrary data objects, are secured using keys that are ultimately protected by the SRK.

All TPM key objects may be described as migratable or non-migratable. Migratable keys may be generated outside the TPM and infinitely replicated by their creator, or, alternatively, they may also be generated by the TPM. Migration facilitates both the backup and the duplication of migratable keys. The migration operation, however, will allow owners to migrate and duplicate migratable keys not just to other TPMs but to anywhere. Therefore, migratable keys can only be trusted by their creator and manager, who knows the history of the key [4]. Non-migratable TPM keys, by contrast, are created inside the TPM, are locked to an individual TPM and are never duplicated. They are never available in plaintext outside of the TPM.

If the physical roots of trust, essentially the TPM and the CRTM, once integrated in a platform, are to be implicitly trusted, there is an obvious need for validation that they are working as expected. Conformance credentials may be issued for the TPM or any Trusted Building Block (TBB), where a TBB is defined as a root of trust component that does not have shielded locations or protected capabilities, for example, the RTM functions, used in the construction of a TP. These conformance credentials verify that the evaluator accepts the TPM or TBB design, and that the implementation is in accordance with established TCG guidelines. An endorsement credential is also created and signed by the entity that generated the TPM EK. It attests that the EK was properly created and embedded within a valid TPM. Finally, a platform credential attests that a platform containing a particular TPM (with its associated EK) is a genuine TP.

Although the EK is unique to a TPM, this key pair is used for encryption/decryption purposes rather than signature generation/verification. It is not considered to represent a TPM identity. In conjunction with this, overuse of this key for encryption/decryption operations may result in privacy concerns [4].

Attestation Identity Keys (AIKs) may also be associated with TPs. In this instance, a trusted party attests to the fact that a particular AIK belongs to a specified TPM, and that the AIK is essentially linked to valid endorsement, platform and conformance credentials. TPMs may have numerous AIKs, which are used for signature generation.

The TCG has also produced a TCG Software Stack (TSS) specification document, which addresses software on a TP that supports the TPM. As these additional functions are not roots of trust, it becomes the responsibility of the challenger to determine whether TSS functions can be trusted, by examining platform integrity measurements [4].

Some generic TSS components include Measurement Agents (MAs) and TP agents [4]. MAs have similar functionality to the RTM but do not constitute roots of trust. They must therefore be measured before they are executed. They are used to build up a chain of trust with respect to integrity measurements. That is, the RTM is made responsible for completing only a few simple operations and measuring the next piece of software to be executed, the RTM then stores the measurement result and passes control onto that next piece of software, which has an MA embedded in it [4]. The embedded MA then continues the measurement process.

Trusted platform agents co-ordinate the supply of integrity measurements, described below, to the challenger of the TP, and may typically be an OS component [4].

The fundamental services offered by a TP include: platform integrity measurement; integrity reporting or platform attestation and protected storage.

Measurement of a TP's integrity by the RTM and MAs results in the generation of measurement events, which are made up of two classes of data: measured values, which are representations of embedded data or program code; and measurement digests, which are hashes of these values [5]. The measurement digests are stored in PCRs on the TPM using RTR and RTS functionality. The measurement values are stored to the Stored Measurement Log (SML), which is outside the TPM but within the TSS.

The first function of the RTR is to expose shielded locations for the storage of integrity measurement digests in the above process. Its second function is to attest to the authenticity of stored digests using AIKs. This permits the TPM to sign PCR digests for challengers of the TP, so that, based on this data, a decision can be made by a challenger as to the trustworthiness of a platform for a particular purpose.

Finally, the RTS protects keys and data entrusted to the TPM. These protected key objects and arbitrary data objects are labelled TPM-protected objects. The RTS manages a small amount of volatile memory where keys are held while performing signing and decryption operations. Inactive keys may be encrypted and moved off-chip. Use of the appropriate TPM keys from the protected TPM key hierarchy, previously mentioned, in conjunction with stored integrity measurement digests allows various forms of protected storage to be facilitated. Binding allows for data to be encrypted so that it can only be decrypted by a particular TPM, whereas sealing allows for data to be bound to a set of platform configuration register values and encrypted such that it can only be decrypted by a particular TPM when the platform is in a particular state.

Many TPM capabilities require 20 bytes of authorisation data to be correctly input and verified by the TPM before their use is authorised. Certain TPM functions require knowledge of the 20 bytes of TPM owner authorisation data to be demonstrated before they can be executed. In conjunction with this, TPM-protected objects, both key and data objects, may require knowledge of 20 bytes of associated authorisation data to be demonstrated prior to their decryption and use. This authorisation data may be input into the TPM through the use of challenge–response protocols. This ensures that authorisation data need never be directly input into the TPM.

The TPM can also be controlled without the use of authorisation data. TPM commands that permit this are labelled 'physical presence' commands. They require proof of the physical presence of a user at the platform to be demonstrated before they may be used, for example, through the use of a hidden dedicated physical switch.

We will now move on to explore the fundamental entities, components, mechanisms and protocols that constitute the TCG's TP in further detail, where core reference material consists of References 4, 5, 10–14, that is, the recently published version 1.2 of the TCG specification set.

3.3.4 Entities involved

We begin with an description of the critical entities involved in the use and endorsement of a TP.

From the end-user point of view, entities include:

- the TP owner, who is in full control of the TP's TPM;
- a TP user, who may differ from the TP owner; and
- a challenger, who needs to decide whether or not a particular TP can be trusted for a particular purpose.

We also consider all entities involved in the establishment of trust in the platform:

- The Trusted Platform Module Entity (TPME) attests to the fact that the TPM is genuine by digitally signing an endorsement credential containing the public EK belonging to a particular TPM. The TPME is likely to be the TPM manufacturer.
- The Conformance Entity (CE) guarantees, through the generation of conformance credentials, that the TP design, and the design of the TPM and other TBBs, when integrated into a particular design of platform, meet the TCG specifications. The method of incorporating the TPM into the platform must also satisfy requirements outlined by the TCG.

- The Platform Entity (PE) offers assurance in the form of a platform credential that a particular platform is an instantiation of a TP design as described in conformance credentials and that the platform's TPM is indeed genuine. The PE may be the Original Equipment Manufacturer (OEM).
- The Validation Entity (VE) certifies integrity measurements, that is, measured values and measurement digests, which correspond to correctly functioning or trustworthy platform components, for example, embedded data or program code, in the form of validation certificates. The VE may be the component supplier. These validation certificates can be used by a challenger wishing to evaluate the state of a challenged TP based on signed integrity measurements provided to it, that is, measured values and measurement digests from the TPM PCRs.
- A privacy certification authority (P-CA) is responsible for the generation of identity certificates, which confirm that particular identities (asymmetric key pairs, AIKs) belong to a genuine TP.
- In addition to the P-CAs, used in version 1.1 protocols to acquire attestation identities, version 1.2 has seen the addition of a new zero-knowledge-based Direct Anonymous Attestation (DAA) protocol, constructed in order to allow TPs to authenticate themselves as a genuine TP while preserving their anonymity (see also Chapter 5). Issuers are responsible for the creation of DAA credentials for particular TPMs, via interaction between the issuer and the TPM, using a TPM unique secret that remains within the TPM. Verifiers can use these DAA credentials to decide whether or not a TPM is genuine.

Other important entities include intermediaries, which may be utilised in either the migration or maintenance procedures.

3.3.5   Trusted platform components

The Trusted Platform Subsystem (TPS) is composed of three fundamental elements:

- The RTM.
- The TPM, which is the RTS and the RTR.
- The TSS, which encompasses the software on the platform that supports the platform's TPM.

3.3.5.1   Roots of trust

The RTM, the RTS and the RTR are defined as the roots of trust for a TP, and function as follows.

3.3.5.1.1   The RTM

The RTM is a computing engine which accurately generates at least one integrity measurement event representing a software component running on the platform [4]. The measurement digest is then recorded to a Platform Configuration Register (PCR) in the TPM, and details of the measuring process, namely the measured value, are then recorded to the SML outside the TPM.

For the foreseeable future, it is envisaged that the RTM will be integrated into the normal computing engine of the platform with minimum protection [4], where the provision of additional BBB or BIOS instructions (the CRTM) causes the main platform processor to function as the RTM. Ideally, however, for the highest level of security, the CRTM would be part of the TPM [4].

3.3.5.1.2   *The RTS and RTR*
The TPM is the RTS and the RTR, where:

- The RTS is a collection of capabilities which must be trusted if storage of data inside a platform is to be trusted. The RTS provides integrity and confidentiality protection to data used by the TPM but that is stored externally. It also provides a mechanism to ensure that the release of certain data only occurs in a named environment.
- The RTR is a collection of capabilities that must be trusted if reports of integrity measurements which represent the platform state are to be trusted.

3.3.5.2   **The TCG software stack**
The TSS [14] is the software on the platform which supports the TPM. The challenger must determine whether TSS functions can be trusted by examining integrity metrics. The TSS architecture consists of a number of software modules, which provide fundamental resources to support the TPM, as defined in [14].

3.3.5.2.1   *The TPM device driver*
The TPM Device Driver (TDD) is a kernel mode component which is TPM- and OS-specific and is likely to be provided by the TPM manufacturer. It contains code that has an understanding of TPM behaviour. Because user mode executables cannot directly access kernel mode executables, the manufacturer must also provide the TCG Device Driver Library (TDDL).

The standard interface to the TDDL is called the Tddli. This facilitates the transition between user mode and kernel mode. This Tddli is defined such that all TPMs will support the same interface.

The TDD receives byte streams from the TDDL, sends them to the TPM and returns any responses.

3.3.5.2.2   *The TSS core services*
The TSS Core Services (TCS) software module resides in user mode, executes as a system service and provides threaded access to the TPM.

The interface to this module is the TCS interface (Tcsi). In most environments it resides as a system process, separate from the application and service provider processes.

- The TCS context manager provides dynamic handles that allow for efficient use of both the service provider's and the TCS's resources.
- The TCS key and credential manager stores and manages keys and credentials associated with the platform, the user or individual applications, preventing unauthorised access to them.
- The TCS event manager provides the functions to store, manage and report PCR event structures and their associated PCRs.
- The TCS parameter block generator converts the parameters passed to the TCS into the byte stream expected by the TPM.

3.3.5.2.3   The TSS service provider module

The TSS Service Provider (TSP) software module provides a common set of services for applications running on the TCG-enabled platform, and may be accessed via the TSP interface. This is an object-oriented interface that resides within the same process as the application. It provides high-level TCG functions required by applications, as well as a small number of auxiliary functions not provided by the TPM, such as hashing.

- The TSP context manager provides dynamic context handles that allow for efficient use and management of both the application's and the TSP's resources.
- The TSP cryptographic functions provide auxiliary cryptographic functionality not provided by the TPM, such as hashing and byte stream generation.

3.3.6   Properties of the TPM

The TPM is a computing engine which must resist software attack and some forms of physical attack. The TPM must be either physically or cryptographically bound to the CRTM. We have already identified the TPM as the RTS and the RTR; we next examine the functional components offered by a typical TPM in order to support RTS and RTR capabilities.

3.3.6.1   Protected capabilities and shielded locations

Protected capabilities and shielded locations are terms introduced by the TCG to illustrate the protection level required for the implementation of TPM functions and protected TPM data areas, without dictating any TP implementation details.

- Protected capabilities are those capabilities whose correct operation is necessary for the operation of the platform to be trusted; and
- Shielded locations are areas in which data is protected against interference or snooping. Only protected capabilities have access to shielded locations.

A TPM manufacturer must ensure that the required properties of protected capabilities and shielded locations are satisfied by the chosen TPM implementation.

3.3.6.2   TPM functional components

Table 3.1 examines the functional components of an archetypal TPM.

Table 3.1   TPM functional components

Functional component	Contents	Explanation
Input and output		This component manages information flow over the communication bus: • It performs encoding/decoding for communications over external and internal buses • It routes messages to the appropriate TPM components • It also enforces access control policies associated with TPM components
Key generation	Asymmetric key generation	The implementation of the asymmetric key generation function must be in accordance with IEEE P1363 [15] No requirements are made on key generation times The generate function is defined as a protected capability
	Nonce creation	All nonces must use the n next bits in the RNG
Cryptographic co-processor:	RSA engine	Used for digital signature generation and encryption RSA 512, 768, 1024 and 2048 [16] must be supported. Use of RSA 2048 is, however, recommended
	Signature Operations	The TPM must use RSA for the generation of signatures to be verified by entities outside the TPM Other algorithms may be used for signature generation, but there is no requirement that other TPM devices either accept or verify such signatures
	Symmetric encryption engine	Symmetric encryption is used to: • Encrypt authentication information • Provide confidentiality in transport sessions • Provide internal encryption of blobs stored off the TPM The TPM does not expose the symmetric operations for general message encryption

Table 3.1   Continued

Functional component	Contents	Explanation
		A Vernam one-time-pad [16] with XOR is used to protect authentication information and transport sessions The shared secret key used for the one-time-pad is constructed from the two nonces exchanged between the parties shared If the data to be protected is larger than the one-time-pad, the MGF1 function [17] is used to expand the entropy to the size of the data For internal encryption the TPM designer may, however, choose any algorithm which provides required level of protection
Execution engine		Runs program code to execute the TPM commands received through the I/O port. It ensures: ● Operations are segregated ● Shielded locations are protected
HMAC engine		The HMAC engine provides two pieces of information to the TPM: ● Proof that the request arriving is indeed authorised ● Proof that the command has not been modified in transit TPM must support HMAC calculation according to RFC 2104 [18] The key size must be 20 bytes The block size must be 64 bytes
SHA-1 engine		SHA-1 must be implemented as defined by FIPS 180-1 [19]
Power detection		This component manages TPM power states and platform power states
RNG	Entropy source	The entropy source provides as much unpredictable data as possible. This data may be either inserted into, or generated inside, the TPM
	Entropy collector	The collector collects the entropy and removes any bias
	State registers:	Hold the most recent RNG state

Table 3.1   Continued

Functional component	Contents	Explanation
	The volatile register	The volatile register is affected by all input from entropy sources and the mixing function
	The NV register	The volatile register is loaded from the NV register at start-up, and saved to the NV register at power down
	Mixing function	Takes the value from the volatile register, puts it through a mixing function to make it truly random and produces the RNG output
		Results are also recorded to the volatile state register
		Output must conform to FIPS 140-1 [20] PRNG requirements
NV memory		Will hold persistent state and identity information, for example, the EK or SRK
Volatile memory		Used for storing keys in use by the TPM (active TPM keys) for signature generation or decryption
Opt-in		The opt-in component maintains the state of persistent and volatile flags, whose values signify whether or not an entity is, or needs to be, physically present at the TP at a given instance, and how this physical presence may be demonstrated. This component also enforces the semantics associated with these flags

3.3.6.3   Platform configuration registers

A TPM must contain a minimum of sixteen 20-byte PCRs, so that integrity measurement digests collated by the RTM can be securely stored. PCRs are examined in greater detail later in this chapter.

3.3.6.4   The endorsement key

A unique 2048-bit RSA key pair, known as an EK, must exist within every genuine TPM, where the private key is used for decryption only. This EK is generated before the end customer receives the platform, and is stored in a TPM-shielded location. The EK may be generated inside the TPM, using the TPM_CreateEndorsementKeyPair command, or alternatively by an outside generator. The entity that initiates EK pair generation is also the entity that creates a credential attesting to its validity and to the validity of the TPM.

The private EK must never be exposed outside the TPM. While the public EK may be revealed outside the TPM, overuse of the public EK may result in privacy issues. These issues will also be explored in more detail later in this chapter.

3.3.7   Initialising the TPM

Before the TPM becomes fully operational, it passes through several operational states. The events or triggers which prompt the TPM to begin and complete the initialisation process and to enter a fully operational state are summarised below.

First, the TPM must be initialised. The TPM_Init command, a protected capability, is a physical method of initialising the platform and may be executed by applying power to the platform, or by physically resetting it. This physical method of initialising the TPM puts it into a state where it waits for the TPM_Startup command.

After the TPM has been initialised, limited self-tests are performed by the TPM on a minimal set of TPM commands in order to ensure that they are working properly. The TPM commands examined include:

- TPM_SHA1xxx;
- TPM_Extend, used for the extension of platform configuration (PCR) values;
- TPM_Startup; and
- TPM_ContinueSelfTest.

The TPM_Startup command then transfers the TPM from an initialisation state to a limited operational state. The type of start up state, or the mode the TPM will start up in, must also be defined when the start-up command is submitted, where the three possible modes include

- 'Clear' state, which results in the TPM values being set to a default or NV operational state;
- 'Save' state, in which the TPM recovers saved state, including PCR values, saved to NV memory following the successful execution of the TPM_SaveState command; or
- 'Deactivated' state, which informs a TPM that any further operations should not be allowed. The TPM turns itself off and can only be reset by performing another TPM_Init command.

Finally, the TPM is transformed to a fully operational state after the successful completion of all remaining self-tests. This can be accomplished in one of two ways:

- a test of the additional functionality can be explicitly called, using the TPM_SelfTestFull command; or
- the TPM_ContinueSelfTest command can be called, which causes the TPM to test all the TPM internal functions that were not tested at start-up.

The option of using the TPM_CertifySelfTest command also exists, where the TPM completes a full self-test and signs the result, thereby enabling a caller to verify that a full self-test was completed.

Although the TPM is now deemed fully operational, not all TPM functions are available until the TPM acquires an owner.

3.3.8   Enabling, activating and taking ownership of the TPM

Once the above processes have been completed, the TPM is ready for operation. Eight possible operational modes exist, based on whether the TPM is enabled or disabled, active or inactive and owned or unowned. The TPM command sets which enable/disable the TPM, enable/disable the process of taking ownership of the TPM and activate/deactivate the TPM, can be used in combination so that taking ownership of the TPM can be accomplished without the risk of malicious TPM use.

3.3.8.1   Enabling the TPM

Initially a TPM must be enabled so that the process by which a prospective owner takes ownership of the TPM can be completed. A single NV TPM flag, tpmDisabled, which is asserted in hardware, is used to represent the enablement status. This flag cannot initially be changed to 'tpmDisabled = FALSE' with normal computer controls. It may only be changed via the execution of the physical command TPM_PhysicalEnable, which may be achieved by flicking a dedicated switch on the platform, which is kept hidden from main view. The effect of physically enabling the TPM persists between boot cycles.

There are three fundamental commands associated with enabling a TPM.

- TPM_PhysicalEnable physically enables an unowned TPM.
- TPM_PhysicalDisable physically disables an owned TPM. Both of these commands may be used by anyone who can prove that they are physically present at the platform, for example, by accessing and changing a dedicated switch or jumper, either before or after the TPM has acquired an owner.
- TPM_OwnerSetDisable is used to put a TPM in either an enabled or disabled state after the TPM has acquired an owner. The input of the correct TPM owner authorisation data is required via a challenge–response protocol before this command can be executed.

Once ownership has been established, 'tpmDisabled = TRUE' causes all TPM functionality to be turned off, with the exception of PCR value tracking. In this way, the TPM always has an accurate record of the platform state. Changing the 'tpmDisabled' flag to 'FALSE' permits the TPM to act normally, even after a period where the 'tpmDisabled' flag was set to 'TRUE' in the current boot cycle.

3.3.8.2   Enabling ownership of the TPM

The 'OwnershipEnabled' flag must be set to TRUE if the process by which a prospective owner can take ownership is to succeed. In order for the TPM_TakeOwnership command to succeed, however, the TPM must also be enabled. A single NV TPM flag is used to represent the 'ownership-enabled' status. This flag must be changed via a physical presence command, but software may be used to demonstrate 'physical presence', for example, by using normal computer controls (e.g., by using the keyboard).

After the TPM has an owner, the status of this flag has no effect.

3.3.8.3   Activating the TPM

When a TPM is deactivated, the execution of commands that utilise TPM resources is not permitted. A deactivated TPM is in a similar state to a disabled TPM, with the exception that the TPM_TakeOwnership command may be executed on a deactivated TPM.

There are two activate flags, a NV TPM flag, which requires physical presence to change, and a volatile TPM flag, which is set to the same state as the NV flag at power up. There is also a TPM_SetTempDeactivated command which will set the volatile flag, 'tpmDeactivated', of an activated TPM, to true, that is, 'tpmDeactivated = TRUE', thereby deactivating the platform until it is rebooted. This command requires that physical presence at the platform be demonstrated before it may be executed, or alternatively, proof of knowledge of operator authorisation data may be demonstrated prior to the command's execution (this can only occur after the operator authorisation data has been set).

If a physical presence was demonstrated before the TPM_SetTempDeactivated command was executed, for example, through the use of a dedicated switch or jumper, then the TPM will remain deactivated until this jumper or switch is changed again. This can be done by anyone with physical access to the platform. The TPM may be activated and deactivated without destroying secrets protected by the TPM. When the TPM is deactivated, integrity measurements are still calculated by the TPM.

The activate commands are designed for use in conjunction with the 'enabling ownership' command, described above, in order to prevent rogue software taking ownership of a platform before the true owner does, and in turn taking control of all TPM functionality [4].

When the TPM is enabled, that is, 'OwnershipEnable = TRUE', and permanently deactivated, that is, the value of NV flag 'tpmDeactivated = TRUE', the genuine TPM owner can execute the taking ownership process, and then turn on the remaining TPM functions by physically activating the TPM. However, if a remote entity (software) successfully executes the takes ownership command on a deactivated TP before the legitimate owner, he will gain only restricted access to TP functionality until the platform is activated. As physical presence is required for TPM activation, the remote software cannot perform this step, and thus the potential control that rogue software may have over a hijacked TPM is limited.

3.3.8.4   Taking ownership

By default, a TPM is shipped with no owner, and taking ownership of TPM is achieved in the following manner. Once the TPM has been enabled and the 'OwnershipEnabled' flag has been set to 'TRUE':

- twenty bytes of TPM owner authorisation data, which is to be shared between the owner and the TPM, is inserted into the TPM under the protection of the TPM's public endorsement key. This data is labelled the 'owner authorisation secret' and will enable the TPM owner to gain access to TPM commands that require the owner authorisation data to be input before they are executed;

- the owner then informs the TPM which type of asymmetric key to create as the SRK;
- the authorisation secret for the SRK is sent to the TPM under the protection of the TPM's public EK;
- the TPM then generates a nonce (tpmProof), that is, a 160-bit secret value. This nonce is later associated with non-migratable TPM key objects by the TPM, so that, when this value is later found associated with a particular TPM key, the TPM knows that it generated the key. Non-migratable TPM keys are created inside the TPM, are locked to an individual TPM and are never duplicated. They are never available in plaintext outside of the TPM.

The owner's authorisation secret, the private part of the SRK, the SRK's authorisation secret and the nonce tmpProof are all kept in NV storage on the TPM.

If the TPM owner should forget his authorisation value, the old value may be removed and a new one installed. The removal of the old value does, however, invalidate all information associated with the previous value.

3.3.8.5   Clearing the TPM

In order to clear a TPM, two command sets are defined.

- The first is the owner clear command, TPM_OwnerClear, which requires the authorisation of the TPM owner in order to be executed. This command remains available for use by the TPM owner unless the disable clear function, TPM_DisableOwnerClear, is executed. Once this has been invoked, the only way to clear the TPM is via physical presence.
- The second command set is composed of a force clear command, TPM_ForceClear, which requires the assertion of physical presence. As above, this command is available unless the owner executes the disable force clear command, TPM_DisableForceClear. In this instance, however, the force clear command only remains disabled until the next start-up.

The clearing of the TPM results in the following actions:

- Invalidation of the SRK.
- Invalidation of the tmpProof.
- Invalidation of the TPM owner authorisation data.
- A reset of both volatile and NV data to manufacturer defaults.
- The PCRs become undefined.

The EK pair, however, is not affected.

3.3.9   *Platform identification and certification*

We next explore the notion of platform identity and certification.

3.3.9.1   An endorsement credential

A TPME vouches that a TPM is indeed genuine via the installation of an asymmetric key pair in the TPM, called an EK pair. The public representation of this EK pair takes the form of an endorsement credential, which includes TPM type information and the public EK, and which is signed by the TPME. The private EK is held securely in the TPM and is non-migratable.

As mentioned earlier in this chapter, the EK has the following properties:

- it is an asymmetric key pair located in a TPM's internal persistent memory;
- each TPM has exactly one such key pair;
- the private key is used for decryption only, and cannot be exported from the TPM;
- the public encryption key can be exported from the TPM for use by other parties;
- generally, it will be installed by the manufacturer before shipping.

The TPME, which embeds the EK pair in a TPM, certifies the public encryption key from the pair in an endorsement credential. This credential contains:

- a statement reflecting the fact that it is an endorsement credential;
- the public EK value;
- the TPM type and security properties; and
- a reference to the TPME.

3.3.9.2   A conformance credential

We now also examine two other credential types, the conformance credential and the platform credential. A conformance credential has the following properties:

1. It references the documents which vouch that a particular design of TPM and platform meets the TCG's specifications;
2. The TCG has two protection profiles, which are methods used to describe the security properties of equipment with respect to the common criteria [21]:
    - the first describes the TPM; and
    - the second describes the attachment of a TPM to the platform.
3. Manufacturers write security targets describing their equipment designs and how they meet particular protection profiles;
4. These security target documents are then scrutinised by conformance labs that issue a corresponding conformance credential for each security target that meets the protection profile.

3.3.9.3   A platform credential

The PE offers assurance in the form of a platform credential that a particular platform is an instantiation of a TP design, as described in conformance credentials. In order to create a platform credential, a PE examines the endorsement credential; the conformance credentials; and the platform to be certified.

Following this, the PE signs a credential containing:

- a statement that it is a platform credential;
- a reference to the EK in the TPM, for example, the identifier of endorsement certificate;

- a reference to conformance credentials;
- a platform type and security property description; and
- a reference to the PE.

3.3.9.4 Attestation identities

Privacy Certification Authorities (P-CAs) enable identities and AIKs to be assigned to TPs. A P-CA will verify all TP credentials to ensure that a particular TP is indeed genuine, and then create an attestation certificate which binds a public AIK to a TP identity label and generic TP information. The private AIK may then be used by the TPM to generate signatures.

A platform may have multiple TP identities, where a TPM identity or TP identity is synonymous with an attestation identity or AIK pair. Such an identity is:

- Statistically unique.
- Difficult to forge.
- Verifiable to a local or remote entity.

The TP or attestation identity guarantees that certain properties hold for the platform associated with the identity. That is, it proves that a platform is a given type of TP. AIKs also allow for past behaviour, linked to a particular TP identity, to be collated. Information associated with a particular AIK can only be correlated with other TP identities by the P-CA, thereby providing a level of anonymity to the platform.

3.3.9.5 AIK uses

TPM private AIKs can only be used to sign data created by the TPM, where fundamental uses include:

1. Proving data existed within a particular platform when that platform was in a particular state, the platform creates a digital signature using the private AIK over the data in question and the current PCR values, that is,

    Data || PCR values || signature (data || PCR values) || and certificates vouching for TPM identity

    are sent to the peer entity, who then validates the signature and PCR values.
2. Certifying other keys:
   - private AIKs can be used to sign statements about the properties of secondary asymmetric keys available to the TPM;
   - these secondary keys must be fixed to the platform and cannot be migrated.

3.3.9.6 AIK credentials

An identity credential is constructed in the following way.

1. A P-CA uses the endorsement credential, the platform credential and the conformance credential, to verify that the platform is a TP with a genuine TPM.
2. The P-CA then creates an identity credential containing:
   - a statement that it is an identity credential;
   - the identity allotted by the TPM owner to the public key;

- the public key to be associated with this identity;
- the TPM type and the security property description from the endorsement certificate;
- the platform type and the security property description from the platform certificate; and
- a reference to the P-CA.

The procedure used to allow the TPM owner to create a TPM identity and obtain an identity credential has two main steps: identity creation and identity activation.

- The platform sends a message to the TPM requesting that an AIK be generated under the SRK;
- The TPM signs the newly generated AIK (the private portion of which is encrypted with the SRK) and AIK control information; the TP identity name chosen by the TPM owner; and the identity of the P-CA chosen to attest to the AIK;
- A TSS command is called to assemble all data needed by the P-CA, that is, the credentials and the identity binding;
- The assembled data is then sent to the chosen P-CA, encrypted under the public key of that P-CA;
- The P-CA inspects the credentials and checks whether they have been sent by a genuine TP and whether the identity binding is consistent with the information supplied;
- The P-CA then creates an attestation credential, encrypts it with a symmetric key and encrypts the symmetric key such that it can only be decrypted by that specific TPM, verified as genuine;
- An encrypted hash of the public key from the identity binding signature is also sent;
- The TPM decrypts the hash of the public key from the identity binding signature and the symmetric key with its private EK;
- The TPM checks the decrypted hash against its identity keys (if the data was intended for the TPM, the hash will equal the hash of a public key belonging to an identity of the TPM);
- If a match is found the TPM releases the decrypted P-CA symmetric key to the host platform;
- Release of the symmetric key allows decryption of the attestation credential.

After public release of the specifications describing P-CA use, controversy arose regarding the P-CA role. It was suggested that they represented a point of weakness in the system, since, in order to assign attestation identities to TPMs, P-CAs must collate an abundance of information about the specific TPM. This information, if disclosed, could potentially compromise TPM user privacy.

In order to address this criticism and the potential threat, the TCG introduced an additional protocol in version 1.2 of the specifications, namely the DAA protocol (see also Chapter 5).

Direct anonymous attestation is based on a family of cryptographic techniques known as zero-knowledge proofs (ZKP) [13]. It allows a TPM to convince a remote 'verifier' that it is indeed valid without the disclosure of the TPM public EK, thereby removing the threat of a Trusted Third Party (TTP) collating data which may jeopardise the privacy of the TPM user. In order to complete a DAA protocol-run:

- The TPM must first generate a set of DAA credentials through interaction with a DAA 'credential issuer'. This can be done multiple times. The DAA credentials are generated in an interaction between the TPM and the issuer using a TPM-unique secret that remains within the TPM. This TPM-unique secret is used in every instance of DAA-credential creation, and is distinct from, but analogous to, the EK [13].
- The DAA credentials are then used during an interaction with a second party called the verifier. At the end of the protocol the verifier can determine if the TPM contains a valid set of DAA credentials from a particular issuer, and may therefore decide whether the TPM is genuine. The verifier will, however, have no knowledge that might allow it to distinguish one particular TPM from others that also have valid DAA credentials [13].

While DAA offers a more secure way of demonstrating that a TPM is valid, the trusted third party model using the P-CA and disclosure of the public EK described above is still valid.

3.3.10   Demonstrating privilege

As previously mentioned, in order to demonstrate the level of privilege necessary to operate the various TPM commands, two possible options exist:

- demonstration of physical presence at the platform, or, alternatively,
- authorisation may be achieved via cryptographic means.

3.3.10.1   Physical presence

There are three particular occasions where demonstration of physical presence at the platform may be necessary in order to execute particular TPM commands, usually in the case when cryptographic authorisation is unavailable. These occasions include the operation of commands that control the TPM before an owner has been installed; when the TPM owner has lost cryptographic authorisation information; or when the host platform cannot communicate with the TPM.

The 'PhysicalPresenceV' flag in volatile memory indicates whether physical presence has been confirmed, that is, whether a particular dedicated switch or jumper has been manipulated. If this flag is set to 'TRUE', then the following commands may be executed:

- TPM_ForceClear;
- TPM_PhysicalEnable;
- TPM_PhysicalDisable;
- TPM_PhysicalSetDeactivated; and
- TPM_SetOwnerInstall, which enables the take ownership process.

It is advised that TPM designers take precautions to ensure that this flag is not maskable, so that physical presence cannot be faked.

3.3.10.2   Cryptographic authorisation

As an alternative to physical presence, cryptographic authorisation mechanisms may be used to authenticate an owner to their TPM, or to authorise the release and use of TPM-protected objects. The authorisation value must be 20 bytes long, for example a hashed password or 20 bytes from a smartcard. It must always be treated as shielded data and only ever used in the authorisation process.

A variety of authorisation data is held by a TPM, including:

- Unique TPM owner authorisation data, required to be input before any TPM command which requires TPM owner authorisation may be used;
- TPM object usage authorisation data, which maybe required before an object protected by the TPM may be accessed; and
- TPM object migration authorisation data, required before a TPM key object may be migrated. Migratable objects, be they keys or data objects, may be generated outside the TPM and infinitely replicated by their creator, or, in the case of migratable keys, may also be generated by the TPM. Migration facilitates both the backup and the duplication of migratable objects on input of the correct TPM object migration authorisation data. The migration operation, however, will allow owners to migrate and duplicate migratable objects not just to TPMs but also to anywhere. Therefore, migratable keys can only be trusted by their creator and manager, who know the history of the key [4].

In order to demonstrate knowledge of the relevant authorisation data, one of two challenge–response protocols, namely the Object Independent Authorisation Protocol (OIAP) or the Object-Specific Authorisation Protocol (OSAP) may be deployed. These protocols are described below.

3.3.10.3   Proving knowledge of authorisation data: OIAP

The OIAP is the more flexible and efficient of the two authorisation protocols. OIAP is a challenge–response protocol. Once an OIAP session has been established, it can be used to prove knowledge of the relevant authorisation data associated with any TPM object.

It proceeds as follows:

1. A TPM_OIAP command is used to start an OIAP authorisation session; execution of this command requires no authorisation to be input;
2. The TPM creates a handle to track the authorisation session and a nonce, and sends these to the caller;
3. The caller then requests the use of a specific TPM command, for example TPM_example1, where TPM_example1 is a TPM command that uses the key

K1, which implies that, in order to use the command, the caller must demonstrate knowledge of the authorisation data for K1;

4. To prove knowledge of this authorisation data, the caller sends to the TPM:
   - the key handle of the key to be accessed;
   - the plain text elements from which m is generated and
   - an HMAC on message m, where the authorisation data needed for access to and use of the key, K1, is used as the HMAC key, and message m is composed of:

   SHA1 (ordinal: fixed value of TPM_example1 || first input argument || second input argument); concatenated with (the handle assigned to the authorisation session by the TPM || the nonce sent by the TPM || the nonce generated by the caller above || an indication as to whether or not the session is to be kept open)

5. If the TPM successfully verifies this, and it is indicated that the session is to be kept open:
   - a new nonce is generated by the TPM to replace the last TPM nonce;
   - the command TPM_example1 is executed;
   - the plain text elements from which $m1$ is generated are returned to the caller in conjunction with the HMAC on message, $m1$, where the authorisation data needed for access to and use of the key K1 is used as the HMAC key, and message $m1$ is composed of:

   SHA1 (the returnCode || the command ordinal representative of TPM_example1 || the output argument); in conjunction with (the handle assigned to the authorisation session || the newly generated TPM nonce || the caller nonce received || an indication as to whether the session is to be kept open or not)

6. The caller verifies that the returnCode and the output parameters are correct;
7. The session may end here or, alternatively, if it has been indicated that the session is to be kept open, the caller saves the new TPM nonce received, creates a new caller nonce, calls a new command (e.g., TPM_example1 or TPM_example2 which use key, K2) and the process continues, as described above.

3.3.10.4 The OSAP

The second protocol defined in the TCG specifications is the OSAP. This protocol allows for the establishment of a session to prove knowledge of the authorisation data for a single TPM object, and minimises the exposure of long-term authorisation values. It may be used to authorise multiple commands without additional session establishment but, as we discuss below, the TPM_OSAP handle specifies a specific object to which all authorisations are bound.

During this protocol, an ephemeral secret is generated (via the HMAC of the session nonces exchanged at the beginning of the protocol, with the target TPM object's authorisation data used as the HMAC key) by the TPM and the caller, which is used to prove knowledge of the TPM object authorisation data. This particular protocol is necessary for operations that set or reset authorisation data.

In conjunction with the terms defined above for the OIAP protocol, two extra nonces are defined for use with OIAP: the nonceOddOSAP and nonceEvenOSAP. These nonces are HMACed with the authorisation data for the protected object or the authorised command, to generate the shared secret key. OSAP proceeds as follows:

1. A TPM_OSAP command is used to start an OSAP authorisation session, and this command is sent to the TPM in conjunction with the handle associated with the object, K1, to be accessed and utilised, and an OSAP nonce;
2. The TPM generates:
    *   A handle in order to track the authorisation session;
    *   An OSAP nonce;
    *   A shared secret by HMACing the caller OSAP nonce and the TPM OSAP nonce, where the authorisation data needed for access to and use of the key, K1, is used as the HMAC key; and
    *   A TPM replay nonce.
3. The authorisation handle, the TPM OSAP nonce and the TPM replay nonce are then sent to the caller who also generates the shared secret key as above; (this can only be accomplished by the caller if it knows the authorisation data for K1);
4. The caller then requests use of a specific TPM command, TPM_example1, where;
    *   TPM_example1 is a TPM command that uses the key, K1, which implies that the caller must demonstrate knowledge of the authorisation data for key K1 in order to use the command;
5. In order to prove knowledge of this data, the caller sends to the TPM:
    *   the key handle;
    *   the plaintext from which *m* is generated and
    *   the HMAC on message *m*, where the shared secret is used as the HMAC key, and message *m* is composed of:

        SHA1 (ordinal: fixed value of TPM_example1 || first input argument || second input argument); concatenated with (handle assigned to the authorisation session by the TPM || the replay nonce sent by the TPM || the replay nonce generated by the caller above || an indication as to whether or not the session is to be kept open)

6. If this can be verified by the TPM, and it is indicated that the session is to be kept open:
    *   A new replay nonce is generated to replace the last TPM replay nonce;
    *   The command is executed;
    *   The plaintext elements from which *m*1 is generated are returned to the caller; in conjunction with the

- HMAC on message $m1$, where the shared secret is used as the HMAC key, and message $m1$ is composed of:

    SHA1 (returnCode || the command ordinal representative of TPM_example1 || output argument); concatenated with (handle assigned to the authorisation session || the newly generated TPM nonce || the caller replay nonce received || an indication as to whether or not the session is to be kept open)

7. The caller verifies the correctness of the returnCode and parameters;
8. The session may end here or, alternatively, if it has been indicated that the session is to be kept open, the caller saves the new TPM replay nonce, creates a new caller replay nonce, calls a new command (e.g., TPM_example2) which uses the same protected object key, K1, and the process continues as described above.

3.3.10.5   Changing authorisation data

Once an object's authorisation data has been set up, it can be securely changed at any stage. Three mechanisms were originally supported in order to accomplish this objective, but the third of these, the Asymmetric Authorisation Change Protocol (AACP), has been phased out in the version 1.2 specification set.

The first mechanism is the Authorisation Data Change Protocol (ADCP):

- The ADCP is used for changing authorisation data bound to TPM objects that have a parent. For example, it can be used to change the authorisation data associated with data (the child object) encrypted under a TPM key (the parent object) which in turn has authorisation data associated with it;
- In this instance the owner of the parent object co-operates to set up an OSAP session for parent object;
- The OSAP ephemeral secret that is generated, as described in the previous section, is then sent to the child object owner so that it can enter the new child authorisation data into the TPM confidentially;
- This OSAP ephemeral secret is then XORed with the newly generated authorisation data for the child object;
- However, the parent object owner can gain access to the new authorisation information for the child object by eavesdropping on TPM commands.

The second mechanism is a variant of ADCP:

- This protocol is specifically used in order to change the TPM owner's authorisation data, or the authorisation data associated with the SRK (TPM objects with no parents);
- In this instance, the TPM owner acts as the parent to the SRK, and also as its own parent;
- The new authorisation value, be it for the TPM owner or the SRK, is rendered confidential by XORing it with the ephemeral secret, generated using an OSAP session based on the TPM owner's authorisation data.

The third mechanism is the AACP:

- This is a two-step mechanism adopted so that the owner of the parent object can not eavesdrop on the insertion of the child object's authorisation data;
- In this protocol the owner of the parent object is required to authorise the authorisation data change of the child object, and then to release all knowledge of the child object authorisation data to the child object owner alone;
- The TPM generates an asymmetric key pair and returns a public key to the parent object owner with proof that the private part of the key is known only to the TPM;
- The parent object owner then presents this to the child object owner, which uses the public key to encrypt and send the new child object's authorisation data to the TPM.

In version 1.2 of the TPM specifications, use of AACP has been deprecated. It is advised that, instead of AACP, a normal TPM_ChangeAuth command (the ADCP) is used inside a transport session with confidentiality, as described later in this chapter.

3.3.10.6   Authorisation Data Insertion Protocol (ADIP)

The protocol used to insert new TPM object authorisation data during the creation of a TPM object is called the ADIP. A new TPM object must always be created under an existing parent TPM object but, in order to use the required parent object, knowledge of the associated parent object's authorisation data must be proved.

To demonstrate knowledge of the parent object's authorisation data, an OSAP authorisation session is established, and the OSAP nonce to be used for shared secret key generation is sent to the TPM. The TPM then chooses a random OSAP nonce and generates the OSAP shared secret from the TPM and caller OSAP nonces and the authorisation data associated with the parent object. A nonce to be used for freshness is also chosen. The caller then generates the shared secret using the same method used by the TPM.

- The parent object owner then passes K, the SHA-1 (of the shared secret key and the freshness nonce sent by the TPM), to the child object creator;
- The creator of the child object then chooses 20 bytes of authorisation data to be associated with the child object and protects it via XORing it with K, received above;
- All information is verified by the TPM and, if all is in order, the new authorisation data is extracted, the command used to create a new entity is executed, the new entity is created, the new authorisation data is securely associated with it and the output parameters are delivered to the caller.
- In order to protect the child object's authorisation data against eavesdropping by the parent object's owner, it was previously recommended that ADIP should be closely followed by AACP, but since this has been deprecated, the execution of ADIP followed by a normal TPM_ChangeAuth command used inside a transport session with confidentiality is advocated.

3.3.11   Integrity measuring, recording and reporting

In this section, we will examine how the integrity of a TP may be measured, recorded and reported, so that a challenger can verify that a platform is in a software state trusted by the challenger for a particular purpose. Following this, we will explore how these integrity measurements may be used in the provision of authenticated and secure boot mechanisms.

3.3.11.1   Platform configuration registers

As previously stated, measuring the TP's integrity results in the generation of measurement events. These events are made up of two classes of data: measured values, which are representations of embedded data or program code, and measurement digests, which are hashes of these values. The measurement digests are stored in PCRs on the TPM using RTR and RTS functionality. The measurement values are stored to the SML outside the TPM.

- A TPM must provide 16 or more PCRs each of which is used to record different aspects of the platform's state;
- Each storage register has a length equal to the SHA-1 digest, 20 bytes;
- Each PCR holds a summary value of all the measurement values presented to it, as this is less expensive than holding all the individual measurements in the TPM. This also enables an unbounded number of measurements to be stored;
- A PCR value is defined as the SHA-1 digest (of the existing PCR value || latest measurement digest);
- A PCR must be held in a TPM-shielded location, protected from interference and prying;
- A PCR is initialised to all zeros during initial boot, but keeps existing values during sleep; in fact a record may be kept as to whether the platform went to sleep (to avoid rogue activity during sleep);
- The fewer the PCRs, the more difficult it is to determine the meaning of the PCR. The more there are, the more costly it is to store sequences in the TPM.

Potential uses of the PCR values include the following [4]:

1. To provide an 'integrity signature', which gives evidence of the state of the TP at the time of signing;
    - In this instance, the TPM concatenates arbitrary data (usually a digest of data to be signed and a nonce to provide freshness) and the PCR values and then signs them.
2. They are also used in the protected storage mechanism so that it can be determined whether secrets should be revealed to the platform in its present state.
    - In this instance the current PCR values are compared with the intended PCR values stored with the data.
    - Access is only granted, and data unsealed, if no discrepancy is found between the two.

3.3.11.2   Data integrity register

Data Integrity registers (DIRs) are storage registers that hold digest values. Version 1.1 of the TCG specifications [38] only requires that the TPM contains one 20-byte DIR in a TPM-shielded location. A specific use of the DIR was not given. However, a DIR may, for example, be used to aid the implementation of a secure boot process [4].

If a TPM contains multiple data integrity registers holding values representing all of the expected PCR values, then the following secure boot implementation may be deployed. Every time a PCR is filled and its final value computed, its value is compared with the equivalent DIR value. If the two values match, the boot process continues; otherwise, an exception is called and the boot process halted.

Alternatively, if the TPM has access to NV memory, all expected PCR values may be held in unprotected NV memory and their summary or accumulative digest held in a single DIR. Every time a PCR is filled and its final value computed, it is checked that:

1. Each PCR value, when calculated, matches the expected value held in the NV memory; and
2. The accumulative digest of the expected table of PCR values matches the value held in the DIR.

As is clear from the above, read access to DIRs must be provided without the requirement for any authorisation process, as typically no authorisation information is available early in the boot process when the DIR value must be read.

In the version 1.2 specifications, however, use of the DIR is deprecated. The TPM must still, however, provide a general-purpose NV storage area.

3.3.11.3   Measuring integrity metrics

In a PC, where the CRTM may be integrated into part of the BIOS called the BIOS Boot Block (BBB), integrity metrics may be measured as follows for example, and the associated PCR values computed [4]:

*   The BBB starts the boot process, measures its own integrity and integrity of entire BIOS and stores the measured values to the SML, saving the measurement digests to PCR-0, for example;
*   The BBB then passes control to the BIOS which contains an MA responsible for measuring the option ROMs, storing the measured values to the SML and the measurement digests to PCR-1;
*   Control is then passed from the BIOS to the option ROMs, which carry out their normal operations and pass control back to the BIOS;
*   The BIOS then measures the OS loader, stores the measured value to the SML and the measurement digest to PCR-2;
*   Control is then passed to the OS loader, also containing an integrated MA, which carries out its normal functions and then measures the OS;
*   Finally, the OS MA generates and stores the measured values and measurement digests of OS components and any additional software loaded onto the platform.

- This MA will remain running on the OS, measuring additional software loaded onto the platform.

Details of all events measured and recorded in PCRs are detailed in the SML, stored outside the TPM.

3.3.11.4 Assessing the software state of a platform

Once the measurement digests of the platform have been generated and stored to the PCRs, and their corresponding measured values stored to the SML, a challenger may use these PCR values to assess whether the software state of a platform can be trusted for its purposes.

A challenger presents the TP with an integrity challenge or nonce, which the TPM signs in conjunction with the relevant PCR values using an AIK. The TP agent then forwards this signed blob on to the challenger, in conjunction with the relevant SML entries and TP credentials. The challenger validates the response, and makes a decision as to whether the challenged TP can be trusted for its intended purpose.

It must be noted, however, that in any transaction that requires a challenged platform to demonstrate its current state before any further interaction occurs, there will be a window between the beginning and the end of the communication in which time the platform's configuration may be changed. Therefore, the challenger must request signed integrity metrics both before and after the transaction is completed.

Alternatively, an exclusive transport session may be instigated between the challenger and the TPM, such that only requests initiated by the challenger of the TPM can be made within this session; otherwise, the session will be aborted. As a change in the software state would lead to a TPM_Extend command being called, such that the platform PCRs can be updated/extended, the exclusive session between the challenger and the TPM would be aborted. This prevents the platforms configuration being changed throughout the duration of the exclusive transport session. This mechanism is described in further detail in Section 3.3.14.

In order to simplify the verification that must be completed by the challenger in the generic protocol run described above, various methods can be used to deal with problems that may occur due to the existence of a large number of entries in the TCS event log, cumulative PCRs and validation certificate store, and the possibility that many different validation entities may be in use. A selection of these methods is described in Reference 4.

- In a constrained environment, where the acceptable software states are limited to a small number, the PCR representations that correspond to these software states may be directly certified by a VE. In this way a challenger can check the whole software state of the challenged platform in a single step;
- Instead of this, a third party could carry out intermediate validation at regular intervals. In this instance, the chosen third party would then certify that integrity information validated at a particular point complies with a particular policy. Integrity information could then be replaced by this single entry representing all of the previous certified history;

● Alternatively, a TTP may be trusted to evaluate the whole software state on behalf of a challenger.

3.3.12   Locality

In the version 1.2 specifications, the concept of locality is introduced. The possible introduction of platforms facilitating the execution of trusted processes in sheltered execution environments, as described in Sections 3.4 and 3.5 of this chapter, is increasingly being discussed. The locality concept permits trusted processes communicating with the TPM to indicate to the TPM that a particular command has originated from a trusted process, the definition of which is platform specific.

Using the locality feature, the trusted process sends the commands to be executed by the TPM in conjunction with a modifier, which indicates that the process from which the command has originated exists, for example, within a trusted system partition.

The TPM cannot, however, validate the modifier received, but the TCG specifications require that, in order to spoof a modifier to the TPM, some expertise and possibly specialist hardware should be required. The TPM is initially expected to be capable of understanding four modifiers.

3.3.12.1   Locality and platform configuration

Until now, we have presented the idea that the PCRs allow the definition of a platform configuration. With the addition of localities however, the definition of what is represented in a platform configuration register becomes somewhat more complex. Rather than allocating a specific PCR to record integrity metrics for a particular subset of platform components, PCR attributes fields may be defined at manufacturing time such that particular PCRs may be:

● reset at times other than TPM start-up, by calling processes in particular localities, such that trusted processes running in protected memory locations can be started up and shut down without resetting the entire PC; and
● extended only by processes running in particular localities.

3.3.13   Protected storage

Protected storage was designed such that an unlimited number of secrets could be protected on behalf of the platform. The protected storage feature only provides functions to access these protected secrets. The functionality to control how they are used, or to protect them from deletion, is not provided.

Protected storage provides data confidentiality via asymmetric encryption of data, where asymmetric cryptography is deployed for two reasons:

● asymmetric cryptography is already required to implement TPM identities, and therefore its reuse minimises the cost of a TPM;

- if plaintext originates outside the TPM it can be encrypted there without revealing the decryption key (ensures that the TPM does not become a bottleneck for encryption operations); and
- it facilitates the easy import/export of TCG-enabled products, as the strength of bulk encryption algorithms can be varied.

Protected storage also provides implicit integrity protection of data objects in the form of an authorisation check [4]:

- A TPM-protected object may includes encrypted authorisation data, which is compared to the authorisation data (size of SHA-1 digest: 20 bytes) submitted to the TPM when access to a protected object is requested; by this means, access is refused to entities without the proper authorisation;
- The fact that 20 bytes of authorisation data is required before a TPM-protected object can be accessed implicitly protects it from tampering; however, the associated plaintext which may accompany a protected object, which could, for example, be:

    descriptive information associated with protected data; or

    descriptive information and the public key portion associated with a protected key object;

is not protected. In order to protect this associated data, a digest of the associated plaintext is contained in the TPM-protected object.

3.3.13.1 Key hierarchy

Following this we examine the various key types that may be used in association with protected storage.

The only TPM storage key to be permanently loaded in the TPM is the SRK, a non-migratory storage key, created inside the TPM. The public portion of the storage root asymmetric key pair is used to wrap the first layer of TPM key objects, and the corresponding private key is used to unwrap the same objects when their use is required. The entire key hierarchy of a TPM will essentially be protected by the SRK.

All other keys within a TP can be divided into two fundamental categories, non-migratable keys and migratable keys:

- In the case of non-migratable asymmetric key pairs, the private key is only known to the TPM that created it. Non-migratable keys may be certified using the AIKs of the TPM, or by general-purpose signing keys.

    They are locked to a given TPM;

    They are never duplicated;

    They must be created by the TPM; and

    tpmProof, which is known only to the specific TPM, is attached to all non-migratable objects in the placeholder of migration authorisation information.

- In the case of migratable asymmetric key pairs, there are no guarantees about the origin or use of the private key.

    Migratable objects may be replicated ad infinitum by owner;

    Migratable objects can be created outside the TPM or by the TPM;

    They are protected by the TPM; and

    The owner of a migratable TPM object creates the migration authorisation information.

- The Version 1.2 TCG specifications include a third type of key, namely the Certifiable Migratable Key (CMK), which is described as a key that allows for migration but still has properties which the TPM can certify. When CMKs are created, control of their migration is appointed to a migration (selection) authority. Their migration will be examined later in the chapter.

There are many different genres of keys defined by TCG including:

- Storage keys, used to wrap or unwrap other keys in the protected storage hierarchy;
- Signature keys, used for signing operations;
- Identity keys, used by TPM-aware applications to prove that data came from a genuine TPM;
- Binding keys, used for TPM bind and unbind operations, as described below;
- Legacy keys, which are for systems that wish to use the same key for signing and encryption; and
- Change authorisation keys, which are ephemeral keys used during the process of changing authorisation information.

3.3.13.2   Sealing

Sealing is an important aspect of protected storage. The seal and unseal operations, TPM_SEAL and TPM_UNSEAL, are used in order to encrypt and decrypt arbitrary data. The tpmProof field in the sealed data structure binds the arbitrary data to be protected to an individual TPM, proving that the data was wrapped on that particular TPM. In conjunction with this, there is an optional field, the sealed info parameter, whose contents allow data to be stored in such a way that it can only be revealed by the TPM when the platform is in a particular software state.

When TPM_SEAL is executed, a TPM_STORED_DATA structure is used to represent the protected data, and is composed of:

- the TPM version;
- the size of the sealed info parameter;
- the sealed info parameter, which contains PCR information. The value of this element may be set to null if the data is not bound to specified PCRs. Alternatively it will contain:

    the selection of PCRs to which the data or key is bound;

    the digest at release; and

    the digest at creation.

Both digest at creation and digest at release consist of:

> the indication of which PCR values are active;

> the size of the PCR value field; and

> an array of PCR value structures in the order specified in the first 'active PCR' field, concatenated into a single blob.

- The size of the encrypted data, encDataSize;
- The encrypted TPM_SEALED_DATA structure, encData, which contains the following fields:

> the payload type;

> the authorisation data for the sealed object;

> the tpmProof;

> STORED_DIGEST: a digest of the TPM_STORED_DATA fields excluding the encDataSize and encData fields;

> the size of the data parameter to be sealed; and

> the data to be sealed.

3.3.13.3 Binding

In the case of binding, external data, created outside of the TPM, is encrypted under a TPM parent bind key. Binding is not a TPM function, but a bound object can only be unbound (unencrypted) by the target TPM using a TPM command. A TPM bind key must always be used to create a bound object. The bound data structure contains the following elements:

- TCPA version number;
- the payload type; and
- the bound data.

The TPM unbind function takes the resulting stored data structure, decrypts it and exports it for use by the caller. The caller, however, must initially authorise the use of the decryption key.

3.3.13.4 Wrapping

Wrapping is a TSS capability which allows an externally generated key to be encrypted under a TPM parent key. The TSS_WrapKey command allows the creation of a migratable blob for a key presented externally. The key creator can, however, prevent migration of the key by a user, by wrapping the key using a non-migratable storage key and loading random data for the migration authorisation data.

TSS_WrapKeyToPCR is a TSS command which allows for an externally generated key to be concatenated with the value of specified PCRs and encrypted under a parent key.

Finally, the TPM_CreateWrapKey command allows for the generation of a key inside the TPM, after which it is concatenated with the value of specified PCRs and encrypted under a parent key.

3.3.14   *Transport security*

The latest version 1.2 of the TCG TPM specifications introduces the concept of transport protection, not previously dealt with in earlier stipulations made for TPM manufacture. This feature facilitates the establishment of a secure channel between the TPM and secure processes, which offers confidentiality and integrity protection of commands sent to the TPM. It also provides a logging function such that all commands sent to the TPM during a transport session can be recorded.

Central to transport security is the concept of session creation, where the creation of a session allows for:

- a set of commands to be grouped;
- a log of all commands to be recorded; and
- the protection of command confidentiality and integrity using the session to be facilitated.

3.3.14.1   Session establishment

The session establishment process launches a transport session, and, depending on the attributes specified for the session, this process may lead to the creation of shared keys, and session logs.

Session establishment involves the generation by the caller of 20 bytes of transport authorisation data, for use between the caller and the TPM. This transport authorisation data has two purposes:

- It is used as input when generating an encryption key for use between the TPM and the caller to provide command confidentiality; and
- It is also used as a HMAC key when sending the TPM_ExecuteTransport command, so that the command can be authorised.

The authorisation data is generated by the caller and encrypted under a public key whose corresponding private key is available only to the TPM. The key used is pointed to in the encHandle field of the TPM_EstablishTransport command sent.

The TPM then decrypts the authorisation data and creates an internal transport structure, which contains the following fields:

- authData, is set to the authorisation data received and decrypted;
- tranPublic, consists of:

    transAttributes, where information regarding the encryption of the session, logging of the session and whether the session is to be exclusive is set;

    algoId, which refers to the properties that the symmetric key to be generated will have; and

    encScheme, which refers to the encryption scheme to be used;

- transHandle, to which a value is assigned;
- transEven, is set to the value of the nonce generated, transNonce;
- transDigest, is initially set to NULL but is then used to reflect all logged transport events.

If transport encryption is required, the TPM must validate that the requested key algorithm and encryption scheme are supported. If logging is required, the log in and log out structures must be created for each logged event. If an exclusive session is requested, then the relevant flag must be set in the transAttribute field.

3.3.14.2 Transport encryption and authorisation

Confidentiality protection of data transmitted inside the transport session is provided through the encryption of the command to be protected or, more specifically, encryption of the input and output parameters associated with the command.

Authorisation of the execute transport command is provided by the calculation of an HMAC on a subset of elements from the wrapped command, the command ordinal, header information and data fields, where the transport authorisation data fixed during session establishment is used as the HMAC key. This HMAC also allows the integrity of the bundle to be verified and a link made between the established session and execute transport commands.

3.3.14.2.1   Transport encryption

Following session establishment, the trusted process can call the execute transport command which delivers a wrapped command to the TPM, which can, in turn, unwrap and execute the command.

The execute transport command has the following structure:

- (Execute transport header || wrapped command || execute transport trailer), where:

  Wrapped command = (ordinal and header information || key and other handles || data || authorisations), where the authorisations represent the usual authorisation data, as described in the OIAP and OSAP protocols, required in order to utilise the specified wrapped command.

Due to resource management issues, encryption of the entire wrapped command is impossible. Therefore, the command data field contains the only information to be encrypted.

Confidentiality of the transport session is generally provided by XORing the command data with the output of an MGF1 function, where input into the MGF1 function consists of:

- Transport session authorisation data, as generated by the caller, the oddnonce provided by the trusted process, the evennonce provided by the TPM and either the number 1 or 2, used to indicate the direction of the communication.

3.3.14.2.2   Execute transport authorisation
The output from an HMAC computation is used, so that knowledge of the transport authorisation data required for use of the execute transport command can be demonstrated and the integrity of the wrapped command assured. It is calculated as follows.

The challenger:

- calculates H1 = SHA-1 (ordinal and header information || decrypted command data), both from the wrapped command above; after which he
- generates the HMAC (of execute transport header and ordinal information || H1 || Transport Nonce Even || Transport Nonce Odd || Continue Transport Session value), where the transport authorisation data set up between the caller and the TPM for this session is used as the key;
- this value is then sent to the TPM which validates it.

The TPM then:

- unwraps the command, validates the ExecuteTransport authorisation HMAC, validates the wrapped command authorisation data and executes the command;
- calculates H2 = SHA-1 (The return code || ordinal and header information || output data) of the wrapped command;
- calculates S2 = SHA-1 (The return code for the execute transport || the ordinal and header information for execute transport || current ticks|| H2);
- the returned execute transport authorisation data = HMAC (S2 || Transport Nonce Even || Transport Nonce Odd || Continue Transport Session value), where the transport authorisation data set up between the caller and the TPM for this session is used as the key.

3.3.14.3   Transport logging

A session log provides a record of each command using a particular session, using a structure that includes the parameters and current tick count for each logged command.

If transport logging functionality is set, entries are written to a TPM_TRANSPORT_LOG_IN structure on the receipt of each wrapped command to be logged.

Similarly, for outgoing data, after the execution of the wrapped command, entries are written to a TPM_TRANSPORT_LOG_OUT structure.

The summaries of these internal structures are stored to the transDigest field of the internal transport structure described above.

3.3.14.4   Error handling and exclusive transport sessions

Provisions are also made for both error messages and the results of commands to be passed back to the callers.

The concept of exclusive transport sessions is also discussed. In this case, if a caller establishes an exclusive session with the TPM, the session is invalidated if any TPM command outside the established session should attempt to execute. Only one exclusive session may be supported by the TPM at any one time.

3.3.15   Monotonic counter

A monotonic counter provides an increasing incremental value. The TPM must support at least four concurrent monotonic counters which may be implemented as:

- four unique counters; or as
- one counter with pointers which keep track of the current values of the other counters.

The fundamental counter components include the internal base and the external counters. The internal base represents the main counter. It is used internally by the TPM, and is not accessible to processes running outside the TPM.

External counters are used by external processes, and each TP will contain a minimum of four. They may be related to the main counter via pointers, via difference values or, alternatively, they may be unique. The values of these counters are not affected by any use, incrementation or deletion of any other external counter. External counters must allow for seven years of increments taking place every five seconds. The output of the counters is a 32-bit value. To create an external counter, TPM owner authorisation is required. In order to increment an external counter, knowledge of the correct authorisation data must be demonstrated. Finally, manufacturers are free to implement monotonic counters using any chosen mechanism.

3.3.16   Context manager

Because the TPM has limited resources, caching of resources may occur without the knowledge or assistance of the application which has loaded the resource.

In version 1.1 two types of resources needed this mechanism, namely keys and authorisation sessions, both of which had separate load and restore operations.

Version 1.2 introduced the concept of the transport session, which also requires management.

In order to consolidate context management, a single context manager is defined in the version 1.2 specifications, which all resources may use. In this instance a resource manager can request that a resource be wrapped in a manner that:

- securely protects the resource when it is evicted from the TPM; and
- allows for the resource to be restored onto the same TPM during the same operational cycle.

The encryption scheme used to protect these cached blobs may be symmetric or asymmetric and the keys used for protecting the blobs may be temporary, regardless of whether they are 2048-bit RSA keys or 128-bit AES keys; for example, a new key could be generated at start-up or, could alternatively, be more permanent. For example, the TPM could generate a key and store it persistently in 'TPM persistent data'.

Resources may need to be evicted from the TPM, for example, because the resources in use by the TPM exceed the available space.

3.3.17   Delegation

Prior to the version 1.2 specifications, the TPM owner had the privilege to control all aspects of the TPM's operation, that is, use of all TPM commands including the 'owner-authorised' command set, the set of TPM commands that requires TPM owner authorisation data to be entered before their execution is authorised. Therefore, if any aspect of the TPM required management, it became the direct responsibility of the TPM owner. As an alternative, privileged information belonging to the TPM owner (the 20 bytes of TPM owner authorisation data) would have to be forwarded to another entity, trusted to perform only a particular subset of operations, thereby potentially leaving the platform vulnerable to attack.

In order to alleviate the risk associated with the above management method, a delegation model has been included in the version 1.2 specifications, so that a TPM owner can delegate particular privileges to individual entities or trusted processes, through the construction of new authorisation data and the association of specified TPM ownership rights with this authorisation data. The delegation process differs depending on the entity to which the specified privileges are being given.

The delegation process is summarised in Table 3.2.

3.3.17.1   Family and delegation tables

In order to implement this delegation model, two tables, a family table and a delegate table, are required. The delegate table must have a minimum of two rows, whereas the family table must have a minimum of eight rows and may have many more. The size of these tables, however, does not restrict the number of delegations because the TPM facilitates the caching of delegations off the TPM, should the number of table rows become limited. This uses a mechanism which protects both the confidentiality and integrity of the delegations. A counter mechanism is also used such that encrypted cached delegations, or 'blobs', can be validated as fresh when they are loaded back onto the TPM.

Each entry in the delegate table contains six fields:

- PCR information, which defines a particular process to which the privileges have been delegated;
- Authorisation data for delegated capabilities, which defines a particular authorisation value to which delegated privileges have been associated;
- A delegation label;
- The family ID, identifying the family to which the delegation belongs;
- The verification count, which specifies the version of this row; and
- A profile of the capabilities delegated to the trusted process identified by the PCR information or the authorisation data.

The TPM owner can also delegate the management of tables to particular entries. Entities belonging to a particular family of delegation processes may be authorised to edit delegate entries which belong to that family.

The family table provides a method of grouping rows in the delegate table. It supports the validation and revocation of exported delegate table rows and those stored

Table 3.2   The delegation process

Delegation to	Requires	Additional information
A generic entity	If privileges are to be delegated to a generic entity, privileges may be associated with a particular entity by: • Dictating PCRs which define a particular process; and/or • Stipulating a particular authorisation value to which privileges are associated	The resultant blob is then passed to the chosen entity
An external entity	If privileges are to be delegated to a specified external entity: • A null PCR selection; and • An authorisation value; are required	The authorisation value may, however, be sealed to a set of PCRs on the remote platform
A trusted process provided by the local OS	If privileges are to be delegated to a trusted process provided by the local OS: • A PCR that defines the specific trusted process; and • A known authorisation value; are required 0x111 111 is suggested by the TCG specifications as the known authorisation value	Generic authorisation data is sufficient, since the OS has no means of securely storing the authorisation token without sealing the token to the PCR representing the trusted process; therefore to associate a randomly chosen authorisation value adds no security value

in the table. The family table must have at least eight rows, and each entry in the family table contains the following four fields:

• The family ID;
• The family label, which helps identify information associated with the family;
• The family verification count, which represents the sequence number identifying the last outside verification and attestation of family information; and
• The family flags.

In order to validate delegation rows, the following process is described. The TPM produces a signed blob, grouping all delegations from the same family. This signed blob then allows a verification agent to examine the delegations and the processes involved, and then to make an assessment as to the validity of the delegations.

Before any signed blob is produced, the verification counter is incremented and inserted into selected table elements (all of which are from the same family), including temporarily loaded blobs. Copies of these elements are then made, signed and sent to a chosen TTP.

Alternatively, the counter may not be incremented before the platform delegations are sent for validation. This, however, leads to the possible use of undesirable blobs which have not been validated, permitting undesirable delegations when loaded onto the delegate table. This occurs because these undesirable blobs were not on the platform when its delegation state was validated, but have the same counter value as blobs that were, as no increment of the verification counter took place prior to the validation process. In this case, there is no way, therefore, of differentiating between validated blobs and undesirable, unvalidated, blobs.

The platform owner also requires assurance that no management of the table is possible during the validation process. In order to ensure this occurs, the transport session established during this verification process will have the 'no other activity' attribute value set. This ensures that no other TPM operations can occur during the validation process. The TTP then returns the results of the assessment.

3.3.17.2   Delegate-specific authorisation protocol

In order to delegate privileges, the delegation creation entity must know the required authorisation data for the key object or command in question. The delegation creation entity must then demonstrate knowledge of the authorisation information associated with the key or command to which access will be delegated.

The delegation entity then creates a TPM_Delegate_Key_Blob or a TPM_Delegate_Owner_Blob, depending on whether key use or TPM owner command execution is being delegated.

This TPM_Delegate_Key_Blob, TPM_Delegate_Owner_Blob or, alternatively, a pointer to an entry in the internal delegation table, which contains the authorisation data necessary for use of delegated command or key use is encrypted such that only the TPM can decrypt it, and then sent to the entity being granted delegated usage of the key or command in conjunction with the authorisation data necessary for use of delegated command or key use.

The entity which has been delegated restricted privileges can now start a TPM_DSAP session using TPM_Delegate_Key_Blob, TPM_Delegate_Owner_Blob or a pointer to an entry in the internal delegation table, as input. The protocol proceeds as follows:

1. The TPM_DSAP command is used to initiate the protocol. In conjunction with the command ordinal, input parameters for this command include:
    *   a key handle associated with the object, K, to be accessed and utilised or a handle to the privileges that have been delegated;

- a caller OSAP nonce;
- an entity type element; and
- an entity value element, where the entity type and entity value elements represent the delegation structure which has been allotted to the caller, be it a TPM_Delgate_Owner_Blob, a TPM_Delegate_Key_Blob or a TPM delegation table index value.

2. If a TPM_Delgate_Owner_Blob or a TPM_Delgate_Key_Blob is received, its integrity is initially checked. Alternatively, if entityType is TPM_ET_DEL_ROW or TPM_ET_DEL_KEY, the entityValue will consist of a TPM_DELEGATE_ INDEX, which points to a delegation entry in the delegate table.

3. The encrypted authorisation data necessary for use of delegated command or key is extracted by the TPM from either the TPM_Delegate_Key_Blob, TPM_Delegate_Owner_Blob or, alternatively, from an entry in the internal del-egation table and decrypted. When the authorised data has been decrypted by the TPM, it is used along with the TPM and caller OSAP nonces to generate a shared key between the caller and the TPM.

4. The DSAP authorisation protocol then proceeds as did the OSAP protocol where the shared key generated by the TPM and the entity requesting access, by the process described above, is used by the entity requesting access to prove to the TPM that usage of a particular command or key should be granted.

3.3.18   Time-stamping

The version 1.2 specifications of the TCG's TPM advocate that the TPM provides a service enabling time-stamps to be applied to various blobs. The time-stamp provided, however, is not a universal clock time but a representation of the number of ticks the TPM has counted. The caller can then have this value associated with a universal time clock value externally.

No requirements are made regarding how the tick counter mechanism is chosen and implemented; neither are any requirements made regarding the ability of the TPM to continually increment the tick counter. This is convenient, in that a PC with continual power supply may deploy a more continuous reliable timing method than a mobile platform with a limited battery, whose timing tick maintenance capability may be limited because of power limitations.

For each tick session, the values specified in Table 3.3 are maintained by the TPM.

A basic tick stamp result consists of a TPM digital signature computed over:

- the data to be time-stamped (a digest of the data to be time-stamped);
- the current tick counter value;
- the TSN; and
- some fixed text.

An example of a protocol illustrating how a tick counter value can be associated with a universal time clock value by employing the functionality of a time-stamping

Table 3.3   Tick session values

Value maintained by TPM for tick session	Description
The tick count value, TCV	Counts the ticks for the session Must be set to 0 at the start of every tick session If the TPM loses the ability to increment the TCV in accordance with the TIR, the TCV must be set to null and a new tick session started
The tick increment rate, TIR	The rate at which the TCV is incremented (its relationship with seconds is set during TPM manufacture)
The tick session nonce, TSN	The TSN is set at the start of each tick session Must be set to the next value of the TPM RNG at the beginning of each new tick session If the TPM loses the ability to increment the TCV in accordance with the TIR, the TSN must be set to null

authority is described in the specifications. The protocol specified, however, is merely illustrative; no particular protocol is mandated.

3.3.19   Migration mechanisms

Migration mechanisms are used for the backup and cloning of migratable TPM-protected key objects. They allow the private keys from TPM-protected key objects to be attached to other TPM-protected storage trees. Two methods for the migration of the private part of a TPM-protected key object are described in the TCG specifications [4].

Both mechanisms initially require that:

- The TPM owner has authorised a particular migration destination, that is, the use of a particular destination or intermediary public key for a particular migration method, be it migrate or rewrap;
- The authorisation data to use the parent key currently wrapping the key that is to be migrated has been submitted; and
- The authorisation data required for key migration has been submitted [4].

Once the TPM owner has authorised the use of a particular destination or intermediary public key for a particular migration method, the target key may be unwrapped at any stage and migrated, if the appropriate authorisation data to enable access to the parent key currently wrapping the key that is to be migrated and the authorisation data required for key migration are submitted by the target key owner.

The first migration method (rewrap) then requires the source TPM to rewrap the target key under the destination public key. This is then forwarded to the destination TPM in conjunction with a plaintext object describing the public key from the key pair to be migrated.

The alternate migration method involves the use of an intermediary. In this instance, the private key to be migrated is OAEP encoded and XORed with a one-time-pad. The resultant data is then encrypted under the public key of the intermediary, which unwraps the key and rewraps it under the public key of the destination TPM. The XOR encryption prevents the intermediary from gaining unauthorised access to the migrated key. The one-time-pad must, however, be made available to the destination TPM so that the migrated key can eventually be integrated into the protected storage hierarchy of the destination TPM.

While the TPM will check that a particular destination or intermediary public key is at least as strong as 2048-bit RSA, it is up to the TPM owner to ensure that the public key does actually represent the desired destination TPM or intermediary [4]. A migratory key can essentially be sent to any arbitrary platform, not necessarily a TP.

With respect to CMKs:

- the TPM owner must authorise the use of a particular destination public key;
- the authorisation data to use the parent key currently wrapping the key that is to be migrated must be submitted;
- the authorisation data required for key migration must be submitted [4]; and
- in conjunction with this, a chosen migration (selection) authority must authorise the migration destination.

In this way, controlled migration of keys is made possible, where an entity other than the TPM owner may have input into the decision as to where CMKs are destined.

3.3.20   Maintenance mechanisms

Maintenance mechanisms are used to clone a broken TP. This cloning process can only be completed with the co-operation of the TPM owner and the platform manufacturer, and the process must only be performed between two platforms of the same manufacturer and model. Maintenance mechanisms are optional, but if they are provided by the TPM, certain functionality is required. The maintenance capability may be disabled until the current owner is erased.

3.3.21   Audit

The audit function allows the TPM owner to determine whether or not certain operations on the TPM have been executed.

The audit function in earlier versions of the TCG specifications, TCPA main specification, version 1.1, 2001, was shown to have security weaknesses [4], so an updated method of audit is described in the version 1.2 document set. In version 1.2 of the specifications, the audit mechanism consists of:

- a digest held internally to the TPM; and
- a log of all audited commands held externally to the TPM.

In this instance, the securely stored internal digest allows for verification of the external log, so that tampering of any kind can be detected. Re-synchronisation functionality is also provided by the TPM, so that the internal digest and the external logs may be kept consistent with each other.

The TPM owner has the capability to choose which functions generate an audit log entry, and to alter this choice at any stage.

The auditing process itself consists of two fundamental steps:

- auditing of the command and input parameter received; and
- auditing of the response to the command and output parameters.

This method was chosen to diminish the amount of memory required to complete the auditing process, as no memory is required to save any audit information while the command is executing.

An internal audit record consists of:

- a NV counter, which increments once per session when the first audit event of a session occurs; and
- a digest, which holds the digest of the current session, most probably volatile.

The audit process may therefore proceed as follows:

- An auditable command is called;
- The audit session opens when the volatile digest is extended from its null state with the input parameter from the command;
- When this audit session is opened, the NV counter is incremented;
- When the command has executed, the response to the command (the return code) and the output parameters are then used to further extend the digest value;
- The audit session closes when the TPM receives the command to get the audit event signed and the close audit parameter. The explicit closing of an audit session addresses the potential threat of undetectable audit log truncation;
- The TPM then signs the concatenation of the NV counter and the volatile digest, and exports the following three values:

    The NV counter value;

    The volatile digest value; and

    The signature.

3.3.22   Conclusions

As is clear from the discussion above, the TCG TP roots of trust, namely the CRTM and the TPM, offer a great deal of functionality.

Realistically however, in order to implement a TP which may be used both efficiently and securely, we must consider not only the trusted foundations of the platform but also the entire system architecture; otherwise practical problems arise in relation to TP implementation.

We examine, for example, the issues surrounding platform integrity verification. If, through the addition of the relevant roots of trust, a PC becomes a TP, and PCRs are set to reflect all software running on that platform, integrity verification may quickly become a hugely complex procedure because of the variety and quantity of processes in existence on the platform. Various measures can be taken to simplify platform integrity verification, for example, deploying validation authorities as described in Section 3.3.11.4, but the procedure remains difficult. A compromise must be reached between the open and diverse operating environment required in practical use, and the closed, constrained operating environment in which the functionality of the CRTM and TPM may be best deployed.

The most sensible solution in terms of an open platform is to utilise a form of memory management such that the platform can be partitioned and PCRs set to reflect only the subset of all software running in the protected partition. This can be achieved in various ways, ranging from traditional virtual memory protection to hardware memory protection.

In conjunction with this, we must also consider how the CRTM and TPM functionality may be leveraged at different levels in the software stack, from standalone applications to fully TCG-aware OS. The architecture outlined by Microsoft, as discussed in the next section, provides an example of how this may be achieved.

3.4 NGSCB

3.4.1 Introduction

In June 2002 [22], Microsoft released information on Palladium, a system which combined software and hardware controls to create a Trusted Computing Platform (TCP). It was initially stated that Palladium was due to be shipped with the next major version of Windows, the Longhorn OS, then planned for release in 2004.

The name 'Palladium', however, has since been abandoned in favour of NGSCB. According to John Lettice of the Register [23], this change was made for two fundamental reasons: the name 'Palladium' had already been used for another product, and because of the initial controversy and misdirected criticism surrounding the project. To date, however, few technical details regarding Palladium or NGSCB have been published. Primary reference material used in the writing of this chapter includes References 6, 7, 24 and 25. Certain details of Microsoft's NGSCB are explored in Chapter 4.

3.4.2 The relationship between the TCG and NGSCB

Microsoft was one of the founding members of the TCG and actively participates in the organisation [4]. The version 1.1 TPM is, however, not supported by Microsoft Windows, nor will it be used as the basis of NGSCB functionality. Version 1.1 TPMs may be supported on a Microsoft windows machine with addition of a Cryptographic Service Provider (CSP), provided by the hardware manufacturer, which has been written to support the Windows Cryptographic Applications Programming Interface

(CAPI).[3] The TPM, as defined in version 1.2 of the specifications, is, however, expected to fulfil the role of the Security Support Component (SSC) in a NGSCB, described below.

The NGSCB architecture encompasses a broader set of capabilities than the TCG's TP. In addition to the functionality offered by the TCG, NGSCB provides:

- an extended CPU to enable the efficient implementation of a minimal isolation kernel;
- a minimal isolation kernel;
- memory controller or chipset extensions such that Direct Memory Access (DMA) can be controlled; and
- hardware components enabling input and output to be efficiently secured.

NGSCB is essentially an entire system supporting high assurance or trusted computing, based upon the three rudimentary roots of trust, namely the RTM, the RTS and the RTS, previously described.

3.4.3   The NGSCB architecture

An NGSCB platform includes three fundamental components:

- The SSC, implemented in hardware and either physically or cryptographically bound to the platform;
- The isolation kernel, which facilitates the execution of several OSs in parallel on the same machine, and controls the access of these OSs to system resources; and
- Hosted by this isolation kernel, an optional mass-market OS in conjunction with one or more High Assurance Components (HACs), previously called 'nexuses', where trusted applications, previously called Nexus Computing Agents (NCAs) are hosted.

3.4.3.1   The SSC

SSC is a tamper-resistant cryptographic chip, the functionality of which is summarised in Table 3.4. It is required to implement a variety of cryptosystems, a RNG, a small amount of memory and a monotonic counter. It must also contain at least one Process Control Register (PCR), for storing the image of system components, for example, the isolation kernel or a HAC. A TPM conforming to version 1.2 of the TCG specifications is a concrete implementation of an NGSCB SSC.

Details of the fundamental SSC primitives are described in Table 3.5.

If a TPM version 1.2, as described in Section 3.3, is used to provide the SSC, the RTM mechanism described in Section 3.3 provides authenticated initialisation of lowest level system software, the isolation kernel. In conjunction with this, services, such as sealed storage and attestation, as described in Sections 3.3.13.2 and 3.3.11.4, are provided to the isolation layer.

---

[3] http://www.microsoft.com/technet/security/news/ngscb.asp

Table 3.4   The NGSCB SSC: an overview

Component	Definition	Capabilities	Provision
NGSCB SSC	Security support component	The following functionality must be provided to HACs hosted by the isolation kernel The capabilities described below need not be directly implemented by the SSC. They may be implemented in the higher layers but will have their security foundation rooted in the SSC Seal Unseal Quote PKSeal PKUnseal GetMonotonicCounter IncrementMonotonicCounter GetEntropy GetCertificate	The SCC will be inextricably linked to the motherboard

This isolation kernel then offers similar services to OSs, or more specifically HACs that it hosts, and, in turn, these HACs offer these same services to their hosted applications.

In the scenario where a trusted application wishes to demonstrate the state of the platform to a challenger, the following process may be utilised rather than the TPM directly signing PCR values which reflect the entire software stack.

1. When a trusted application wishes to attest to its identity/code configuration, the hosting HAC signs the trusted application's identity concatenated with arbitrary data, for example, a challenger nonce. This is then sent to the challenger in conjunction with two further attestation statements, as listed in steps 2 and 3.
2. In the second attestation statement, the isolation kernel has digitally signed:
    the HAC identity; and

    the public key corresponding to the private key used for attestation in step 1.
3. In the third attestation statement, the TPM has digitally signed:
    the isolation kernel identity (which has been measured and stored in TPM PCRs); and

    the public key corresponding to the private key used for attestation in step 2 above.

Table 3.5 SSC capabilities

Primitive	Input	Output	Description
Seal	Source_Identity (Identity/hash of the isolation kernel or OS currently running) AC_Information (The access control information, e.g. the identity/hash of the isolation kernel or OS allowed to decrypt the sealed secret) Data to be sealed/protected	C = Store (Source_Identity | AC_Information | Data)	A cryptographic implementation of the store operation, which satisfies the 'standard' requirements for an authenticated encryption scheme, and which encrypts the input data and returns it to the caller Implementations require the SSC to have the functionality to securely store and access cryptographic keys, so that encryption and integrity protections can be performed
Unseal	C (an identifier for the sealed bundle)	Source_Identity Data Only output if the access control information, AC_Information, is fulfilled: For example it may be required that the identity of the HAC currently running equates to the AC_Information	This sealed storage capability may be extended to contain more sophisticated access control policies than AC_Information equating to the identity of the HAC currently running
Quote	Data (arbitrary data block)	S_K (Data | Source_Identity) A public key signature is output on the above data using key K, which is protected by the SSC	

Table 3.5   Continued

Primitive	Input	Output	Description
PKSeal	Target_Identity Data (data to be protected) K (a public key, whose corresponding private key is held in the SSC)	$D = \text{AsymmetricEncrypt}_K$ (Target_Identity | Data)	PKSeal allows a remote entity to encrypt a secret such that it is only accessible by a specified entity, the Target_Identity with private key, K, protected by the SSC PKSeal does not need to be implemented in the SSC
PKUnseal	D	Decrypts D and returns data If Target_Identity is equal to the identity of the caller identity	
ReadCounter		V	Gets the value, V of the monotonic counter
IncrementCounter			Increments the value, V of the monotonic counter
GetEntropy			Returns a random octet sequence

4. In conjunction with the three attestation statements listed in steps 1–3, a certificate is provided in which a trusted certification authority attests to the fact that:

> The TPM public key corresponding to the private key used to sign the statement in step 3 belongs to a genuine TPM.

A similar chaining scheme may be used for protected storage operations, which must be deployed in the implementation of the attestation chain described above to securely store the private signing keys.

As an example, we examine the symmetric seal functionality as defined by Microsoft. In this case, a host, that is, the isolation layer or a HAC, may facilitate the symmetric encryption of arbitrary data and its associated access control information (seal). In turn, at the lowest layer in the stack, the keys used in this symmetric sealing mechanism will be protected by the TPM using, for example, the TPM_SEAL command.

3.4.3.2   The isolation kernel

Following this we examine the fundamental properties of the NGSCB isolation kernel; further details on concepts introduced below can be found in Chapter 4.

The isolation kernel [7] will execute in a CPU mode more privileged than the existing mode 0, effectively in ring −1, which will be introduced in forthcoming versions of the x86 processors. This allows for the isolation kernel to operate in ring −1 and all guest OSs to execute in ring 0. Thus problems that may occur with virtualisation, in the scenario where the isolation kernel executes in ring 0 and guest OSs or HACs must execute in ring 1, will be avoided.

The isolation kernel is described as combining the merits of both Virtual Machine Monitors (VMMs) and exokernels [24]. It resembles a minimised VMM, in that it allows mass-market OSs to operate with few changes. However, rather than necessitating the virtualisation of all devices, as a VMM does, the exokernel approach to devices is adopted, where devices are assigned to guest OSs which contain drivers for the devices they choose to support. Guest OSs may then efficiently operate directly on the chosen device.

This does, however, leave the problem of uncontrolled DMA devices, which by default have access to all physical memory. In order to prevent DMA devices gaining unauthorised access to virtual memory-based protected environments, chipset extensions are required of the hardware manufacturers. A DMA policy map [24] is set by software with write access to the memory region which holds the policy map, usually the isolation kernel, and it is then stored in main memory. The DMA policy map is then read and enforced by hardware, where this policy map decides, given the state of the system, if a particular subject (DMA device) has access (read or write) to a specified resource (physical address).

The isolation kernel utilises a page table edit control (PTEC) algorithm in order to partition memory among guests executing on the isolation kernel. Any attempt made to edit the page map traps to the isolation kernel, which consults its security policy in order to decide whether or not the action may proceed.

3.4.3.3   High assurance components and trusted applications

Trusted applications are hosted by the protected execution environments (high assurance components), and may constitute an application, part of an application or a service. In the protected execution environments (HACs), trusted and untrusted applications are isolated from each other by the isolation kernel. A trusted application can make requests of the HAC for security-related services and for services such as memory management and inter-process communication.

3.4.4   NGSCB components

In order to implement all aspects of the NGSCB architecture, Microsoft stipulates that modifications must be made to the following components of the traditional computing platform.

- In conjunction with the addition of an SSC, the memory controller or chipset must be specially designed to facilitate DMA protection.

- CPU modifications allow the newly designed isolation kernel to execute in a new ring −1, thereby facilitating the execution of legacy OSs with few modifications. This also means that problems usually associated with virtualising OS instruction sets may be avoided.
- Enhancements to input devices, such as keyboards and mice, may be deployed to facilitate the MACing and encryption of data as it is communicated to a trusted application on the platform. Secure graphics hardware may also be deployed in parallel to the complex mass-market graphics system, and used only by the isolation kernel and high assurance guests.

In a fundamental sense, however, these input and output hardware changes are not strictly necessary. In principle, a piece of trusted code could be given physical control of the keyboard and the graphics card by the isolation kernel, and thus guarantee that input and output will not be observed or corrupted. There are two reasons, however, why new hardware for input and graphics is desirable:

- Minimising the size of the Trusted Computing Base (TCB), which should ideally be kept as small as possible to preserve security; graphics drivers, for example, typically contain millions of lines of code.
- Performance and ease of running off-the-shelf legacy OSs; OSs expect to have direct access to the graphics card. While VMMs routinely solve this problem by exposing a virtual graphics card to their guest OSs, in practice this solution entails significant performance degradation.

3.5 LaGrande

3.5.1 Introduction

Following the description of NGSCB, we briefly examine LT, born out of Intel's initiative to address the challenges of trusted computing. LaGrande is defined as 'a set of enhanced hardware components designed to help protect sensitive information from software-based attacks, where LT features include capabilities in the microprocessor, chipset, I/O subsystems, and other platform components' [26]. As was the case with NGSCB, detailed information on LT remains limited.

LaGrande Technology essentially provides all the components needed to meet the requirements defined by Microsoft for hardware enhancements and extensions necessary to support their NGSCB architecture.

3.5.2 The architecture

The generic LT architecture consists of two fundamental concepts. These are the notions of standard and protected partitions, and the domain manager.

The standard partition provides an environment identical to today's Intel Architecture-32 (IA-32) environment [26]. In this standard partition, users may freely run software of their choice. The existence of this standard partition implies that, despite the addition of supplementary security mechanisms to the platform, code already in existence will retain its value, and software unconcerned with security will have somewhere to execute unaffected.

The protected partition provides a parallel environment, in which hardened software can be executed with the assurance that it cannot be tampered with by software executing in either the standard or protected partition. This protected partition is hardened against software attacks by the implementation of a number of components, described below, which provide domain separation; memory protection; protected graphics; and a trusted channel to peripherals.

The existence of a domain manager, which facilitates this domain separation, is also assumed. This domain manager may be constructed in various ways, depending on the architecture implemented. A concrete example of this domain manager is the isolation kernel as described in Section 3.4. The domain manager is physically protected via processor and chipset extensions and, in turn, protects standard and protected partitions from each other.

3.5.3   Hardware enhancements and extensions

In order to facilitate the implementation of the above partitions, in conjunction with protected input and output and TPM functionality to a platform, Intel are in the process of extending and enhancing the following hardware components:

- the CPU;
- the memory controller or chipset;
- the keyboard and mouse;
- the video graphics card; and
- the graphics adaptor.

A version 1.2 TPM must also be added.

3.5.3.1   The CPU

The CPU extensions facilitate the efficient generation of standard and protected execution environments or partitions, as described above. CPU enhancements, in conjunction with chipset extensions, also provide more stringent access control enforcement with respect to the use of hardware resources, such as memory, thereby thwarting the threats caused by DMA devices.

Secure event management may also be facilitated. Through the extension of the CPU and chipset, the situation where an abnormal event may result in the transfer of control to a malicious agent outside the protective environment's boundaries, can be detected and handled appropriately.

Instructions to manage the protected execution environment and to establish a more secure software stack are also added. Samples of these instructions are given in the following description of the protected partition launch.

At any stage after the platform has been booted, a protected partition is launched by a request to an LT-aware OS component, as follows:

1. Ordinary software running on an LT processor executes a new SENTER instruction to initiate the launch process;
2. This instruction triggers a sequence of handshakes; after which

   the processor and chipset are ready to be brought into the protected environment; and

   memory spaces are then allocated for the protected partition and marked protected.
3. The processor then:

   loads an authenticated code module (AC module) into internal private memory;

   authenticates it via signature verification;

   registers its identity in a PCR in the TPM; and

   invokes it.
4. It is then the responsibility of the AC module to:

   check that there is no improperly configured hardware running;

   enable memory protection for the proposed domain manager;

   record the identity of the domain manager in a TPM PCR; and then

   transfer execution control to the domain manager.
5. The domain manager is then in control.
6. When protected memory is no longer needed:

   the domain manager ensures that no secrets are left behind in either memory or registers:

   > it must re-seal secrets to be placed in persistent storage; and

   > scrub the contents of protected partitioned memory pages.

   the SEXIT instruction is then executed by the domain manager, which triggers another sequence of handshakes and an exit from the protected environment [26].

3.5.3.2 The chipset

Chipset extensions allow for a memory protection policy to be enforced; facilitate the creation of protected channels to and from input/output devices; include enhancements, which protect against DMA; and provide interfaces to the version 1.2 TPM.

3.5.3.3 The keyboard and mouse

The keyboard and mouse extensions support secure communication between the mouse and keyboard and trusted applications. Protected input allows for protected channels to be established between input devices and applications running in the protected environments. This protects the confidentiality and integrity of input data against unauthorised or malicious software running on the platform.

Keystrokes and mouse clicks may be encrypted or MACed, or both, using keys shared between the protected domain's input manager and the input device. Only applications with the correct encryption key can then decrypt and use the transported data [26].

3.5.3.4   The video graphics card

The video graphics card extensions allow for display information to be sent to the graphics frame buffer without observation or compromise [26]. Protected output allows applications running in protected execution environments to securely send display information to the graphics frame buffer, with the assurance that it cannot be observed or tampered with by malicious software running on the platform [26].

3.5.3.5   TPM version 1.2

Intel also manufactures TPM version 1.2 chips, as described in Section 2.

3.6   ARM TrustZone

3.6.1   Introduction

The conversion of generic platforms into trusted computing platforms has been largely focused on open systems, such as the personal computing and server environments. Moreover, the majority of today's TPM implementations are chip-based, such as Intel's TPM-chip implementation, constructed as part of the LaGrande project (see Section 3.5), or the TPM chip manufactured by Infineon as part of their TPM professional package.

The necessity, however, for equivalent trusted computing functionality in embedded systems, such as smart phones and PDAs, has also become apparent [27] and these issues are being tackled within the TCG, particularly within the mobile phone working group. ARM TrustZone™ Technology focuses on the security of embedded systems rather than open platforms such as PCs and servers, where power consumption, performance and area are all issues that must be taken into account when implementing security mechanisms. ARM TrustZone is also illustrative of the key enabling technologies being developed so that software instantiations of TPMs may be deployed.

We briefly examine ARM's TrustZone technology,[4] which offers a safe execution environment or 'secure world' for security critical functions, through the extension of an ARM CPU. By this means, security critical functions, for example, TPM functions, can be securely implemented and reliably protected from non-secure code running in the 'non-secure world' on the platform [28].

ARM software technology is focused on enabling the TrustZone hardware, and providing a common environment for development of higher-level security services (such as TPMs) across all ARM platforms.

---

[4] http://www.arm.com/products/CPUs/arch-trustzone.html

We focus here on the hardware extensions, which may facilitate a software implementation of trusted computing technology in embedded systems. Core reference material for this chapter consists of References 27 and 28.

3.6.2   Fundamental components

The fundamental additions [27] made to the current ARM processor architecture include:

1. A new permission level, which supplements current user and privileged modes.
2. The resources required to enter and exit that permission level in a secure manner:
    *   One new instruction;
    *   A new configuration bit, that distinguishes between secure and normal operation, that is, between secure and non-secure 'worlds';
    *   A new 'gatekeeper' CPU operating mode, called monitor mode.
3. A set of new guards and controls to facilitate secure exception handling.

Rather than being implemented in firmware or software, these extensions are hard wired into the microprocessor core [27].

3.6.2.1   The additional permission level

TrustZone works by adding a special permission domain [27] to the existing user and privileged modes. To try to avoid confusion with the current use of the terms domain, mode and state, this new domain is referred to as the 'secure world'.

This secure world is more privileged than the privileged mode in which the OS runs. It is not, however, an exclusive operating mode. Both privileged code and user code can run in TrustZone's secure world. ARM describes the TrustZone security level as a parallel permission domain, not as new layer in the stack of domains.

3.6.2.2   The new instruction

In order to enter TrustZone (the secure world), the OS must invoke the single new TrustZone instruction: the Secure Monitor Interrupt (SMI) [27]. Only an OS running in privileged mode can invoke the SMI, and any attempt by an application running in user mode to directly execute the SMI results in an exception.

To enter TrustZone legitimately, therefore, an application must request permission to do so by calling an API routine in the OS. This API is commonly installed as a driver. When this API routine is called, the API call gives the OS a chance to perform any checks it considers necessary to ensure that the application is not attempting any malicious activities. The extent of the checks completed, however, is left entirely up to the OS vendor. The only requirement made of the OS is the provision of a vector to the SMI instruction. The extent to which the secure world trusts the checks made by the OS is up to the TrustZone implementation. The TrustZone implementation is also capable of carrying out its own checks, and these can be used to decide the degree of trust in the OS checks.

When the SMI instruction executes, it causes a branch to the software controlling the exchange between the secure and non-secure worlds, and switches the processor into the TrustZone domain or 'secure world' [27].

3.6.2.3   The new configuration bit

To make the switch, the SMI sets a new security bit, called the S-bit, in one of the 15 coprocessor secure status registers, which are part of the core's extended configuration system [27]. This bit is then propagated into the hardware system to enable that hardware to react to the different security 'worlds'.

3.6.2.4   The secure monitor mode code

The secure monitor is defined as a small, self-contained program that is completely independent from the regular OS, the secure OS kernel and the secure device drivers that are also required [27]. Its fundamental responsibility consists of switching contexts between secure and non-secure worlds.

The first duty of the secure monitor is to maintain and protect the state of the currently running non-secure process, before switching contexts to the new secure process. The contents of the non-secure process's registers may be saved to Tightly Coupled Memory (TCM), and configuration settings saved to an extra bank of coprocessor registers.

When switching contexts, the flushing of the instruction cache, data cache, tightly coupled memory or any other memory, is a redundant activity within the TrustZone architecture because all these structures are divided into secure and non-secure partitions. The caches, Memory-Management Unit (MMU) and Translation Lookaside Buffer (TLB) have additional tag bits, the S-bit tags, to keep track of those partitions [27].

These tags [27] are then used to ensure that only secure processes can access secure memory partitions or cache lines. If a non-secure process should attempt to access the restricted cache lines or memory, a cache miss and/or an external abort will be generated.

3.6.2.5   Interrupts

Interrupts originating from potentially malicious programs must be handled to prevent use of an interrupt to divert execution to a bogus interrupt handler. One solution to this problem, although not a very realistic or practical one, would be to block all interrupts while the processor is running in secure mode.

Another suggested approach is to secure all the interrupt handlers, thereby requiring the system to switch into secure mode to handle every interrupt. This may benefit security, but not to the point where it justifies the probable interrupt–response latencies incurred.

It is the opinion of ARM, however [27], that most systems will need separate interrupt vector tables and interrupt handlers for their secure and non-secure modes, with different interrupt policies for each mode. The secure vector table would reside in secure memory and might point to interrupt handlers that are likewise secure. The non-secure vector table and handlers would reside in regular memory. Although this solution might duplicate a few handlers and impose some redundancy on the system, it would prevent a malicious program overwriting the secure vector tables and handlers.

In the ARM architecture, where two kinds of interrupts are supported, namely fast interrupts and regular interrupts, the simplest solution, if interrupts are required in both worlds, is for nFIQ on an ARM processor, the fast interrupt request input, to be dedicated to interrupt handling from secure devices, and nIRQ on an ARM processor, the interrupt request input, to be dedicated to handling interrupts from normal devices.

3.7 The PERSEUS system architecture

We now move to explore PERSEUS[5] [5,29,30], an open source trusted computing project, the main contributors to which include Riordan and Waidner of IBM, Pfitzmann and Stüble of Saarland University and Weber from the Karlsruhe Research Centre. Their work aims to address some of the negative social, economic and technical concerns which have been raised with respect to trusted computing platforms. Of particular significance are issues regarding the loss of user control over their personal systems or personal information, and issues concerning commercial censorship. Their efforts have focused on the construction of a TP which fulfils both end-user needs and the needs of the content provider, through the integration of TCG/NGSCB hardware features with an open source security kernel which they have developed.

3.7.1 Introduction

As stated above, the fundamental motivation for the development of the PERSEUS system architecture was born from concerns regarding the power that content providers may potentially attain over a user's privacy, and the use of digital content. Stüble *et al.* [29] point out, however, that the hardware functionality provided for by NGSCB and TCG technologies is under the control of the OS. The user can therefore benefit from its functionality and also remain protected from threats outlined above as long as the OS is indeed trustworthy, thereby preserving the interests of both the content providers and the end users.

---

[5] http://www.perseusos.org/

They propose a new architecture for a trustworthy security platform which combines NGSCB/TCG hardware features with a newly developed open source security kernel which they claim [29] has the following properties:

- Backward compatibility with the Linux OS;
- A layered design; and
- Lightweightness such that migration to platforms such as PDAs or mobile phones is simple.

This project also provides an example of an open source security kernel, subject to the GNU GPL open source license, that allows every user to verify the implementation or, indeed, compile their own trusted system. Work of this nature may help prevent one company from obtaining a monopoly in this field.

Fundamental reference material for PERSEUS includes References 5, 29, 30.

3.7.2   Trusted platform functionality

Sadeghi and Stüble [8] state that a TP should satisfy the following requirements.

1. All components capable of breaking the security policy, that is, the TCB, should be trustworthy.
    - They highlight the fact that in every 1000 lines of code there is approximately one critical bug, and therefore the TCB should be kept as small as possible;
    - It is also emphasised that, where possible, evaluation of critical components should be completed against the common criteria; and
    - Finally, they state that source code should be made publicly available.
2. It is also desirable that the confidentiality and integrity of code and data during execution and during storage can be assured:
    - In order to protect the confidentiality and integrity of code and data during execution, virtual memory protection mechanisms may be deployed. In conjunction with this, the system must shield against any mechanism which may be utilised by untrusted components to bypass memory protections. If an untrusted process gains control over a DMA-enabled device, which permits direct access to all physical memory, memory protection mechanisms may be bypassed. One possible solution to this problem is to place all critical code, including device drivers, in the TCB;
    - For protection of code and data during storage, cryptographic mechanisms should be deployed, where the master key is stored in a tamper-resistant component.
3. The integrity of the TCB is important if the enforcement of security policies is to be guaranteed.
    - In order to prevent tampering of the TCB while it is inactive, a secure bootstrap architecture should be deployed; and
    - A method of securely verifying the results of the integrity check should also be provided to users.

4. In the majority of OSs, the concept of least privilege is not enforced thereby leading to possible security violations.
5. A trusted path to the user should be provided.
6. Secure channels between devices and applications are required in order to prevent malicious applications from deceiving honest applications.
7. With existing computer architectures, the generation of secure random numbers is difficult or impossible, but it is necessary in a platform if it is to be considered trustworthy.

3.7.3 The PERSEUS security kernel

PERSEUS itself is defined as a minimal, open source, security kernel, which provides all OS services required to protect security critical applications executed on top of it [29]. OSs are intended to run as applications on top of the security kernel, thereby providing the user with:

- A common and familiar user interface; and
- A backward compatible interface to re-use all uncritical standard applications and services [29].

The above design decision was also motivated by the fact that the development of a new secure OS without backward compatibility would be too costly [29]. From these assumptions development work was carried out with the objective of designing a security kernel that was:

- Minimal;
- Manageable;
- Stable; and
- Easy to evaluate [29].

3.7.3.1 The L4 microkernel

We begin our discussion of the PERSEUS security kernel with a brief examination of the L4 microkernel, on which the PERSEUS security kernel is based.

Security kernel design is based upon the same concepts as used in OS kernel design, where four broad categories can be identified: the monolithic kernel, the hybrid kernel, the exokernel and the one which we are most interested in, namely the microkernel.

Large monolithic kernels represented the means by which the earliest OSs were implemented, where the complete OS, including services, such as scheduling, file system, networking, device drivers, memory management and paging, were all packaged into a single kernel [31]. The later, microkernel, approach involves a radically different design, aimed to minimise the size of the kernel as much as possible, and to implement the majority of services outside the kernel.

This design principle led to the development of a kernel implementing only address spaces, IPC and basic scheduling. All servers outside the kernel are then run in user mode, and treated exactly like any other application by the kernel, each with their own address space and thereby protected from all other objects [31]. This modular design greatly simplifies the structure and design of the kernel; consequently, should a service server fail, the entire system is not brought down. Instead, the specific module can be restarted independently of the rest [31]. The L4 microkernel family is an example of a microkernel implementation.

The L4 microkernel is a second-generation microkernel designed and implemented by Liedtke to run on i486 and Pentium CPUs [31]. There are now numerous implementations of the L4 API on a variety of hardware architectures.

Whereas the first-generation microkernels were criticised for their inefficiency and inflexibility, second-generation microkernels (such as L4) have been widely praised. More specifically, L4 microkernels are claimed to possess the following properties [31]:

- They are message-based;
- They offer synchronous IPC;
- They have a simple-to-use external paging mechanisms; and a security mechanism based on secure domains (tasks, clans and chiefs);
- The kernels try to implement only a minimal set of abstractions on which OSs can be built flexibly.

These properties ensure that [31]:

- errors in one component are prevented from affecting others;
- only authorised processes can access hardware; and
- only the microkernel is executed in the supervisor mode of the CPU.

3.7.3.2   The security kernel
The PERSEUS security kernel consists of the components described in Table 3.6.

3.7.3.3   Security analysis
If this security kernel is extended to support TCG and NGSCB hardware, thereby combining security functionality as defined in Table 3.6 with security functionality provided by NGSCB/TCG hardware, Stüble *et al.* [8] claim that the requirements that should be met by a TP can be fulfilled. In order to utilise the security functionality offered, security critical applications do, however, have to be adapted to the PERSEUS interface.

Table 3.6   The PERSEUS security kernal

Component	Lines of code	Description	Implementation

Microkernel	7100	Provides:
		  Basic process support
		  IPC support
		  Thread support
		  Memory support and
		  Exception support
		Also provides capabilities to:
		Processes
		Interrupts
		I/O ports
		A process level AC mechanism is also provided
			Use of Fiasco or L4KA L4 microkernel
			Offers fast IPC; and uses clan and chief method of message redirection on top of hardware (process level access control)

Resource manager	5600	Enforces security policies on low level hardware resources, such as interrupts, processes and I/O ports	The resource manager, RMGR, which comes with the Fiasco distribution is utilised It controls access to interrupts; and manages capabilities to start new tasks Services to manage DMA channels and to access I/O ports are under development
Memory manager	654	Ensures that different services and applications do not share memory pages	The memory pager from the Fiasco distribution is used
Device drivers	Size depends on the size of the original drivers	Every device driver that accesses DMA-enabled devices has to be isolated in the secure environment to prevent malicious modifications	Not yet addressed
Trustworthy user interface	5400	Provides a trusted path by controlling the hardware of input devices Ensures only the active application receives user input	

Table 3.6   Continued

Component	Lines of code	Description	Implementation
Application manager	5000	Controls installation and removal of security critical applications based on code signing It enforces user-defined installation policies and assigns predefined sets of permissions to new applications	
Storage manger	500	Encrypts and decrypts memory pages of other applications and services and persistently stores them in the file system of the client OS	Encrypts memory pages and then passes them to a Linux task for storage.
Boot manager		Currently only marginally provided due to lack of hardware support	
DGD		A specific PERSEUS application Provides user compatibility to PGP	

Table 3.7 indicates how the requirements, as outlined in Section 3.7.2, are fulfilled with the combination of functionality provided by the minimal PERSEUS kernel and TCG/NGSCB hardware.

3.8   Secure coprocessors

In parallel to the development of trusted computing technologies described above, numerous alternative architectures, whose aim is also to develop a more secure and trustworthy platform, have been developed.

The most familiar of these alternative architecture types involves platforms which contain secure coprocessors. A secure coprocessor provides a tamper-resistant computing environment in which functions may be executed without interference,

Table 3.7   Security service provision

Security requirement	Method of fulfilment
Trustworthiness improved	Size and complexity of TCB is small, that is, 25 000 lines of code Also, the attestation functionality provided by TCG and NGSCB hardware allows external entities to trust the architecture
Application code and data protection during runtime	Existing CPU memory protection mechanisms, e.g. virtual address space separation, are used They are enforced by the PERSEUS security kernel memory manager To allow for the reuse of existing device driver implementations, DMA has to be tamed using methods as described in papers, such as Reference 32. In this paper, the authors advocate the use of I/O memory management unit hardware, available in modern platforms, to extend the encapsulation of device drivers as user processes. This allows DMA to be controlled making it infeasible for device drivers to access data other than the DMA buffers registered with the kernel
Protection of application code and data protection during storage	Protected by the extended storage manager, which uses sealing to ensure that security mechanisms cannot be bypassed by the booting of another, potentially malicious, OS
TCB integrity	The boot manager ensures that both the TCB and application code are protected while the system is switched off
A trusted path	Provided by the TCB that controls common user I/O components, such as the keyboard, display and mouse
Secure channel between devices and applications	A secure channel to devices and between applications is provided through the secure IPC communication mechanism
RNG	TCG/NGSCB hardware provide for secure random number generation

despite physical or logical access to the device. The IBM 4758 is an example of a user configurable, tamper-resistant coprocessor with the following properties [33]:

- A hardware tamper response;
- RNG;
- A layered design, where each device should have at least two layers, one responsible for implementing the code load security policy, which should be validated as correct, and a subsequent layer or layers for device personalisation;
- Self-initialisation, which implies that a programmable device must leave the factory ready to respond to tampering;

- Outbound authentication, which allows external entities to determine the exact applications running on the device;
- General coprocessor and auxiliary processors, which, for example, allow the efficient implementation of DES and modular arithmetic;
- Persistent storage, which may protect application data or arbitrary data directly using the 4758 tamper response in battery backed RAM, or indirectly by encrypting the data using keys stored in battery backed RAM; and also
- A third party programmable interface, which is as useable as possible.

Coprocessors essentially provide a tamper-resistant secluded area on a platform in which particular applications may be securely executed. As highlighted above, a variety of security services may be offered to applications executing or data processed within this region. In conjunction with this, outbound authentication is often permitted, allowing external entities to verify the exact applications running on the device. Coprocessors, however, are essentially separate from the generic platform processor, providing specialised protection for a limited set of applications and data, independently of what occurs outside of the device on the generic platform with which the coprocessor is associated. A challenger need only trust the specified coprocessing environment. This segregated protection is expensive to provide.

3.9   Hardened processors

The concept of hardened processors has also been widely discussed. Rather than implementing a secure coprocessor, which runs in parallel to the general platform processor, the primary processor is extended such that certain applications can be run securely in on-chip protected compartments. A process running in one compartment has only strictly controlled access to application code or data from another compartment. Off-chip compartment application code and data is also protected through the deployment of encryption and integrity mechanisms.

We begin with a brief examination of the XOM architecture [34] which provides protected environments/compartments for XOM code to execute in. The XOM architecture essentially provides on-chip protection of caches and registers, protection of cache and register values during context switching and on interrupts and confidentiality and integrity protection of application code and data when transferred to external memory.

In order to implement practically and efficiently a XOM machine, extensive hardware additions must be made to the CPU. In a hardware implementation of the XOM machine, all trust is put in the modified CPU hardware. Everything transmitted outside the main CPU is encrypted.

On the other hand, however, the XOM virtual machine monitor (XVMM) Implementation of the XOM machine, described below, significantly reduces necessary CPU hardware extensions. A software XVMM, whose integrity is validated via secure boot, is used to provide an abundance of the security services provided directly by the CPU in the hardware implementation.

We subsequently explore the AEGIS architecture [35], which builds upon concepts developed in the XOM architecture. Given the abstract AEGIS architecture, two potential architecture implementations are explored: an untrusted OS solution, which involves implementing all security mechanisms within the hardened AEGIS processor, and a trusted security kernel solution, where some of the core OS functionality is trusted, thereby enabling the minimisation of CPU modifications.

As is the case with the more efficient hardware implementation of the XOM architecture, the untrusted OS implementation of the AEGIS architecture puts all the trust in the CPU hardware, and therefore requires a complete overhaul of current system architectures.

The 'security kernel implementation' of AEGIS, while also requiring CPU modifications to be made, utilises a security kernel so that the requisite hardware adjustments may be minimised. Through the addition of secure boot and security services, loosely coupled with the sealing and platform attestation mechanisms as described in Section 3.3, the boundaries of trust may be moved from the trusted hardware core to encompass the security kernel running on the hardware.

3.9.1   Executable only memory (XOM)

Executable only memory [34] was proposed with the objective of preventing software consumers from examining executable code, thereby protecting any algorithms incorporated into the code. It also aimed to thwart the unauthorised execution of software through the deployment of XOM security mechanisms, described below. While, as stated above, the XOM architecture is not an implementation of trusted computing methodologies, it presents concepts closely linked to the notion of trusted computing. These concepts were later adopted and extended by the developers of the AEGIS processor are described in Section 3.9.2. Fundamental reference material for our discussion of XOM includes References 34 and 36.

3.9.1.1   The abstract XOM machine

In order to facilitate the execution of XOM code, an XOM machine, which supports internal compartments, is proposed. Within this XOM machine, 'a XOM process executing in one compartment cannot read data from another compartment', and all data that leaves a particular compartment on the XOM machine is integrity and confidentiality protected, as it is assumed that external memory is not secure.

An XOM machine, as defined by Lie *et al.* [34], has three fundamental tasks to fulfil:

- Decryption of the symmetric compartment key used to protect an incoming application, using the private key from the asymmetric key pair embedded in that particular XOM machine;
- Decryption of the program code using the symmetric compartment key; and

- Isolation of the active principal, for example, the decrypted code and its data, where principals are separated into compartments between which only strictly controlled information flow is possible.

3.9.1.2   XOM machine implementation

Throughout the course of their paper [34], Lie *et al.* consider two potential XOM machine implementations: a virtual machine implementation of a XOM machine and a hardware implementation of a XOM machine.

The virtual machine implementation of the XOM architecture involves running a special XOM virtual machine monitor (XVMM) on a slightly modified CPU, which integrates special microcode that incorporates [34]:

- a private key from a unique asymmetric key pair assigned to the XOM hardened processor;
- on-chip memory, which contains tagged shadow registers and the XOM key table;
- the ability to trap on instruction cache misses (to the XVMM); and
- a privileged mode under which XVMM runs.

The actual XVMM may be implemented either in software, where implementations must be authenticated via a secure boot, or in microcode. However, only the microcode XVMM implementation is explored by the authors.

The XVMM must execute as an authorised privileged program. It requires the processor to be configured to trap on instruction cache misses, so that the XVMM can then decrypt data and instructions coming from external memory. The XVMM then stores decrypted instructions to the instruction cache. On interrupts or context switches, where a copy of the encrypted XOM program instructions remains in external memory, the instruction cache may be flushed, as it contains no modified data.

While decrypted instructions may be saved to the instruction cache by the XVMM, the XVMM may not, however, store decrypted XOM program data to the data cache. Unlike decrypted XOM instructions, there are two types of program data: shared data, that is, data generated during XOM program execution, which an XOM program may authorise other programs to access; and XOM program private data. Shared data may be pushed from the caches unencrypted, whereas XOM private data needs to be both confidentiality- and integrity-protected when evicted from the data cache. As there is no way to differentiate between data types held in the data cache, without additional hardware extensions, the data cache is not used by the XVMM to store decrypted XOM program data.

In order to facilitate compartment access control in an XOM machine which contains no cache or register tags, the XVMM must facilitate interrupts and context switching by flushing instruction caches and clearing all registers. In order to support register clears, the XVMM must maintain a set of shadow registers for each compartment, where each of these registers stores a compartment ownership bit indicating whether the register is in the private or shared compartment and a saved bit indicating which registers we saved by the OS after the interrupt. When a compartment is interrupted, private compartment register values are copied to protected shadow registers by the processor, and then cleared; thereby protecting values from OS interrupt handlers. When the compartment is restarted, the values are returned.

In order to support the above functionality, the XVMM must implement the following eight additional instructions:

- enter_xom, which facilitates the initial decryption of the symmetric XOM application compartment key and decryption of the XOM program code and data, the registration of a handler for cache miss events and re-vectoring of all CPU exceptions and interrupts;
- exit_xom, which unregisters the handler for cache misses and restores handlers for all CPU exceptions and interrupts;
- secure_store, used to move data between private registers (where register status is stored in shadow registers) and the data cache and ultimately external memory. The XVMM MACs and encrypts register values before eviction;
- secure_load, used to import values into registers. The XVMM decrypts the value from memory and verifies the MAC. If the MAC can be verified, the register value is written and its 'private' status written to the shadow registers;
- move_from_shared and move_to_shared, which change the status of the registers in the status register to and from 'private';
- save_register, which moves all register values whose status is 'private' to the shadow registers; a record of the source register from which the value has been saved is also stored; and
- restore_register, which restores shadow register values to the source registers.

Only the XXVM can access the private key and secure on-chip memory. The alternative hardware implementation:

- Facilitates the use of data caches;
- Alleviates the necessity to flush the instruction cache every time there is a trap;
- Eliminates the overhead incurred through the use of the XVMM for cryptographic operations; and, finally,
- XOM instructions are both interpreted and implemented in hardware, thereby decreasing overhead.

Additional CPU hardware modifications required to facilitate a hardware implementation of the XOM machine include:

- a private key from a unique asymmetric key pair assigned to the XOM hardened processor;
- on-chip memory, which contains tagged shadow registers and the XOM key table;
- on-chip cache and register ownership tags; and
- a hardware cryptographic engine for symmetric encryption/decryption and MACing.

Because of the efficiency and performance issues associated with the XVMM implementation of the XOM machine, we now examine the concept of XOM in further detail, focusing particularly on its hardware implementation when exploring XOM machine concepts and instructions.

3.9.1.3   Compartments

As stated above, each XOM processor chip has an embedded asymmetric key pair, where the private decryption key is protected on-chip and the public encryption key is made available such that anyone can encrypt code for the particular chip. If, however, code for a particular chip were encrypted under its public key, instruction loading would be extremely inefficient. Therefore, the header block of the message contains a symmetric key, encrypted under the public key of the XOM chip, and the program image is encrypted under this symmetric session key. Each application will be encrypted under a different symmetric key.

In order to support trusted or secure execution environments, a 'compartment' is used to isolate independent software applications running on the same processor, where a compartment is built from, and defined by, the symmetric compartment key used originally by the service provider in order to protect distributed program image. The null compartment is defined as one where regular unencrypted code may run; it has no associated session key.

It is worth noting that, in order to protect the incoming XOM program image, not only should it be encrypted by the service provider before being communicated to the host, but it should also be integrity-protected via the use of a MAC or digital signature. According to Reference 34, there is no mechanism deployed in order to protect the integrity of the incoming program image while in transit from the service provider to the mobile host. The same may be said of the more recent thesis of Lie [36], where the deployment of an integrity protection mechanism is not explicitly mentioned in their software distribution model. The integrity verification of an incoming application, is however, implicitly implied in the instruction definition, where Lie states that the enter_xom instruction, described below, must always be followed by an encrypted and MACed application. No mention is made of how the MAC key is derived.

When a symmetric compartment key has been decrypted, the XOM machine associates it with an arbitrary XOM ID and a 128-bit hash of the encrypted compartment key in a key table stored in the XOM machine.

More specifically, the isolation of active principals through the use of compartments, as defined above, may be achieved by the provision of three fundamental services, secure storage, external memory protection and security over interrupts.

3.9.1.3.1   Secure storage

On-chip, all XOM data and code in caches and registers are tagged with a unique XOM identifier, which is mapped to the code's decrypted symmetric compartment key in a session key table. Programs that run in the clear have a XOM identifier of 0. The size of the session key table and the number of XOM identifier tags depend on how many concurrently executing principals can have data in the machine.

At any one time, only one program will be executing, therefore there will be only:

- one active principal;
- one active XOM identifier; and
- one active compartment key.

When this active principal produces data, it is automatically tagged with the active XOM identifier. Subsequently, when an attempt is made by an active principal to read data, the tag on the data is compared with the active XOM identifier, and access is only permitted if these values are identical.

In order to implement the proposed functionality, a series of instructions and additional functionality must be added to the abstract machine. Two basic instructions are initially required of the abstract machine to facilitate compartment establishment, namely enter_xom and exit_xom, as described in Table 3.8. These instructions facilitate the decryption and integrity verification of XOM code and data from external memory into the instruction stream.

The instructions defined for use when moving data between caches and registers in the active compartment on the abstract machine include those indicated in Table 3.9. These instructions act as normal load and store instructions for XOM processes.

Although isolation of principles is required, complete isolation, where principals are separated by compartments, and between which no information flow is possible, would prove impractical and a hindrance. In order to facilitate communication between protected principals, two further instructions are also defined (see Table 3.10). The mv_to_null and mv_from_null instructions provide a controlled way of changing tags associated with data values.

Executing these commands on data that was not originally tagged, results in an exception.

3.9.1.3.2   Interrupts

Extra consideration must also be given to interrupts, so that an untrusted OS can save the register state of an XOM process without leaving the register contents vulnerable to attack. Two further instructions are necessary in order to protect register values. These instructions, described in Table 3.11, package data in such a way that any principal, for example, the OS, may be permitted to move the data with the knowledge that it cannot be tampered with in any way by the moving principal. This, therefore, provides the OS with a means of scheduling XOM processes without violating compartment security.

3.9.1.3.3   External memory

The mechanisms described above would prove sufficient in the implementation of XOM code if either external memory was secure or, alternatively, if there were no need to use external memory. Either case rarely holds, however, and it therefore became clear that the compartments, as defined above, would have to be extended to incorporate external memory. In order to extend a compartment:

- Tagged data in caches is MACed and then encrypted with the appropriate compartment key before it leaves the abstract machine;

Table 3.8   XOM enter_xom and exit_xom instructions

enter_xom	exit_xom
All XOM code is preceded by an enter_xom instruction	This instruction changes the active identifier back to null and the machine stops decrypting
The source register holds the starting memory address of the encrypted session key for the XOM code	If an abnormal 'trap' or 'interrupt' occurs, an implicit exit_xom is executed before the instructions from the interruption handler are executed
The enter_xom instruction indicates that all the following code belongs to a principal associated with the session key	
The machine checks to see if the session key has already been decrypted by comparing the 128-bit hash of the encrypted symmetric key with those stored in the XOM key table	
If the compartment key is already in the table, the active identifier is set to that entry and the encrypted XOM code is fetched	
If no matching entry is found:	
A free entry in the XOM key table is found	
An XOM ID is assigned to the key	
The active identifier is set to this entry	
The encrypted symmetric key is loaded and the asymmetric decryption algorithm is run on the key	
The 128-bit hash of the encrypted compartment key and the decrypted compartment key is then entered into the key table	
All instructions following the enter_xom instruction must be encrypted and accompanied by a valid MAC; otherwise, they are not loaded into the instruction cache for execution	

- A secure hash is generated on regions of memory and stored in on-chip registers so that the replay of data in external memory can be detected. In turn, register keys prevent the replay of registers in which the memory hashes are stored.

3.9.2   AEGIS

Suh *et al.* [35] describe the architecture for a single chip AEGIS processor, which they use in order to build a system secure against physical and software attack, assuming untrusted external memory. As was the case with the XOM architecture, AEGIS is

Table 3.9   XOM secure_load and secure_store instructions

secure_load	secure_store
Used if the required value is found in the cache If a line hits in the cache, the XOM cache tag of the cache line is compared with the active XOM ID If the values match, then the value in the cache and the XOM ID are written to the register	The XOM processor verifies that the source register tags match the active XOM ID If they match, the register value is stored to the cache and the particular cache line is tagged with the active XOM ID ownership tags

Table 3.10   XOM mv_to_shared and mv_from_shared instructions

mv_to_shared	mv_from_shared
Changes the XOM ID tag on a register to the null identifier After execution of this instruction, access to data by the original principal results in an exception	Changes the tag on a register to the tag of the active XOM identifier

Table 3.11   XOM save_register and restore_register instructions

save_register	restore_register
The XOM processor takes the contents of the register and creates an encapsulated version that other principals can move but cannot manipulate To achieve this the register contents are MACed and encrypted with a register key associated with the XOM ID in the XOM key table Each XOM compartment register key is regenerated every time a particular XOM compartment is interrupted, to prevent the replay of saved register values	Used to restore a register value This instruction decrypts the register value, verifies the MAC and then restores it

not an implementation of trusted computing methodologies, but it presents concepts closely linked to the notion of trusted computing and to the development of more trust-worthy and secure platforms. More specifically the security kernel implementation of the AEGIS architecture incorporates concepts such as secure booting and notions loosely coupled with platform attestation, that is, a platform makes a statement about the software environment it is running and the sealing mechanism, where content cannot be decrypted unless a specified environment is running on the platform, as described by the TCG.

It is claimed that, within this AEGIS architecture, both tamper evident and tamper-resistant environments can be provided for multiple mistrusting processes. Tamper evident environments are defined as authenticated environments, where physical or software tampering can be detected [35]. Tamper-resistant environments are defined as private and authenticated environments where an adversary cannot gain any information about data or software within the environment by tampering with or observing system operation [35].

Suh *et al.* also describe two implementations of their architecture:

- In the first implementation it is assumed that the core functionality of the OS is trusted and implemented in a security kernel; and
- In the second implementation the use of an untrusted OS is assumed.

The fundamental reference material for the following description is Reference 35.

3.9.2.1   Secure computing model: assumptions

Before we examine the AEGIS architecture in detail, we highlight suppositions made by the authors with respect to the computing model. Abstractly speaking, the authors reflect upon systems that are built around processing subsystems with external memory and peripherals. The processor chip is assumed to be trusted and protected from physical attacks, implying that the internal state cannot be tampered with or observed by physical means. It may contain secret information that identifies it and allows it to communicate with the outside world securely, such as a physical random function, or the secret key from a certified public key pair [35].

External memory and peripherals are assumed to be untrusted and therefore may be observed and tampered with.

Generally, the OS is assumed to be untrusted and, consequently, attacks by an OS or malicious software are deemed feasible. However, in certain implementations, part of the OS (the security kernel) may operate at a higher level than the remainder of the OS [35].

An adversary may also attack off-chip memory.

3.9.2.2   The AEGIS architecture

We now examine the security services the authors specify as necessary for the provision of both tamper-evident and tamper-resistant environments. Interspersed with the descriptions of these necessary security services, potential mechanisms for their successful provision are explored. Methods of implementing the secure execution environments are highlighted, both in the scenario where a security kernel is in existence within the TCB in conjunction with a hardened AEGIS processor chip; and also in the scenario where no security kernel exists, that is, there is merely an untrusted OS and a hardened AEGIS processor chip (the TCB).

In the first scenario, the security kernel will operate at a higher level of protection than the rest of the OS, in order to prevent attacks from untrusted parts of the OS, such as device drivers.

In the alternate scenario, where no security kernel exists, the processor needs to be aware of all processes running in AEGIS mode so that their states can be securely tracked. In this scenario, a secure context manager (SCM), is added to the hardened AEGIS processor, to ensure protection of secure processes.

- The SCM assigns a Secure Process Identity (SPID) to each secure process, where a zero SPID represents regular processes.
- The SCM then maintains a table for each process running in AEGIS mode containing:

    The SPID of the program;

    The program hash;

    A field used to store architectural register values;

    A field used to store a hash for memory integrity verification;

    A bit which indicates whether the process is in tamper-evident or tamper-resistant mode; and

    A pair of keys for encryption (a static key and a dynamic key).
- A table entry is created by the initial enter_aegis instruction; and deleted by exit_aegis instruction.

This SCM table may be stored on the processor, but this will obviously restrict the number of processes that can be held in the table. Hence, virtual memory space, managed by the OS and stored in off-chip memory, is generally used to store the table, where a memory integrity mechanism, described below, is used to prevent a malicious OS tampering with the SCM table. A special on-chip cache is used to store SCM table entries for recent processes. When encryption keys and register values in the SCM table are moved off-chip, they are protected using a master key held in the processor.

3.9.2.3   Tamper-Evident (TE) processing

A TE environment does not provide for the privacy of code or data. The integrity of programs is, however, guaranteed.

3.9.2.4   Additional instructions

In order to enable TE processing, an application program must be provided with the use of the instruction set given in Table 3.12.

The valid execution of a program on a general-purpose time-sharing processor can be guaranteed, or a TE environment constructed, by securing the program against three potential forms of attack:

- Attacks on initial state;
- Attacks to on-chip caches or off-chip memory; and

Table 3.12   AEGIS additional instructions

Instruction	Description
enter_aegis	Start execution in TE environment
exit_aegis	Exit TE environment
sign_msg	Generate a signature on a message and a program identity/hash with the processor's secret key

- Attacks on state information when interrupts occur or during context switching [35].

3.9.2.5   Protection of initial state

In order to guarantee that the initial state of a program is properly set-up:

1. The enter_aegis instruction is used to enter TE mode;
2. This instruction specifies a region containing stub code, which is used to generate the program's hash;
3. This hash, when calculated, is then stored in protected storage for later use;

   This stub code gets executed directly after the enter_aegis instruction, and is responsible for verifying the hashes of any applications or data upon which the application relies by comparing their hashes with hashes stored in the stub region;

   The stub code also checks the sanity of the environment it is running in, that is,
   - the processor mode it is running in;
   - the virtual address of the stub code; and
   - the position of stack must all be checked and validated.

This is summarised in Table 3.13.

3.9.2.6   Protection of state on interrupts

The integrity of the register state of the program must also be protected and guaranteed to be preserved over an interrupt – see Table 3.14.

3.9.2.7   Memory

The integrity of on-chip caches and off-chip memory must be protected against both physical and software attacks. Due to different intrinsic physical attributes of each of the memory locations, on-chip caches and off-chip memory are examined separately.

3.9.2.7.1   On-chip cache integrity

By virtue of the fact that on-chip caches are on-chip, they should be implicitly secure from physical attack and therefore need only to be protected form buggy software – see Table 3.15.

Table 3.13 AEGIS – protection of initial state

	Implementation containing a security kernel	Untrusted OS solution
Security kernel start-up	The kernel identity should be verifiable by a user, where a user can identify a TCB by the security kernel hash and the processor's public/private key pair The processor computes the hash of kernel at boot time, as is the case in the NGSCB architecture After this, the kernel's integrity is protected using the same methods used for the protection of other secure processes, that is, Trusted VM management: Off-chip integrity verification	N/A
Initial start-up of programs	Managed by the security kernel Ensures initial state is correct	The SCM implements the enter_aegis operation as a processor instruction A hash of the program code and data are calculated The hash is then stored in the SCM table (In architectures, such as x86, the initial stack pointer is checked to avoid stack overflow should an interrupt occur)

3.9.2.7.2 Off-chip memory integrity

Off-chip memory (see Table 3.16) is vulnerable to both physical and software attack. Therefore, the integrity of a block needs to be verified whenever it is read from off-chip memory.

1. Memory integrity verification mechanisms operate as a layer between the L2 cache and the encryption mechanisms;
2. Merkle trees or hash trees as they are sometimes called are used in order to verify the integrity of dynamic data in untrusted storage, where;
   - the memory space is divided into multiple chunks;
   - a parent is the hash of the concatenation of its children, where in this system, every hash covers one L2 cache block;
   - the tree root is stored in the SCM, where it cannot be tampered with.

Table 3.14   AEGIS – protection of state on interrupts

	Implementation containing a security kernel	Untrusted OS solution
Interrupts	Managed by the security kernel, which ensures that states are correctly restored after an interrupt	The untrusted OS handles all aspects of multitasking The processor must, however, verify that a TE process's state is preserved when it is not executing, so the SCM stores all process register values in the SCM table when the interrupt occurs and restores them later

3.   In order to check the integrity of a node:
   - the processor reads the node hash and its siblings from memory;
   - concatenates the values; and
   - checks the resultant hash matches that of the parent.

This process is repeated until tree root is reached.

If, however, the entire memory space is protected, no sharing is permitted between processes; and no input from I/O device is allowed. Therefore, a program should be able to access a part of memory with no integrity protection [35].

The solution involves the use of the most significant bit (MSB), which is used to determine whether the integrity of the address should be protected or not. This allows for the upper half of virtual memory only to be protected. In view of this, the program must lay out its code and data appropriately. This static division of memory restricts processes to only half of the memory space for secure data, although this is not a problem for 64-bit architectures [35].

3.9.2.8   Trusting program execution results

In order that the results of a program's execution by a system can be trusted, in spite of the fact that communication channels from a processor may be untrusted:

- the sign_msg operation is used (see Table 3.17)
- the signature of the security processor is provided on the message (results) concatenated with the identity/hash of the program from which the message originated;

   If there is a security kernel within the TCB, the signature of the security processor will be calculated on the message concatenated with both the hash of the security kernel and the hash of the program from which the message originated.

Table 3.15   AEGIS – cache integrity

	Implementation containing a security kernel	Untrusted OS solution
Protection of on-chip caches	Physical attacks: The processor chip is assumed to be tamper resistant, therefore on-chip caches are assumed safe from physical attacks Software attacks: The security kernel protects on-chip caches from software attacks Virtual memory and privileges are considered adequate to protect applications from each other A virtual memory manager is included within the security kernel to protect the integrity of memory from software attack	Physical attacks: The processor chip is assumed to be tamper resistant, therefore on-chip caches are assumed safe from physical attacks Software attacks: On-chip caches are protected using SPID tags When a process accesses an on-chip cache block, the block is tagged with the owners SPID This specifies the owner of the cache block Each block will also contain the virtual address used by the owner process on last accessing the block If a secure process later wants access to a cache block which requires integrity protection, the processor verifies the block before using it: If the active SPID = SPID of the cache block; and The accessing virtual address = virtual address of cache block, access is permitted

3.9.2.9   Private Tamper-Resistant (PTR) processing

In order to allow for the provision of tamper-resistant processing, the tamper-evident environment described above may be extended to support private and authenticated operation [35].

3.9.2.9.1   *Additional instructions*
As described in Table 3.18, one new instruction is added to support this mode.
In a PTR environment:

- all register values are considered private and protected;
- whether instructions and data exported to external memory are protected is dependent on the value of the second MSB of the address. Data stored in virtual addresses with the second MSB set is privacy-protected.

Table 3.16   AEGIS – off-chip memory integrity

	Implementation containing a security kernel	Untrusted OS solution
Protection of off-chip memory	Physical attacks: To protect off-chip memory from physical attacks, hardware memory integrity verification, is applied to physical memory space	Physical and software attacks: To protect off-chip memory from physical attacks, hardware memory integrity verification, is applied to physical memory space
	Software attacks: The security kernel protects off-chip memory from software attacks	Software attacks: In this instance, the memory verification algorithm is applied to each secure process's virtual memory space.
	Virtual memory and privilege levels are considered adequate to protect applications from each other	Each TE process uses a separate hash tree to protect its own virtual memory space where changes made by different processes are detected as tampering
	Therefore, a virtual memory manager is included within the security kernel to protect the integrity of memory from software	

Table 3.17   AEGIS – sign_msg operation

	Implementation containing a security kernel	Untrusted OS solution
Signing operation	Sign_msg is implemented as a system call	Sign_msg is implemented as a processor instruction

3.9.2.9.2   *Protection of initial state*
The set_aegis_mode is used to enable or disable privacy from tamper-evident mode see Table 3.18. The initial state is therefore validated when the initial enter_aegis instruction is called.

3.9.2.9.3   *Protection of state on interrupts*
In order to ensure the privacy of registers against software attacks when interrupts occur, the TCB saves the register values in private storage in the TCB, and then clears the registers before the untrusted interrupt handler starts – see Table 3.19.

Table 3.18   AEGIS – set_aegis_mode

Instruction	Description
set_aegis_mode	Used to enable or disable the PTR environment from TE mode
	After this instruction, a static key, concatenated with the protected program identity/hash, encrypted under the public key of the security processor, must be provided. The static key can only be decrypted by a particular AEGIS processor. It is set as the static key for the protected program if and only if the encrypted program hash received matches the hash of the program decrypted by the AEGIS processor
	If there is a security kernel, the input to set_aegis_mode must include the concatenation of the security kernel hash, the program hash and the static key encrypted under the public key of the security processor
	In this instance, the processor will only decrypt the static key if the security kernel hash matches the encrypted hash of the security kernel received
	This static key may then be used to decrypt the accompanying application, as above

Table 3.19   AEGIS – protection of state on interrupts

	Implementation containing a security kernel	Untrusted OS solution
Interrupts	Managed by the security kernel which ensures that states are correctly restored after an interrupt	The untrusted OS handles all aspects of multitasking As was the case in the TE environment, the SCM stores all process register values in the SCM table when the interrupt occurs, and restores them at the end. In addition, for a PTR process, once the values have been stored in the SCM table, the working copy is cleared such that interrupt handlers cannot see previous values

3.9.2.9.4   On-chip/off-chip memory

The TCB also protects on-chip caches and off-chip memory so that no process can read the private data belonging to another process.

On-chip cache privacy. Once again, since on-chip caches are on-chip, they should be implicitly secure from physical attack and therefore need only to be protected from buggy software. The issues are summarised in Table 3.20.

Table 3.20   AEGIS – on-chip cache privacy

	Implementation containing a security kernel	Untrusted OS solution
On-chip caches	Physical attacks: The processor chip is deemed tamper resistant, and therefore on-chip caches are assumed safe from physical attacks Software attacks: The security kernel protects on-chip caches against software attacks Virtual memory and privileges are considered adequate to protect applications from each other Therefore, a virtual memory manager is included within the security kernel to protect the integrity of memory from software attach	Physical attacks: The processor chip is deemed tamper resistant, and therefore on-chip caches are assumed safe from physical attacks Software attacks: In PTR mode, accesses to private cache blocks are allowed if and only if the cache block SPID = active SPID; and the active process is in the PTR mode Otherwise, the block is evicted from the cache and reloaded

Off-chip memory encryption. When data needs to leave the chip but remain privacy-protected, it is encrypted by the TCB using symmetric encryption. Each process uses:

- A *static key* to decrypt instructions and data from the received program binary. It is obtained, encrypted under the processor public key, as input to the set_aegis_mode instruction. Following its initial use, it is used to protect instructions and data from the program binary when exported to off-chip memory.
- A *dynamic key* to encrypt data generated during program execution. It is randomly chosen by the TCB when enter_aegis instruction is called.

The authors advocate the use of AES as the symmetric encryption algorithm, although this is not compulsory. The functions are summarised in Table 3.21.

3.10   Conclusions

In this chapter, the state of the art in trusted computing technology has been examined. Various initiatives, projects and specification sets have been explored. It is clear that, despite the negative criticism often associated with this particular area of computing, trusted computing technologies offer a wide range of functionality which may be leveraged to improve computer security.

It must also be noted, however, that this chapter reflects these technologies as they are currently documented. This area is the subject of much current research and

Table 3.21 AEGIS – off-chip memory encryption

	Implementation containing a security kernel	Untrusted OS solution
Off-chip memory	A hardware engine is placed between the integrity checker and off-chip memory bus For the PTR, the security kernel executes the set_aegis_mode operation with: the static key, kernel hash and program hash encrypted under the processor public key, as input The instruction decrypt_key is then used by the security kernel, so that it can retrieve the program hash and the static key if the security kernel hash matches that received as input to the set_aegis_mode instruction Once the kernel decrypts the hash(es) and the static key, the static key is set for the program if its calculated hash matches the one returned with the key During context switching between processes, the security kernel must clear the static key of the process being interrupted and, if appropriate, load the key of the new process	Also achieved via the placement of a hardware engine between the integrity checker and off-chip memory bus

development, and the specifications, functionality, architectures, mechanisms and implementations associated with trusted computing technologies are evolving and changing very rapidly.

Acknowledgements

The work reported in this paper has formed part of the Core 3 Research Programme of the Virtual Centre of Excellence in Mobile & Personal Communications, Mobile VCE, www.mobilevce.com, whose funding support, including that of EPSRC, is gratefully acknowledged. More detailed technical reports on this research are available to Industrial Members of Mobile VCE.

I would also like to thank Graeme Proudler, HP (TCG); Marcus Peinado, Microsoft; David Grawrock, Intel; Don Felton, ARM; and Edward Suh, who made themselves available to answer any questions and clarify any queries that arose in relation to the respective technologies with which they are involved.

Appendix

Further information on the Trusted Computing Group, including access to all specifications and additional documentation, is available at www.trustedcomputinggroup.org

The original Trusted Computing Platform Alliance website is also still available at www.trustedcomputing.org

The latest information detailing Microsoft's NGSCB can be found at http://www.microsoft.com/resources/ngscb/default.mspx

Microsoft's NGSCB technical frequently asked questions may also be found at http://www.microsoft.com/technet/security/news/ngscb.mspx

Intel's LaGrande Technology document set can be found at www.intel.com/technology/security

Ross Anderson's frequently asked questions on trusted computing are available at http://www.cl.cam.ac.uk/~rja14/tcpa-faq.html

Further information on ARM's TrustZone technology is available at http://www.arm.com/products/CPUs/arch-trustzone.html

The PERSEUS project official website is http://www.perseusos.org/

References

1 S. Schoen. Trusted computing: promise and risk. Electronic Frontier Foundation White Paper, October 2003. Available at http://www.eff.org/Infra/trusted_computing/20031001_tc.php

2 R. Anderson. Cryptography and competition policy – issues with 'trusted computing'. In *Proceedings of PODC'03*, July 13–16, Boston, MA, pp. 3–10, ACM Press, 2003.

3 R. Anderson. *Security Engineering – A Guide to Building Dependable Distributed Systems*. John Wiley and Sons, New York, 2001.

4 B. Balacheff, L. Chen, S. Pearson, D. Plaquin, and G. Proudler. In S. Pearson, ed., *Trusted Computing Platforms: TCPA Technology in Context*. Prentice Hall PTR, Upper Saddle River, NJ, 2003.

5 Trusted Computing Group. TCG specification architecture overview, version 1.2, April 2004.

6 P. England, B. Lampson, J. Manferdelli, M. Peinado, and B. Willman. A trusted open platform. *IEEE Computer*, 36(7): 55-62, 2003.

7 M. Peinado, Y. Chen, P. England, and J. Manferdelli. NGSCB: a trusted open system. In H. Wang, J. Pieprzyk, and V. Varadharajan, eds, *Proceedings of the 9th Australasian Conference on Information Security and Privacy (ACISP 2004)*, July 13–15, Sydney, Australia, *volume 3108 of Lecture Notes in Computer Science*, pp. 86–97, Springer-Verlag, Berlin, 2004.

8 A. R. Sadeghi and C. Stüble. Bridging the gap between TCPA/Palladium and personal security. Technical Report, Saarland University, 2003. Available at http://www-krypt.cs.uni-sb.de/download/papers/SadStu2003.pdf

9 Trusted Computing Group. Work group charter summary, 2004.

10 Trusted Computing Group. Main specification: design principals, version 1.2, October 2003.

11 Trusted Computing Group. Main specification: data structures, version 1.2, October 2003.

12 Trusted Computing Group. Main specification: commands, version 1.2, October 2003.

13 Trusted Computing Group. Main specification: specification changes, version 1.2, October 2003.

14 Trusted Computing Group. TCG software stack (TSS) specification, version 1.1, August 2003.

15 IEEE. IEEE P1363 Standard specifications for public key cryptography. Available at http://grouper.ieee.org/groups/1363/

16 A. Menezes, P. van Oorschot, and S. Vanstone. *Handbook of Applied Cryptography, volume 6 of Discrete Mathematics and its Applications*, CRC Press, Boca Raton, Fl, 1997.

17 B. Kaliski and J. Staddon. PKCS #1: RSA cryptographic specifications – version 2, Internet request for comments 2437. RFC 2437, October 1999.

18 H. Krawczyk, M. Bellare, and R. Canetti. HMAC – keyed hashing for message authentication, Internet request for comments 2104, RFC 2104, February 1997.

19 NIST. Secure hash standard. Federal Information Processing Standards Publication FIPS PUB 180 – 1, National Institute of Standards and Technology (NIST), April 1997.

20 NIST. Security requirements for cryptographic modules. Federal Information Processing Standards Publication FIPS PUB 140 – 1, National Institute of Standards and Technology (NIST), January 1994.

21 NIST. Common criteria of information technology security evaluation, version 2.1, August 1999.

22 R. Walsh. Q &A: Microsoft seeks industry wide collaboration for 'Palladium' initiative. Press Pass – Information for Journalists, July 2002. Available at http://www.microsoft.com/presspass/features/2002/jul02/07-01palladium.asp

23 J. Lettice. Bad publicity: clashes trigger MS Palladium name change. *The Register*, 27 January 2003. Available at http://www.theregister.co.uk/2003/01/27/bad_publicity_clashes_trigger_ms/

24 Y. Chen, P. England, M. Peinado, and B. Willman. High assurance computing on open hardware architectures. Technical Report MSR-TR-2003-20, Microsoft Research, Microsoft Corporation, March 2003.

25 E. Cram. NGSCB: development considerations for nexus computing agents. Microsoft Corporation, October 2003. Available at http://msdn.miscrosoft.com/library/en-us/dnsecure/html/nca_considerations.asp

26 Intel. LaGrande Technology architectural overview, September 2003. Available at http://www.intel.com/technology/security/downloads/LT_Arch_Overview.htm

27 T. Halfhill. ARM dons armour, Microprocessor report article, Reed Electronics Group. Available at http://www.arm.com/miscPDFs/4136.pdf

28 T. Alves and D. Felton. TrustZone: integrated hardware and software security, enabling trusted computing in embedded systems. ARM White Paper, July 2004.

29 A. R. Sadeghi and C. Stüble. Taming 'trusted platforms' by operating system design. In K. Chae and M. Yung, eds, *Proceedings of the 4th International Workshop on Information Security Applications (WISA 2003)*, August 25–27, Jeju Island, Korea, *Revised Papers, volume 2908 of Lecture Notes in Computer Science*, pp. 286–302, Springer-Verlag, Berlin, 2004.

30 B. Pfitzmann, J. Riordan, C. Stüble, M. Waidner, and A. Weber. The PERSEUS system architecture. Technical Report RZ 3335 (#93381), IBM Research Division, Zurich Laboratory, April 2003.

31 J. Liedtke. Toward real microkernels. *Communications of the ACM*, 39(9): 70–77, 1996.

32 B. Leslie and G. Heiser. Towards untrusted devices drivers. Technical Report UNSW-CSE-TR-0303, School of Computer Science and Engineering, March 2003.

33 J. G. Dyer, M. Lindemann, R. Perez, R. Sailer, L. van Doorn, S.W. Smith, and S. Weingart. Building the IBM 4758 secure coprocessor, *IEEE Computer*, 34(10): 57–66, 2001.

34 D. Lie, C. Thekkath, M. Mitchell, P. Lincoln, D. Boneh, J. Mitchell, and M. Horowitz. Architectural support for copy and tamper resistant software. In *Proceedings of the 9th International Conference on Architectural Support for Programming Languages and Operating Systems (ASPLOS-ix)*, pp. 168–177, ACM Press, New York, 2000.

35 G. E. Suh, D. Clarke, B. Gassend, M. van Dyke, and S. Devadas. AEGIS: architecture for tamper evident and tamper resistant processing. In *Proceedings of the 17th International Conference on Supercomputing*, pp. 160–171, ACM Press, New York, 2003.

36 D. Lie. Architectural support for copy and tamper-resistant software, Ph.D. thesis, Stanford University, December 2003.

37 D. Safford. The need for TCPA. IBM Research White Paper, October 2002. Available at http://www.research.ibm.com/gsal/tcpa/why_tcpa.pdf

38 Trusted Computing Platform Alliance. Main specification, version 1.1b, February 2003.

Chapter 4

An overview of NGSCB

Marcus Peinado, Paul England and Yuqun Chen

4.1   Introduction

A major challenge the computer industry is facing today is how to effectively protect end users against a plethora of email viruses and network intrusions. An obvious solution is to make the desktop Operating System (OS) and applications flawless and bug-free. However, experience shows that this is an impractical goal [1]. The reasons are threefold: the rich functionality users expect from mass market OSs makes these systems so large and complex that security bugs will exist even after rigorous testing and the use of advanced quality assurance methodology during the development process; similar problems apply to applications and device drivers; finally, configuration and maintenance are non-trivial, such that users often mis-configure the system.

Security vulnerabilities exist largely due to software bugs, some of which are in the operating systems. Commercial OSs have rapidly grown in size in order to provide ever richer user experiences. Rigorous development and testing can uncover and eliminate a large percentage of these bugs. However, a small number will always remain. The problem is further compounded by the necessity to support an arbitrary number of devices in a consumer desktop OS. A bug in a device driver may be exploited to subvert the system. Again, although stringent testing standards are successful at reducing the number of driver bugs, security vulnerabilities cannot be completely eliminated in complex device drivers.

These problems were recognised decades ago and led to the development of systems that focused on simplicity, correctness and security, rather than rich mass market functionality [2–4]. In spite of their security merits, none of these systems was successful in the mass market. Given today's personal computers, it appears extremely unlikely that a system that provided significantly less functionality than existing systems would be accepted by users, irrespective of how secure it was. The system has to provide all existing functionality to users. In addition, it should provide strong protection for the limited set of tasks that needs such protection (e.g., electronic banking).

In light of the virtual impossibility of providing ultimate security for a large mass market operating system, we opt to construct a safe execution environment that coexists with the mass market operating system on a desktop – a tight security sanctuary on an otherwise bug-prone system. Such a platform would allow the user to run a few highly trusted applications without having to worry about interference from malicious applications, compromised OSs and subverted hardware devices. This alternative has a pragmatic attraction: the secure execution environment only has to support a few trusted applications. Its construction can therefore be highly specialised, reducing the code size by orders of magnitude, and lending itself to close scrutiny.

NGSCB, the Next-Generation Secure Computing Base being developed by Microsoft, provides exactly this high-assurance runtime environment for trustworthy applications on a regular Personal Computer (PC). This chapter describes NGSCB system architecture and some aspects of its implementation.

Section 4.2 lists the requirements under which the system was designed. Sections 4.3 and 4.4 describe how a safe execution environment and a mass market OS can coexist on a single computer, with Section 4.3 summarising existing approaches and their shortcomings and Section 4.4 providing a detailed description of our solution. Section 4.5 explains how we use code identities to enable robust mechanisms for authentication and the protection of persistent data. Section 4.6 describes a concrete hardware-based implementation of these mechanisms. Section 4.7 describes how a complete system can be configured. Section 4.8 discusses related work.

4.2   Requirements

NGSCB strives for a general-purpose, secure computing environment for running trusted applications. The task would be much simpler if we were only to concentrate on providing a set of application-specific hardware systems, for example, a custom-designed terminal that allows secure, authenticated remote access by bank customers. This narrow approach may be suitable for a limited set of applications but would not meet the security demands of the majority of corporate customers and home users. From both the ergonomic and the economic point of view, it is safe to argue that most people would prefer a unified computing environment to an ever increasing number of home and office gadgets.

On such a system, security mechanisms must be devised to protect the trusted applications from the rest of the system, and to protect the interaction between the user and a trusted application, that between a trusted application and a remote service and that between a user and a remote service.

4.2.1   Security requirements

More specifically, the execution environment must possess the following properties.

- No interference. The execution environment must provide a program that executes in it with the same underlying machine interface every time the program executes. The program must be isolated from external interference. A necessary condition is that a deterministic sequential program that does not access devices or persistent state should always reach the same result, irrespective of other programs that might have executed earlier or at the same time on the same machine.
- No observation. The computations and data of a program should not be observable by other entities, except for data the program chooses to reveal (e.g., through Inter Process Communication (IPC)).
- Trusted paths. A program should be able to receive data from a local input device (keyboard, mouse), such that only the program and the user of the input device share the data. Data integrity must be assured. A similar requirement applies to local output devices (video).
- Persistent storage. A program should be able to store data (e.g., cryptographic keys) persistently, such that the integrity and the confidentiality of the data are ensured.
- Communication. A program should be able to exchange data with another program, such that the integrity and the confidentiality of the data are ensured.
- Local authentication. A local user should be able to determine the identity of a program.
- Remote authentication. A program should be able to authenticate itself to a remote entity. For example, a corporate network administrator should be able to verify that all machines on his network are running the latest security patches and virus checker files.

4.2.1.1   Threat model

The security properties listed above must hold in the presence of adversarial code (e.g., viruses) executing on the machine. We assume an adversary may execute his code not only in user mode but also in kernel (supervisor) mode. The adversarial code may also program certain devices (e.g., Direct Memory Access (DMA) controllers) to assist in the attack.

Our adversary model is significantly more powerful than common OS security models. These models typically assume that adversarial application code may execute in user mode. Furthermore, they equate adversarial code executing in kernel mode with a complete breakdown of the system's security. These are unrealistic assumptions, for the open architecture of PCs entails the presence of a large number of often very complex device drivers, which are subject to different types of attacks by applications.

4.2.1.2   Assurance

We also require the system to provide high assurance for its security features. Assurance is the confidence one has that a system will behave as specified [5,6]. Given some specified functionality for which high assurance is required, the Trusted Computing Base (TCB) is defined as the collection of hardware and software components, on which this functionality depends. Based on vast empirical evidence and the current state of assurance methodology (formal methods, testing), it is generally believed that high-assurance systems require a TCB that is small, simple and stable over time and centrally controlled and verified.

This chapter focuses not on the assurance methodology,[1] but on the impact of the assurance requirement on system architecture. Several fundamental design choices described in this chapter are the result of the need to keep the TCB small and simple, in order to make it 'assurable'. One such design decision, a salient feature of our system, is to exclude the mass market OS and most device drivers from the TCB.

4.2.2   Commercial requirements

In order to be commercially viable in a mass market environment, our system has to meet the following requirements:

- Open architecture. The system has to host a large class of hardware components and expose them to applications by means of device drivers. Many of the hardware components and peripherals of PCs (Central Processing Units (CPUs), chipsets, graphics, storage, printers, imaging) are produced in different versions and with a variety of hardware interfaces by different vendors. This variety leads to a large number of hardware configurations, which increases continually as new devices become available. The number of software configurations is similarly large due to the fact that each new device requires an associated software driver. Our system has to operate in this very diverse hardware and software environment.
- No central authority. This requirement is closely related to the previous one. The system must not require a central authority (e.g., a certification authority) to 'approve' hardware or software before the system 'admits' it.
- Legacy support. The system must be compatible with existing mass market technology. That is, the system must be compatible with most existing peripheral devices and application programs. For example, most deployed Personal Computer Interface (PCI) cards or Universal Serial Bus (USB) devices should work in the new system. The system may only require very limited changes to core computer hardware (CPU, chipset) and operating system software. These changes must not lead to a significant increase in the production cost of platform hardware.
- Performance. The security-related features of the system must not degrade performance significantly (more than a few per cent).

---

[1] We are using a combination of formal methods (specification, automatic verification) and rigorous testing.

4.3   Existing approaches and problems

The security and assurance requirements call for a simple and constrained operating environment. In contrast, the commercial requirements call for the rich and diverse legacy operating environment of mass market PCs. In particular, the latter must allow arbitrary devices to be attached to the system and support an open device driver model. The former has to exclude most device drivers, in order to be assurable.

The generic resolution to these conflicting requirements is to run at least two different OSs in isolation on the same computer: one rich mass market OS for all uses without special security requirements and one or more constrained OSs that meet our security and assurance requirements. In this setting, it is of critical importance to protect these OSs from each other. This task is performed by a third component: the isolation layer (Figure 4.1). Clearly, the isolation layer is part of the TCB, and it has to meet our assurance and security requirements.

Implementations of isolation layers that have been proposed in the past include microkernels [7], exokernels [8] and virtual machine monitors (VMMs) [9]. In spite of their many merits, these systems fall short of addressing our requirements in several respects. The rest of this section summarises these deficiencies. Section 4.4 describes our isolation layer and how it solves these problems.

4.3.1   Assurance and device support

The VMMs expose devices to their guest operating systems by virtualising them. That is, a VMM intercepts a guest OS's attempt to access a physical device and performs the actual device access on behalf of the guest with possible modifications of the request and/or access-control checks. This allows the VMM to coordinate access requests from different guests and to share devices among them.

However, this approach requires a driver for each virtualised device to be part of the isolation layer (TCB). As described above, the set of devices that have to be supported in today's consumer environment is very large and diverse, and many device drivers are very complex. In this setting, any system that uses device virtualisation for more than a very constrained collection of devices cannot meet the assurance requirement. This problem is worse in the hosted VMM architecture (Type 2 VMM [10]), in which the VMM, rather than being a self-contained system with its own device drivers, executes within a host OS and uses the device drivers of the latter. In the hosted VMM architecture, the TCB of the isolation layer is expanded to include an entire OS.

An alternative to device virtualisation is to export devices to guest OSs. The isolation layer controls only which guests can access a device. However, device accesses by guests are made directly to the device – without translation by the isolation layer. Thus, the isolation layer does not have to include the device driver.

Unfortunately, this approach does not work on existing PC hardware. Main-stream PCs give any DMA device unrestricted access to the full physical address space of the machine. Thus, a guest in control of a DMA device can circumvent any protections put in place by the isolation layer to protect guests from each other.

It will have unrestricted access to most resources on the machine, including the parts of main memory that belong to the isolation layer or other guests. Some hardware modifications are required.

In summary, any existing implementation of an isolation layer for mainstream PCs suffers from at least one of the following problems: (1) It may severely restrict the set of devices that can be accessed on the machine. This solution does not meet our commercial requirements. (2) It may virtualise devices. This solution does not meet our assurance requirements. (3) It may export DMA devices. On existing PC hardware, this solution does not meet our security requirements.

4.3.2   Operating system compatibility

There are two options regarding the interface between the isolation layer and its guests. VMMs try to expose the original hardware interface. This has the important benefit that existing off-the-shelf operating systems can be used as guests, but increases the complexity of the isolation layer. This increase in complexity is especially severe on PC hardware, since the instruction set of x86 CPUs is not virtualisable [10,11].

Other implementations of isolation layers (e.g., exokernel, microkernels) expose different interfaces, requiring new guest OSs to be written [8] or existing OSs to be modified [7,12]. These solutions, while possible in principle, are not appealing under our requirements, because of the development overhead they entail.

4.4   The isolation kernel

In light of the conflict between commercial and security requirements, we follow the approach outlined above of allowing several OSs to execute on the same machine. Accesses by these OSs to system resources (e.g., memory, devices) are controlled by an isolation layer. Figure 4.1 gives a high-level view of the system. The OS layer consists of copies of Windows or other OSs with their device drivers and applications as the mass market operating environment and instances of a much smaller OS that provides higher assurance. The hardware layer consists of standard hardware resources (CPU, Random Access Memory (RAM), Memory Management Unit (MMU), etc.) which are shared among the software components. Furthermore, the system contains a collection of devices and their device drivers.

This section describes the isolation layer and focuses on the design decisions we took to minimise its complexity. More precisely, we describe the design employed in a system prototype we built. At the time of writing, it is hard to predict how the commercial product will relate to the prototype described in this chapter.

The isolation layer exposes the original hardware interface to one guest. This allows us to run Windows (almost) unmodified. Other guests have to adhere to a somewhat different hardware interface. At the expense of some complexity, it is possible to extend our isolation layer to expose the original hardware interface to all guests. We will call our isolation layer the isolation kernel for the rest of the chapter.

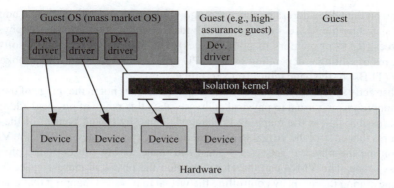

*Figure 4.1   The figure shows a system in which an isolation layer isolates guest
OSs. The isolation encompasses DMA devices, which are controlled by
guests.*

4.4.1   CPU

We mentioned above that VMMs for the x86 CPU incur significant complexity due
to the fact that the instruction set of the x86 is not virtualisable. A CPU instruction
set is called virtualisable if every instruction whose behaviour depends on the ring in
which it executes causes a trap into the most privileged ring [11]. The x86 CPU has
four protection rings (rings 0–3). Existing operating system kernels typically execute
in ring 0 (supervisor mode), while applications execute in ring 3 (user mode).

The VMMs execute in the most privileged ring (ring 0 on the x86) and execute
guest OSs in a less privileged ring (ring 1 or 3). On a CPU with a virtualisable
instruction set, the VMM can hide this ring change from the guest by appropriately
reacting to all instruction traps it receives. However, the x86 instruction set contains
17 instructions that should trap, but do not [10], leaving the VMM with the complex
task of identifying these instructions at runtime before they execute and compensating
for their changed behaviour.

In connection with NGSCB, upcoming versions of the x86 processor will introduce a new CPU mode that is strictly more privileged than the existing ring 0.
Effectively, this amounts to a new ring −1. Our isolation kernel executes in this
ring. Executing the isolation kernel in ring −1 allows us to execute guest OSs in
ring 0, thus avoiding the problems entailed by the fact that the x86 instruction set is
not virtualisable.

4.4.2   Memory

A VMM has to partition the physical memory of the machine among multiple guests.
That is, it must allow each guest to access some portion of memory that no other guest
can access. Furthermore, it has to reserve some memory for its own use. On most
platforms, VMMs can use existing virtual memory hardware in CPUs and MMUs
to enforce memory partitioning efficiently. Under virtual memory, instructions that

execute on the CPU address memory through virtual addresses. Each virtual address is translated by the MMU into a physical address, which is used to access physical resources (RAM or memory mapped devices). The mapping is defined by software by means of editing – depending on the CPU type – either the translation lookaside buffer (TLBs) or the page tables (on x86 processors).

Abstractly speaking, if a range of physical addresses is not in the image of the current mapping from virtual to physical addresses then this range of physical addresses is inaccessible unless the mapping is changed. Thus, by taking control of the data structures that control the virtual to physical mapping (page tables, TLBs), the VMM can confine the physical accesses a guest can make to any subset of the physical address space. The VMM can therefore partition the physical address space of the machine among its guests by controlling the virtual to physical mapping that is active for each guest.

Our isolation kernel uses an algorithm called Page Table Edit Control (PTEC) to partition physical memory among its guests [13]. In summary, the machine is set up such that any attempt by a guest to edit its page map (or CPU registers that control the behaviour of virtual memory) traps into the isolation kernel, which consults its security policy to decide if the instruction may proceed. This provides isolation and memory partitioning among guests, since guests can only access memory through their page maps.

Under the PTEC algorithm, guests see the true physical address space of the machine. The physical memory available to any given guest will, in general, not be contiguous nor begin at address 0. It is shown in Reference 12 that existing operating systems require only modest modifications to be able to execute in this environment. At the expense of some additional complexity (shadow page table algorithm [14]), our solution can be extended to provide zero-based contiguous address spaces for all guests.

4.4.3   Devices

The isolation kernel does not support a general device driver model. It contains device-specific code for a very small collection of devices. This collection includes devices that are required in the configuration or operation of the isolation kernel.

However, almost all devices – in particular consumer peripherals (cameras, scanners, printers, etc.) – are assigned to and managed by guest OSs. This obviates the need for driver code in the isolation kernel. The rest of this section describes these approaches in more detail and explains how we avoid the problems outlined in Section 4.3.

4.4.3.1   Exporting non-essential devices

On PC hardware, many devices are memory-mapped. That is, the control registers of a given device can be accessed by writing to or reading from certain physical addresses. The isolation kernel makes a device accessible to a guest by allowing the guest to map the control registers of the device into its virtual address space (cf. Section 4.4.2) – thus enabling the guest to read and write to these addresses. The isolation kernel controls which guest can access the device, but does not contain any device-specific knowledge (device driver).

As mentioned above, on existing PC hardware, DMA devices have unrestricted access to the full physical address space. In this situation, a guest in control of a DMA device can circumvent the virtual memory-based protections described in Section 4.4.2. In order to solve this problem, we have encouraged chipset manufacturers to change the hardware as follows.

Conceptually, we require an access control system [15]. In light of the need to minimise hardware cost and impact on performance, the system has to be very lightweight. We will begin by outlining the general concept and then discuss simplifications and implementation options.

Consider a set of resources (physical addresses), a set of subjects (software components or DMA devices) and a set of access modes (read, write). Given a state X of the system, the current access control policy is given by the function f that decides which access requests are allowed. More precisely, in state X, subject s should be allowed to access a resource r in mode a if and only if $f_X(r, s, a)$ is true.

Our general strategy is to store the DMA policy map f in main memory. The DMA policy is set by software (e.g., the isolation kernel) with write access to the memory region that stores f. The DMA policy map f is read and enforced by hardware: in the case where the protected resource is main memory, the memory controller or bus bridges can enforce the security policy. The policy will typically include the requirement that no DMA device under the control of a guest OS has write access to the memory that stores f.

In the most general case, the isolation kernel could assign each DMA device read or write access rights to an arbitrary set of memory pages. In the other extreme, if all DMA devices are under the control of one guest OS then it would be sufficient to allow the isolation kernel to deny all device access to a subset of main memory. A very simple concrete example of f, which is still useful, addresses resources at the granularity of pages and does not depend on subjects and access modes. This reduces the storage requirements for f to one bit per page and allows for very simple control logic in the memory controller: a page is inaccessible to all DMA devices if the bit is false. Otherwise, all DMA devices have read and write access to the page.

4.4.3.2   Persistent storage

Applications, OSs and possibly the isolation kernel must be able to store data persistently, such that the confidentiality and integrity of the data are ensured. In light of the variety of interfaces (e.g., IDE (Integrated Device Electronics), USB, IEEE 1394 and SCSI (Small Computer Systems Interface)), the isolation kernel assigns all persistent storage devices (e.g., hard disks, Flash memory cards) to a guest. In the simplest case, this guest could be a mass market OS. The isolation kernel relies on helper code in this guest to store data on these devices. Other guests can use cryptographic tunnelling [16] (encryption, MAC) to protect the confidentiality and integrity of the data. In addition, the stored data must be protected against replay attacks, in which subverted helper code returns an old version of the data. Furthermore, the cryptographic keys used to protect the data must themselves be managed using a different mechanism. We solve the latter two problems using the monotonic counter and sealed storage primitives described in Section 4.5.

Our prototype implementation of the cryptographic solution comprises only a few hundred lines of C code. Direct support for an interface such as SCSI would have required at least 50000 lines of code.

4.4.3.3 Graphics

Trusted software must be able to establish an output path to the screen that ensures the confidentiality and integrity of the displayed data. This problem is made more challenging by the performance requirements of graphics.

Our assurance requirement rules out any design that includes a regular graphics driver (whose size can easily exceed one million lines of code) in the TCB. A similar assurance problem exists for the graphics hardware, which is typically highly complex and optimised for performance.

In light of these constraints, we require new graphics hardware that consists of two largely isolated and independent subsystems: (1) the existing complex mass market graphics system and (2) a much simpler component that provides a single graphics surface without most popular performance optimisations. The only hardware connection between the two subsystems is a relatively simple circuit that combines their outputs. The main requirements for subsystem (2) are to provide a simple standardised interface and to display the data in the surface on the screen without corruption and without leaking. This includes the protection of its frame buffer.

The isolation kernel assigns subsystem (1) to a mass market OS and subsystem (2) to itself or to a high-assurance guest. The code required to expose a raw frame buffer of subsystem (2) comprises several hundred lines of C code in our prototype. The traditional device driver controls subsystem (1) and is contained in the mass market operating system (typically about one million lines of code).

4.4.4 Prototype implementation

We have implemented a prototype of the system. The system runs on prototype hardware from various vendors. The isolation kernel comprises the isolation component that allows memory and devices to be assigned to a particular guest for its exclusive use. Furthermore, the isolation kernel prototype exposes interfaces that allow a guest to be booted, the system to be shut down and resources to be assigned to a different guest. The isolation kernel prototype consists of 2000 lines of C code, whose correctness has been verified with a theorem prover. Initial performance measurements on a regular PC (2.5 GHz Pentium 4) using standard benchmarks show that the impact of the isolation kernel on the performance of Windows XP is small. For example, the performance of Windows XP on the Winstone 2002 Content Creation benchmark [17] when hosted by our isolation kernel prototype comes within 5 per cent of the native performance of Windows XP on the same benchmark. The prototype and the performance measurements are described in detail in Reference 13.

4.5 Code authentication

This section describes how we solve the remaining security requirements of Section 4.2. In particular, we describe how to implement remote authentication (Section 4.5.3), persistent storage (Section 4.5.2) and an isolated execution environment that is free from interference and observation (Section 4.5.1).

In order to satisfy these requirements on an open system, we need an access control mechanism that is beyond the reach of software. In practice, this mechanism is implemented by means of a crypto chip attached to the motherboard [18] and limited changes to the chipset. In order to minimise cost, this chip has to be cheap. The access control mechanism it implements is simple. A large part of the problem is to bootstrap a solution to our requirements on the full PC from a small collection of simple primitives.

In the remainder of this section, we provide an abstract description of the primitives we use in connection with code authentication. In Section 4.6 we describe an implementation of these primitives based upon the Trusted Platform Module (TPM) cryptographic processor.

4.5.1 *Execution environment and code identities*

In order to provide a predictable execution environment for software, we have to set at least parts of the hardware into a fixed initial state and allow the isolation kernel to initialise itself (boot). For the core platform components (CPU, chipset, crypto chip), initialisation can be implemented by an instruction akin to a reset that removes microcode patches and other state that may affect basic machine behaviour.

Isolation is implemented by different mechanisms depending on the layer. The crypto chip is physically isolated from software in the sense that it does not share memory or similar resources with the main platform. An isolation kernel can isolate itself from higher layers using CPU ring protections. The isolation kernel can isolate its guest OSs as outlined in Section 4.4.3.

Before we can describe the boot procedure, we have to define program identities. We follow the approach of Reference 19. Given a fixed, well-defined execution environment, the behaviour of a program is defined by its instruction sequence, its initial state and its input. In practice, the instruction sequence and the initial state are given by an executable file. We define the code identity of a program as the digest (cryptographic hash) of the concatenation of the executable file and an input string.

Figure 4.2 summarises the steps of the authenticated boot procedure. It assumes that the executable file and its input string have previously been laid out in memory. After being reset to its initial state, the hardware records the code identity and transfers control to the executable file. This code identity will be used to identify the program when it tries to access hardware keys (Sections 4.5.2 and 4.5.3).

The authenticated boot algorithm is implemented as a new CPU instruction. The hardware (chipset) must ensure that this operation is atomic. That is, other processors or devices must not be able to interrupt it or modify relevant state. These protections must remain in place until after additional memory-isolation mechanisms are

1. Set the core platform hardware into a well-defned state (similar to reset).

2. Protect the program from DMA devices.

3. Compute the code identity of the program by hashing the contents of the memory region in which it was previously laid out.

4. Record this code identity into a special, otherwise unmodifiable register of the crypto chip.

5. Ensure the program can initialise itself without interruption.

6. Transfer control to the entry point of the program.

Figure 4.2   The authenticated boot instruction

initialised (e.g., the DMA protections mentioned in Section 4.4.3). Any external event, such as a reset, that might remove these protections or otherwise corrupt the execution environment can only proceed after the memory used in the execution environment has been erased (overwritten). This can be implemented in the memory controller.

4.5.2   Persistent protected storage

This section addresses the problem of providing persistent storage, whose confidentiality and integrity are protected from non-TCB code without including disk device drivers in the TCB. The cryptographic approach to managing the disk described in Section 4.4.3.2 only reduces the amount of data we have to handle from files of arbitrary size to cryptographic keys.

4.5.2.1   Sealed storage

This section describes the sealed storage primitive [13] through which the crypto chip allows software to store data, such that their confidentiality and integrity are protected. Let the function ID( ) return the code identity that was recorded during the authenticated boot procedure. That is, ID( ) identifies the isolation kernel or OS that is currently running. We expose sealed storage through the following functions.

Seal
Input: a secret s, the code identity of a target program t
Output: c – an opaque identifier for s
Description:
        return $c = \mathrm{store}(s|t|\mathrm{ID}(\,))$

Unseal
Input: c an identifier for secrets
Output: a number s, the code identity of a program d

Description:
$$s|t|d = \text{retrieve}(c)$$
$$\text{if } t = \text{ID}(\,) \text{ then return } (s, d)$$
$$\text{else fail}$$

The | symbol represents concatenation. The function store( ) processes its argument, such that only the layer implementing Seal and Unseal on this particular machine – and no other entity – can recover it by calling retrieve(c). The Seal operation attaches the identity of the caller and access control information (t) to its argument (s) and makes the result inaccessible by means of store( ). The function Unseal( ) retrieves the data associated with its input (c), decides if the caller is authorised to read s and, if so, returns s and the identity of the source of s. Sealed storage can easily be extended to support more sophisticated access control policies than the simple $t = \text{ID}(\,)$ equality check described here.

We rely on a cryptographic implementation of store( ) and retrieve( ) and, thus, of Seal( ) and Unseal( ). The cryptographic requirements regarding confidentiality and integrity are identical to those of authenticated encryption schemes, as defined in Reference 20. Several authors describe and analyse implementations of authenticated encryption schemes, based on the generic composition of a block cipher and a message authentication code [20,21]. These implementations require the crypto chip to have access to cryptographic keys to perform encryption and integrity verification. The same keys can be used for all software callers of Seal and Unseal.

4.5.2.2 Monotonic counters

Sealed storage does not require persistent storage in the crypto chip – beyond, of course, for cryptographic keys. Being effectively stateless, sealed storage is by itself incapable of providing the storage semantics of regular hard disks. We provide hardware-based monotonic counters as a primitive to enable stronger storage semantics. An isolation kernel (identified by its code identity) can obtain exclusive access to a monotonic counter. The two access operations IncrementCounter and ReadCounter allow software to increment and read the current counter value.

Given this additional primitive, software can implement a 'write' operation with stronger semantics as follows: upon a request to write a data item a, it increments its counter, reads the new counter value c, seals the concatenation of a and c and writes the output of Seal to unprotected persistent storage (e.g., disk). The corresponding 'read' operation is implemented by retrieving the sealed ciphertext from the disk, calling Unseal( ) to obtain the payload a, c and its originator d. If d is unexpected or c is not the current counter value, the read function returns an error. Otherwise, it returns a.

In general, the number of different data items that an operating system has to store is likely to exceed the number of available hardware counters. This problem is solved by virtualising one or more hardware counters. For example, in order to implement a collection of n virtual counters using a single hardware counter, an OS can maintain an array of n integers, initialised to zero. IncrementCounter(i), where $i \leq n$ is the ith virtual counter, is implemented by incrementing the ith integer in the array and performing a 'write' operation on the entire array. ReadCounter(i) returns the ith array element. Upon boot, the OS performs a 'read' operation to restore the virtual counter values.

4.5.3   Attestation

We introduce the following primitive, implemented and exposed by the crypto chip, in order to enable attestation:

Quote
Input: an arbitrary data block a
Output: a public key signature s
Description:
> return $s = \text{Signature}_K(\text{ID}(\ )|a)$

Quote(a) generates a signature s [22] over the string a supplied by the caller concatenated with the caller's code identity. The key K used by the Quote operation is held by the crypto chip.

A second primitive to enable attestation is called PkUnseal; it is a variant of public key decryption [22]. The corresponding decryption key K_d is held in the crypto chip. Remote entities implement the PkSeal operation, and pass the generated ciphertext to the PkUnseal operation of the crypto chip on the target machine.

PkSeal
Input: a number s, a code ID d, a public key K
Output: a ciphertext block c
Description:
> Return $x = \text{Encrypt}_K(s|d)$

PkUnseal
Input: a ciphertext block c
Output: a number s
Description:
> $(d, s) = \text{Decrypt}_{K_d}(c)$
> if $d = \text{ID}(\ )$ then return s
> else fail

These operations allow a remote entity to encrypt a secret for a particular machine that will only be revealed if the code ID of the caller is as stated by the PkSealer.

4.5.3.1   Use of attestation in cryptographic protocols

Cryptographic protocols (e.g., for authentication or key transport) are typically formulated in a setting in which each principal can be represented by a cryptographic key to which it has exclusive access. However, the principals we are interested in are programs which, at least initially, do not have access to a key. Instead, we have to identify each program by the combination of the machine key and its code identity. This difference requires small modifications to standard public key-based cryptographic protocols (e.g., Reference 22).

Typically, we can adapt encryption-based protocols by replacing calls to public key decryption by calls to PkUnseal and including the code identity of the intended receiver in the corresponding encryption. Similarly, most signature-based protocols can be adapted by replacing signing operations by calls to Quote and testing for code identities in connection with signature verification.

For example, consider the popular one-pass key transport protocol, in which a sender A wishes to expose a secret k to a recipient B. A obtains implicit key authentication by sending the message $P_B(k)$ to B, where $P_B(k)$ is the result of encrypting k with B's public key [22]. If B does not have a key, but is a program with identity d executing on a machine with key K, then A can replace $P_B(k)$ by PkSeal(d, k). The adapted protocol still provides implicit key authentication. Other popular protocols, such as the Needham–Schroeder public key protocol [23], Beller–Yacobi [24] and different versions of the protocols described in the ISO/IEC 9798-3 [25] and ITU-T X.509 [26] standards can be similarly adapted.

When used in connection with a key agreement or key transport protocol, attestation can be used to provide a program with a certified cryptographic key for its exclusive use. After this initialisation step, the program can use protocols of its choice without requiring modifications to the protocol. In practice, this allows attestation to be integrated into legacy protocols and infrastructures (e.g., Kerberos or commerce web servers using SSL). Thus, an attestation aware key server or certification authority is only required to perform the initialisation. The legacy infrastructure at large can remain unchanged. Furthermore, the system does not require a common root of trust (central authority).

4.6   The TPM

In this section we provide an overview of a concrete implementation of the abstract crypto chip of the previous section: the TPM.

The TPM is a cryptographic coprocessor that is attached to the chipset complex in a way that allows it to authenticate system software running on the main processor. The TPM specification is currently being developed by the Trustworthy Computing Group [18], and was originally developed by the Trustworthy Computing Platform Alliance. At the time of writing, the TPM 1.2 specification is nearing completion.

The TPM provides functionality in the following areas:

- Support for authenticated operation.
- TPM administration.
- Cryptographic operations and cryptographic key protection.
- Non-volatile storage.
- Monotonic counters.

In the following section, we describe the features of the TPM that support authenticated operation. Other features are not described further here.

4.6.1   *TPM support for authenticated operation – initialisation*

Implementation responsibilities for authenticated boot on TPM-based platforms are divided between the TPM and other platform components: typically the processors and chipset. It is the responsibility of the processor and chipset to perform steps 1, 2, 5 and 6 in Figure 4.2. Step 3 (hashing the program), is split between the chipset and the TPM. Compliant chipsets must (a) indicate to the TPM that boot is being initiated using a signal that cannot be forged by software; and (b) send the program bytes to the TPM. At the initiation signal, the TPM starts to hash the incoming program. When complete, the 20-byte SHA-1 hash [22] is written into a register called a platform configuration register, or PCR (step 4). PCR registers are used to implement ID( ). PCR registers cannot be directly reset or written: they are only settable as part of the boot operation.

In addition, the TPM also has a bank of PCR registers that support the 'static root of trust'. On compliant platforms these registers are reset on reboot, and are initialised by platform microcode, for example, the BIOS. These registers also support authenticated operation, but by necessity, the TCB in this case includes the BIOS, loader and option ROMs.

4.6.1.1   Sealed storage

The TPM implements a generalisation of the sealed storage implementation described in Section 4.5. The corresponding TPM commands are called Seal and Unseal. However, these commands can name any PCR register set as the configuration to 'seal to'. Furthermore, Seal can be called with a password. In this case, Unseal will only succeed if the same password is provided.

The TPM implementations of sealed storage are typically based upon RSA (Rivest, Shamir and Adleman) public key encryption [22]. Since it is a requirement that sealed data can only be generated on the platform that can unseal them, seal implementations embed a per-platform secret in externally stored sealed data to ascertain that they were generated by the same TPM.

The root key that supports TPM sealed storage is called the Storage Root Key (SRK). It is randomly generated by the TPM and is never revealed outside the TPM. In order to support resale of the platform without risk of revealing secrets, the TPM allows the SRK to be reset.

4.6.1.2   Attestation

The TPM support for attestation is considerably more complex than the abstract description given earlier. The complexity is almost entirely in support of privacy and owner control. To support attestation, TPMs are furnished with an RSA key pair at manufacture called the Endorsement Key. Vendors will provide endorsement key certificates with the TPMs, that indicate that the TPM was embedded in a compliant platform. This certificate or chain is called the Platform Credential.

The endorsement key is an RSA decryption key. It is not (typically) used in attestation protocols directly, but instead is used in conjunction with a third party to certify another key – called an identity key – that is used for attestation. Simplistically, the endorsement key is used to prove to the certifying party that a freshly generated identity key is securely held within the TPM. If the certifying party is satisfied with the proof, then it generates a certificate for the newly generated identity key. The newly generated identity key can then be used in 'quote' operations, essentially exactly as described in Section 4.5.3. This two-step process is designed to limit the rate at which the endorsement key is used, to stop the endorsement key being used as a 'super-cookie' to track a user's actions on the Internet. A typical use model is that a client obtains identity keys from a third party trusted by Internet commerce sites only to certify legitimate TPM keys and by the clients themselves not to reveal privacy compromising information.

The TPM 1.2 specification also introduces an alternative mechanism for obtaining identity keys called Direct Anonymous Attestation, or DAA [27]. DAA allows a client to prove membership in a group (e.g., one of a class of trusted platforms) without revealing which member it is. DAA is used to obtain identity keys, which are then used as described earlier.

4.6.2   *Authenticated operation in practice*

We have described how authenticated initialisation allows hardware to authenticate lowest-level system software, and allows that software to store secrets and authenticate itself. Lowest-level system software could be an isolation kernel, or an operating system.

It is often the case that higher-level software – a guest OS of an isolation kernel or an application running on an OS – will require similar services. In this section we describe how similar services can be made available to higher-level software. We use the terms host and guest to describe the hosting program and hosted program, regardless of whether the host is an isolation kernel or operating system.

We assume that the lowest layer host has been initialised as described in Section 4.5, and has access to the TPM. This means that the host may use the TPM to authenticate itself to others, and may protect data by sealing this data either to itself or to other programs.

A host that wishes to provide authenticated operation services to guests must authenticate and assign a code identity to guests, and start them in a deterministic fashion. However, in this case, the host can be more sophisticated, because it is not implemented in a low-cost hardware module. This means that it is reasonable to provide more sophisticated authentication and naming: for instance, by allowing the use of certificate chains in the specification of program identities.

Once an identity for a guest has been established by the host, there are several ways to allow the guest program access to authenticated operation services. One way in which this can be accomplished is for the host to implement authenticated operation services, in macrocode software for the programs that it hosts, and use the underlying layer to allow the host-authenticated operation module to keep secrets and to certify its keys. Once again, since the hosting layer can be more sophisticated macrocode, it is reasonable to offer richer services than simple sealing of a key. For example, a cryptographically protected file system or other data store could be used.

4.7 System overview

We are now ready to outline how the components and concepts described so far can be combined into a complete system. Beyond the fact that the isolation kernel has to expose the crypto chip like any other device, the missing pieces are OSs and applications that execute on the isolation kernel.

Possibly the most intuitive configuration would be to execute an existing mass market OS alongside an existing high-assurance OS, such as in References 28 and 29. The former provides access to most mass market devices and allows mass market applications to execute. The latter can be used for a reduced set of applications with special security needs (e.g., electronic banking).

Alternatively, the isolation kernel can host several instances of an existing mass market operating system, where some of these instances execute applications with special security needs. This configuration is similar to systems such as that in Reference 30.

Given sufficiently strong isolation between Virtual Machines (VMs) and appropriate security policies on the VMs, the need for high assurance in the OS may be relaxed. For example, the VMM of Reference 30 implemented mandatory access control for VMs running largely unmodified VMS. This approach is appealing for several reasons:

- The amount of code that requires high assurance is reduced. While the isolation kernel becomes somewhat more complex (see below), this added complexity does not amount to that of a full operating system.
- Being able to use a regular operating system simplifies application compatibility and provides more functionality to applications.

Clearly, reducing the assurance level of the OS has implications for the rest of the system. If the isolation kernel implements mandatory access control (e.g., [31]), even corrupted OSs are prevented from leaking information by the isolation kernel. However, in practice, it is extremely difficult to mitigate the covert channels of the PC platform to an acceptable level.

Any application that can compromise the OS can compromise all applications running in the same VM. Even so, and even if the isolation kernel does not implement mandatory access control, several useful configurations exist. For example, the problem disappears if each VM can run exactly one application, and combinations of operating system and application cannot impersonate each other.

4.8 Applications

4.8.1 Enhanced smart-card applications

Smart cards provide cryptographic services such as signing, encryption or decryption. A smart card stores keys, which it uses to perform these operations and which are never revealed outside the smart card. Smart cards are used as authentication and authorisation tokens in applications such as user authentication (log on). When compared to other common authentication schemes, such as passwords, smart cards have the following security advantages:

- Compromising the credential (stealing a smart card) requires physical contact.
- The victim can usually detect that the credential has been compromised (i.e., that her smart card has been stolen).
- Cloning a credential (extracting the keying material from the smart card) requires physical intervention and at least a modest amount of sophistication.
- Unlike most passwords, the credential is cryptographically strong.

Unfortunately, the following problem severely limits the value of smart cards in mainstream computer security applications: most applications require interaction with the user. For example, signing an electronic document requires the user to see the document (and have assurance that the document she sees is indeed the document she is authorising the smart card to sign). The user must be able to provide input that cannot be spoofed, such that the smart card will not sign the document unless the user instructs the smart card to do so. On PCs, this lowers the assurance level of most smart-card-based operations to the assurance level of the mass market OSs that control the interaction with the user.

The provisions for high-assurance isolated execution environments and trusted input and output paths described earlier in this chapter can be used as a generic foundation for increased assurance for a broad range of smart-card applications. For example, a VM in control of a smart-card reader and of trusted input and output paths may act as a smart-card terminal for interactions between the user and the smart-card. Alternatively, an application may not use a physical smart-card, but perform cryptographic operations directly with keys that are secured under sealed storage with the help of the TPM – thus effectively implementing a soft smart-card. Concrete smart-card applications include network log on, e-commerce transaction authorisation and document signing.

4.8.1.1 Network log on

As outlined above, smart-card based user authentication offers a number of benefits over simpler schemes, such as passwords. User authentication on a corporate network might involve an NGSCB-based (soft or hard) smart-card terminal, whose trusted input path protects smart-card PINs from adversaries. The application may be further strengthened by using attestation to authenticate the smart-card terminal software to the server.

4.8.1.2   E-commerce or e-banking transaction authorisation

The Internet has become an important medium for financial transactions, such as stock purchases, money transfers and purchases of a broad range of goods and services. Typically, users have to log on to a server (e.g. using passwords). Once a user has logged in, there is a presumption that the software that provided the password and is requesting subsequent transactions is acting in the best interest of the authenticated user. With the advent of widespread viruses and Trojans, this assumption may not always be well founded.

Our system can strengthen transaction authorisation. A transaction authorisation application could use a trusted output path in conjunction with a trusted renderer to indicate to the user exactly the transaction being requested and use a trusted input path to obtain authorisation from the user. Again, additional protection can be gained by using attestation to authenticate the client application to the server.

4.8.1.3   Document signing

Paper is being replaced by email and other forms of electronic documents. However, the ease of modification of electronic documents places them at a disadvantage compared to physical media. If document integrity must be assured, digital signature technologies can be used to make documents tamper evident after they are signed. However, the open nature of client computers makes signing key compromise easy. Even smart-card-based signing applications are only as strong as the computer's output system that displays the document to the user and the input system that transmits the user's decision to sign the document to the smart card. As in the other applications, trusted paths in conjunction with sealed storage and attestation can significantly raise the robustness of document signing applications.

4.8.2   Rights management

If a user places a data file on a known and well-administered server, she can be assured that the access control provisions placed on that file will be honoured. However, the world is moving away from centrally located and administered data repositories, and towards a very large collection of locally administered peers. In this model users have very little assurance that documents, email or media content sent to others will remain secure. Attestation allows peers to authenticate the platform and software to which they are revealing data. If the sender can authenticate the receiver, then the sender has some assurance that access restrictions he or she placed on the data will be honoured by the recipient. The next section describes some of the limitations of using attestation to protect data that is outside the physical control of the owner.

4.8.3   Threat models

This chapter describes techniques for improving the robustness of computers especially with respect to data confidentiality and integrity. It is important to understand the strengths and limitations of these techniques in the context of broadly deployed distributed systems.

In principle, individual machines should be unconditionally robust against software attack. More precisely, on computers with uncompromised hardware and correctly configured software (isolation kernel, relevant guest OS), no action performed by external software (applications, other guests) should lead to a violation of the access control policy. The potential benefits of this property are clear: the confidentiality of data is protected even in the presence of viruses, Trojans, worms, etc., spreading throughout the Internet.

Whether the goal of unconditional robustness against software attacks can be achieved in practice will depend critically on the ability to build hardware and software that is free from security-relevant bugs. While this is true for many systems, we have taken a range of measures to reduce the number of hazards, even given the constraint of having to build a commercially viable system. For example, decisions at the architectural level have allowed us to exclude entire operating systems, device drivers and the BIOS from the TCB.

However, even under the assumption that the software TCB is bug-free, there exist a whole range of physical attacks on the hardware, requiring different degrees of sophistication and equipment from the adversary. Sufficiently sophisticated attacks will succeed. We are not aware of security-relevant hardware to which this general statement does not apply, even though the level of sophistication required from the adversary may differ. Hence, we expect that some fraction of machines will be compromised.

In the worst case, the adversary can gain knowledge of all data a compromised machine was guarding (sealed storage) and of the attestation private key. The latter allows the adversary to impersonate a legitimate system in communications with remote computers. If the compromised information is used broadly (e.g., the attestation private key is posted on the Internet), the compromise can be detected and the attestation key revoked. Otherwise, detecting the break requires some out-of-band mechanism (e.g., regular inspections of the hardware on a corporate network by a security officer).

In summary, the system holds the promise of protecting data stored on computers that are under the physical control of the owner of the data. In practical terms, consumers will enjoy increased security and privacy protection on their PCs for activities such as online banking, online shopping and storing arbitrary personal information.

Similar benefits apply in corporate settings. In addition, well-managed corporate networks have the character of distributed systems that are under the physical control of the corporation. In such settings, data can be distributed to a controlled set of corporate machines with reasonable assurance that the data will not be compromised.

Applications of the system that distribute confidential data to machines in potentially hostile physical environments have to take into account that some of these machines will be compromised and that the confidential data will be exposed. The consequences of this fact for the application depend on many application-specific factors. For example, in the case of broadly distributed, copy-protected entertainment content, the distributor must assume that some fraction of the recipients operate compromised machines and are able to circumvent the copy protection system and redistribute the data. The commercial impact of this depends among other things on the efficiency of the redistribution channel [32].

4.9   Related work

Traditionally, high-assurance systems have been built for settings (e.g., military) in which security concerns were paramount and existing mass market requirements were of little importance and not addressed. Examples include References 2, 4, and 30. Nevertheless, the SCOMP system [4] included hardware protection against DMA devices that allowed it to move the corresponding device drivers from the base layer to less critical parts of the system. The nature of the measures used by SCOMP differs from those described in this chapter. SCOMP made DMA devices operate on virtual addresses. In contrast, we use hardware protection directly on physical addresses, which requires fewer changes to PC hardware.

More recently, several secure OSs, such as Eros [29], have been built for personal computers. SE/Linux [33] adds security features to a mass market OS. None of these systems reconciles the conflict between the requirements of assurance (a manageable TCB) and those of the mass market (a large and complex set of device drivers as well as performance and functionality requirements on the OS).

The Perseus system [7] uses a microkernel to host a modified version of Linux and 'secure applications'. The assurance problems posed by DMA device drivers in the base layer (microkernel) on open architectures are recognised in Reference 7 but not solved. Similar systems built by using regular VMMs [34] or Exokernels to host mass market and secure operating systems suffer from the same problem. In contrast, we have presented a solution that allows all DMA device drivers to be excluded from the TCB without violating safety or restricting the openness of the architecture.

Several recent papers [12,35] describe new VMMs or isolation kernels for PC hardware. In each case, simplifications of the VMM software and performance improvements are obtained by exposing a simplified virtual hardware interface to guest OSs. While we have also described a modified VMM, our goals and our solutions differ from those of References 12 and 35. For example, neither system addresses the problem of supporting a large and diverse set of device drivers in a security setting. Xen [12] addresses the fact that the x86 CPU is not virtualisable by requiring modifications in guest OSs. In contrast, we make use of hardware enhancements that make the x86 virtualisable and to which we have contributed.

4.9.1   Code authentication

Code authentication appears in a variety of contexts. Lampson *et al*. [19] study authentication in distributed systems, including the authentication of executable OS and application code. Our attestation primitives are functionally similar to the method described in Reference 19, in which the hardware generates and certifies a public private key pair during each boot of an OS. The different implementation of our attestation primitives allows key management to be decoupled from the boot operation. Furthermore, we enable protected persistent storage for any collection of OSs without assuming an inherent trust relationship between them.

Secure boot systems rely on code identities to authenticate an operating system upon boot. For example, the Aegis system [36,37] modifies the BIOS of PCs to verify a signature on the image of an OS before booting it. If the signature cannot be verified the OS is not allowed to boot. Aegis does not perform key management. Thus, all OSs that are allowed to boot have equal access to persistent storage and attestation keys. This requires all OSs to be in a mutual trust relationship, which is incompatible with our requirements.

Secure coprocessors typically use a mechanism akin to secure boot to initialise themselves [38–41]. At a high level, there are a number of parallels between our system and the secure coprocessor described in Reference 41. For example, our requirements on the execution environment and attestation are similar to the safe execution and authenticated operation requirements of Reference 41. However, the underlying security models are different. For example, the definition of safe execution in Reference 41 includes the notion of an authority that has ownership of a particular software layer. While these authorities can be distributed, they are ultimately rooted in a central certification authority. In contrast, our system does not involve a central authority. Other differences include the implementation of persistent storage and attestation.

Systems with secure coprocessors use hardware to isolate a trusted computing environment from the rest of the machine. This hardware approach yields higher robustness against attacks on hardware and eliminates many covert channels. The advantages of our software-based approach are cost, performance and application compatibility. While our system also requires a cryptographic chip, this chip is effectively a smart card and far simpler than a programmable secure coprocessor. Furthermore, the software approach allows the high-assurance code to execute at full processor speed. Given economies of scale, there is typically a large performance gap between mainstream high-performance CPUs and secure coprocessors.

Several systems use code authentication to secure code distribution over the Internet. Authenticode [42] allows users to decide whether a program should execute based on the names of a program and its publisher. Wallach *et al.* [43] describe a fine-grained access control mechanism based on the identity of Java programs. Grimm and Bershad [44] study code authentication in the context of operating system extensions. Each of these systems authenticates software components at a single system layer. The system described in this chapter bootstraps code authentication from simple hardware primitives to all higher system layers.

Other work related to code identities includes References 45 and 46. Wobber *et al.* [47] describe a number of applications that make use of code authentication and attestation.

4.10   Conclusions

We have described a system that reconciles the conflicting requirements of high assurance and the mass market. Our general approach has been to preserve the open architecture of mass market computers with its large and diverse hardware and software base and to build an execution environment that is isolated from it and requires only a far smaller trusted computing base. In particular, we have shown how device drivers can be excluded from the TCB in an open hardware environment and how memory can be protected efficiently from unauthorised CPU and device accesses. A common design choice has been to introduce simple hardware protections in order to exclude large bodies of code from the TCB. While working within the constraints of legacy PC hardware and software has been a challenge throughout the project, it is also a prerequisite for our main goal: bringing high-assurance computing to the broad mass market.

References

1 B. Lampson. Computer security in the real world, 2000. http://www.research.microsoft.com/lampson/64-SecurityInRealWorld/Abstract.html.

2 T. Berson and G. Barksdale. KSOS – a development methodology for a secure operating system. In *Proceedings of the 1979 AFIPS National Computer Conference*, pp. 365–371. AFIPS Press, Montvale, NJ, 1979.

3 R. Schell, T. Tao, and M. Heckman. Designing the GEMSOS security kernel for security and performance. In *Proceedings of the 8th DoD/NBS Computer Security Conference*, pp. 108–119, 1985.

4 L. Fraim. Scomp: a solution to the multilevel security problem. *IEEE Computer*, 16:26–34, July 1983.

5 DOD, Washington, DC. *Department of Defense Trusted Computer System Evaluation Criteria*. DOD 5200.28-STD, December 1985.

6 NIST. *Common Criteria for Information Technology Security Evaluation*, version 2.1 edition, August 1999. http://www.commoncriteriaportal.org/public/files/ccpart1V2.2.pdf

7 B. Pfitzmann, J. Riordan, C. Stüble, M. Waidner, and A. Weber. The Perseus system architecture. Technical Report, IBM Research Division, 2001.

8 D. Engler, M. F. Kaashoek, and J. O'Toole, Jr. Exokernel: an operating system architecture for application-level resource management. In *Proceedings of the 15th Symposium on Operating Systems Principles (SOSP'95), Operating Systems Review*, pp. 251–266. ACM Press, New York, 1995.

9 T. Garfinkel, M. Rosenblum, and D. Boneh. Flexible OS support and applications for trusted computing. In *Proceedings of the 9th USENIX Workshop on Hot Topics in Operating Systems (HotOS-IX)*, pp. 145–150. USENIX, Berkeley, CA, 2003.

10 J. Robin and C. Irvine. Analysis of the Intel Pentium's ability to support a secure virtual machine monitor. In *Proceedings of the 9th USENIX Security Symposium (SECURITY-00)*, pp. 129–144. The USENIX Association, Berkeley, CA, 2000.

11 G. Popek and R. Goldberg. Formal requirements for virtualizable third generation architectures. *Communications of the ACM*, 17(7):412–421, 1974.

12 P. Barham, B. Dragovic, K. Fraser, S. Hand, T. Harris, A. Ho, R. Neugebauer, I. Pratt, and A. Warfield. Xen and the art of virtualization. In *Proceedings of*

the 19th Symposium on Operating Systems Principles (SOSP'03), pp. 164–177. ACM Press, New York, 2003.

13 Y. Chen, P. England, M. Peinado, and B. Willman. High assurance computing on open hardware architectures. Technical Report MSR-TR-2003-20, Microsoft Research, 2003.

14 R. Parmelee, T. Peterson, C. Tillman, and D. Hatfield. Virtual storage and virtual machine concepts. *IBM Systems Journal*, 11(2):99–130, 1972.

15 B. Lampson. Protection. *ACM Operating Systems Review*, 8(1):18–24, 1974.

16 H. Härtig. Security architectures revisited, 2002. http://os.inf.tu-dresden.de/ papers_ps/secarch.pdf.

17 eTestingLab. Business Winstone 2002 and Multimedia Content Creation Winstone 2002, 2002. http://www.winstone.com.

18 Trusted Computing Group. TCG TPM specification version 1.2. http://www. trustedcomputinggroup.org, 2004.

19 B. Lampson, M. Abadi, M. Burrows, and E. Wobber. Authentication in distributed systems: theory and practice. *ACM Transactions on Computer Systems*, 10:265–310, November 1992.

20 M. Bellare and C. Namprempre. Authenticated encryption: relations among notions and analysis of the generic composition paradigm. In *Proceedings of the Advances in Cryptology – Asiacrypt'00*, pp. 531–545. Springer-Verlag, Berlin, 2000.

21 H. Krawczyk. The order of encryption and authentication for protecting communication (or: how secure is SSL?). In *Proceedings of Advances in Cryptology (Crypto 2001)*, pp. 310–331. Springer-Verlag, Berlin, 2001.

22 A. Menezes, P. van Oorschot, and S. Vanstone. *Handbook of Applied Cryptography*. CRC Press, Boca Raton, FL, 1997.

23 R. Needham and M. Schroeder. Using encryption and authentication in large networks of computers. *Communications of the ACM*, 21:993–999, 1978.

24 M. Beller and Y. Yacobi. Fully-fledged two-way public key authentication and key management for low-cost terminals. *Electronics Letters*, 29:999–1001, 1993.

25 ISO/IEC 9798-3. Information technology – Security techniques – Entity authentication mechanisms – Part 3: mechanisms using digital signature techniques, 1998.

26 ISO/IEC 9594-8. Information technology – Open systems interconnection – The directory: public-key and attribute certificate frameworks, 2001.

27 E. Brickell, J. Camenisch, and L. Chen. Direct anonymous attestation. In *Proceedings of the 11th ACM Conference on Computer and Communications Security*, pp. 132–145. ACM Press, New York, 2004.

28 H. Härtig, M. Hohmuth, J. Liedtke, S. Schönberg, and J. Wolter. The performance of μ-kernel-based systems. In *Proceedings of the 16th Symposium on Operating Systems Principles (SOSP'97)*, pp. 66–77. ACM Press, New York, 1997.

29 J. Shapiro, J. Smith, and D. Faber. EROS: a fast capability system. In *Proceedings of the 17th Symposium on Operating Systems Principles (SOSP-99)*, Operating Systems Review, pp. 170–185. ACM Press, New York, 1999.

30 P. Karger, M. Zurko, D. Bonin, A. Mason, and C. Kahn. A restrospective on the VAX VMM security kernel. *IEEE Transactions on Software Engineering*, 17(11):1147–1165, November 1991.

31 D. Bell and L. La Padula. Secure computer systems: mathematical foundations and model. Technical Report M74-244, Mitre Corporation, 1975.

32 P. Biddle, P. England, M. Peinado, and B. Willman. The Darknet and the future of content protection. In *Proceedings of the 2nd ACM CCS Workshop on Digital Rights Management*, pp. 155–176. Springer-Verlag, Berlin 2002.

33 C. Wright, C. Cowan, S. Smalley, J. Morris, and G. Kroah-Hartman. Linux security modules: general security support in the Linux kernel. In *Proceedings of the 11th USENIX Security Symposium*, USENIX, Berkeley, CA, 2002.

34 T. Garfinkel, B. Pfaff, J. Chow, M. Rosenblum, and D. Boneh. Terra: a virtual-machine based platform for trusted computing. In *Proceedings of the 19th Symposium on Operating Systems Principles (SOSP'03)*, pp. 193–206. ACM Press, New York, 2003.

35 A. Whitaker, M. Shaw, and S. Gribble. Scale and performance in the Denali isolation kernel. In *Proceedings of the 5th Symposium on Operating Systems Design and Implementation (OSDI'02)*, pp. 195–209. USENIX, Berkeley, CA, 2002.

36 W. A. Arbaugh, D. J. Faber, and J. M. Smith. A secure and reliable bootstrap architecture. In *Proceedings of the 1997 IEEE Symposium on Security and Privacy*, pp. 65–71. IEEE Computer Society, Los Alamites, CA, 1997.

37 N. Itoi, W. A. Arbaugh, S. J. Pollack, and D. M. Reeves. Personal secure booting. In V. Varadharajan and Y. Mu, eds, *Proceedings of 6th Australasian Conference on Information Security and Privacy (ACISP 2001)*, pp. 130–144. Springer-Verlag, Berlin, 2001.

38 B. Yee. *Using Secure Coprocessors*. Ph.D. thesis, Carnegie Mellon University, 1994.

39 S. W. Smith, E. R. Palmer, and S. Weingart. Using a high-performance, programmable secure coprocessor. In *Proceedings of the Second International Conference on Financial Cryptography*, pp. 73–89. Springer-Verlag, Berlin, 1998.

40 S. W. Smith and V. Austel. Trusting trusted hardware: towards a formal model for programmable secure coprocessors. In *Proceedings of the Third USENIX Workshop on Electronic Commerce*, pp. 83–98. USENIX, Berkeley, CA, 1998.

41 S. W. Smith and S. Weingart. Building a high-performance, programmable secure coprocessor. *Computer Networks*, 31(8):831–860, April 1999.

42 P. Johns. Signing and marking Active X controls. In *Developer Network News*, 1996. http://msdn.microsoft.com/library/default.asp?url=library/ends/dnaxctrl/html/msdn_signmark.asp

43 D. Wallach, D. Balfanz, D. Dean, and E. Felten. Extensible security architectures for Java. Technical Report 546-97, Princeton University, Princeton, NJ, 1997.

44 R. Grimm and B. Bershad. Access control in extensible systems. Technical Report UW-CSE-97-11-01, University of Washington, 1997.

45 A. Fraser. File integrity in a disk-based multi-access system. In C. A. R. Hoare and R. H. Perrot, eds, *Operating Systems Techniques*. Academic Press, 1972.

46 P. England and M. Peinado. Authenticated operation of open computing devices. In *Proceedings of 2002 Australian Conference on Information Security and Privacy (ACISP 2002)*, pp. 346–361. Springer-Verlag, Berlin, 2002.

47 E. Wobber, M. Abadi, M. Burrows, and B. Lampson. Authentication in the Taos operating system. *ACM Transactions on Computer Systems*, 12(1):3–32, February 1994.

Chapter 5

The DAA scheme in context

Ernie Brickell, Jan Camenisch and Liqun Chen

5.1   Introduction

This chapter describes the Direct Anonymous Attestation (DAA) scheme in the context of its development and use within the TCG specification. This scheme was originated by Brickell, Camenisch and Chen and published in [9,10]. It was adopted by the Trusted Computing Group [47] as the method for remote anonymous authentication of a Trusted Platform Module (TPM). In this chapter, we first talk about how the work of designing DAA started from a conflict between the need for security and the need for privacy in TPM authentication. In the historical context, we acknowledge various schemes which have been developed in response to this TCG problem, and which eventually led to the DAA scheme. In the context of a solution to the problem, we focus on explaining how the DAA scheme proposed in [9,10] works. For more information on the security model of DAA, the security proof of the DAA scheme and its implementation analysis, we refer the reader to these two papers. In the context of further consideration, we discuss some options for the reissue of DAA keys and some possible improvements to increase the performance of the DAA scheme.

5.1.1   The privacy issue in TCG technology

As discussed in many other articles (e.g., [1,2]), the goal of the Trusted Computing Group (TCG) architecture[1] is to provide high security and high privacy solutions for users. However, an obstacle in achieving this goal is that security and privacy are seemingly incompatible. Suppose that a TCG-specified platform with a Trusted Platform Module (TPM) is used to communicate with a remote user (called a remote verifier). To achieve high security, TCG requires that the remote verifier must be

---

[1]   TCG is the successor organisation of the Trusted Computing Platform Alliance (TCPA).

convinced that he or she is talking to a TCG-specified TPM. However, to achieve high privacy, TCG requires that neither the remote verifier, nor any other service provider, such as the TPM issuer, nor any two of these working together, can discover which TPM the remote verifier is actually communicating with.

A TPM is used to provide platform attestation to the remote verifiers, that is, the TPM can prove that the platform of which it forms part has properties attested to by some third party. To achieve this, each TPM has a unique Endorsement Key (EK), created in the TPM manufacturing process and certified by the TPM manufacturer. Since the EK is unique and long-term, if a remote verifier obtains the EK, he or she learns the identity of the TPM. To avoid revealing the TPM identity, the TCG has designed another level of key, called the Attestation Identity Key (AIK). This key is short-term and is generally used for only one particular application requiring the TPM to communicate with a remote verifier. The TPM can have multiple AIKs for different applications. The requirement here is that the remote verifier be unable to discover which TPM the AIK belongs to.

When applied in a TCG setting, the external verifier is only happy to talk to a TCG-specified TPM. We assume that the certified EK is the only information which can prove that the TPM is TCG-specified. Clearly, there is a gap between the EK and AIK, and we need a bridge that would allow the TPM, using the EK, to introduce the AIK to the external verifier. The most recent solution bridging this gap is Direct Anonymous Attestation (DAA).

5.1.2   What is DAA?

The short answer is that DAA is a signature scheme. It is useful to look at different categories of signature schemes in order to see where DAA fits in. The following is one way of categorising signature schemes from a verifier's point of view, that is, by looking at what type of authenticated public information of the signers a verifier holds for signature verification. We have three different categories of signature scheme:

- 1-from-1 signature. Given an authenticated public key of a signer, a verifier is convinced that a given signature was signed by someone knowing the private signing key corresponding to the public key.
- 1-from-n signature. Given the authenticated public keys or other public information of all potential signers, say from a set of size n, a verifier is convinced that a given signature was signed by one of these n candidate signers; that is the signer knows at least one of the private signing keys belonging to one of the n signers. However, the verifier does not know which of the n candidates is the real signer. Examples are ring signatures and concurrent signatures.
- 1-from-group signature. Given an authenticated group public key, but not any individual signer's public key, a verifier is convinced that a given signature was signed by a member of the group, but does not know which member of the group is the real signer. DAA belongs to this category of signature scheme.

We next need to look at the difference between ordinary group signature schemes and the DAA scheme. A group signature scheme offers a designated Trusted Third

Party (TTP) the power to 'open', that is, de-anonymise, the signer's identity from a group signature. Clearly this TTP must be trusted by all signing parties not to compromise signer privacy. The problem is that it might be difficult to find such a commonly trusted on-line TTP when the scheme is used as part of a TCG system. If such a TTP existed, it could play the role of the privacy Certificate Authority (privacy-CA) specified in one of the early TCG solutions, discussed below. On the other hand, if a signature is completely untraceable, it can offer high privacy but low security, because there is no way to stop a compromised signer providing a valid signature. Hence a new solution is needed which not only removes the need for a single TTP (and hence improves privacy) but also permits revocation of compromised signing keys.

The DAA has been proposed as a solution to this dilemma. It has different revocation properties than group signatures. The issuer who issues DAA certificates is not able to identify the signer of a DAA signature, unlike the group manager in a group signature scheme who can open any signature and identify the signer.

The primary revocation method is used when a TPM has been compromised, the DAA secret key has been removed from the secure storage of the TPM and the DAA signature key has become known. If the DAA signature key is known to a verifier, the verifier can add that signature key to a revocation list. Then, when the verifier receives a DAA signature, he can check that signature against each revoked key on his list to determine if that signature was created by that revoked key.

There is another revocation method in DAA that can be made available, which we will refer to as user-controlled linkability. The signer and the verifier can negotiate about whether to enable verifier-specific linkability. If they agree to this, then the signer creates self-certified revocation evidence that can only be used by that specific verifier, as identified by the name of the verifier. In this case, that verifier is able to link the DAA signatures that the TPM creates using the name of this verifier. Then, if that verifier suspects that the DAA key of that TPM has been compromised, the verifier can stop accepting signatures using that DAA key. However, the verifier will not be able to identify the DAA key to another verifier who is using a different name.

In the DAA scheme, we denote a 'basename' for such a verifier's name used in a DAA signature. In the protocol descriptions that follow, the verifier provides a basename for the signer to use in creating a signature to enable verifier-specific linkability. When a verifier name is not provided, the signer creates a random value instead, and verifier-specific linkability is not enabled.

In TCG, a DAA signer is a TPM, a DAA issuer could be a manufacturer of TPMs, and a DAA verifier could be any external partner. To bridge the gap between an EK and an AIK, the TPM first creates a DAA key and then authenticates itself to the issuer using the EK. When the issuer is convinced of the validation of the EK, the issuer generates a DAA certificate on the DAA key and gives the certificate back to the TPM. During this process, the issuer learns nothing about the DAA key. To allow an external verifier to check an AIK, the TPM signs the AIK under the DAA key and DAA certificate, and sends the DAA signature to the verifier. The DAA signature provides anonymity-preserving assurance that the TPM contains a valid DAA key and certificate. By verifying the DAA signature, the verifier is convinced that the signature was signed by a TPM which knows both an unspecified EK and a DAA certificate that was issued by the designated DAA issuer. A DAA key and DAA certificate can be used not only to sign multiple AIKs, but also any other arbitrary messages.

As mentioned before, although neither the verifier nor the issuer can tell which TPM is the signer, the DAA scheme allows the signer to offer user-controlled linkability. With this property, the verifier can build its own revocation list and find out whether or not different DAA signatures constructed using that verifier's basename were signed by the same TPM.

5.1.3   *A simple example of DAA use*

The following is a simple example of the use of DAA. A user, Alice, has a TCG platform with a TPM. Inside the TPM is a DAA algorithm. Alice wants to communicate with a music service provider, Bob, and a stock broker, Charlie. To protect their communications, Alice is required to send an authenticated AIK to each of the two service providers. The service provider requires that the received AIK is created by a TPM, and that the private part of the AIK is stored and used by the TPM. Alice's requirement is to prevent either Bob or Charlie learning the identity of the TPM. Furthermore, she does not want them to be able to determine that they are both dealing with the same platform.

Alice requests the TPM to create two AIKs, AIK_1 and AIK_2, respectively. The TPM creates a DAA signature on AIK_1 and sends it to Bob, and then creates another DAA signature on AIK_2 and sends it to Charlie. After verification of the received DAA signature, Bob (and Charlie) is convinced that AIK_1 (and AIK_2) was issued by a TPM, but does not know which TPM it is. Even if Bob and Charlie cooperate, they cannot determine whether or not they have talked to the same TPM.

As DAA offers the property of user-controlled linkability, if Alice decides to permit this, then Alice would use Bob's basename when computing signatures for Bob, and would use Charlie's basename when computing signatures for Charlie. Then Bob could link multiple signatures he receives from Alice. Similarly, Charlie could link multiple signatures he receives from Alice. Therefore, if either Bob or Charlie is unhappy with Alice's behaviour, they can reject any DAA signature from her. However, Bob and Charlie still cannot link the signatures Alice generates for Bob with the ones she generates for Charlie.

5.2   History of DAA

5.2.1   *The privacy-CA solution*

Before the development of the DAA scheme, the privacy properties required for TCG were achieved by invoking a privacy-CA, which issues a certificate on a randomly chosen AIK, after verifying the validation of an EK. An external verifier authenticates the TPM by verifying the certificate of the AIK from the privacy-CA instead of the original certificate of the EK from the TPM manufacturer.

This privacy-CA solution is suitable for many applications, including those which have a central controller, for example, the internal communications of a big company. However, for many other applications, for example, communications between individual users and individual service providers, this solution is not good enough, because the privacy-CA solution is a likely bottleneck and also a single point of failure/attack – it potentially enables a mapping between a TPM's EK and AIK. If the privacy-CA reneges on a promise to keep such a mapping secret, or if the privacy-CA is willing to keep such mappings confidential but its database is compromised, it becomes possible to match the AIK certificates to the EKs of all TPMs certified by that privacy-CA.

It is therefore desirable that a TPM is able to assure a remote verifier that it is a TCG-specified TPM without revealing the identity of the TPM to the verifier or to any TTP. The following subsections contain descriptions of four proposals for achieving this property.

5.2.2   The DP protocol

Brickell was the first to discover that an anonymous attestation scheme could be used instead of a privacy-CA to meet the privacy requirements of the TCG. He submitted a proposal he called the Direct Proof (DP) protocol to TCG in April 2003 [3].

The DP protocol

Setup. The DP issuer does the following:

1. Create a public Rivest, Shamir and Adlenan (RSA) key, (e, n) with secret exponent d. Select an integer K, such that $P = Kn + 1$ is a prime and $K < 2^{2 \log_2 n}$. If no such K is found, then a new RSA key pair can be selected.
2. Select two prime numbers q and p, such that $2^{159} < q < 2^{160}$, $2^{2047} < p < 2^{2048}$ and q divides $(p - 1)$.
3. Select security parameters, W and Z, satisfying $\log W = O(\log n)$ and Z is between 0 and $n - W$. In practice, values of $W = 2^{160}$ and $Z = 0$ should be sufficient. Select W_{IP3}, such that $W_{IP3} > W2^{\log p}$.

Join. TPM and the DP issuer run a one-round protocol as follows:

1. TPM picks a random number m, such that $0 < m - Z < W$.
2. TPM picks a random number a, such that $1 < a < n$, computes $f = ma^e \bmod n$, and sends f to the issuer.
3. The issuer computes $c' = f^d \bmod n$, and sends c' to TPM.
4. TPM computes $c = c'a^{-1} = m^d \bmod n$.
5. TPM stores m, c secretly as the DP key and certificate.

Prove. TPM proves the DP key and certificate with a committed message k to a verifier as follows:

1. TPM first randomly chooses $a \in [1, p]$, if a random base is allowed; or computes $a = \text{MGF1}((\text{VerifierBaseName}), \log P)$, if a verifier name base is required.

2. TPM computes $h = a^K \bmod p$ and $k = h^m \bmod p$.

3. The verifier supplies an assurance parameter, α, to TPM. A recommended value for α is 80.

4. TPM and the verifier perform the following α times:
   - TPM randomly selects $y \in \mathbb{Z}_n^*$.
   - TPM computes $x = cy \bmod n$.
   - TPM randomly selects $r \in [0, W_{\text{IP3}}]$.
   - TPM computes $v = h^r \bmod p$.
   - TPM picks t at random in $[1, n-1]$.
   - TPM computes $z_x = x^e t \bmod n$, $z_y = y^e r + t \bmod n$ and $z = z_x + z_y \bmod n$.
   - TPM hashes individually v, y, z_x, z_y, z, t, r and sends all hashed values to the verifier.
   - The verifier makes a choice of b from $\{0, 1, 2, 3\}$ and sends b to TPM.
   - If $b = 0$, TPM sends x, t to the verifier. The verifier computes $z_x = x^e - t \bmod n$, and verifies the hashes of t, z_x.
   - If $b = 1$, TPM sends y, t, r to the verifier. The verifier computes $z_y = y^e r + t \bmod n$, $v = h^r \bmod p$, and verifies the hashes of y, t, r, z_y, v and $r \in [0, W_{\text{IP3}}]$.
   - If $b = 2$, TPM sends z_x, z_y to the verifier. The verifier computes $z = z_x + z_y \bmod n$ and verifies the hashes of z_x, z_y, z.
   - If $b = 3$, TPM sends y, z, v to the verifier. The verifier checks the hashes of y, z, v and $h^z = (kv)^{y^e \bmod n} \bmod p$. The verifier computes $s = zy^{-e} \bmod n$ and checks $s \in [Z, Z + W + W_{\text{IP3}}]$.

5. If the above steps all pass, the verifier accepts the proof of knowledge of c and m and that m is in the correct interval. The verifier also accepts k as an anonymous key, which can be used as an AIK or to sign an AIK.

The DP protocol was the first submission to TCG to challenge the privacy-CA solution and to meet the TCG requirement on privacy. The security of the DP protocol is based on the interval RSA assumption, that is, that the following problem is hard to solve by any polynomial algorithms: For a fixed $\epsilon > 0$, given a randomly chosen RSA modulus, n, a public exponent e, W such that $W < n^{(1/2)-\epsilon}$, and a $Z \in [0, n]$, find y such that for $x = y^e \bmod n$, $x - Z \in [0, W]$. The main disadvantage of this protocol is its relatively poor performance.

5.2.3 The GSRE scheme

After reviewing the proposal by Brickell, Chen submitted an alternative in May 2003 [4]. This proposal takes the idea of user-controlled linkability from the DP protocol but provides a more efficient direct proof, which benefits from the existing cryptographic primitive of group signatures. The scheme is called Group Signatures with Revocation Evidence (GSRE).

For the following two reasons, this proposal recommends using the group signature scheme in Reference 5. First, this scheme was the most efficient group signature scheme available at that time, and second, this scheme is based on the strong RSA assumption, and the TCG specifications have already recommended using RSA technology to implement many other TCG algorithms.

The GSRE scheme

Setup. The setup algorithm takes security parameters

- $\ell_1, \ell_2, \ell_3, \ell_4 \in \mathbb{Z}$ (e.g., $\ell_1 = 1024, \ell_2 = 160, \ell_3 = 400$ and $\ell_4 = 380$)
- two collision-resistant hash functions $H_1 : \{0,1\}^* \rightarrow \{0,1\}^{2\ell_1}$, for example, MGF1 [6]; and $H_2 : \{0,1\}^* \rightarrow \{0,1\}^{\ell_2}$, for example, one of the hash functions specified in [7].

It then does the following:

1. Select random secret l_1-bit primes p', q' such that $p = 2p' + 1$ and $q = 2q' + 1$ are prime, and set the modulus $n = pq$.
2. Select a random number $r \in \mathbb{Z}_n^*$, and compute $R = H_1(r\|1)^2 \bmod n$, $S = H_1(r\|2)^2 \bmod n$, $g = H_1(r\|3)^2 \bmod n$ and $h = H_1(r\|4)^2 \bmod n$.
3. Output the public parameters (R, S, g, h, n), along with evidence r that R, S, g, h were created properly, as a GSRE issuer's public key. The issuer's private key is $p'q'$.

Join. To let a TPM become a member of the TPM group, TPM and the issuer engage in the following one-round protocol (both are given the public parameters (R, S, n)):

1. TPM generates a secret exponent $f \in]1, 2^{l_2}]$ at random as its private key, computes $U = R^f \bmod n$ and sends U to the issuer.
2. The issuer generates the key certificate (A, e) by selecting a random prime $e \in_R [2^{l_3} + 1, 2^{l_3} + 2^{l_2}]$ and computing $A = (US)^{1/e} \bmod n$. The issuer sends (A, e) to TPM.
3. TPM stores (A, e, f) satisfying $A^e = R^f S \bmod n$.

Revocation evidence create. Assume that two users, the TPM owner and the verifier, have agreed to use the value *bsn* as a base, which could be generated with an application's attribute and the verifier's identifier, or which could be a random number. The revocation evidence E with respect to this base is created as follows:

1. Compute $B = H_1(bsn)^2 \bmod n$.
2. Compute revocation evidence $E = B^f \bmod n$.
3. Output E.

Sign. TPM generates a GSRE signature on a given message $m \in \{0,1\}^*$ (which could be the public key of an AIK) by performing the following steps: Private input: (A, e, f), public input (R, S, g, h, n, m, E, B) and output σ.

1. Randomly choose $w_1, w_2 \in \{0,1\}^{\ell_2}$.
2. Compute $T_1 = Ah^{w_1} \bmod n$, $T_2 = g^{w_1} \bmod n$ and $T_3 = h^e g^{w_2} \bmod n$.
3. Randomly choose $r_1, r_2, r_3, r_4 \in \{0,1\}^{\ell_4}$.
4. Compute $d_1 = T_1^{r_1} R^{r_2} T_2^{r_3} T_3^{r_4} \bmod n$, $d_2 = h^{r_1} g^{r_3} \bmod n$, $d_3 = g^{r_4} \bmod n$ and $d_4 = B^{r_2} \bmod n$.
5. Compute $c = H_2(T_1 \| T_2 \| T_3 \| d_1 \| d_2 \| d_3 \| E \| d_4 \| m)$.
6. Compute $s_1 = r_1 - c(e - 2^{\ell_3})$, $s_2 = r_2 + cf$, $s_3 = r_3 - cw_2$ and $s_4 = r_4 + cw_1$ (all in $\mathbb{Z}$).
7. Output $\sigma = (T_1, T_2, T_3, E, c, s_1, s_2, s_3, s_4)$.

Verify. A verifier checks the validity of a signature σ of the message m by performing the following steps: Input $\sigma = (T_1, T_2, T_3, E, c, s_1, s_2, s_3, s_4)$, m, (R, S, g, h, n, E, B).

1. Check if E is in a revocation list maintained by the verifier; if yes reject the signature, otherwise carry on.
2. Compute $d_1' = S^c T_1^{s_1 - c 2^{\ell_3}} R^{s_2} T_2^{s_3} T_3^{s_4} \bmod n$, $d_2' = h^{s_1 - c 2^{\ell_3}} g^{s_3} T_3^c \bmod n$, $d_3' = g^{s_4} / T_2^c \bmod n$ and $d_4' = B^{s_2} / E^c \bmod n$.
3. Compute $c' = H_2(T_1 \| T_2 \| T_3 \| d_1 \| d_2 \| d_3 \| E \| d_4 \| m)$.
4. Accept the signature if and only if $c = c'$ and $s_1, s_2, s_3, s_4 \in \{0,1\}^{\ell_4 + 1}$.

To ensure security, the issuer must provide proof that its public key has been correctly created. This will guarantee $R, S, g, h \in \mathrm{QR}_n$ of order $p'q'$, and will also ensure that no one knows the discrete logarithm of one element of (R, S, g, h) with respect to the base using any other element.

The GSRE scheme is a Schnorr-like signature [8], and a large part of the signature can be pre-computed. The GSRE scheme recommends pre-computing all stages of the signature signing process except c, s_1, s_2, s_3, s_4 and d_4.

Because the TPM is a small chip with limited resources, the GSRE scheme also recommends minimising the operations carried out in the TPM by delegating many stages of the signature computation to the TPM's host (i.e., to software that is run on the host). The security requirement for this delegation is that a host should not be able to create a GSRE signature without interacting with the TPM. However, privacy/anonymity can only be guaranteed if the host is not corrupted. As the host controls all the communications of the TPM to the outside, a corrupted host can always break privacy/anonymity by just adding an identifier to each message sent by the TPM.

5.2.4   The set signature scheme

Another proposal to accomplish anonymous attestation was the set signature scheme due to Boneh *et al.* [9]. We call this the BBS set signature scheme.

The BBS set signature scheme

Setup. In the setup process, a set signature issuer takes security parameters $\ell_1, \ell_2, \ell_3, \ell_4 \in \mathbb{Z}$ (we require $\ell_1 > \ell_3 > \ell_4 > 2\ell_2$) and does the following:

1. Generate two distinct ℓ_1-bit safe primes p and q, that is, such that $p = 2p' + 1$ and $q = 2q' + 1$, with p' and q' prime. Let $n = pq$ and QR_n denote the group of quadratic residues modulo n.
2. Pick random $R, S \in \mathrm{QR}_n$.
3. Output the public parameters (n, R, S), along with evidence that R, S were selected randomly. The issuer's secret key is the pair of factors p, q of n.
4. The system also requires two hash functions $H_1 : \{0,1\}^* \to \mathrm{QR}_n$ and $H_2 : \{0,1\}^* \to [1, 2^{\ell_2}]$. Note that hashing into QR_n is done by hashing into $\mathbb{Z}_n^*$ and squaring the result modulo n.

Join. To certify a new TPM, the issuer and TPM engage in the following one-round protocol (both are given the public parameters (n, R, S)):

1. TPM picks a random $f \in [1, 2^{\ell_2}]$ and sends $T = R^f$ to the issuer.
2. The issuer picks a random odd prime $e \in [2^{\ell_3} + 1, 2^{\ell_3} + 2^{\ell_2}]$ and computes $A = (S/T)^{1/e} \bmod n$ and sends (A, e) to TPM.
3. TPM now has (A, e, f) such that $A^e R^f = S \bmod n$.

Sign. TPM is given a message m to sign and has the public parameters (n, R, S) and its secret key (A, e, f). TPM signs m as follows:

1. Pick a random $r \in [1, 2^{\ell_2}]$. Set $h = H_1(0\|r\|m)$ and $g = H_1(1\|r\|m)$.
2. Pick a random integer $w \in [1, 2^{\ell_2}]$ and compute $T_1 = Ah^w \bmod n$, $T_2 = h^e g^f \bmod n$ and $T_3 = g^w \bmod n$.
3. Pick random integers $r_1, r_2, r_3 \in [1, 2^{\ell_4}]$ and compute $V_1 = T_1^{r_1} R^{r_2} T_2^{r_3} T_3^{r_2} \bmod n$, $V_2 = h^{r_1} g^{r_2} \bmod n$ and $V_3 = g^{-r_3} \bmod n$.
4. Compute $c = H_2(m\|g\|h\|V_1\|V_2\|V_3) \in [1, 2^{\ell_2}]$.
5. Set $s_1 = (e - 2^{\ell_3})c + r_1$, $s_2 = fc + r_2$ and $s_3 = wc - r_3$ (all in $\mathbb{Z}$).
6. Output the signature $\sigma = (r, c, T_1, T_2, T_3, s_1, s_2, s_3)$.

Verify. When verifying a signature $\sigma = (r, c, T_1, T_2, T_3, s_1, s_2, s_3)$ on a message m, the verifier is also given a list of revoked private keys $\{(A_i, e_i, f_i)\}_{i=1}^k$. The verifier works as follows:

1. If s_1 is not in the range $[1, 2^{\ell_4+1}]$ then reject the signature.
2. Set $h = H_1(0\|r\|m)$ and $g = H_1(1\|r\|m)$.
3. Compute $U_1 = T_1^{s_1+2^{\ell_3}c} R^{s_2} T_2^{-s_3} T_3^{s_2} / S^c \bmod n$, $U_2 = h^{s_1+2^{\ell_3}c} g^{s_2} / T_2^c \bmod n$ and $U_3 = g^{s_3} / T_3^c \bmod n$.
4. Compute $c' = H_2(m\|g\|h\|U_1\|U_2\|U_3)$.
5. Test if $c = c'$. If not, reject the signature.
6. Finally, the verifier checks that the signature was not generated using a revoked private key. For $i = 1, \ldots, k$ the verifier checks if $T_2 = h^{e_i} g^{f_i} \bmod n$. If equality is satisfied for some i reject the signature. Otherwise, accept the signature.

5.2.5   The modified set signature scheme

In order to improve performance, Boneh, Brickell, Chen and Shacham (BBCS) collaborated to develop the GSRE scheme [4] and the set signature scheme [9], and created a modified scheme [10], which is more efficient than either. We call this the BBCS set signature scheme.

The BBCS set signature scheme

Setup. In the setup process, a set signature issuer takes security parameters $\ell_1, \ell_2, \ell_3, \ell_4 \in \mathbb{Z}$ (we require $\ell_1 > \ell_3 > \ell_4 > 2\ell_2$) and does the following:

1. Generate two distinct ℓ_1-bit safe primes p and q, that is, such that $p = 2p' + 1$ and $q = 2q' + 1$, with p' and q' prime. Let $n = pq$ and QR_n denote the group of quadratic residues modulo n.
2. Pick random $R, S, h \in \mathrm{QR}_n$.
3. Output the public parameters (n, R, S, h), along with evidence that R, S, h were selected randomly. The issuer's secret key is the pair of factors p, q of n.
4. The system also requires two hash functions $H_1 : \{0, 1\}^* \to \mathrm{QR}_n$ and $H_2 : \{0, 1\}^* \to [1, 2^{\ell_2}]$. Note that hashing into QR_n is done by hashing into $\mathbb{Z}_n^*$ and squaring the result modulo n.

Join. The same as in the set signature scheme.

Sign. TPM is given a message m to sign and has the public parameters (n, R, S, h) and its secret key (A, e, f).

TPM signs m as follows:

1. Pick a random $r \in [1, 2^{\ell_2}]$. Set $g = H_1(1\|r\|m)$.
2. Pick a random integer $w \in [1, 2^{\ell_2}]$ and compute $T_1 = Ah^w \bmod n$ and $T_2 = h^e g^f \bmod n$.

3. Pick random integers $r_1, r_2, r_3 \in [1, 2^{\ell_4}]$ and compute $V_1 = T_1^{r_1} R^{r_2} h^{r_3}$ mod n and $V_2 = h^{r_1} g^{r_2}$ mod n.

4. Compute $c = H_2(m\|g\|h\|V_1\|V_2) \in [1, 2^{\ell_2}]$.

5. Set $s_1 = (e - 2^{\ell_3})c + r_1$, $s_2 = fc + r_2$ and $s_3 = r_3 - wec$. In the computation of s_1, s_2, s_3, the arithmetic is over the integers.

6. Output the signature $\sigma = (r, c, T_1, T_2, s_1, s_2, s_3)$.

Verify. When verifying a signature $\sigma = (r, c, T_1, T_2, s_1, s_2, s_3)$ on a message m, a verifier is also given a list of revoked private keys $\{(A_i, e_i, f_i)\}_{i=1}^k$. The verifier works as follows:

1. If s_1 is not in the range $[1, 2^{\ell_4+1}]$ then reject the signature.

2. Set $g = H_1(1\|r\|m)$.

3. Compute $U_1 = T_1^{s_1 + 2^{\ell_3}c} R^{s_2} h^{s_3} / S^c$ mod n and $U_2 = h^{s_1 + 2^{\ell_3}c} g^{s_2} / T_2^c$ mod n.

4. Compute $c' = H_2(m\|g\|h\|U_1\|U_2)$.

5. Test if $c = c'$. If not, reject the signature.

6. Finally, the verifier checks that the signature was not generated using a revoked private key. For $i = 1, \ldots, k$ the verifier checks if $T_2 = h^{e_i} g^{f_i}$ mod n. If equality is satisfied for some i reject the signature. Otherwise, accept the signature.

The security of the GSRE, BBS and BBCS schemes [4, 9, 10] is based on the strong RSA assumption and the bounded decision Diffie–Hellman assumption. This is the same as for the DAA scheme.

Although these three schemes obtain performance benefits from use of the group signature scheme due to Ateniese *et al.* [5], none of them (nor the DP protocol [3]) are proven to possess the property of insider-security, that is, to protect against a corrupted TPM when issuing certificates. This may be acceptable in the case that a TPM does not leave the control of a secure manufacturing facility before a certificate is issued. However, to meet a requirement that certificates may be issued to TPMs after they have been released to an insecure environment, it is desirable to use a scheme in which the signature scheme used to issue certificates is proven to be secure against adaptive chosen message attacks.

Instead of using the Ateniese *et al.* group signature scheme [5], the DAA scheme makes use of the Camenisch–Lysyanskaya (CL) signature scheme [11] to create a group signature, which is the major difference between the DAA scheme and the above three schemes. The major benefit from this difference is that we can prove that the DAA scheme has the property of insider-security.

5.3 Related prior work

In this section, we briefly review other related prior work that is used to build the DAA scheme. DAA draws on techniques that have been developed for group signatures [5, 12, 13], identity escrow [14] and credential systems [15, 16]. In DAA we also use various protocols to prove knowledge of, and relations among, discrete logarithms, such as those in References 12, and 17–24. Furthermore, we use the Fiat–Shamir heuristic [23, 25] to turn proofs into signatures. The security of these proofs can be proved in the random oracle model [26].

The issuer setting in the DAA scheme shares many properties with one of group signatures [5,12,13], identity escrow [14] and credential systems [15,16] and we employ many techniques [5,11,15] used in these schemes.

The DAA scheme makes use of the CL signature scheme [27, 28] as the DAA certificate. This signature scheme offers the property of discrete logarithm-based proofs to prove possession of a certificate. We have proved that unforgeability of the certificates holds under the strong RSA assumption and that privacy and anonymity is guaranteed under the decisional Diffie–Hellman assumption. Our security proof is in the random oracle model. The CL signature scheme works as follows.

The CL signature scheme

Key generation. On input 1^k, choose a special RSA modulus $n = pq$, $p = 2p' + 1$, $q = 2q' + 1$. Choose, uniformly at random, $R_0, \ldots, R_{L-1}, S, Z \in QR_n$. Output the public key $(n, R_0, \ldots, R_{L-1}, S, Z)$ and the secret key p. Let ℓ_n be the length of n.

Message space. Let ℓ_m be a parameter. The message space is the set $\{(m_0, \ldots, m_{L-1}) \colon m_i \in \pm\{0, 1\}^{\ell_m}\}$.

Signing algorithm. On input $m_0, \ldots, m_{L-1}$, choose a random prime number e of length $\ell_e > \ell_m + 2$, and a random number v of length $\ell_v = \ell_n + \ell_m + \ell_r$, where ℓ_r is a security parameter. Compute the value A such that $Z \equiv R_0^{m_0} \cdots R_{L-1}^{m_{L-1}} S^v A^e \pmod{n}$. The signature on the message $(m_0, \ldots, m_{L-1})$ consists of (e, A, v).

Verification algorithm. To verify that the tuple (e, A, v) is a signature on message $(m_0, \ldots, m_{L-1})$, check that $Z \equiv A^e R_0^{m_0} \cdots R_{L-1}^{m_{L-1}} S^v \pmod{n}$ and check that $2^{\ell_e} > e > 2^{\ell_e - 1}$.

Theorem 1 ([27]). *The CL signature scheme is secure against adaptive chosen message attacks [29] under the strong RSA assumption in the random oracle model.*

The original scheme considered messages in the interval $[0, 2^{\ell_m} - 1]$. In the DAA scheme, we allow messages from $[-2^{\ell_m} + 1, 2^{\ell_m} - 1]$. The only consequence of this is that we need to require that $\ell_e > \ell_m + 2$ holds instead of $\ell_e > \ell_m + 1$.

The reason this signature scheme is particularly suited to our purposes is that it can be used to sign a message blindly and prove knowledge of a signature anonymously by using discrete logarithm-based proofs of knowledge [27, 28]. However, in the DAA scheme, we use somewhat different (and also optimised) protocols for blind signing and anonymous verification than those provided in References 27 and 28.

Another property that distinguishes DAA from the CL signature scheme and all the prior Strong RSA-based proposals is that DAA does not require that the modulus be a product of safe primes. This assumption is required for the other schemes in order to guarantee privacy to the users. The issue is that the user needs to be assured that the values of the signature lie in the right subgroup (i.e., the A value in DAA). Otherwise the signer could choose the values to be in another subgroup and thereby break privacy. However, proving that the modulus is the product of two safe primes is not practical! So, DAA is indeed the first scheme that is practical from this point of view.

5.4   The DAA scheme

This section, we recall the DAA scheme in Reference 30.

5.4.1   Entities

The DAA scheme involves the following four kinds of entities:

- A DAA issuer. This could be any third party but most likely is a manufacturer of TPMs.
- A TPM. This is the entity that generates DAA signatures.
- A host. This is the platform of which the TPM forms part, and assists in the DAA join and signing processes. The reason for involving the host in the DAA scheme is because the TPM will typically have a very limited capacity for computation and storage.
- A DAA verifier. This could be any external partner.

5.4.2   Notation

We employ the following notation:

- $\{0, 1\}^\ell$: the set of non-negative binary strings of length ℓ, that is, the set $[0, 2^\ell - 1]$ of integers.
- $\pm\{0, 1\}^\ell$: the set of all binary strings of length ℓ, that is, the set $[-2^\ell + 1, 2^\ell - 1]$ of integers.
- $\text{LSB}_u(x)$: the integer corresponding to the u least significant bits of the binary representation of x, that is, $\text{LSB}_u(x) := x - 2^u \lfloor x/2^u \rfloor$.
- $\text{CAR}_u(x)$: the integer obtained by taking the binary representation of x, and deleting the u right-most bits, that is, $\text{CAR}_u(x) := \lfloor x/2^u \rfloor$.

5.4.3   Security parameters

We employ the following security parameters (where the numbers in parentheses are proposed values for these parameters):

- ℓ_n (2048): the size of the RSA modulus.
- ℓ_f (104): the size of the f_i's (information encoded into the certificate).
- ℓ_e (368): the size of the e's (exponents, part of certificate).

- ℓ'_e (120): the size of the interval that the e's are chosen from.
- ℓ_v (2536): the size of the v's (random value, part of certificate).
- $\ell_\varnothing$ (80): the security parameter controlling the statistical zero-knowledge property.
- $\ell_{\mathcal{H}}$ (160): the output length of the hash function used for the Fiat–Shamir heuristic.
- ℓ_r (80): the security parameter needed for the reduction in the proof of security.
- ℓ_s (1024): the size into which to split large exponents for simpler computations on the TPM.
- ℓ_Γ (1632): the size of the modulus Γ.
- ℓ_ρ (208): the size of the order ρ of the subgroup of $\mathbb{Z}^*_\Gamma$ that is used for rogue-tagging.
- $\mathcal{H}$: a collision resistant hash function $\mathcal{H} : \{0, 1\}^* \rightarrow \{0, 1\}^{\ell_{\mathcal{H}}}$.
- $H_\Gamma(\cdot)$ and $H(\cdot)$: two collision-resistant hash functions $H_\Gamma(\cdot) : \{0, 1\}^* \rightarrow \{0, 1\}^{\ell_\Gamma + \ell_\varnothing}$ and $H(\cdot): \{0, 1\}^* \rightarrow \{0, 1\}^{\ell_{\mathcal{H}}}$.

We require that:

$$\ell_\rho = 2\ell_f,$$
$$\ell_e > \ell_\varnothing + \ell_{\mathcal{H}} + \max\{\ell_f + 4, \ell'_e + 2\}$$

and

$$\ell_v > \ell_n + \ell_\varnothing + \ell_{\mathcal{H}} + \max\{\ell_f + \ell_r + 3, \ell_\varnothing + 2\}.$$

The parameters ℓ_Γ and ℓ_ρ should be chosen such that the discrete logarithm problem in the subgroup of $\mathbb{Z}^*_\Gamma$ of order ρ with Γ and ρ being primes such that $2^{\ell_\rho} > \rho > 2^{\ell_\rho - 1}$ and $2^{\ell_\Gamma} > \Gamma > 2^{\ell_\Gamma - 1}$, has about the same difficulty as factoring ℓ_n-bit RSA moduli [31].

5.4.4   Setup for the issuer

This section describes how the issuer chooses its public key and secret key. The key generation procedure also produces a non-interactive proof (using the Fiat–Shamir heuristic) that the keys were chosen correctly. The latter will guarantee the security requirements of the host (and its user), that is, that privacy and anonymity of signatures will hold.

The issuer setup

1. The issuer chooses a RSA modulus $n = pq$ with $p = 2p' + 1$, $q = 2q' + 1$ such that p, p', q, q' are all primes and n has ℓ_n bits. We refer to Reference 32 for an efficient algorithm to select such a modulus.

2. The issuer also chooses a random generator g' of QR_n (the group of quadratic residues modulo n).

---

3. Next, it chooses random integers $x_0, x_1, x_z, x_s, x_h, x_g \in [1, p'q']$ and computes

$$g := g'^{x_g} \bmod n, \quad h := g'^{x_h} \bmod n, \quad S := h^{x_s} \bmod n,$$

$$Z := h^{x_z} \bmod n, \quad R_0 := S^{x_0} \bmod n, \quad R_1 := S^{x_1} \bmod n.$$

4. It produces a non-interactive proof *proof* that R_0, R_1, S, Z, g and h are computed correctly, that is, that $g, h \in \langle g' \rangle$, $S, Z \in \langle h \rangle$ and $R_0, R_1 \in \langle S \rangle$, as follows. It chooses random

$$\tilde{x}_{(g,1)}, \ldots, \tilde{x}_{(g,\ell_{\mathcal{H}})} \in_R [1, p'q'] \quad \tilde{x}_{(h,1)}, \ldots, \tilde{x}_{(h,\ell_{\mathcal{H}})} \in_R [1, p'q']$$

$$\tilde{x}_{(s,1)}, \ldots, \tilde{x}_{(s,\ell_{\mathcal{H}})} \in_R [1, p'q']$$

$$\tilde{x}_{(z,1)}, \ldots, \tilde{x}_{(z,\ell_{\mathcal{H}})} \in_R [1, p'q'] \quad \tilde{x}_{(0,1)}, \ldots, \tilde{x}_{(0,\ell_{\mathcal{H}})} \in_R [1, p'q']$$

$$\tilde{x}_{(1,1)}, \ldots, \tilde{x}_{(1,\ell_{\mathcal{H}})} \in_R [1, p'q']$$

and computes

$$\tilde{g}_{(g,i)} := g'^{\tilde{x}_{(g,i)}} \bmod n \qquad \tilde{h}_{(h,i)} := g'^{\tilde{x}_{(h,i)}} \bmod n$$

$$\tilde{S}_{(s,i)} := h^{\tilde{x}_{(s,i)}} \bmod n$$

$$\tilde{Z}_{(z,i)} := h^{\tilde{x}_{(z,i)}} \bmod n \qquad \tilde{R}_{(0,i)} := S^{\tilde{x}_{(0,i)}} \bmod n$$

$$\tilde{R}_{(1,i)} := S^{\tilde{x}_{(1,i)}} \bmod n$$

for $i = 1, \ldots, \ell_{\mathcal{H}}$.

It then computes

$$c := H(n, g', g, h, S, Z, R_0, R_1, \tilde{g}_{(g,1)}, \ldots, \tilde{g}_{(g,\ell_{\mathcal{H}})}, \tilde{h}_{(h,1)}, \ldots, \tilde{h}_{(h,\ell_{\mathcal{H}})},$$

$$\tilde{S}_{(s,1)}, \ldots, \tilde{S}_{(s,\ell_{\mathcal{H}})}, \tilde{Z}_{(z,1)}, \ldots, \tilde{Z}_{(z,\ell_{\mathcal{H}})}, \tilde{R}_{(0,1)}, \ldots, \tilde{R}_{(0,\ell_{\mathcal{H}})},$$

$$\tilde{R}_{(1,1)}, \ldots, \tilde{R}_{(1,\ell_{\mathcal{H}})}),$$

and

$$\hat{x}_{(g,i)} := \tilde{x}_{(g,i)} - c_i x_g \bmod p'q' \quad \hat{x}_{(h,i)} := \tilde{x}_{(h,i)} - c_i x_h \bmod p'q'$$

$$\hat{x}_{(s,i)} := \tilde{x}_{(s,i)} - c_i x_s \bmod p'q'$$

$$\hat{x}_{(z,i)} := \tilde{x}_{(z,i)} - c_i x_z \bmod p'q' \quad \hat{x}_{(0,i)} := \tilde{x}_{(0,i)} - c_i x_0 \bmod p'q'$$

$$\hat{x}_{(1,i)} := \tilde{x}_{(1,i)} - c_i x_1 \bmod p'q'$$

for $i = 1, \ldots, \ell_{\mathcal{H}}$, where c_i is the ith bit of c.

$$proof := (c, \hat{x}_{(g,1)}, \ldots, \hat{x}_{(g,\ell_{\mathcal{H}})}, \hat{x}_{(h,1)}, \ldots, \hat{x}_{(h,\ell_{\mathcal{H}})},$$

$$\hat{x}_{(s,1)}, \ldots, \hat{x}_{(s,\ell_{\mathcal{H}})}, \hat{x}_{(z,1)}, \ldots, \hat{x}_{(z,\ell_{\mathcal{H}})},$$

$$\hat{x}_{(0,1)}, \ldots, \hat{x}_{(0,\ell_{\mathcal{H}})}, \hat{x}_{(1,1)}, \ldots, \hat{x}_{(1,\ell_{\mathcal{H}})}).$$

5. It generates a group of prime order: Choose random primes ρ and Γ such that $\Gamma = r\rho + 1$ for some r with $\rho \nmid r$, $2^{\ell_\Gamma - 1} < \Gamma < 2^{\ell_\Gamma}$ and $2^{\ell_\rho - 1} < \rho < 2^{\ell_\rho}$. Choose a random $\gamma' \in_R \mathbb{Z}_\Gamma^*$ such that $\gamma'^{(\Gamma - 1)/\rho} \not\equiv 1 \pmod{\Gamma}$ and set $\gamma := \gamma'^{(\Gamma - 1)/\rho} \bmod \Gamma$.

6. Finally, it publishes the public key $(n, g', g, h, S, Z, R_0, R_1, \gamma, \Gamma, \rho)$ and the proof *proof* and stores $p'q'$ as its secret key.

5.4.5 Verification of the issuer's public key

This section describes how a host verifies the proof described in Section 5.4.4. The purpose of the mechanism is to guarantee that the privacy and anonymity properties of the scheme will hold.

The proof uses binary challenges (the c_i's) and it is easy to see that it is indeed a zero-knowledge proof that R_0 and R_1 lie in $\langle S \rangle$, that Z and S lie in $\langle h \rangle$ and that g and h lie in $\langle g' \rangle$. We note that if some RSA modulus was available whose factorisation is not known to the issuer, this proof could be performed using non-binary challenges, which would make it about $\ell_\mathcal{H}$ times more efficient. We do not pursue this issue further here.

The verification of the issuer's public key

1. A verifier first verifies the proof

$$\text{proof} = (c, \hat{x}_{(g,1)}, \ldots, \hat{x}_{(g,\ell_\mathcal{H})}, \hat{x}_{(h,1)}, \ldots, \hat{x}_{(h,\ell_\mathcal{H})}, \hat{x}_{(s,1)}, \ldots, \hat{x}_{(s,\ell_\mathcal{H})},$$
$$\hat{x}_{(z,1)}, \ldots, \hat{x}_{(z,\ell_\mathcal{H})}, \hat{x}_{(0,1)}, \ldots, \hat{x}_{(0,\ell_\mathcal{H})}, \hat{x}_{(1,1)}, \ldots, \hat{x}_{(1,\ell_\mathcal{H})})$$

as follows.
The verifier computes

$$\hat{g}_{(g,i)} := g^{c_i} g'^{\hat{x}_{(g,i)}} \bmod n \quad \hat{h}_{(h,i)} := h^{c_i} g'^{\hat{x}_{(h,i)}} \bmod n$$

$$\hat{S}_{(s,i)} := S^{c_i} h^{\hat{x}_{(s,i)}} \bmod n$$

$$\hat{Z}_{(z,i)} := Z^{c_i} h^{\hat{x}_{(z,i)}} \bmod n \quad \hat{R}_{(0,i)} := R_0^{c_i} S^{\hat{x}_{(0,i)}} \bmod n$$

$$\hat{R}_{(1,i)} := R_1^{c_i} S^{\hat{x}_{(1,i)}} \bmod n$$

for $i = 1, \ldots, \ell_\mathcal{H}$, where c_i is the ith bit of c.
It then checks

$$c \stackrel{?}{=} H(n, g', g, h, S, Z, R_0, R_1, \hat{g}_{(g,1)}, \ldots, \hat{g}_{(g,\ell_\mathcal{H})}, \hat{h}_{(h,1)}, \ldots, \hat{h}_{(h,\ell_\mathcal{H})},$$
$$\hat{S}_{(s,1)}, \ldots, \hat{S}_{(s,\ell_\mathcal{H})}, \hat{Z}_{(z,1)}, \ldots, \hat{Z}_{(z,\ell_\mathcal{H})},$$
$$\hat{R}_{(0,1)}, \ldots, \hat{R}_{(0,\ell_\mathcal{H})}, \hat{R}_{(1,1)}, \ldots, \hat{R}_{(1,\ell_\mathcal{H})}).$$

2. It then checks whether Γ and ρ are primes, $\rho \mid (\Gamma - 1)$, $\rho \nmid (\Gamma - 1)/\rho$, and $\gamma^\rho \equiv 1 \pmod{\Gamma}$.
3. Finally it checks whether all public key parameter have the required length.

If R_0, R_1, S, Z, g and h are not formed correctly, it could potentially mean that the security properties for the TPM/host do not hold. However, it is sufficient if the platform/host (i.e., owner of the TPM) verifies the proof that R_0, R_1, g and h are computed correctly just once. In principle, it is sufficient if just one representative of platform users checks this proof. Also, if γ does not generate a subgroup of $\mathbb{Z}_\Gamma^*$, the issuer could potentially use this to link different signatures.

As the anonymity/pseudonymity properties have been addressed in the security proof of the DAA scheme [30, 33], it is not important for the security of the platform that n is a product of two safe primes.

5.4.6 Join protocol

Let $\text{PK}_I := (n, g', g, h, S, Z, R_0, R_1, \gamma, \Gamma, \rho)$ be the public key of the issuer, and let CK_I be a long-term public key of the issuer used to authenticate PK_I for the DAA. Let $\zeta_I \equiv (H_\Gamma(1\|\text{bsn}_I))^{(\Gamma-1)/\rho} \bmod \Gamma$, where bsn_I is the issuer's long-term basename, which is used to provide an issuer-specific linkability, as described in Section 5.1.2.

We assume that, prior to running the Join protocol, the TPM and host both verify that PK_I is authenticated by CK_I.

Let DAAseed be the secret seed used by the TPM in the computation of f_0 and f_1. Note that the reason for using DAAseed, instead of generating f_0 and f_1 from a unique random number every time, is that this means that in the DAA scheme it is only necessary to store a single secret value inside the TPM.

Let cnt be the current value of the counter, which is used to keep track of the number of times that the TPM has run the Join protocol. The TPM is allowed to re-run the Join protocol with the same cnt value many times. In that case, both the number of times that the TPM has run the Join protocol to re-certify the same f_0 and f_1 pair, and the number of times that the TPM has run the Join protocol to get certificates for different f_0 and f_1 pairs, could be traced. More detailed discussion of re-issuing DAA keys and certificates can be found in Section 5.6.

We assume that the TPM and the issuer have established a one-way authentic channel, that is, the issuer needs to be sure that it is talking to the right TPM. Note that authenticity of the channel is enough, that is, we do not require secrecy, in fact we can even assume that the host reads all messages and may choose not to forward some messages sent by the issuer to the TPM. In fact, it is sufficient that the value U be transmitted authentically from the TPM to the issuer. In the TCG setting, one can achieve this using the EK pair that was issued to the TPM as follows.

The issuer must be sure that the value U stems from the TPM that owns a given endorsement public key EK. In this chapter we just assume that the issuer receives U in an authentic manner; the following protocol could be used to achieve this.

A protocol to authenticate a TPM with respect to an EK

1. The issuer chooses a random $n_e \in \{0,1\}^{\ell_\varnothing}$ and encrypts n_e under the EK and sends the encrypted value to the TPM.
2. The TPM decrypts this and thereby retrieves some string n_e. Then, the TPM computes $a_U := H(U\|n_e)$ and sends a_U to the issuer.
3. The issuer verifies if $a_U = H(U\|n_e)$ holds.

This protocol should be executed between the steps 2 and 4 of the Join protocol. This protocol is in the same spirit as the protocol to 'authenticate' the AIK in the TCG TPM 1.1b specification [34].

The Join protocol

1. The host computes $\zeta_{\mathrm{I}} := (H_\Gamma(1\|\mathrm{bsn}_{\mathrm{I}}))^{(\Gamma-1)/\rho} \bmod \Gamma$ and sends ζ_{I} to the TPM. The host also selects $\mathtt{cnt}$ and sends $\mathtt{cnt}$ to the TPM and to the issuer.

2. The TPM checks whether $\zeta_{\mathrm{I}}^\rho \equiv 1 \pmod{\Gamma}$. Let $i := \lfloor (\ell_\rho + \ell_\varnothing)/\ell_{\mathcal{H}} \rfloor$ (i will be 1 for the values of the parameters suggested in Section 5.4.3). The TPM computes

$$f := H(H(\mathrm{DAAseed}\|H(\mathrm{CK}_{\mathrm{I}}))\|\mathtt{cnt}\|0)\| \cdots$$

$$\times \|H(H(\mathrm{DAAseed}\|H(\mathrm{CK}_{\mathrm{I}}))\|\mathtt{cnt}\|i) \pmod{\rho},$$

$$f_0 := \mathrm{LSB}_{\ell_f}(f), \quad f_1 := \mathrm{CAR}_{\ell_f}(f), \quad v' \in_R \{0,1\}^{\ell_n+\ell_\varnothing},$$

$$U := R_0^{f_0} R_1^{f_1} S^{v'} \bmod n, \quad N_{\mathrm{I}} := \zeta_{\mathrm{I}}^{f_0+f_1 2^{\ell_f}} \bmod \Gamma$$

and sends U and N_{I} to the host who forwards them to the issuer.

3. The issuer checks whether values of $N_{\mathrm{I}} \overset{?}{\neq} (\zeta_{\mathrm{I}}^{f_0+f_1 2^{\ell_f}}) \pmod{\Gamma}$ for each (f_0, f_1) on the rogue list. The issuer also checks this for the N_{I} this platform had used previously. If the issuer finds the platform to be rogue, it aborts the protocol.

4. The TPM proves to the issuer knowledge of f_0, f_1 and v': it executes as prover the protocol

$$\mathrm{SPK}\{(f_0,f_1,v'): \ U \equiv \pm R_0^{f_0} R_1^{f_1} S^{v'} \pmod{n}$$

$$\wedge \ N_{\mathrm{I}} \equiv \zeta_{\mathrm{I}}^{f_0+f_1 2^{\ell_f}} \pmod{\Gamma}$$

$$\wedge \ f_0, f_1 \in \{0,1\}^{\ell_f+\ell_\varnothing+\ell_{\mathcal{H}}+2}$$

$$\wedge \ v' \in \{0,1\}^{\ell_n+\ell_\varnothing+\ell_{\mathcal{H}}+2}\}(n_t\|n_i)$$

with the issuer as the verifier. This protocol is implemented as follows, where some non-critical operations are performed by the host and not by the TPM.

(a) The TPM picks random integers $r_{f_0}, r_{f_1} \in_R \{0,1\}^{\ell_f + \ell_\varnothing + \ell_\mathcal{H}}$ and $r_{v'} \in_R \{0,1\}^{\ell_n + 2\ell_\varnothing + \ell_\mathcal{H}}$, computes

$$\tilde{U} := R_0^{r_{f_0}} R_1^{r_{f_1}} S^{r_{v'}} \bmod n \text{ and } \tilde{N}_\mathrm{I} := \zeta_\mathrm{I}^{r_{f_0} + r_{f_1} 2^{\ell_f}} \bmod \Gamma, \text{ and sends } \tilde{U}$$

and $\tilde{N}_\mathrm{I}$ to the host.

(b) The issuer chooses a random string $n_i \in \{0,1\}^{\ell_\mathcal{H}}$ and sends n_i to the host.

(c) The host computes $c_h := H(n\|R_0\|R_1\|S\|U\|N_\mathrm{I}\|\tilde{U}\|\tilde{N}_\mathrm{I}\|n_i)$ and sends c_h to the TPM.

(d) The TPM chooses a random $n_t \in \{0,1\}^{\ell_\varnothing}$ and computes $c := H(c_h\|n_t) \in [0, 2^{\ell_\mathcal{H}} - 1]$.

(e) The TPM computes $s_{f_0} := r_{f_0} + cf_0$, $s_{f_1} := r_{f_1} + cf_1$ and $s_{v'} := r_{v'} + cv'$ and sends the host $(c, n_t, s_{f_0}, s_{f_1}, s_{v'})$.

(f) The host forwards $(c, n_t, s_{f_0}, s_{f_1}, s_{v'})$ to the issuer.

(g) The issuer verifies the proof by computing $\hat{U} := U^{-c} R_0^{s_{f_0}} R_1^{s_{f_1}} \times S^{s_{v'}} \bmod n$ and $\hat{N}_\mathrm{I} := N_\mathrm{I}^{-c} \zeta_\mathrm{I}^{s_{f_0} + 2^{\ell_f} s_{f_1}} \bmod \Gamma$ and checking if $c \stackrel{?}{=} H(H(n\|R_0\|R_1\|S\|U\|N_\mathrm{I}\|\hat{U}\|\hat{N}_\mathrm{I}\|n_i)\|n_t)$, $s_{f_0}, s_{f_1} \stackrel{?}{\in} \{0,1\}^{\ell_f + \ell_\varnothing + \ell_\mathcal{H} + 1}$ and $s_{v'} \stackrel{?}{\in} \{0,1\}^{\ell_n + 2\ell_\varnothing + \ell_\mathcal{H} + 1}$.

5. The issuer chooses $\hat{v} \in_R \{0,1\}^{\ell_v - 1}$ and a prime $e \in_R [2^{\ell_e - 1}, 2^{\ell_e - 1} + 2^{\ell'_e - 1}]$ and computes $v'' := \hat{v} + 2^{\ell_v - 1}$ and

$$A := \left(\frac{Z}{U S^{v''}} \right)^{1/e} \bmod n.$$

6. To convince the host that A was correctly computed, the issuer as prover runs the protocol

$$\mathrm{SPK} \left\{ (d) : A \equiv \pm \left(\frac{Z}{U S^{v''}} \right)^d \pmod{n} \right\} (n_h)$$

with the host:

(a) The host chooses a random integer $n_h \in \{0,1\}^{\ell_\varnothing}$ and sends n_h to the issuer.

(b) The issuer randomly chooses $r_e \in_R [0, p'q']$, computes

$$\tilde{A} := \left(\frac{Z}{U S^{v''}} \right)^{r_e} \bmod n, \quad c' := H(n\|Z\|S\|U\|v''\|A\|\tilde{A}\|n_h)$$

and

$$s_e := r_e - c'/e \bmod p'q',$$

and sends c', s_e and (A, e, v'') to the host.

(c) The host verifies whether e is a prime and lies in $[2^{\ell_e-1}, 2^{\ell_e-1} + 2^{\ell'_e-1}]$, computes $\hat{A} := A^{c'}(Z/US^{v''})^{s_e} \bmod n$ and checks whether

$$c' \stackrel{?}{=} H(n\|Z\|S\|U\|v''\|A\|\hat{A}\|n_h).$$

7. The host forwards v'' to the TPM.
8. The TPM receives v'', sets $v := v'' + v'$ and stores (f_0, f_1, v).

As a result of the protocol, the TPM will have obtained secret values f_0, f_1 and v, the host will have values A and e and the issuer will have values N_I such that $A^e R_0^{f_0} R_1^{f_1} S^v \equiv Z \pmod{n}$ and $N_I \equiv \zeta_I^{f_0+f_1 2^{\ell_f}} \pmod{\Gamma}$ hold.

Our protocol differs from that given in Reference 27 mainly in that our protocol requires the issuer to prove that A lies in $\langle h \rangle$. The host can conclude that $A \in \langle h \rangle$ from the proof the issuer provides in step 6, the fact that $A^e US^{v''} \equiv Z \pmod{n}$ and the proofs the issuer provides as part of the setup that $S, R_0, R_1, Z \in \langle h \rangle$. We refer to the security proof of Theorem 5.5 provided in Reference 33 for the details of this. The reason for requiring $A \in \langle h \rangle$ is to assure that later, in the signing algorithm, A can be statistically hidden in $\langle h \rangle$. Otherwise, an adversarial signer could, for example, compute A as $b(Z/US^{v''})^{1/e} \bmod n$, using some b such that $b^e = 1$ and $b \notin \langle h \rangle$. As a DAA-signature contains the value $T_1 = Ah^w$ for a random w (see DAA-signing protocol), an adversarial signer would be able to link T_1 to A, for example, by testing $T_1 \in \langle h \rangle$. Prior schemes [5, 15, 27] have prevented this by ensuring that n is a safe-prime product and that all elements are cast into QR_n. However, proving that a modulus is a safe-prime product is rather inefficient [35] and hence the setup of these schemes is not really practical. We note that the proof in step 6 is zero-knowledge only if the issuer has chosen n as a safe-prime product. This is a property that the issuer is interested in, and not the TPM, host or users of a platform.

Because our security proof requires rewinding to extract f_0, f_1 and v' from an adversarial TPM, the join protocol can only be run sequentially, that is, not in parallel with many TPMs. At some loss of efficiency, this drawback could, for example, be overcome by using the verifiable encryption [36] of these values.

5.4.7 DAA-signing protocol

We now describe how a platform can prove that it possesses an anonymous attestation credential and at the same time authenticate a message. Suppose that the platform gets as input a message m to DAA-sign. We remark that in some cases the message m will be generated by the TPM and might not be known to the host. For example, the TPM may sign an AIK, an RSA public key that it has generated, which the TPM will later use to sign its internal registers.

Let $n_v \in \{0,1\}^{\ell_{\mathcal{H}}}$ be a nonce and bsn$_V$ a basename value provided by the verifier. Let b be a byte describing the use of the protocol, that is, $b = 0$ means that the message m is generated by the TPM and $b = 1$ means that the message m was input to the TPM.

The DAA-sign procedure is a protocol between the TPM and its host.

The signing algorithm

1. (a) Depending on the verifier's request (i.e., whether the verifier's basename $\mathrm{bsn_V}$ is included or not), the host computes ζ as follows:

$$\zeta \in_R \langle \gamma \rangle \qquad \text{or} \qquad \zeta := (H_\Gamma(1\|\mathrm{bsn_V}))^{(\Gamma-1)/\rho} \bmod \Gamma$$

and sends ζ to the TPM.

   (b) The TPM checks whether $\zeta^\rho \equiv 1 \pmod{\Gamma}$.

2. (a) The host picks random integers $w, r \in \{0,1\}^{\ell_n + \ell_\varnothing}$ and computes $T_1 := Ah^w \bmod n$ and $T_2 := g^w h^e (g')^r \bmod n$.

   (b) The TPM computes $N_V := \zeta^{f_0 + f_1 2^{\ell_f}} \bmod \Gamma$ and sends N_V to the host.

3. Now, the TPM and the host together produce a 'signature of knowledge' that T_1 and T_2 commit to a certificate and that N_V was computed using the secret key going with that certificate. That is, they compute the 'signature of knowledge'

$$\mathrm{SPK}\{(f_0, f_1, v, e, w, r, ew, ee, er):$$

$$Z \equiv \pm T_1^e R_0^{f_0} R_1^{f_1} S^v h^{-ew} \pmod{n} \ \wedge \ T_2 \equiv \pm g^w h^e g'^r \pmod{n}$$

$$\wedge \ 1 \equiv \pm T_2^{-e} g^{ew} h^{ee} g'^{er} \pmod{n} \ \wedge \ N_V \equiv \zeta^{f_0 + f_1 2^{\ell_f}} \pmod{\Gamma}$$

$$\wedge \ f_0, f_1 \in \{0,1\}^{\ell_f + \ell_\varnothing + \ell_\mathcal{H} + 2}$$

$$\wedge \ (e - 2^{\ell_e}) \in \{0,1\}^{\ell'_e + \ell_\varnothing + \ell_\mathcal{H} + 1}\}(n_t\|n_v\|b\|m).$$

Most of the secrets involved are actually known by the host; in fact only the values involving f_0, f_1, and v need to be computed by the TPM, as the reader can see below.

(a) i. The TPM picks random integers $r_v \in_R \{0,1\}^{\ell_v + \ell_\varnothing + \ell_\mathcal{H}}$ and $r_{f_0}, r_{f_1} \in_R \{0,1\}^{\ell_f + \ell_\varnothing + \ell_\mathcal{H}}$ and computes

$$\tilde{T}_{1t} := R_0^{r_{f_0}} R_1^{r_{f_1}} S^{r_v} \bmod n \qquad \tilde{r}_f := r_{f_0} + r_{f_1} 2^{\ell_f} \bmod \rho$$

$$\tilde{N}_V := \zeta^{\tilde{r}_f} \bmod \Gamma.$$

The TPM sends $\tilde{T}_{1t}$ and $\tilde{N}_V$ to the host.

   ii. The host picks random integers

$$r_e \in_R \{0,1\}^{\ell'_e + \ell_\varnothing + \ell_\mathcal{H}}, \quad r_{ee} \in_R \{0,1\}^{2\ell_e + \ell_\varnothing + \ell_\mathcal{H} + 1},$$

$$r_w, r_r \in_R \{0,1\}^{\ell_n + 2\ell_\varnothing + \ell_\mathcal{H}}, \quad r_{ew}, r_{er} \in_R \{0,1\}^{\ell_e + \ell_n + 2\ell_\varnothing + \ell_\mathcal{H} + 1}$$

and computes

$$\tilde{T}_1 := \tilde{T}_{1t}T_1^{r_e}h^{-r_{ew}} \bmod n, \quad \tilde{T}_2 := g^{r_w}h^{r_e}g'^{r_r} \bmod n,$$

$$\tilde{T}_2' := T_2^{-r_e}g^{r_{ew}}h^{r_{ee}}g'^{r_{er}} \bmod n.$$

(b) i. The host computes

$$c_{\mathrm{h}} := H((n\|g\|g'\|h\|R_0\|R_1\|S\|Z\|\gamma\|\Gamma\|\rho)\|\zeta\|(T_1\|T_2)\|N_V\|$$

$$(\tilde{T}_1\|\tilde{T}_2\|\tilde{T}_2')\|\tilde{N}_V)\|n_v)$$

and sends c_{h} to the TPM.

ii. The TPM chooses a random $n_t \in \{0,1\}^{\ell_\varnothing}$, computes $c := H(H(c_{\mathrm{h}}\|n_t)\|b\|m)$, and sends c, n_t to the host.

(c) i. The TPM computes (over the integers)

$$s_v := r_v + cv, \quad s_{f_0} := r_{f_0} + cf_0 \quad \text{and} \quad s_{f_1} := r_{f_1} + cf_1$$

and sends (s_v, s_{f_0}, s_{f_1}) to the host.

ii. The host computes (over the integers)

$$s_e := r_e + c(e - 2^{\ell_e - 1}), \quad s_{ee} := r_{ee} + ce^2,$$

$$s_w := r_w + cw, \quad s_{ew} := r_{ew} + cwe,$$

$$s_r := r_r + cr, \quad s_{er} := r_{er} + cer.$$

4. The host outputs the signature $\sigma := (\zeta, (T_1, T_2), N_V, c, n_t, (s_v, s_{f_0}, s_{f_1}, s_e,$
$s_{ee}, s_w, s_{ew}, s_r, s_{er}))$.

As a result of the protocol, the host will have obtained a signature $\sigma := (\zeta, (T_1, T_2), N_V, c, n_t, (s_v, s_{f_0}, s_{f_1}, s_e, s_{ee}, s_w, s_{ew}, s_r, s_{er}))$ on the message m.

Let us give some intuition about why this signature should convince a verifier that N_V links to secrets that were certified. The first term in the SPK can be rewritten as $Z \equiv (\pm T_1/h^{ew/e})^e R_0^{f_0} R_1^{f_1} S^v \pmod{n}$, if e divides we (see the proof of security [33]). The second two terms show that e indeed divides we, so the rewriting works. Therefore, because the last terms that show that the f_i's and e satisfy the length requirements, $(T_1/(h^{ew/e}), e, v)$ is a valid certificate for f_0 and f_1. The remaining term shows that N_V is based on the same f_0 and f_1.

The main difference between this DAA-signing protocol and the signature generation in prior schemes such as References 5, 15 and 27 is that here we have distributed the necessary operation to two parties, the TPM and the host. Basically, the TPM only produces the proof-signature $\mathrm{SPK}\{(f_0, f_1, v) : (Z/A^e) \equiv R_0^{f_0} R_1^{f_1} S^v$ $\pmod{n}) \wedge N_V \equiv \zeta^{f_0 + f_1 2^{\ell_f}} \times \pmod{\Gamma}\} (n_t \|n_v\|b\|m)$, which the host then extends to the full DAA-signature (note that (Z/A^e) is known to the host). Note that the SPK produced by the TPM is not anonymous (even with a random ζ) as the value (Z/A^e) would fully identify the TPM. While it is intuitively obvious that the host cannot generate such signatures on its own, or turn one by a TPM into one on a different message, a formal proof of this is given in Reference 33.

5.4.8   *Verification algorithm*

A signature

$$\sigma = (\zeta, (T_1, T_2), N_V, c, n_t, (s_v, s_{f_0}, s_{f_1}, s_e, s_{ee}, s_w, s_{ew}, s_r, s_{er}))$$

on a message m with respect to the public key $(n, g, g', h, R_0, R_1, S, Z, \gamma, \Gamma, \rho)$ and the selection-bit b is as verified as follows.

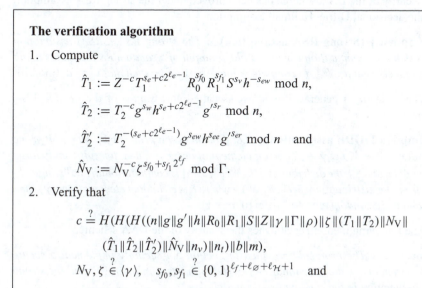

The verification algorithm

1.   Compute

$$\hat{T}_1 := Z^{-c} T_1^{s_e + c2^{\ell e - 1}} R_0^{s_{f_0}} R_1^{s_{f_1}} S^{s_v} h^{-s_{ew}} \bmod n,$$

$$\hat{T}_2 := T_2^{-c} g^{s_w} h^{s_e + c2^{\ell e - 1}} g'^{s_r} \bmod n,$$

$$\hat{T}_2' := T_2^{-(s_e + c2^{\ell e - 1})} g^{s_{ew}} h^{s_{ee}} g'^{s_{er}} \bmod n \quad \text{and}$$

$$\hat{N}_V := N_V^{-c} \zeta^{s_{f_0} + s_{f_1} 2^{\ell_f}} \bmod \Gamma.$$

2.   Verify that

$$c \overset{?}{=} H(H(H((n\|g\|g'\|h\|R_0\|R_1\|S\|Z\|\gamma\|\Gamma\|\rho)\|\zeta\|(T_1\|T_2)\|N_V\|$$

$$(\hat{T}_1\|\hat{T}_2\|\hat{T}_2')\|\hat{N}_V\|n_v)\|n_t)\|b\|m),$$

$$N_V, \zeta \overset{?}{\in} \langle \gamma \rangle, \quad s_{f_0}, s_{f_1} \overset{?}{\in} \{0,1\}^{\ell_f + \ell_\varnothing + \ell_\mathcal{H} + 1} \quad \text{and}$$

$$s_e \overset{?}{\in} \{0,1\}^{\ell_e' + \ell_\varnothing + \ell_\mathcal{H} + 1}.$$

3.   If ζ was derived from a verifier's basename, check whether $\zeta \overset{?}{=} (H_\Gamma(1\|\text{bsn}_V))^{(\Gamma - 1)/\rho} \pmod{\Gamma}$.

4.   For all (f_0, f_1) on the rogue list, check whether $N_V \overset{?}{\neq} (\zeta^{f_0 + f_1 2^{\ell_f}}) \pmod{\Gamma}$.

The check $N_V, \zeta \overset{?}{\in} \langle \gamma \rangle$ can be done by raising N_V and ζ to the order of γ (which is ρ) and checking whether the result is 1. If ζ is random, one can apply so-called batch verification techniques (cf. [37]) to obtain a considerable speed-up of verification step 4. Note also that the involved exponents are relatively small. Finally, if ζ is not random, one could precompute $\zeta^{f_0 + f_1 2^{\ell_f}}$ for all (f_0, f_1) on the rogue list.

5.4.9   *On rogue tagging*

When a certificate (A, e, v) and values f_0 and f_1 are found (e.g., on the Internet or embedded in some software), they should be distributed to all potential verifiers.

These verifiers can then check whether $A^e R_0^{f_0} R_1^{f_1} S^v \equiv Z$ (mod n) holds and then put f_0 and f_1 on their list of rogue keys. Note that this does not involve a certificate revocation authority.

5.5   Security results

The security of the DAA scheme has been proved under the strong RSA assumption and the decisional Diffie–Hellman assumption.

Assumption 1 (Strong RSA assumption).   *The strong RSA (SRSA) assumption states that it is computationally infeasible, on input of a random RSA modulus n and a random element $u \in \mathbb{Z}_n^*$, to compute values $e > 1$ and v such that $v^e \equiv u$ (mod n).*

The tuple (n, u) generated as above is called an *instance* of the *flexible* RSA problem.

Assumption 2 (DDH assumption).   *Let Γ be an ℓ_Γ-bit prime and ρ an ℓ_ρ-bit prime such that $\rho | \Gamma - 1$. Let $\gamma \in \mathbb{Z}_\Gamma^*$ be an element of order ρ. Then, for sufficiently large values of ℓ_Γ and ℓ_ρ, the distribution $\{(\delta, \delta^a, \delta^b, \delta^{ab})\}$ is computationally indistinguishable from the distribution $\{(\delta, \delta^a, \delta^b, \delta^c)\}$, where δ is a random element from $\langle \gamma \rangle$, and a, b and c are random elements from $[0, \rho - 1]$.*

The following theorem establishes the security of the DAA scheme.

Theorem 2.   *The protocols provided in Section 5.4 securely implement a secure DAA system under the decisional Diffie–Hellman assumption in $\langle \gamma \rangle$ and the strong RSA assumption in the random oracle model.*

A proof of this theorem has been given in Reference 33.

5.6   Options for re-issue of DAA keys

The TPM needs to support the re-issue of DAA keys. The two primary reasons for this are to replace a DAA key that has been lost, and to change DAA keys in the case that a platform is sold. In this section, we will explain these motivations and present a method for supporting re-issue.

The TPM specifications allow multiple issuers to issue DAA keys for the TPM. However, the TPM has limited non-volatile storage. Therefore, the TPM needs to be able to encrypt DAA keys so that they can be stored off of the TPM. This introduces the possibility that the DAA keys may be lost or destroyed.

If a platform containing a TPM is sold, both the seller and the buyer would want to be assured that the DAA keys had been changed. To see why this is true, suppose that the DAA keys were not changed, and suppose also that the buyer went to a verifier using the same DAA keys. Assuming that the seller had cleaned his or her system before selling it, the buyer would be using a different AIK. But, because the buyer would be using the same DAA keys as the seller, and if the verifier is still using the same basename value, then the verifier will know that the TPM is the same one that had previously been used by the seller. In such a case the verifier should have a privacy policy such that he would not reveal to the buyer any previous transactions that had been performed with those DAA keys. However, if the verifier did not have such a privacy policy, then the verifier could reveal to the buyer the transactions that had previously been performed by the seller. To protect against this possible scenario, the seller would like to know that the buyer cannot use the same DAA keys as were used by the seller. Similarly, the buyer would like to be assured that the DAA keys had been changed so that a verifier collaborating with the seller could not link transactions to the buyer.

5.6.1 Requirements for the re-issue of DAA keys

We next give four fundamental requirements for the re-issue of DAA keys.

Mitigate issuer private key compromise. For any private key held by the issuer for the purpose of issuing DAA keys, there should be a plan to mitigate the risk that the key is compromised or lost. Any such private key should be able to be deleted after some fixed period of time.

Recover from user loss of DAA certificate. There must be a method for recovering from the loss of all data stored externally to the TPM, which could include the DAA certificate. In the recovery procedure the f_0 and f_1 pair used with an issuer should remain the same, so that an adversary would not be able to pretend that he had lost his or her DAA certificate and obtain multiple f_0 and f_1 pairs. The reason for this is that if an adversary had reverse engineered a TPM and removed the EK, the adversary would be able to misuse the DAA certificate issued by this EK. Suppose the adversary had used the DAA certificate in such a way that the misuse was detected by a verifier using a particular basename value. The adversary would like to get a new DAA certificate with a new f_0 and f_1 pair so that he could establish a new account with the verifier that was not traceable to the misused DAA certificate. Since the issuer would not be able to determine which DAA certificate was the bad one, even if the verifier told him, without using the verifier basename value, the best method to resolve this issue would be to be sure that when the issuer re-issues a DAA certificate, the f_0 and f_1 pair remains the same.

Privacy protection for the buyer of a platform. If a person buys a PC from a previous owner, then there should be a method for the new owner to establish a new DAA certificate for an issuer, so that the new owner is convinced that a verifier could not link use of the new DAA certificate to the DAA certificate of the previous owner.

Privacy protection for a seller of a platform. If a person sells a PC to a new owner, then there should be a method for the previous owner to be assured that if the new owner establishes a DAA certificate with an issuer, then the previous owner is convinced that a verifier could not link use of the new DAA certificate to the DAA certificate of the previous owner.

5.6.2 Method implemented in the TPM

In this section we describe the method implemented in the TPM to support key re-issue, which addresses the requirements listed above.

The issuer will select a certificate key pair for an ordinary signature scheme, with CK_I as the public verification key and SK_I as the private signature key. A certificate key pair is either used to issue a certificate for another certificate key pair or to issue a certificate for an issuer key, PK_I. The reason we allow a multi-level certification hierarchy is to mitigate the risk that an issuer key pair is compromised. The issuer can change the issuer key with some frequency. When a new issuer key is created and certified, the previous private portion of the issuer key can be deleted. If an issuer key is compromised, then the issuer can certify a new issuer key with a certificate key, and only the TPMs that were issued DAA keys by the compromised issuer key would be affected. The issuer can keep the certification keys in a more secure environment, since they are not used often. With some frequency, the issuer can create a new certification key, certify it with the previous certification key and then delete the previous private portion SK_I of the certification key. Prior to the Join protocol, the TPM will receive CK_I, PK_I and a certificate chain linking PK_I to CK_I. The TPM will validate the certificate chain.

During the Join protocol, a value cnt is input to the TPM. In step 2 of the Join protocol, f is computed as the hash of DAAseed, $H(CK_I)$, cnt. The DAAseed is a random secret constant held in the TPM. During the re-issue of a DAA certificate, the CK_I will be the same as before. As long as the same cnt is used, the same f will be computed. The issuer can check that the same f was computed, since the value of $N_I = \zeta_I^{f_0 + f_1 2^{\ell_f}} \mod \Gamma$ is sent to the issuer in step 2 of the Join protocol, and in step 4(g), the issuer verifies that the f value used in the computation of N_I is the same as the f value used in the generation of the DAA certificate.

The value of cnt will be sent to the issuer, so that if the user loses the value of cnt, the issuer can give him or her that value.

So if a DAA certificate is lost, the owner of the TPM can request a re-issue using the same cnt as was used before, and will thus receive a new DAA certificate with the same f value.

Note that, in order to avoid an adversary letting the TPM use a wrong CK_I and then compromising the DAA key, the TPM should tell the issuer which CK_I is used to compute the DAA key. To achieve this, in step 4 of the Join protocol, the TPM should include the value $H(CK_I)$ in the signed message, that is, signing $(n_t \| n_i \| H(CK_I))$ instead of $(n_t \| n_i)$. This potential weakness was pointed out by Challener and Zimmermann [38].

5.6.3   Re-issue upon sale of TPM

If the TPM is sold, then both the seller and the buyer would like assurance that a new cnt was used. When the seller sells the platform, he or she will inform the issuer that he or she is selling the platform and wants to start using a new cnt. The issuer may want to do some additional checking to be assured that the platform really is being sold, or he or she may allow one or two sales in the lifetime of a platform without any checking. After the issuer has accepted that the platform was sold, then he or she will no longer accept a DAA certificate request using the previous f value, and will only accept a DAA certificate request using a new f value. When the new owner makes a new DAA certificate request, he can choose a random value for cnt. In this way, there is a low probability that the previous owner had used this value, even if the previous owner and the issuer had collaborated, and the issuer had allowed the previous owner to make many certificate requests.

This method does make the seller dependent upon the issuer. If the issuer so wanted, the issuer could release the previous cnt value to the new owner. So the issuer and the new owner could collaborate so that the new owner could use the same f value as the seller. There is a tradeoff that the owner of a platform can make. If the owner thinks that at some point they will sell the platform, if they are worried about the integrity of the DAA issuer and they are worried that some verifiers will collaborate with the new owner to trace their transactions, then when they apply for a DAA certificate, they can lie about the cnt value to the issuer. They could then write down the cnt value and store it in a safe place. Then, if they ever lose their DAA certificate and need to recover, they can retrieve their cnt value and use it again. This will give them the same f value that was used in the previous DAA issuing, so the issuer will accept it. When they sell their platform, the new owner will not be able to determine the correct cnt, even if collaborating with the issuer, without trying all possibilities for cnt until the correct one is used. However, if the original owner loses the cnt values and also loses his or her DAA certificate, he or she will need to argue with the issuer to obtain a new DAA certificate without selling his or her platform. In the TPM 1.2 implementation [39], the cnt value is only 32 bits long, so in theory an exhaustive search on cnt is possible in a collaborative effort between the new owner and the issuer, but it would be quite time-consuming.

5.7   Increasing efficiency

In this section, we apply a recent observation made by Camenisch and Groth [40] that CL signatures [27] are randomisable which allows one to more efficiently prove knowledge of a signature on a hidden message [40].

Now, if (A, e, v) is a signature on a message-tuple (f_0, f_1), then so is $(T = AS^w, e, \bar{v} = v - we)$ for any integer w. Moreover, if w is suitably chosen, T will be randomly distributed in $\langle S \rangle$. Hence, the value T could be revealed and thence proving knowledge of a signature on (secret) messages becomes equivalent to proving knowledge of the representation of Z with respect to the bases T, R_0, R_1 and S. We are now ready to present a more efficient DAA signing algorithm that uses these facts.

The modified signing algorithm

1. (This step remains unchanged from Section 4.7.)
2. (a)   The host picks random integers $w \in \{0, 1\}^{\ell_n + \ell_\varnothing}$ and computes $T := AS^w \bmod n$.
    (b)   The TPM computes $N_V := \zeta^{f_0 + f_1 2^{\ell_f}} \bmod \Gamma$ and sends N_V and T to the host.

---

3. Now, the TPM and host together produce a 'signature of knowledge' that T commits to a certificate and N_V was computed using the secret key going with that certificate. That is, they compute the 'signature of knowledge'

$$\text{SPK}\{(f_0, f_1, \bar{v}, e):$$

$$Z \equiv \pm T^e R_0^{f_0} R_1^{f_1} S^{\bar{v}} \quad (\text{mod } n)$$

$$\wedge \ N_V \equiv \zeta^{f_0 + f_1 2^{\ell_f}} \quad (\text{mod } \Gamma)$$

$$\wedge \ f_0, f_1 \in \{0, 1\}^{\ell_f + \ell_\varnothing + \ell_\mathcal{H} + 2}$$

$$\wedge \ (e - 2^{\ell_e}) \in \{0, 1\}^{\ell'_e + \ell_\varnothing + \ell_\mathcal{H} + 1}\}(n_t \| n_v \| b \| m)$$

as follows (note that the value $\bar{v} = v - we$ is shared by the TPM and then host, that is, the TPM knows $\bar{v}$ and the host knows w and e).

(a) i. The TPM picks random integers $r_v \in_R \{0, 1\}^{\ell_v + \ell_\varnothing + \ell_\mathcal{H}}$ and $r_{f_0}, r_{f_1} \in_R \{0, 1\}^{\ell_f + \ell_\varnothing + \ell_\mathcal{H}}$ and computes

$$\tilde{T}_t := R_0^{r_{f_0}} R_1^{r_{f_1}} S^{r_v} \text{ mod } n \quad \tilde{r}_f := r_{f_0} + r_{f_1} 2^{\ell_f} \text{ mod } \rho$$

$$\tilde{N}_V := \zeta^{\tilde{r}_f} \text{ mod } \Gamma.$$

The TPM sends $\tilde{T}_t$ and $\tilde{N}_V$ to the host.

ii. The host picks random integers

$$r_e \in_R \{0, 1\}^{\ell'_e + \ell_\varnothing + \ell_\mathcal{H}} \quad \text{and} \quad r_{\bar{v}} \in_R \{0, 1\}^{\ell_e + \ell_n + 2\ell_\varnothing + \ell_\mathcal{H} + 1}$$

and computes $\tilde{T} := \tilde{T}_t T^{r_e} S^{r_{\bar{v}}} \text{ mod } n$.

(b) i. Host computes

$$c_h := H((n \| R_0 \| R_1 \| S \| Z \| \gamma \| \Gamma \| \rho) \| \zeta \| T \| N_V \| \tilde{T} \| \tilde{N}_V) \| n_v)$$

and sends c_h to the TPM.

ii. The TPM chooses a random $n_t \in \{0, 1\}^{\ell_\varnothing}$, computes $c := H(H(c_h \| n_t) \| b \| m)$ and sends c, n_t to the host.

(c) i. The TPM computes (over the integers)

$$s_v := r_v + cv, \quad s_{f_0} := r_{f_0} + cf_0 \quad \text{and} \quad s_{f_1} := r_{f_1} + cf_1$$

and sends (s_v, s_{f_0}, s_{f_1}) to the host.

ii. The host computes (over the integers)

$$s_e := r_e + c(e - 2^{\ell_e - 1}) \quad \text{and} \quad s_{\bar{v}} := s_v + r_{\bar{v}} - cwe.$$

4. The host outputs the signature $\sigma := (\zeta, T, N_V, c, n_t, (s_{\bar{v}}, s_{f_0}, s_{f_1}, s_e))$.

It is not hard to verify that the generation (as well as the verification) of modified DAA-signatures has a computational complexity that is less than half that of the original algorithm. Note that the modified signing algorithm only affects the host part of the signing algorithm (i.e., the TPM part is unaffected). Moreover, we no longer require the bases g, g' and h, and we can omit them from the key generation of the signer. As the signatures produced by the modified signing algorithm are different from the ones produced by the original scheme, we need to modify the verification algorithm as well. A signature

$$\sigma = (\zeta, T, N_V, c, n_t, (s_{\bar{v}}, s_{f_0}, s_{f_1}, s_e))$$

on a message m with respect to the public key $(n, R_0, R_1, S, Z, \gamma, \Gamma, \rho)$ and the selection-bit b is as verified as follows.

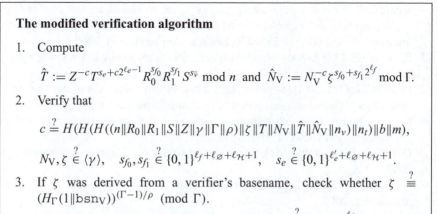

The modified verification algorithm

1. Compute

   $$\hat{T} := Z^{-c} T^{s_e + c2^{\ell_e - 1}} R_0^{s_{f_0}} R_1^{s_{f_1}} S^{s_{\bar{v}}} \bmod n \quad \text{and} \quad \hat{N}_V := N_V^{-c} \zeta^{s_{f_0} + s_{f_1} 2^{\ell_f}} \bmod \Gamma.$$

2. Verify that

   $$c \stackrel{?}{=} H(H(H(H((n\|R_0\|R_1\|S\|Z\|\gamma\|\Gamma\|\rho)\|\zeta\|T\|N_V\|\hat{T}\|\hat{N}_V\|n_v)\|n_t)\|b\|m),$$

   $$N_V, \zeta \stackrel{?}{\in} \langle \gamma \rangle, \quad s_{f_0}, s_{f_1} \stackrel{?}{\in} \{0,1\}^{\ell_f + \ell_\varnothing + \ell_H + 1}, \quad s_e \stackrel{?}{\in} \{0,1\}^{\ell'_e + \ell_\varnothing + \ell_H + 1}.$$

3. If ζ was derived from a verifier's basename, check whether $\zeta \stackrel{?}{=} (H_\Gamma(1\|\text{bsn}_V))^{(\Gamma-1)/\rho} \pmod{\Gamma}$.

4. For all (f_0, f_1) on the rogue list, check whether $N_V \stackrel{?}{\neq} (\zeta^{f_0 + f_1 2^{\ell_f}}) \pmod{\Gamma}$.

With regard to the security of DAA with the modified signing and verification procedures, it is not too hard to see that the proof given for the original scheme still applies. The only difference is the method needed to argue that one can extract a valid certificate from a modified DAA signature. This argument, however, is analogous to argument given by Camenisch and Groth for their group signature scheme [40].

5.8 Conclusion and acknowledgements

Since the DAA scheme was accepted by TCG, it has received a lot of attention in both industry and academia, including Grossman's article in *Scientific American* discussing the general issue of anonymous trust [41].

The authors would like to take this opportunity to thank the TPM working group in TCG for successfully introducing the DAA scheme into the TPM specification. In particular, we would like to thank Dave Challener and Roger Zimmermann for pointing out a potential weakness in the DAA implementation, as mentioned in Section 5.6.2.

References

1 B. Balacheff, L. Chen, S. Pearson, D. Plaquin, and G. Proudler. *Trusted Computing Platforms: TCPA Technology in Context*. Prentice Hall PTR, New York, 2003.

2 Trusted Computing Group website. www.trustedcomputinggroup.org.

3 E. Brickell. An efficient protocol for anonymously providing assurance of the container of a private key. Submitted to the Trusted Computing Group, April 2003.

4 L. Chen. A scheme of group signatures with revocation evidence – a proposal for TCG. Submitted to the Trusted Computing Group, May 2003.

5 G. Ateniese, J. Camenisch, M. Joye, and G. Tsudik. A practical and provably secure coalition-resistant group signature scheme. In M. Bellare, ed., *Proceedings of the Advances in Cryptology, (CRYPTO 2000), volume 1880 of Lecture Notes in Computer Science*, pp. 255–270, Springer-Verlag, Berlin, 2000.

6 IEEE. IEEE 1363A-2004: standard specifications for public key cryptography – amendment 1: additional techniques.

7 ISO/IEC. ISO/IEC 10118-3 (3rd edn): 2004. Information technology – Security techniques – Hash-functions – Part 3: Dedicated hash-functions.

8 C. P. Schnorr. Efficient signature generation by smart cards. *Journal of Cryptology*, 4(3):161–174, 1991.

9 D. Boneh, E. Brickell, and H. Shacham. Set signatures. Unpublished manuscript, 2003.

10 D. Boneh, E. Brickell, L. Chen, and H. Shacham. Set signatures. Unpublished manuscript, 2003.

11 J. Camenisch and A. Lysyanskaya. Dynamic accumulators and application to efficient revocation of anonymous credentials. In M. Yung, ed., *Proceedings of the Advances in Cryptology, (CRYPTO 2002), volume 2442 of Lecture Notes in Computer Science*, pp. 61–76, Springer-Verlag, Berlin, 2002.

12 J. Camenisch and M. Stadler. Efficient group signature schemes for large groups. In B. Kaliski, ed., *Proceedings of the Advances in Cryptology, (CRYPTO '97), volume 1296 of Lecture Notes in Computer Science*, pp. 410–424, Springer-Verlag, Berlin, 1997.

13 D. Chaum and E. van Heyst. Group signatures. In D. W. Davies, ed., *Proceedings of the Advances in Cryptology, (EUROCRYPT '91), volume 547 of Lecture Notes in Computer Science*, pp. 257–265, Springer-Verlag, Berlin, 1991.

14 J. Kilian and E. Petrank. Identity escrow. In H. Krawczyk, ed., *Proceedings of the Advances in Cryptology, (CRYPTO '98), volume 1642 of Lecture Notes in Computer Sciences*, pp. 169–185, Springer-Verlag, Berlin, 1998.

15 J. Camenisch and A. Lysyanskaya. Efficient non-transferable anonymous multi-show credential system with optional anonymity revocation. In B. Pfitzmann, ed., *Proceedings of the Advances in Cryptology, (EUROCRYPT 2001), volume 2045 of Lecture Notes in Computer Science*, pp. 93–118, Springer-Verlag, Berlin, 2001.

16 D. Chaum. Security without identification: transaction systems to make big brother obsolete. *Communications of the ACM*, 28(10):1030–1044, October 1985.

17 F. Boudot. Efficient proofs that a committed number lies in an interval. In B. Preneel, ed., *Proceedings of Advances in Cryptology, (EUROCRYPT 2000), volume 1807 of Lecture Notes in Computer Science*, pp. 431–444, Springer-Verlag, 2000.

18 E. F. Brickell, D. Chaum, I. B. Damgård, and J. van de Graaf. Gradual and verifiable release of a secret. In C. Pomerance, ed., *Proceedings in Advances in Cryptology, (CRYPTO '87), volume 293 of Lecture Notes in Computer Science*, pp. 156–166, Springer-Verlag, Berlin, 1988.

19 J. Camenisch and M. Michels. Separability and efficiency for generic group signature schemes. In M. Wiener, ed., *Proceedings of the Advances in Cryptology, (CRYPTO'99), volume 1666 of Lecture Notes in Computer Science*, pp. 413–430, Springer-Verlag, Berlin, 1999.

20 D. Chaum. Zero-knowledge undeniable signatures. In I. B. Damgård, ed., *Proceedings of the Advances in Cryptology, (EUROCRYPT'90), volume 473 of Lecture Notes on Computer Science*, pp. 458–464, Springer-Verlag, Berlin, 1991.

21 D. Chaum, J.-H. Evertse, and J. van de Graaf. An improved protocol for demonstrating possession of discrete logarithms and some generalizations. In D. Chaum and W. L. Price, eds, *Proceedings of the Advances in Cryptology, (EUROCRYPT '87), volume 304 of Lecture Notes in Computer Science*, pp. 127–141, Springer-Verlag, Berlin, 1988.

22 D. Chaum and T. P. Pedersen. Wallet databases with observers. In E. F. Brickell, ed., *Proceedings of the Advances in Cryptology, (CRYPTO '92), volume 740 of Lecture Notes in Computer Science*, pp. 89–105, Springer-Verlag, Berlin, 1993.

23 A. Fiat and A. Shamir. How to prove yourself: practical solutions to identification and signature problems. In A. M. Odlyzko, ed., *Proceedings of the Advances in Cryptology, (CRYPTO '86), volume 263 of Lecture Notes in Computer Science*, pp. 186–194, Springer-Verlag, Berlin, 1987.

24 E. Fujisaki and T. Okamoto. Statistical zero knowledge protocols to prove modular polynomial relations. In B. Kaliski, ed., *Proceedings of the Advances in Cryptology, (CRYPTO '97), volume 1294 of Lecture Notes in Computer Science*, pp. 16–30, Springer-Verlag, Berlin, 1997.

25 D. Pointcheval and J. Stern. Security proofs for signature schemes. In U. Maurer, ed., *Proceedings of the Advances in Cryptology, (EUROCRYPT '96), volume 1070 of Lecture Notes in Computer Science*, pp. 387–398, Springer-Verlag, Berlin, 1996.

26 M. Bellare and P. Rogaway. Random oracles are practical: a paradigm for designing efficient protocols. In *Proceedings of the 1st ACM Conference on Computer and Communications Security*, pp. 62–73, ACM Press, New York, 1993.

27 J. Camenisch and A. Lysyanskaya. A signature scheme with efficient protocols. In S. Cimato, C. Galdi, and G. Persiano, eds, *Proceedings of the Third International Conference, Security in Communication Networks, (SCN 2002), volume 2576 of Lecture Notes in Computer Science*, pp. 268–289, Springer-Verlag, Berlin, 2003.

28 A. Lysyanskaya. Signature schemes and applications to cryptographic protocol design. Ph.D. thesis, Massachusetts Institute of Technology, Cambridge, MA, September 2002.

29 S. Goldwasser, S. Micali, and R. Rivest. A digital signature scheme secure against adaptive chosen-message attacks. *SIAM Journal on Computing*, 17(2):281–308, 1988.

30 E. Brickell, J. Camenisch, and L. Chen. Direct anonymous attestation. In B. Pfitzmann and P. Liu, eds, *Proceedings of the 11th ACM Conference on Computer and Communications Security*, pp. 132–145, ACM Press, New York, October 2004.

31 A. K. Lenstra and E. K. Verheul. Selecting cryptographic key sizes. *Journal of Cryptology*, 14(4):255–293, 2001.

32 R. Cramer and V. Shoup. Signature schemes based on the strong RSA assumption. *ACM Transactions on Information and System Security*, 3(3):161–185, 2000.

33 E. Brickell, J. Camenisch, and L. Chen. Direct anonymous attestation. Available at http://eprint.iacr.org/2004/205/.

34 Trusted Computing Group. Trusted computing platform alliance (TCPA) main specification, version 1.1a. Republished as Trusted Computing Group (TCG) main specification, Version 1.1b, Available at www.trustedcomputinggroup.org, 2001.

35 J. Camenisch and M. Michels. Proving in zero-knowledge that a number n is the product of two safe primes. In J. Stern, ed., *Proceedings of the Advances in Cryptology, (EUROCRYPT '99), volume 1592 of Lecture Notes in Computer Science*, pp. 107–122, Springer-Verlag, Berlin, 1999.

36 J. Camenisch and V. Shoup. Practical verifiable encryption and decryption of discrete logarithms. In D. Boneh, ed., *Proceedings of the Advances in Cryptology, (CRYPTO 2003), volume 2729 of Lecture Notes in Computer Science*, pp. 126–144, 2003.

37 M. Bellare, J. A. Garay, and T. Rabin. Fast batch verification for modular exponentiation and digital signatures. In K. Nyberg, ed., *Proceedings of Advances in Cryptology, (EUROCRYPT '98), volume 1403 of Lecture Notes in Computer Science*, pp. 236–250, Springer-Verlag, Berlin, 1998.

38 D. Challener and R. Zimmermann. Private communications, November 2004.

39 Trusted Computing Group. TCG TPM specification 1.2. Available at www.trustedcomputinggroup.org, 2003.

40 J. Camenisch and J. Groth. Group signatures: better efficiency and new theoretical aspects. In C. Blundo and S. Cimato, eds, *Proceedings of the 4th International Conference on Security in Communication Networks, (SCN 2004), volume 3352 of Lecture Notes in Computer Science*, pp. 122–135, Springer-Verlag, Berlin, 2005.

41 W. M. Grossman. Anonymous trust: making trusted computer work with privacy. *Scientific American*, August 2004.

Chapter 6

Single Sign-On using TCG-conformant platforms

Andreas Pashalidis and Chris J. Mitchell

6.1   Introduction

In this chapter we examine an application that can potentially benefit from trusted computing, namely Single Sign-On (SSO). SSO gives the user the ability to log into systems and applications without the need to maintain separate authentication credentials for each such system and application. In other words, an SSO scheme allows the user to log into (ideally) all relevant systems and applications, using only one set of authentication credentials (e.g., only one username/password pair). In the remainder of the chapter, we will use the generic term 'Service Provider' (SP) to refer to systems and/or applications in the context of SSO.

SSO has been the target of research for more than 20 years. During this period, many different SSO schemes have been proposed. Some of those have been implemented and deployed. However, none has been widely adopted (at least not in an open environment) and none has been able to provide a service to a large number of existing SPs. We examine the reasons behind this failure in Section 6.1.3 below. First, however, we outline the motivation behind SSO in Section 6.1.1, and explain how it works in Section 6.1.2. We then examine, in Section 6.2, how platforms that conform to the Trusted Computing Group (TCG) specifications could be used to enhance existing SSO schemes. Section 6.3 deals with the issue of privacy. Other issues that arise in the SSO context, such as associated costs and cross-platform mobility, are discussed in Section 6.4. Finally, Section 6.5 concludes with thoughts on the future of SSO.

6.1.1   Why SSO?

Before continuing we should first convince ourselves that implementing SSO is really something desirable. Roughly speaking, there are three main motives for SSO.

- Usability: This is probably the most obvious advantage of SSO. The user no longer has to maintain a set of authentication credentials for each SP. Moreover, he does not have to do so securely.
- User management: In a certain type of SSO scheme (see Section 6.2.2) a supporting management system can enforce a global policy. Apart from unifying rules and trust relationships among a group of entities, such a system has the potential to reduce operational costs enormously. For instance, users could be added to, or removed from, the system by being granted or having revoked, respectively, their (single) authentication credential. This feature can be particularly useful in an corporate environment.
- Security: SSO has the potential, while maintaining its usability benefits, to increase the overall level of security. First, from the user perspective, it is arguably easier to securely maintain only one set of authentication credentials, rather than many. Second, from the SP perspective, a globally enforceable policy is highly desirable because it significantly mitigates the threat of human error and abuse.

A scheme that achieves the above in practice would be useful indeed. So why have none of the schemes that have so far been developed been more widely adopted? In order to answer this question we need to take a brief look at how an SSO scheme works.

6.1.2   How SSO works

In this section we sketch a high level overview of an SSO scheme. Although concrete schemes differ in many, often fundamental, aspects, the description here is generic; whilst it omits the technical details, it applies to virtually all such existing schemes.

SSO schemes depend on the notion of authentication sessions. In order to start a session, the user needs to authenticate himself using an authentication credential. He has to do so to a special entity which we call the 'Authentication Service' (AS). (The AS may either be some program that is running locally on the user's machine, or a service that is running on another machine somewhere in the network. At this stage, however, we do not care which of these two is the case.) If this 'initial' authentication is successful, the session is started.

For as long as the session lasts, the AS provides the following service to the user: it *automatically* logs him into the SPs he uses, as necessary. How exactly this is done again differs from scheme to scheme. In all schemes, however, it involves the AS (and possibly the user) executing a protocol with the SP; we call this the 'SSO protocol'. The objective of the SSO protocol is to identify and authenticate the user to the SP in a manner that does not (necessarily) require further manual interaction from the user. During its execution, the SP performs tests that are designed to detect certain attacks that may be launched against the scheme. In particular, these tests enable the SP to detect if an attacker is trying to login as someone else; such an attack is known as an impersonation attack. Only if the SP's tests are passed successfully, as dictated by its policy, is the claimed identity of the user deemed to have been successfully authenticated.

At some point in time the authentication session is terminated. The reasons for this termination may vary from system to system. Terminating a session is, of course, subject to the AS's, the SP's or, indeed, the user's policy and may be triggered by events, such as extended periods of inactivity, a maximum number of logins performed or a simple time limit. After a session is terminated, the user has to authenticate himself again to the AS in order to start a new one.

The main questions that the designer of an SSO scheme has to answer are the following. What exactly should be the form of the AS and who should control it? How exactly should the SSO protocol operate? In particular, should it involve the user or just the AS and the SP? How should the user be identified at the AS and the different SPs? How should the SSO protocol enable the SPs to authenticate the user's (claimed) identity (i.e., prevent impersonation attacks)? Designers of SSO schemes have answered these questions differently and have, not surprisingly, come up with different schemes.

6.1.3   Why SSO has failed

It turns out that the answer to the first of the above questions is probably the most crucial. This is because the AS is central to the scheme and, as such, needs to be trustworthy. There are many design decisions to be taken concerning the AS that affect the properties of the resulting SSO scheme. Some of the questions that need to be answered are the following.

- Provision of AS: Will the AS be provided as a service by a (trusted) third party, or can it be a program that runs on the user machine?
- Trustworthiness of AS: How much damage can a misbehaving, malicious or compromised AS cause? Can it impersonate users to SPs or SPs to users? Can it deny service? How much trust are users and SPs required to have in it?
- Control of AS: Who will be in control of the AS: the user or a third party? How is this control exercised?
- Transparency of AS: Will SPs need to support the SSO scheme (i.e., be required to change their legacy authentication infrastructure), or will the AS operate transparently to SPs?
- Centralisation of AS: Will the functionality of the AS be centralised or distributed? In the first case the AS may constitute a central point of failure; in the second, system efficiency may be impaired.
- Liability of AS: Who is responsible when something goes wrong? That is, in which situations should the AS, the user or the SP(s) be held liable?

The answers to these questions determine the applicability of the resulting scheme. This is because they dictate not only technical limitations, but also associated costs. For example, a scheme that replicates the AS at several locations in the network (in order to avoid a central point of failure and thereby guaranteeing high availability) is likely to be more expensive than one where the AS is centralised. There are several different types of cost associated with an SSO scheme, all of which have to be taken into account at the design phase. They are the following.

- Implementation cost: Complicated schemes are more difficult, and therefore more expensive, to implement and test than simple ones.
- Deployment cost: How much effort needs to be made by the different parties in the scheme (users, AS provider, SPs) in order to support the scheme? Does the scheme require a common security infrastructure (e.g., a Public Key Infrastructure (PKI) that covers the AS as well as SPs)? Does it require legal backup?
- Running costs: How much computation and bandwidth does the scheme consume? How expensive is it to manage its day-to-day operation (e.g., user account management)?
- Maintenance costs: How easily can the scheme accommodate technology changes, extensions, policy changes, etc.?

While theoretical research can afford to ignore (some of) the above costs, the real world cannot. Unfortunately, experience has shown that, the more of the benefits listed in Section 6.1.1 that a scheme provides, the more costly it is likely to be. Moreover, and, again in contrast to some of the theory, no single AS provider/controller that is globally trusted appears to exist in the real world. This is not to say that all existing SSO schemes have failed completely. In fact, SSO systems have been successfully deployed in closed corporate environments. It is hard to say which particular scheme (if any) dominates in this market, as this would require the analysis of information that is not publicly available.

As far as open environments are concerned, the most popular SSO scheme is perhaps Microsoft's Passport service[1] [1]. Although it has millions of registered users, it is not easy to estimate Passport's success as an SSO service. This is because the users of Microsoft's free – and popular – electronic mail service ('Hotmail') are required to register themselves with Passport. It remains unclear how many registered Passport users actually use it for inter-domain SSO (i.e., for logging into non-Microsoft sites). According to an LA Times news report,[2] dated 30 December 2004, Microsoft said that 'it would stop trying to persuade websites to use its Passport service [. . .]' after one of its biggest customers, eBay, 'posted a notice on its site [. . .], saying it would stop using Passport in late January [2005] and rely on its own service'. In that report, eBay spokesman, Hani Durzy, is quoted as saying that 'a pretty small percentage of eBay users regularly signed in using Passport'.

In general it can be said no single SSO system meets the requirements of all real-world situations; different operational environments call for different solutions. In the remainder of this chapter we will examine how trusted computing can offer an approach to SSO that is, in certain ways, distinct from existing approaches. We will

---

[1] www.passport.com
[2] www.latimes.com/business/la-fi-passport30dec30,1,3691923.story

see how this approach leads to novel properties that, in some situations, may prove particularly useful.

6.2 Using trusted platforms for SSO

SSO schemes can be divided into two main types: those that do *not* require SPs to be aware of the SSO scheme (and to support it) and those that do. Consistent with the terminology introduced in Reference 2, we call the two types of SSO scheme 'pseudo-SSO' and 'true SSO', respectively. Both types of scheme can be enhanced using trusted platforms, that is, platforms that conform to the Trusted Computing Group (TCG) specification. We next take a closer look at how this could be done.

6.2.1 Pseudo-SSO

SSO schemes in this category do not require SPs to change their existing user authentication infrastructure in any way. As shown in Figure 6.1, they operate as follows. At the start of a session, the user authenticates himself to the AS using his SSO credential (step 1 in the figure). Subsequently, and throughout the session, the AS intercepts login requests that the user makes to SPs (step 2). It then automatically executes the SP's legacy authentication mechanism on the user's behalf. As this is done automatically, no interaction from the user is required. In addition, the AS operates in a manner transparent to SPs; they do not need to be aware of its existence. In other words, the SSO protocol of pseudo-SSO schemes is simply each SP's respective legacy authentication mechanism. If this legacy mechanism completes successfully, the user is logged in to the SP (step 3).

Although the figure implies that the AS resides on a separate machine, this is not necessarily the case. For example, in some existing pseudo-SSO implementations, typically those that were designed for an open environment, the AS is a program

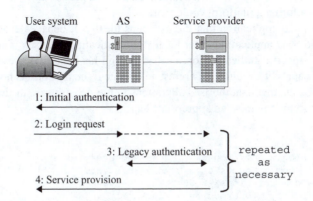

Figure 6.1   Operation of pseudo-SSO

that the user executes locally (e.g., password management applications, automatic form completion functionality of web browsers and a system called v-GO SSO[3]). Other systems, typically those designed for a closed, corporate environment, rely on a server to host the AS. Examples of this type of scheme are cafesoft Cams,[4] eTrust Single SignOn,[5] Entegrity AssureAccess,[6] Entrust GetAccess[7] and Evidian.[8]

From a security standpoint, pseudo-SSO has certain disadvantages, including the following.

- No global security policy can be formulated and enforced. This is because users can directly use an SP's legacy authentication mechanism. They are therefore free to choose whether or not to use the SSO scheme, or use it only for some SPs but not for others.
- There exists no explicit trust relationship between the AS and SPs. Therefore, there is no obvious way to address liability issues in case of security incidents. Even worse, it may even be hard to trace the cause of a security incident. If, for example, it is revealed that a user has been the victim of an impersonation attack, then this may be because the attacker compromised either his SP-specific or his SSO credentials. Which of the two is the case may be hard to find out; however, the cost of rectifying the situation may differ significantly between the two cases.
- Pseudo-SSO does not really remove the need to maintain multiple authentication credentials. This is because, in order to function, the AS needs to have access to the necessary SP-specific authentication credentials of the user (typically his username/password pairs). Thus the problem of securely storing these remains.

It is with respect to the last point – the secure storage of authentication credentials – that TCG-conformant platforms can enhance the security of pseudo-SSO schemes. The two Trusted Platform Module (TPM) services that are relevant in this scenario are secure storage and secure booting (these services have been explained in Chapter 3 of this book). We will now describe how a pseudo-SSO scheme running on a TCG-conformant platform could work.

The AS is an application that the user runs locally. It behaves exactly like any other pseudo-SSO application: after locally authenticating the user, it automatically executes SP-specific authentication mechanisms on his behalf. However, using the secure boot capability, the AS may refuse to operate if the platform is not in a trusted state. This means that unauthorised alterations to the AS software or the underlying operating system may raise an appropriate alarm.

---

[3] www.passlogix.com/products/v-go%5Fsso/overview.asp
[4] cafesoft.com/products/cams/camsOverview.html
[5] www3.ca.com/Solutions/Product.asp?ID=166
[6] www.entegrity.com/products/aa/aa.shtml
[7] www.entrust.com/getaccess/index.htm
[8] www.evidian.com

When combined with the TPM capability of secure storage, the scheme can be implemented such that the AS can access the user's SP-specific credentials only if the following two conditions are met.

- The platform has booted into a trusted state.
- The initial user-to-AS authentication has been performed successfully.

There are two ways to guarantee that the second condition holds. The first is to bind the release of the TPM key that is required to decrypt the user's SP-specific authentication credentials to a particular – trusted – platform state. (See Chapter 3 of this book to see how it can be done.) If this is done properly, only the AS can access these credentials. A trustworthy AS would then access these credentials only after the user completed the initial authentication successfully.

Another, perhaps more elegant, way to guarantee the second condition is by linking the user's initial authentication to the authorisation data that is required to retrieve the decryption key for the user's SP-specific authentication credentials. If, for example, the initial authentication mechanism is based on a passphrase, the authorisation data could be the cryptographic hash value [3] of that passphrase. In this way, not only is the need for the AS to keep a copy of this data removed, but also other software that the user deems trustworthy may gain access to his SP-specific authentication credentials (e.g., to perform a backup).

In the above scenario, no external party needs to challenge the integrity of the platform's software state (using the integrity challenge–response mechanism explained in Chapter 3 in this book). This means that classifying particular software states as 'trustworthy' is solely under the control of the platform owner.

6.2.2   True SSO

A true SSO scheme needs to be supported by the SPs in their user authentication infrastructure. The SSO protocol of such a scheme is identical for all SPs. It involves the AS sending a message to the SP that attests to the fact that the user was successfully authenticated by the AS. We call this message an 'authentication assertion' or simply an 'assertion'. The SP assesses the trustworthiness and content of the assertion; if the assertion satisfies the SP's policy, the user is logged in.

The typical flow of information in such a scheme, depicted in Figure 6.2, is as follows. First, the user authenticates himself to the AS (step 1.1 in the figure). If successful, the session starts and the AS issues an authentication assertion to the user (step 1.2). Afterwards, and throughout the session, whenever the user issues a login request to the SP (step 2.1), the latter requests this assertion (step 2.2). This is then shown to the SP (step 2.3) and, if it passes the SP's tests, the user is logged in (step 3). In some true SSO schemes, steps 2.2 and 2.3 may occur between the SP and the AS, rather than the SP and the user.

Under true SSO, SPs are required to trust the AS to perform the initial user authentication properly. In fact, the trust relationships between user, AS and SPs are well defined. Thus, it is possible to formulate and enforce system-wide policies.

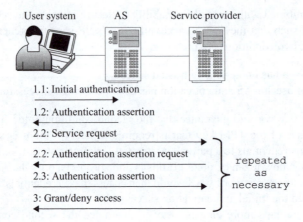

Figure 6.2   Operation of true SSO

In contrast to pseudo-SSO schemes, liability issues that arise whenever some security-related incident is detected can be addressed and resolved. Moreover, user account management can, although does not have to, be centralised.

Virtually all existing true SSO schemes rely on an external third party that provides and controls the AS (e.g., [1,4,5]). This party necessarily has to be trusted by both users and SPs as it can typically impersonate users to SPs at will. It is a challenge to construct true SSO schemes that remove the need for this party, or at least limit the amount of trust that users and SPs are required to have in it. TCG-conformant platforms can help in this direction. In particular, although they do not remove the need for an external party to provide the AS, they can put the platform owner in control of it. This could be done as follows.

The AS will run locally in the user machine, preferably as a continuously running process (daemon). A session starts with the user authenticating himself to the AS, as usual. However, the SSO protocol will provide assurance to the SP that the AS is one that it trusts to behave appropriately. The protocol therefore involves an integrity challenge–response message exchange during which the SP convinces itself that:

- the platform is conformant to the TCG specification, and
- its software state is trustworthy, that is, an AS that the SP trusts is running properly on the platform.

These conditions essentially guarantee to the SP that the software that is running on the user's platform (including the BIOS, the OS and the AS) has not been modified and that it therefore behaves as expected. In particular, since a 'well-behaved' AS only executes the SSO protocol after the user has performed the initial authentication successfully, the integrity challenge–response mechanism guarantees to the SP that attacks that are based on a (maliciously) modified AS, for example, a modification that simply skips the initial authentication, are prevented. (A detailed explanation of the integrity challenge–response mechanism has been given in Chapter 3 in this book.) In this scenario, of course, each individual SP (rather than the platform owner) selects which platform states it deems trustworthy, as part of its policy.

The AS, as part of the SSO protocol, also needs to convey an authentication assertion to the SP, that is, a message containing the user's identifier and a description of his initial authentication act. How this is done needs to be specified carefully. In particular, the integrity response should not be sent prior to the assertion because this would enable the following simplistic impersonation attack. The attacker executes some malicious software just after the integrity response is sent to the SP. This software then simply sends an assertion containing the identifier of a victim user, skipping the initial authentication. Because the modification of the software state took place after the integrity response (which reflects a legitimate state) is sent to the SP, the latter has no means to detect the attack.

Ideally, the assertion should be cryptographically bound to the integrity response. This could be done by having the AS calculate the cryptographic hash [3] of the concatenation of the random number contained in the SP's integrity challenge with the hash value of the authentication assertion. The result should then be input to the TPM as the parameter TPM_NONCE of the TPM_Quote command that is executed during the integrity challenge–response session. (For a detailed description of this command see Reference 6, p. 116.) As long as the authentication assertion is sent to the SP in the clear (along with the integrity response), the SP can verify that the correct random number was used in the calculation of the integrity response, by reconstructing the aforementioned hash chain.

So, by using TCG-conformant platforms, the functionality of the AS, that in virtually all existing true SSO schemes resides on some trusted third party, can be delegated to the user platform. Although the AS still needs to be manufactured and provided by some party that is deemed trustworthy by SPs, the user, although unable to modify it without being detected, is, in some sense, being put in control of it.

Another important aspect that arises from the migration of the AS to the user platform is that of decentralisation. In contrast to existing true SSO schemes, where the party that controls the AS constitutes a central point of failure (and therefore a susceptible target of service denial attacks), a scheme of the above described type effectively distributes that party's functionality among all users; the scheme is therefore decentralised, robust and scalable.

6.3 Privacy

One more aspect of SSO that recently has attracted large amounts of interest in the research community (and the public in general), and that many of the early schemes fail to address satisfactorily, is that of privacy. Although privacy has many facets, here we consider it in the context of SSO in an open environment, such as the Internet.

As discussed earlier, most existing true SSO systems intended for use in an open environment depend on a trusted server. The operator of this server typically obtains access to certain information that might be considered private. This information disclosure is inevitable because otherwise the system would no longer work. According to the Liberty Alliance specifications [4,7–11], for example, the operator of the server hosting the AS (called the 'Identity Provider' in the specifications) gets to know which SPs the users have a relationship with, their identifiers at those SPs, their login times, etc. This is because, every time the user requests to log into an SP, the AS is contacted and a new authentication assertion is issued. Moreover, during registration, the AS provider generates the user's identifier for the SP.

In contrast to these schemes, the TCG-based true SSO scheme described in the previous section is under the control of the user. As no third party needs to be contacted during executions of the SSO protocol, the scheme avoids the aforementioned information disclosure; it is significantly more privacy friendly than existing server-based true SSO schemes.

In the remainder of this section we focus on the case where users are known to different SPs under different pseudonyms. A privacy-protecting SSO scheme should, in this case, prevent SPs working out which pseudonyms belong to the same user – even if they collude with each other and the AS provider. An SSO scheme that protects the user's privacy in this sense is said to offer unlinkability of pseudonyms [12,13]. It turns out that unlinkability is not as easy to achieve as it may seem at first glance. In fact, no existing SSO scheme has managed to achieve it.[9]

In order for pseudonyms to be unlinkable, they should not contain any information that allows them to be linked to each other. Under pseudo-SSO, SPs select the type of user identifier (i.e., pseudonym) that has to be used; a user interested in privacy must select his pseudonyms in a way that obscures the fact that they all belong to him. Apart from this being a tedious task that many users may find impractical, the system cannot guarantee unlinkability in any way; it simply falls outside its scope.

A system that intends to guarantee unlinkability of pseudonyms necessarily needs to provide a suitable mechanism for users and SPs to establish these pseudonyms. A true SSO scheme has this potential. This is because, since the applicability of a true SSO scheme's protocols is system-wide (i.e., all SPs are required to support the same protocols), SPs can be required to support a suitable pseudonym establishment mechanism.

Unfortunately, providing this mechanism is not sufficient; it is also required that subsequent use of the scheme (executions of the SSO protocol in particular) does not compromise pseudonym unlinkability. We will now examine the feasibility of meeting this requirement in the context of the TCG-supported true SSO scheme described in the previous section.

As discussed in Chapters 3 and 5 of this book, the provisions with respect to privacy have changed significantly from version 1.1 to version 1.2 of the TCG specification. In particular, the way a platform is authenticated as TCG-conformant by

---

[9] At the time of writing and to the best of the authors' knowledge.

a verifier (during an integrity challenge–response session between the platform and that verifier), is based on quite different cryptographic primitives in the two versions. Since the true SSO scheme described in Section 6.2.2 above involves TCG's integrity challenge–response mechanism, its privacy properties affect the whole scheme.

6.3.1 Privacy under TCG 1.1

In version 1.1 of the TCG specification, platforms need a so-called 'platform identity' in order to be able to respond to integrity challenges. A platform identity is simply a public/private key pair, called an 'Identity Key' (IDK). The IDK's public part has to be certified by a special entity, the so-called 'Privacy CA' (Privacy Certificate Authority). The integrity response contains (among other things) this certificate. The (public part of an) IDK can be used as a pseudonym. As the IDKs are randomly generated they do not reveal any information about each other (and the platform they were generated on). They are thus unlinkable. Unfortunately, the process by which certificates for IDKs are obtained from the Privacy CA, allows the latter to unambiguously link (the public parts of) all IDKs that originate from the same platform. This is because, during this process, it is required that the platform's so-called 'public endorsement key' is revealed to the Privacy CA; this piece of information is unique to each TCG-conformant platform. (The issues surrounding the concept and the functionality of the Privacy CA are discussed in more detail in Chapter 3 in this book.)

In practical terms this means that, using platforms conformant to TCG version 1.1, it is possible to design a true SSO scheme where pseudonyms are unlinkable, only under the assumption that the Privacy CA does not reveal the links between IDKs (and therefore pseudonyms). Unfortunately, this assumption does not hold for a misbehaving, malicious or compromised Privacy CA.

6.3.2 Privacy under TCG 1.2

In version 1.2 of the TCG specification the need for a Privacy CA is removed. Nevertheless, conformant platforms still need to be able to convince verifiers, during an integrity challenge–response session, that they are indeed conformant. So, the need for an external entity to vouch for a platform's conformity (and therefore trustworthiness) is not removed. The entity that performs this task is called an 'issuer' in version 1.2 of the specification.

The way a platform proves its conformity is no longer based on a traditional PKI. Instead, a new mechanism, called 'Direct Anonymous Attestation' (DAA) is introduced [14]. DAA is based on an anonymous credential system [15]. According to DAA, the platform is required to obtain, only once, a so-called 'attestation credential' from the issuer. Then, during challenge–response sessions, the platform proves to the verifier that it possesses knowledge of such a credential. If it is successful, and if the verifier trusts the issuer, the former is convinced of the platform's conformity. The feature of this procedure that differentiates it from the mechanism of version 1.1 is that the credential itself is not sent to the verifier. In fact, no information at all about the credential is revealed to the verifier (other than the identity of its issuer and the fact that it is possessed by the platform). This means that all executions of the integrity challenge–response protocol that correspond to any particular platform that has obtained an attestation credential from some issuer, could correspond, in the view of (possibly colluding) verifiers, to any platform that has obtained an attestation credential from that issuer. Moreover, because the platform obtains the credential using a special technique called 'blinding', verifiers are not able to gain an advantage by linking together different executions of the integrity challenge–response protocol, even by colluding with the issuer himself. (The fact that the platform's public endorsement key is revealed to the issuer during the issuing of the credential, in similar fashion as it is revealed to the Privacy CA of version 1.1 of the specifications, is irrelevant.) The DAA scheme is described in detail in Chapter 5 of this book.

The DAA scheme requires the platform to establish pseudonyms with verifiers. Every time an integrity challenge–response protocol is executed between the platform and a verifier, the established pseudonym is revealed to the verifier. Although the pseudonyms were included in DAA because of the need to detect compromised platforms, they can be reused in the SSO scenario to identify users. However, care needs to be taken when specifying how this should be done, as DAA pseudonyms are a function of data that is either supplied by the platform alone, or the platform and the verifier of an integrity challenge (which, in the SSO context, coincides with the SP).

In particular, under DAA, each SP can choose for itself whether or not any given platform is allowed to establish with the SP more than one pseudonym for each attestation credential. This can be done because the pseudonym is constructed as ζ^f, where f is a TPM-protected secret that is part of the attestation credential, and ζ is a generator of an algebraic subgroup in which the discrete logarithm problem is believed to be intractable.[10] An SP that requires a specific value for ζ to be used to construct the pseudonym, effectively prevents the establishment of more than one unlinkable pseudonym (per obtained attestation credential) with any given platform. Assuming the case where a platform only has one attestation credential,[11] in practical terms this means that the platform user would be prevented from establishing more than one unlinkable pseudonyms with the SP. Moreover, if the platform has multiple users, the SP would then be able to unambiguously link them.

Perhaps even more seriously, colluding SPs that require the use of the same value for ζ may be able to unambiguously link pseudonyms as corresponding to the same platform. Users who are interested in maintaining the unlinkability of their pseudonyms have to make sure that no SP requires, at any point in time, the same ζ value as any other SP (at any point in time). Depending on the number of SPs

---

[10] This description is rather simplified. Chapter 5 explains the DAA scheme in much greater detail.

[11] Users can obtain multiple attestation credentials for different TPM-generated f values (see Chapter 5), possibly from different issuers, and use different credentials for those pseudonyms that would otherwise be linkable through a common ζ value. However, the number of attestation credentials that a user may obtain is limited by the number of issuers that are willing to issue such credentials to the user's specific platform type. This is likely to impose a strict limit on the number of attestations that any given platform may obtain.

and how often they change the value of ζ they require, this may be prohibitively complex.

One possibility is to derive the value of ζ from the SP's unique name, using a collision-resistant hash function [3]. If done properly, this method prevents SPs with different names to linking pseudonyms. However, in this case care has to be taken when SPs change their names.

From a privacy perspective it would be desirable if the user is free to choose ζ in every execution of the DAA protocol. In this way he can choose the same value for those executions that should involve the same pseudonym and thus be linked to each other, even across SPs. Unfortunately, not imposing a particular value for ζ may leave SPs unable to detect compromised or rogue platforms. However, even if an attacker manages to compromise a platform (i.e., to extract the TPM's secrets), this does not enable him to impersonate users other than those of the compromised platform. The risks and tradeoffs associated with DAA are discussed further in Chapter 5 in this book.

More generally, and as observed in Reference 16, it can be said that the level of privacy offered by TCG version 1.2 is, in certain circumstances, lower than that offered by TCG version 1.1. This is because during DAA (version 1.2) the verifier gets to know the identity of the issuer that attested to a platform's conformity. During a version 1.1 integrity challenge–response session, however, the verifier only gets to know the identity of the Privacy CA.[12] As a Privacy CA would typically correspond to more than one issuer, the information the verifier obtains during DAA (i.e., the identity of the issuer) allows it to identify the platform more effectively than it would be able to if it only knows the identity of the Privacy CA. A scheme that equalises the level of privacy protection provided by DAA to that of the honest-Privacy CA scenario of version 1.1 is proposed in Reference 16. However, as this scheme introduces extra complexity (and potentially a third party), it remains questionable whether it will be used in practice.

6.4 Other issues

In this section we discuss other issues that arise with the SSO schemes described in this chapter. In particular, the issues of cross-platform mobility, complexity of managing trusted states, costs and the use of open-source software are examined.

6.4.1 Cross-platform mobility

Cross-platform mobility refers to a user's ability to use an SSO scheme from more than one platform. In an SSO scheme that offers cross-platform mobility, the user's pseudonyms are independent of the particular platform he is using. In other words, if a scheme offers cross-platform mobility, then the AS that is invoked when the user

---

[12] Assuming that the Privacy CA is honest and not compromised.

is using, say, his office machine, logs him into SPs using the same set of pseudonyms as the AS that is invoked when he is using, say, his home computer.

It is conceptually easy to enable cross-platform mobility in a local pseudo-SSO scheme. This primarily involves copying the user's legacy authentication credentials from one platform to the other. Although these may be encrypted under platform-dependent keys, the AS itself may be extended with a special 'migration' function that allows for this copying to take place. In the context of the local pseudo-SSO scheme described in Section 6.2.1, the key migration mechanisms that are described in the TCG specification could be used for this purpose. (A more detailed discussion of these methods can be found in Chapter 3 of this book.)

In true SSO schemes where the AS resides on a trusted third party, cross-platform mobility is an inherent feature. Unfortunately, the situation is different for the scheme described in Section 6.2.2 above, in particular if pseudonyms are derived from the platform's IDKs or DAA pseudonyms (as described in Sections 6.3.1 and 6.3.2, respectively). Because identity keys and (some factors used to compute) DAA pseudonyms are strictly platform-dependent and non-migratable, so are SSO pseudonyms; different platforms necessarily involve different pseudonyms during integrity challenge–response sessions.

Nevertheless, it is still possible to achieve cross-platform mobility. This, however, needs to be implemented as a separate service 'on top' of the SSO scheme; such a service will allow a user to explicitly link different pseudonyms at an SP. Unfortunately, this solution not only appears to be somewhat unnatural in the TCG context, it also needs to be specified and implemented carefully in order to avoid introducing new attacks. It would appear that, under true SSO using TCG-conformant platforms, there exists a tradeoff between potential unlinkability of pseudonyms and cross-platform mobility.

6.4.2   *Complexity of managing trusted states*

Under pseudo-SSO, it is the platform owner who classifies software states as trustworthy. Since the verification of whether the platform is actually in one of these states only occurs locally, the associated management overhead is not particularly complex. In the simplest case, the platform owner may just record the integrity metrics of a new installation (i.e., one that he is confident is flawless), and specify this to be the only trustworthy state. (For a more detailed discussion of integrity metrics see Chapter 3 of this book.)

Unfortunately, the situation is different under true SSO. There, SPs need to be able to tell apart the software states that they trust from those that they do not, these states being in a remote platform. Depending on how the platform's software stack (BIOS, operating system and other applications) reports integrity metrics to the TPM, this may be a rather complex task. In order to see why this might be so, consider the following scenario.

An SP that trusts the AS manufactured by some company X, decides to classify as trustworthy platform states that reflect a running instance of this particular AS. The AS comes in two different versions, AS_A for operating system A and AS_B for operating system B. Suppose that users of TCG-conformant platforms that run A and B, install AS_A and AS_B, respectively. Let us assume further that the platforms actually come with, say 15 different BIOS versions (or that some users choose to update their BIOS). Furthermore, assume that A is an open-source system that users are free to modify. So, the users who run A, actually run slightly different, although perfectly legitimate, versions (or 'distributions') of it, say A_1 to A_{18}. The problem is that, each combination of BIOS, operating system and AS yields a different set of integrity metrics, even if individual components differ only slightly. In the above example, the SP would have to be aware of $15 \times 18 + 15 = 285$ different software states and classify them as trustworthy, just to be able to recognise acceptable software configurations that include the one AS it has chosen to trust. Imagine what will happen if the AS manufacturer periodically releases new versions of the AS and some users still use older versions. The number of integrity metric sets that represent equally trustworthy software configurations increases at an exponential rate as the number of measured software components grows. Although some efforts have been made to reduce this rate (by grouping the TPM's PCRs together according to functional categories), it remains unclear how complex, or practical, the management of trusted states is going to be in practice.

6.4.3   Costs

The types of cost that apply to SSO schemes were already briefly mentioned in Section 6.1.3. In this section, we re-examine them in the context of the schemes described in Sections 6.2.1 and 6.2.2 above.

6.4.3.1   Implementation costs

Implementing applications that make use of TPM functionality is, at least at the time of writing, much more expensive than implementing 'traditional' software. There are several reasons for this, including the following.

- Platforms that conform to the TCG specifications are not yet widespread.
- The implementation of TPM-aware BIOSs and operating systems is still under development.
- There exist no reusable software libraries that would make it easier for a programmer to interface with the TPM.

Even if an implementer manages to properly interface with the TPM, the current lack of integration and support for reporting integrity metrics (at the BIOS and operating system level) hinders testing in different environments (on platforms with another BIOS or operating system).

When contrasting the implementation costs of the two schemes described in Section 6.2, it appears that, generally speaking, the pseudo-SSO scheme of Section 6.2.1 is cheaper than the true SSO scheme of Section 6.2.2. This is because the latter is more complex than the former; as it includes the integrity challenge–response mechanism, its testing phase requires the cooperation of multiple, preferably different, TCG-conformant platforms.

6.4.3.2   Deployment costs

The main advantage of pseudo-SSO is that it operates transparently to SPs. This means that SPs do not need to change their existing authentication infrastructures; that is, they have zero deployment costs. (This is not unfair as they do not gain any benefit from the pseudo-SSO scheme, either.) In fact, most pseudo-SSO schemes, including the one described in Section 6.2.1, run on the user's machine; deployment costs are low in these cases. Only a minority of schemes involve a third party that stores the user's legacy credentials or some special 'login scripts'. In these cases the deployment costs include the setup of this third party.

True SSO systems, on the other hand, come with a considerable deployment cost. This is because they require some form of supporting security infrastructure to be in place between the AS and SPs (and possibly users as well). If, for example, the scheme requires the AS provider to digitally sign the authentication assertions it issues, a PKI with all its (typically costly) procedures has to be in place that enables SPs to verify the signatures. In the case of the true SSO scheme described in Section 6.2.2, the supporting security infrastructure is the PKI specified by TCG. Although this is an inherently complex (and expensive) PKI, its deployment is independent of any particular scheme and therefore does not count towards its costs. However, the SPs are required to manage trusted software states for the AS. The complexity of this procedure counts towards the scheme's deployment cost and is discussed in Section 6.4.2 above.

Technical deployment is not the only aspect of true SSO schemes that is costly. Because the SPs are required to trust the AS, their relationship is typically governed by contractual agreements. These carry their own cost during the setup phase. Furthermore, policies have to be devised and applied at the AS provider, the SPs and the users.

6.4.3.3   Maintenance costs

The AS of pseudo-SSO schemes has to be able to execute the legacy authentication mechanisms of SPs automatically. Whenever an SP changes this mechanism, the change has to be reflected in the AS. In an environment where SPs often change their legacy authentication mechanisms the AS has to be updated frequently as well. This renders the maintenance costs of pseudo-SSO schemes potentially high. It is worth noting that changing the legacy authentication mechanism does not necessarily mean changing the actual authentication method (e.g., from username/password-based authentication to smartcard-based); a change in merely the user interface may be enough to make it compulsory to update the AS.

True SSO schemes, on the other hand, do not suffer from this deficiency. Since the SSO protocol is common for all SPs, no separate user interfaces exist per SP. The only user interface that exists in the scheme is the one provided by the AS for the initial authentication. Even a change in that method (e.g., from username/password-based to biometrics) does not require changes in the actual SSO protocol or the format of messages. The only change it will cause is in the content in the authentication assertion that now needs to encode a description of the new method; SPs then only need to be able to understand the new description.

In terms of maintenance costs, the schemes described in Sections 6.2.1 and 6.2.2 have no significant differences from existing SSO schemes.

6.4.3.4   Running costs

Running costs of SSO schemes are measured in bandwidth consumption, delays, day-to-day management procedures and the amount of computation required. The latter depends entirely on the technical details of each scheme, pseudo and true SSO alike.

Existing true SSO schemes are, generally speaking, more expensive to run than pseudo ones. This is because the AS is provided by a third party that communicates over the network. This introduces bandwidth overheads and associated delays. Also, since the AS is typically responsible for many users, account and other management procedures may incur significant costs.

While the pseudo-SSO scheme described in Section 6.2.1 does not differ significantly from such existing schemes in terms of running costs, the true SSO scheme described in Section 6.2.2 potentially eliminates all the costs mentioned in the previous paragraph, as it effectively distributes the AS to users.

6.4.4   Open-source software

It is sometimes said that open-source software is, in general, more trustworthy than software for which the source code is not publicly available. This, it is said, is because the source code can be reviewed by security experts who can point out weaknesses. Unfortunately, experience has shown that so can potential attackers. In practice, open-source software is not necessarily less flawed than closed-source software. In fact, commercial software (which typically is not open source) is sometimes supported by contractual agreements that settle liability issues in case of security incidents. In these cases, security-related software flaws may be irrelevant.

However, the situation is perhaps different in the context of the SSO schemes described in this chapter. In Section 6.2.2, in particular, we argued that TCG-conformant platforms enable the user, as opposed to some third party, to be in control of the AS. Although this may be true, in order for this control to be effective, we argue here that it is advantageous for the AS's source code to be publicly available. This is because it can be established, via independent means, how exactly the AS is doing what it claims to be doing, thereby enabling users to exercise their control more effectively.

Public availability of the AS's source code may be even more advantageous in the context of privacy, as discussed in Section 6.3; users who wish their pseudonyms to remain unlinkable are likely to require some form of assurance that the AS does not disclose (at least not in any obvious way) any unnecessary information. Although some may trust the AS provider to properly implement the SSO functionality, this does not necessarily imply that they trust the AS provider to protect their privacy as well. As it is easy to hide information leakage in closed-source software (thereby avoiding the raising of alarms), it would appear potentially easier to convince a wary user that an open-source, as opposed to closed-source, AS will effectively protect their privacy.

6.5   Conclusion and the future of SSO

SSO has been an active research topic for a long time. Nevertheless, no single SSO scheme has been adopted on a wide scale. In this chapter we demonstrated that TCG-conformant platforms enable the construction of SSO schemes that differ in several important aspects from previous efforts. The differences stem from the fact that TCG-conformant platforms come with a tamper-resistant module that accurately reports metrics of software configurations. Using this and other related TCG services, security sensitive functionality, that previously had to reside on an external party, can now be delegated to the user platform.

However, one should keep in mind that providing SSO in an open environment is not only a technical issue. Experience has shown that trust and business issues are major obstacles that a scheme has to overcome in order to be successful. How successful the approaches described in this chapter will be in surmounting these obstacles remains to be seen.

References

1 Microsoft. *Microsoft.NET Passport Review Guide*, November 2002.
2 Andreas Pashalidis and Chris J. Mitchell. A taxonomy of single sign-on systems. In R. Safavi-Naini and J. Seberry, eds, *Proceedings of the 8th Australasian Conference on Information Security and Privacy (ACISP 2003), July 9–11, Wollongong, Australia, volume 2727 of Lecture Notes in Computer Science*, pp. 249–264, Springer-Verlag, Berlin, 2003.
3 A. J. Menezes, P. C. van Oorschot, and S. A. Vanstone. *Handbook of Applied Cryptography*. CRC Press, Boca Raton, FL, 1997.
4 Liberty Alliance. *Liberty ID-FF Architecture Overview v.1.2-03*, April 2003.
5 J. G. Steiner, B. Clifford Neuman, and J. I. Schiller. Kerberos: an authentication service for open network systems. In *Proceedings of the Winter 1988 Usenix Conference*, pp. 191–201, USENIX Association, Dallas, TX, 1988.
6 Trusted Computing Group. TCG TPM Specification, Version 1.2 – TPM Commands, 2003.
7 Liberty Alliance. *Liberty Architecture Glossary v.1.2-04*, April 2003.
8 Liberty Alliance. *Liberty Authentication Context Specification v.1.2-05*, April 2003.
9 Liberty Alliance. *Liberty ID-FF Bindings and Profiles Specification v.1.2-08*, April 2003.
10 Liberty Alliance. *Liberty ID-FF Implementation Guidelines v.1.2-02*, April 2003.
11 Liberty Alliance. *Liberty ID-FF Protocols and Schema Specification v.1.2-08*, April 2003.

12 A. Pfitzmann and M. Köhntopp. Anonymity, unobservability, and pseudonymity – a proposal for terminology. In H. Federrath, ed., *Designing Privacy Enhancing Technologies, Proceedings of the International Workshop on Design Issues in Anonymity and Unobservability, July 25–26, Berkeley, CA, volume 2009 of Lecture Notes in Computer Science*, pp. 1–9, Springer-Verlag, Berlin, 2001.

13 S. Steinbrecher and S. Koepsell. Modelling unlinkability. In R. Dingledine, ed., *Proceedings of the 3rd International Workshop on Privacy Enhancing Technologies (PET 2003), March 26–28, Dresden, Germany, Revised Papers, volume 2760 of Lecture Notes in Computer Science*, pp. 32–47, Springer-Verlag, Berlin, 2003.

14 Ernie Brickell, Jan Camenisch, and Liqun Chen. Direct anonymous attestation. In *Proceedings of the 11th ACM Conference on Computer and Communications Security, (CCS 2004)*, pp. 132–145, ACM Press, New York, 2004.

15 J. Camenisch and A. Lysyanskaya. An efficient system for non-transferable anonymous credentials with optional anonymity revocation. In B. Pfitzmann, ed., *Advances in Cryptology – EUROCRYPT 2001, Proceedings of the International Conference on the Theory and Application of Cryptographic Techniques, May 6–10, Innsbruck, Austria, volume 2045 of Lecture Notes in Computer Science*, pp. 93–118, Springer-Verlag, Berlin, 2001.

16 Jan Camenisch. Better privacy for trusted computing platforms. In P. Saramati, P. Ryan, D. Gollman, and R. Molva, eds, *Proceedings of the 9th European Symposium on Research Computer Security (ESORICS 2004), September 13–15, Sophia Antipolis, France, volume 3193 of Lecture Notes in Computer Science*, pp. 73–88, Springer-Verlag, Berlin, 2004.

Chapter 7

Secure delivery of conditional access applications to mobile receivers

Eimear Gallery and Allan Tomlinson

7.1 Introduction

7.1.1 Motivation

One of the driving forces behind recent developments in mobile communications systems is the potential for such systems to deliver more complex content to consumers. Current 3G systems are capable of delivering multimedia clips to subscribers' mobile telephones. The next generation of communications systems are expected to develop this service, and collaborate with broadcast systems to provide wireless access to video content from a wide range of mobile devices. For a service like this to achieve its full commercial potential, the owners of the content will require assurance that their material is not illegally accessed. Current broadcast systems accomplish this by using conditional access systems to ensure that only bona fide subscribers have access to the content.

The Digital Video Broadcasting (DVB) organisation[1] has developed several standards for conditional access systems. These standards provide a common interface to conditional access systems at both the transmission site and the receiver, while allowing the systems themselves to remain proprietary. Services broadcast today, therefore, are subject to a range of proprietary access control systems. While receivers remain static, and consumers subscribe to one or two service providers, the DVB standards provide a practical solution.

However, if a mobile subscriber requires access to services controlled by several different conditional access systems, then the current solution becomes increasingly impractical. If future wireless devices are to maximise their access to broadcast

---

[1] www.dvb.org

services, then a more practical and cost-effective means will be required to allow consumer products to support this wide range of proprietary conditional access systems.

7.1.2   Purpose and scope

This chapter considers the possibility of downloading legacy conditional access applications on demand to the mobile device. If this solution is to be deployed, two security requirements must be fulfilled with respect to the conditional access application. It is essential that the conditional access application is protected as it is transported from the software provider to the mobile device, and that the mobile device can demonstrate to the application provider that it can be trusted to prevent attacks on the received application.

In this chapter we describe two protocols that meet the above security requirements. These protocols are not intended in any way to supersede or replace the DVB standards or existing conditional access systems. Instead, they are intended to coexist with existing mechanisms, so that the receipt of digital video broadcast may be achieved more efficiently in the mobile environment.

Section 7.2 examines the current mechanisms used to protect broadcast content, and describes some limitations which arise when they are applied in the mobile environment. This is followed in Section 7.3 by a description of the threats introduced by this new environment and identification of the mechanisms required to securely download a conditional access application to a mobile receiver.

An abstract description of our proposed protocols is presented in Section 7.4, followed by an analysis. Section 7.5 then goes on to show how the protocols may be mapped onto specific trusted computing architectures and presents a further analysis for each particular architecture. Sections 7.6 and 7.7 introduce two alternative platform designs that may meet our objectives by using special tamper-proof processors.

7.2   Conditional access systems

The security issues for current broadcast systems may be encompassed in the requirement to provide conditional access to content. That is, to ensure that only bona fide subscribers can access the broadcast services. As can be seen from Table 7.1, there are many proprietary conditional access systems available for broadcasters to choose from. Although the conditional access systems and their security mechanisms remain proprietary, most vendors have adopted the DVB standard protocols. These protocols provide a well-defined interface between the proprietary system and the rest of the broadcast equipment. This gives the consumer some degree of choice over the proprietary system they use with their receiver. The remainder of this section describes DVB protocols and assesses their suitability for use with highly mobile receivers.

7.2.1   DVB standards

The DVB standards specify two mechanisms that aim to provide some flexibility in the application of proprietary conditional access systems to broadcast services [1].

Table 7.1   Conditional access system vendors

Conditional Access System	Vendor	
Viaccess	Viaccess SA	www.viaccess.fr
NagraVision	Kudelski	www.kudelski.com
Videoguard	NDS	www.nds.com
Mediguard	Canal+	www.canalplus-technologies.com
Mcrypt	Irdeto	www.irdetoaccess.com
PiSys	Irdeto	www.irdetoaccess.com
CryptoWorks	Philips	www.digitalnetworks.philips.com
BetaCrypt	BetaResearch	www.betaresearch.de
Conax	Telenor	www.telenorsbc.com
Digicipher	Motorola	broadband.motorola.com
PowerKey	Scientific Atlanta	www.sciatl.com

At the transmission site, the simulcrypt standard [2] allows a service to be controlled by two or more conditional access systems. At the receiver, the common interface standard [3] allows conditional access modules to be plugged into pc-card slots in the receiver to configure the device for the required conditional access system. Both systems rely on the service being scrambled by a standard Common Scrambling Algorithm (CSA) [4]. Figure 7.1 illustrates how these standards would be used to scramble a broadcast service.

The service is scrambled by the CSA under a key known as a Control Word (CW). Since the cryptographic scheme is a symmetric algorithm, the CW must be delivered to the receiver in a secure manner. This is the function of the conditional access system. At the transmission site, the CW is encrypted by the conditional access system, and the encrypted E (CW), or Entitlement Control Message (ECM), is broadcast to the receiver in advance of the scrambled service. The DVB standards define the interface to the conditional access system, and the format of the ECM messages.

7.2.2   Simulcrypt

If a second conditional access system is available to the broadcaster, then the same CW may be encrypted by this system, as shown in Figure 7.2. The simulcrypt standard [2] describes the interface to the conditional access systems and the synchronisation protocols. Both encrypted CWs are then broadcast in advance of the scrambled service. Thus, receivers running either conditional access system are able to recover the CW and access the scrambled service. As far as the consumer is concerned, the operation of this system is completely transparent. The service provider, however, must operate multiple conditional access systems.

While it may be commercially feasible for large networks to operate two or three conditional access systems, the cost and logistics of running many such systems simultaneously could prove to be prohibitive for smaller networks.

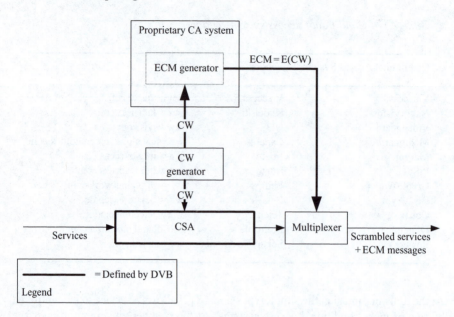

Figure 7.1   Scrambling broadcast services using DVB standards

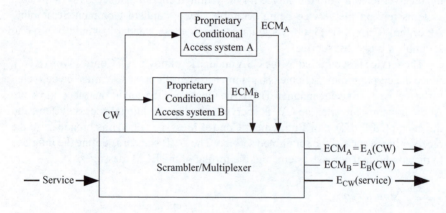

Figure 7.2   Simulcrypt

7.2.3   Common interface

A parallel means of supporting multiple conditional access systems is to provide a solution at the receiver. This is accomplished by specifying a standard interface for the receiver that provides access to the scrambled service and the encrypted CWs [3]. Figure 7.3 shows how the scrambled service and the encrypted CW can be passed to a separate pc-card module containing the hardware and software for a specific conditional access system. The encrypted CWs can be deciphered on the module to provide access to the service.

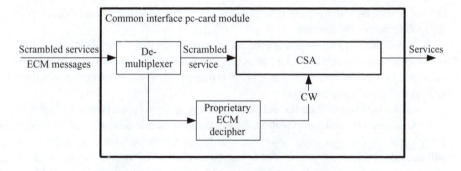

Figure 7.3   Common interface module

By swapping modules, the receiver can thus be configured to match the conditional access system used by the broadcaster. This system is therefore transparent to the broadcaster but not to the subscriber. As is the case with simulcrypt, this mechanism may provide a solution for two or three conditional access systems, but as the numbers increase the cost to the subscriber could become prohibitive.

7.2.4   Limitations of existing mechanisms

The solutions described above are well suited to current technology, where services are generally controlled by one or two conditional access systems and subscribers generally only require authorisation from one or two broadcasters. With a mobile receiver, however, subscribers will require authorisation from an increasing number of service providers as they travel further afield.

The common interface solution would require mobile devices to have a pc-card interface and the user to carry a number of modules. The cost of adding such an interface as well as the practical design issues could make this infeasible. The cost of the modules may also deter some subscribers. The alternative solution using current technology would be to broadcast each service under the control of as many conditional access systems as possible, which could prove prohibitively expensive for many broadcasters, especially those operating in small niche markets. Both current solutions therefore have potential difficulties which will significantly restrict the content available to mobile receivers. These existing solutions do not transfer well to mobile systems and the problem would benefit therefore from some reconsideration in the light of new requirements.

7.2.5   Modifications required for mobile receivers

The objective is to provide access-controlled broadcast content to mobile devices. This should be achieved with minimum impact on existing networks while at the same time minimising the hardware overhead on the mobile device and the cost to the user. An attractive solution is to re-configure a mobile platform to be compatible with the appropriate proprietary conditional access system. The implication of this is that the proprietary application is implemented entirely in software and delivered to the mobile device on demand.

The difficulty lies in convincing the software provider that the application, including any embedded secret keys, will be protected to at least the level offered by current solutions. This contrasts with the more familiar problem of securing the platform against malicious applications.

To address this problem, the delivery mechanism must protect both the integrity and confidentiality of the application. Moreover, the mobile device must be able to demonstrate to the application provider that the platform on which the application will execute is trustworthy. The former can be accomplished by well-known security mechanisms such as encryption and the use of Message Authentication Codes (MACs) [5], while the latter may be achieved by the deployment of trusted computing or closely related technologies.

7.3   Security requirements

To ensure that any solution proposed for use in the mobile environment is at least as secure as currently implemented DVB standard solutions, two fundamental security requirements must be satisfied, namely:

Secure download. The confidentiality and integrity of the application must be protected as it is transported from the software provider to the host platform.

Secure execution. The application must be protected while it is stored and executed on the host platform.

This section summarises the security threats, services and potential mechanisms, which need to be considered when securing the download, storage and execution of the conditional access application.

7.3.1   Security threats

The secure download, storage and execution of a conditional access application is subject to a number of threats including:

1.   Unauthorised reading of the application code and data while in transit.
2.   Unauthorised alteration of the application while in transit.
3.   Unknowingly communicating with an unknown and potentially malicious entity. More specifically, we will primarily concentrate on the threat of a software provider unknowingly communicating with an unknown and potentially malicious mobile platform.
4.   The inability to corroborate the source of the conditional access application.
5.   Replay of communications.
6.   Unauthorised reading or modification of the application while in storage on the mobile host.
7.   Unauthorised reading or modification of the application while it executes on the mobile host.

7.3.2 Security services and mechanisms

The security services required to thwart the first five threats listed above may be provided using standard cryptographic mechanisms [5,6]. The services required to counter the remaining two threats require the application of mechanisms associated with trusted computing or closely related technologies. There is a direct mapping between the above threats and the services and potential mechanisms, outlined below, which may be deployed to prevent their realisation.

1. Confidentiality of the application while in transit. This service may be provided by symmetric or asymmetric cryptography.
2. Integrity protection of the application while in transit. MACs or digital signatures can provide this service.
3. Entity authentication.
    (a) With respect to the mobile host, platform attestation may fulfill this service requirement, where a signature from a Trusted Module (TM) on some external data, for example, anti-replay data and the identity of the signature recipient, and platform state information attests to: the identity of the module, particular capabilities and functionality of the module, and the state configuration of the host in which the TM is embedded [7]. Through signature verification, a challenger wishing to authenticate the mobile host, can verify the platform identity and guarantee that certain properties hold for the platform associated with the identity. This identity verification process 'provides sufficient evidence that a target platform contains capabilities and data that must be trustworthy if reports about the software environment in the platform are to be trusted' [7]. Thus, reports reflecting the specific state of the platform at the time of signature generation can be verified as accurate.
    (b) A unilateral entity authentication protocol may provide this service with respect to the software provider, where the identity of the software provider is proved to the mobile host.
4. Origin authentication. The origin of the conditional access application can be authenticated via the verification of the software provider's signature on the session keys used to protect the integrity and confidentiality of the conditional access application sent from the software provider to the mobile host.
5. Freshness. This can be provided by a nonce or a timestamp.
6. This threat may be countered by providing the following services:
    (a) Confidentiality and integrity protection of the application on the host platform. This service requires the availability of protected storage on the host [7].
    (b) Prevention of unauthorised access to the application while in storage. This service can be provided by binding the application to particular access control information. The protected storage mechanism can be used to ensure that the application is only accessed when the particular execution environment is in a specific state and, optionally, when valid authorisation data is provided. Alternatively, the application may be bound to a

particular hardware component, such as a secure (co-)processor, such that the application can only be decrypted by, or inside, that particular hardware component [8,9].

7. Confidentiality and integrity protection of the application code and data during execution. This service can be provided by using process isolation techniques. These are mechanisms that allow applications and services to run without interference from other processes executing in parallel [10–12].

7.4 Protocols for secure application download using trusted computing technologies

Having established a set of requirements, two protocols are now described which have been designed to meet these requirements. A public key protocol is described in Section 7.4.5 and an alternative secret key protocol is described in Section 7.4.7.

7.4.1 Model

The model under consideration is illustrated in Figure 7.4 and involves three parties: the user, who has a mobile receiver, M; the broadcasters, B; and the software providers, S. A fundamental component in this model is the TM. This tamper-proof module is assumed to be bound physically or cryptographically to the mobile receiver, and is capable of performing a limited number of cryptographic operations as described in the protocols.

The mobile user does not have a long-term relationship with the broadcaster but is aware of the services that are available. Some of these services may be scrambled, in which case access is controlled by a conditional access system. For each scrambled service, the associated conditional access application, A_C, must be acquired by the mobile receiver. The protocol requires that the mobile receiver is able to demonstrate to the software provider that it is a bona fide receiver and not in a malicious state that may attempt to modify, replicate or extract secret data from the downloaded application. Once the receiver has proved itself to be legitimate, the application is made available only to that receiver. Finally, the protocol must protect the confidentiality and integrity of the application as it is transported to the mobile device.

The software provider in this model is required to supply the appropriate conditional access software to the mobile receiver. This software provider may, in practice, be the same entity as the broadcaster; alternatively it may be a third-party broker who provides the application, A_C, to the receiver. The mobile user needs to be aware of which software provider can deliver the application, A_C. He or she may be informed of this by either the broadcaster or the software provider. The mobile receiver is therefore in a position to download A_C from the software provider and descramble the broadcast service, subject to the appropriate commercial agreements.

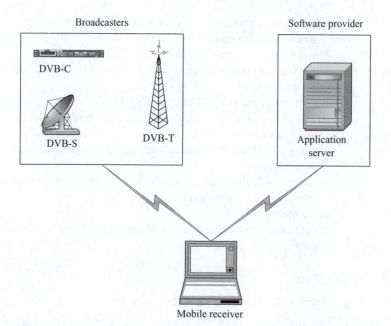

Figure 7.4   Model

7.4.2 *Notation*

The following notation is used in the specification of the protocols:

M	Denotes the mobile receiver
B	Denotes the broadcaster
S	Denotes the software provider
CA	Denotes a Certification Authority (CA) trusted by S and M
TM	Denotes a TM bound to the mobile receiver
A_D	Denotes a trusted application, or agent, responsible for the secure download of conditional access software
A_B	Denotes a trusted broadcast application
A_C	Denotes the conditional access application which is downloaded
Cert_X	Is a public key certificate for entity X
$K_{X,Y}$	Denotes a secret key possessed only by X and Y
R_X	Is a random number issued by entity X
$E_K(Z)$	Is the result of the encryption of data Z using the key K
$\text{Seal}_1(Z)$	Is the result of the encryption of data Z concatenated with integrity metrics, I, such that Z can only be deciphered and accessed if the software state of the platform is consistent with I
$H(Z)$	Is a one-way hash function on data Z
$\text{MAC}_K(Z)$	Is a MAC, generated on data Z using key K

$S_X(Z)$ Is the digital signature of data Z computed using entity X's
                  private signature transformation

X(public)   The public asymmetric key of X

X(private)   The private asymmetric key of X

p Is a prime number

g Is a generator for Diffie–Hellman key exchange modulo p, that is,
                  an element of multiplicative order q (a large prime dividing
                  $p - 1$) modulo p

a_X Is entity X's Diffie–Hellman private key component for secret
                  key generation

b_X Is entity X's Diffie–Hellman public key component for secret key
                  generation $b_X = g^{a_X} \bmod p$

Id_X Is the identity of X

$X \| Y$ Is the result of the concatenation of data items X and Y in that
                  order

7.4.3 Assumptions

In describing the protocols, the following assumptions are made:

1. The TM is inextricably bound to the platform. It is a self-contained processing module with specialist security capabilities such as random number generation, asymmetric key generation, digital signing, encryption capabilities, hashing capabilities, an HMAC [5] engine, monotonic counters as well as memory, non-volatile memory, power detection and I/O. Support for platform integrity measurement, recording and reporting is also provided. One possible implementation of TM is as a hardware chip which is separate from the main platform Central Processing Unit (CPU).

2. The mobile receiver, M, is running at least one protected execution environment. Within this environment, different applications run in isolation, free from being observed or compromised by other processes running in the same protected partition, or by software running in any insecure partition that may exist in parallel. The services described in Section 7.3.2 are assumed to be available in this environment.

3. All secret keys required by the mobile receiver are protected by the TM, either directly or indirectly.

4. A unique asymmetric encryption key pair is associated with the TM.

5. The private decryption key is securely stored in the TM.

6. The associated public key is certified. The certificate contains a general description of the TM and its security properties.

7. Credentials are generated indicating whether the particular design of TM in a particular class of mobile platform meets specified security requirements, and whether a particular mobile host is an instance of this class of mobile platform and incorporates a specific TM which meets this design.

8. A private signing key is securely stored by the TM. This key is used only for entity authentication.

9. The public signature verification key, corresponding to the private key in assumption 8, is certified by a Certification Authority, CA. The certificate issued, Cert$_{TM}$, binds the identity of the TM (the trusted platform containing the module) to a public key used for the verification of digital signatures. This certificate must be obtainable by the software provider S.

10. The software provider, S, has a private signing key that is securely stored within its environment. This key is used only for entity authentication.

11. The software provider, S, has a certificate, Cert$_S$, issued by the certification authority, CA. This certificate associates the identity of the S with a public key value for the verification of digital signatures. This certificate must be available to the mobile platform.

12. For the secret key protocol described in Section 7.4.7, the software provider's certificate, Cert$_S$, contains public Diffie–Hellman parameters g and p.

13. For the secret key protocol described in Section 7.4.7, a Diffie–Hellman key is agreed for each and every protocol run.

14. The TM is capable of generating an asymmetric encryption key pair where the public encryption key is signed/certified using the signature key described in assumption 8. This thwarts the privacy and security threats surrounding routine use of the public encryption key described in assumption 4. The private decryption key from this pair is bound to a particular environment configuration state.

15. For the public key protocol described in Section 7.4.5, an asymmetric encryption key pair, as mentioned above, is generated for each and every protocol run.

16. S is able to verify the claims made by the platform containing a particular TM. S is able to look up, or obtain from a validation authority, an expected set of trustworthy integrity metrics.

17. Every mobile device wishing to receive a video broadcast must have a trusted broadcast application, A_B, running in the protected environment.

18. Every mobile device will also have a download application, A_D, running in the protected environment. This download application will perform two fundamental tasks. It will complete one of the protocols described below. It will also prevent the potential interference of any other application with A_C while it is executing. It may, for example, incorporate a monitoring function which adheres to a specified policy, such that once the conditional access application is running on the device, any attempt by another application to start-up will fail; alternatively the start-up of any additional applications will result in A_D stopping A_C, and erasing it from memory.

19. Finally, it is assumed that one of the following protocol runs, is completed every time a conditional access application is to be downloaded such that either the asymmetric encryption key pair generated in the public key protocol or the Diffie–Hellman key agreed in the secret key protocol are unique to a specific protocol run.

The preceding discussion has identified the essential components of an ideal solution to the download problem. Based on this analysis, two abstract protocols are now defined that aim to meet these requirements. This is followed in Section 7.5 by an exploration of how these protocols may be implemented using specific trusted computing technologies. Each specific technology provides different mechanisms to meet the defined requirements.

7.4.4   Initiation of the protocols

Both protocols begin when the user makes a request to the broadcast application, A_B, to view a specific video broadcast. If reception of this broadcast is controlled by a particular conditional access application, A_C, then A_B carries out the following steps:

1. A_B checks to see if the mobile device has dedicated hardware or software installed to support A_C.
2. If no dedicated hardware, for example, a common interface module, exists on the mobile device, then A_B determines whether A_C has previously been downloaded and is still available in secure storage. If so, the download application, A_D, is called to retrieve A_C from secure storage and execute the application.
3. If A_C is not available on the mobile device, then A_D is called to download the application.
4. The download of A_C will be accomplished by deploying one of the protocols described in Sections 7.4.5 and 7.4.7.

7.4.5   Public key protocol

The public key protocol is described by the following sequence of steps, where $X \rightarrow Y: Z$ is used to indicate that the message Z is sent by entity X to entity Y.

1. $A_D \rightarrow S$: Request for application A_C.
2. $S \rightarrow A_D$: R_S.
3. $A_D \rightarrow$ TM: Request the generation of an asymmetric encryption key pair, A_D(private) and A_D(public), and association of A_D(private) with a specified protected environment state.
4. TM: Generates A_D(public) and A_D(private), where A_D(private) is bound to a specified protected environment state.
5. TM $\rightarrow A_D$: A_D(public).
6. $A_D \rightarrow$ TM: Request to certify A_D(public).
   This involves the TM signing A_D(public), and the integrity metrics, I, reflecting the state of the protected environment when the key pair was generated and the state required for private key use. The value R_S is included in the signed bundle so that the freshness of the operation can be checked by the software provider. Id_S is also signed such that the intended destination of the message can be verified by the software provider.
7. TM $\rightarrow A_D$: $R_S \| \text{Id}_S \| A_D(\text{public}) \| I \| S_{TM}(R_S \| \text{Id}_S \| A_D(\text{public}) \| I)$.
8. $A_D \rightarrow S$: $R_S \| \text{Id}_S \| A_D(\text{public}) \| I \| S_{TM}(R_S \| \text{Id}_S \| A_D(\text{public}) \| I)$.
9. S: Retrieves Cert_{TM} and verifies it.
   S: Verifies $S_{TM}(R_S \| \text{Id}_S \| A_D(\text{public}) \| I)$.

10. S: Verifies R_S to ensure the message is fresh and verifies that the message was intended for S.

11. S: Decides if I represents a sufficiently trustworthy state.

 Given I, S can verify that the A_D is executing as expected, that it has not been tampered with, and that there is also a legitimate broadcast application executing on the mobile host.

12. Assuming the signature from TM verifies correctly, the values of R_S and Id_S are as expected and the integrity metrics, I, if delivered, are acceptable, then:

 S: Extracts A_D(public)

13. S: Generates $K1_{S,A_D}$ used for data encryption.

 S: Generates $K2_{S,A_D}$ used for data integrity protection.

14. $S \rightarrow A_D$: $E_{A_D}(\text{public})(K1_{S,A_D} \| K2_{S,A_D}) \|$
 $S_S(E_{A_D(\text{public})}(K1_{S,A_D} \| K2_{S,A_D})) \| E_{K1_{S,A_D}}(\text{MAC}_{K2_{S,A_D}}(A_C))$.

15. A_D: Verifies $S_S(E_{A_D}(\text{public})(K1_{S,A_D}, K2_{S,A_D}))$.

16. $A_D \rightarrow$ TM: Request to load A_D(private).

17. TM: Decrypts $E_{A_D}(\text{public})(K1_{S,A_D}, K2_{S,A_D})$.

18. A_D: Decrypts $E_{K1_{S,A_D}}(\text{MAC}_{K2_{S,A_D}}(A_C))$.

19. A_D: Verifies $\text{MAC}_{K2_{S,A_D}}(A_C)$.

20. Once A_C is executing, A_D precludes the potential interference of any other application with A_C.

21. A_D: Deletes A_C, and all other keys, when they are no longer required.

 The encrypted copy of A_C may remain stored for future use, space permitting.

Only when the protected execution environment is in a particular state can the short-term keys, $K1$ and $K2$, be decrypted and the application A_C accessed. This state, I, will have been verified by the software provider as being trusted to protect A_C while executing.

7.4.6   Analysis of the public key protocol

The initial analysis focuses on the protection of the application while in transit from the software provider to the mobile host. The threat model is illustrated in Figure 7.5. The attacker in this model is able to observe and modify the messages passing between M and S. The attacker may also record any message passing between M and S and replay this message at any time in the future and as often as desired. Furthermore, the attacker may prevent the transmission of any message passing between M and S. This last assumption allows a trivial denial of service attack which cannot be prevented.

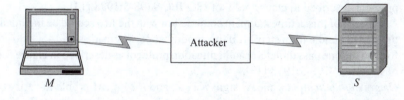

Figure 7.5   Threat model

Protection of the application on the host platform will depend on the specific mechanisms adopted. Consequently, the analysis of this aspect of security is presented in Section 7.5, following the description of each specific technology.

1. *Confidentiality of the application while in transit.* Symmetric encryption is deployed to provide confidentiality of A_C whilst it is in transit. The symmetric key used, $K1_{S,A_D}$, is securely transported to M protected by A_D(public). The corresponding private key is securely stored in TM, and is only useable when the protected partition is in a particular state which has been verified as trustworthy. An attacker would have to extract A_D(private) from TM to decipher A_C. However, $K1_{S,A_D}$ must also be securely managed and protected by S, at least to the same degree as A_C itself is protected.

2. *Integrity protection of the application while in transit.* A MAC is deployed to protect the integrity of A_C in transit. Generation of the MAC requires possession of $K2_{S,A_D}$, which is also delivered to M under the protection of A_D(public). As above, an attacker would have to extract A_D(private) from TM to recover $K2_{S,A_D}$ and tamper with A_C. However, as above, $K2_{S,A_D}$ must be securely managed and protected by S, at least to the same degree as A_C itself is protected.

3. *Entity authentication.* The software provider can verify the identity of TM and the state of the protected execution environment which utilises TM security services, via the platform attestation mechanism. That is, the signature of TM on R_S, Id_S and on the integrity metrics representing the protected execution environment guarantees the platform's state and allows the software provider to authenticate the trusted platform. Steps 2 and 8 of the above protocol conform to the two pass unilateral authentication protocol described in clause 5.1.2 of ISO/IEC 9798-3:1998 [13] where A_D (public) serves as the nonce in the response message sent by M by virtue of the fact that the asymmetric key pair is generated for each protocol run.

   It may be argued that the protocol outlined above also provides entity authentication with respect to the software provider. If a unique A_D(public) is generated for each protocol run, A_D(public) acts as not only a random nonce but also represents the identity of the destination platform. The signature of the software provider on the unique public key, A_D(public), provides entity authentication.

   Alternatively, one of the following additions may be made to the protocol. A random nonce may be included in the signed bundle sent to the software provider in step 8 and returned in conjunction with R_S and Id_M in the bundle signed by the software provider in step 14. If this modification is made to the protocol, steps 2, 8 and 14 conform to the three pass mutual authentication protocol described in clause 5.2.2 of ISO/IEC 9798-3:1998 [13].

   Instead of this, a timestamp, in conjunction with the Id_M, could be included in the signed bundle from step 14. If this modification was made step 14 would conform to the one pass unilateral authentication protocol as described in clause 5.1.1 of ISO/IEC 9798-3:1998 [13].

4. *Origin authentication.* Since S signs $K1_{S,A_D}$ and $K2_{S,A_D}$, M is able to verify that these keys have been sent from S. Also, since $K2_{S,A_D}$ is used to compute the MAC,

M can thus verify that the A_C has been sent from the same source. An attacker attempting to deliver a malicious application would require the collaboration of S.

5. *Freshness.* Platform attestation using the integrity metrics proves that the platform is in a specific configuration, and that S is communicating with a particular TM. This is only useful if proof exists that communications are fresh. This is accomplished by including R_S in the signed bundle sent to S in step 8.

It may be possible for an attacker to replace the message in step 14 with an older message destined for the same mobile host, or with a corresponding message destined for a different mobile host. However, since a unique A_D(public) is generated for each protocol run, the verification in step 19 would detect this.

Alternatively, one of the following additions may be made to the protocol. A random nonce may be included in the signed bundle sent to the software provider in step 8 and returned in the bundle signed by the software provider in step 14. Instead of this, a timestamp could be included in the signed bundle from step 14.

7.4.7 Secret key protocol

Next we describe an alternative protocol based upon symmetric cryptography. As before, the protocol begins when the download application, A_D, in the mobile device makes a request for a conditional access application to be downloaded. The following steps are performed.

1. A_D: Chooses a Diffie–Hellman private value a_M and calculates b_M based on g and p which are retrieved from the public key certificate of the software provider, Cert$_S$.
2. $A_D \rightarrow S$: Request application $A_C \| b_M$.
3. S: Chooses a Diffie–Hellman private value a_S and calculates b_S using g and p which are contained in Cert$_S$.
4. $S \rightarrow A_D$: $b_S \| S_S(b_S \| b_M \| Id_M)$.
5. A_D: Verifies the signature on the message received and verifies $(b_S \| b_M \| Id_M)$ to ensure the message is fresh and was destined for M.
6. A_D: Calculates the shared key K_{S,A_D}.
7. A_D: Uses K_{S,A_D} to derive:
   $K1_{S,A_D}$ used for data encryption and
   $K2_{S,A_D}$ used for data integrity protection, by an agreed method.
8. $A_D \rightarrow$ TM: Request the encryption of $K1_{S,A_D}, K2_{S,A_D}$ and their association with a specified protected environment state: Seal$_I(K1_{S,A_D}, K2_{S,A_D})$.
9. TM: Securely stores $K1_{S,A_D}$ and $K2_{S,A_D}$ using the protected storage mechanism such that $K1_{S,A_D}, K2_{S,A_D}$ can only be decrypted when the protected environment is in a specified state, I.
10. $A_D \rightarrow$ TM: Request platform attestation, that is, the signature of TM on $(b_M \| b_S \| Id_S \| I)$.
11. TM $\rightarrow A_D$: $S_{TM}(b_M \| b_S \| Id_S \| I)$.
12. $A_D \rightarrow S$: $S_{TM}(b_M \| b_S \| Id_S \| I)$.
13. S: Obtains and verifies Cert$_{TM}$ and then verifies $S_{TM}(b_M \| b_S \| Id_S \| I)$.

14. S: Verifies $(b_M \| b_S \| Id_S)$ to ensure the message is fresh and was destined for S.
15. S: Checks that the statement has come from a trustworthy module, and checks that the state information represents a sufficiently trustworthy execution environment.
16. S: Calculates K_{S,A_D} and derives $K1_{S,A_D}$ and $K2_{S,A_D}$ by an agreed method.
17. $S \rightarrow A_D$: $E_{K1_{S,A_D}}(\text{MAC}_{K2_{S,A_D}}(A_C))$.
18. $A_D \rightarrow$ TM: Request to unseal $K1_{S,A_D}$ and $K2_{S,A_D}$.
      $K1_{S,A_D}$ and $K2_{S,A_D}$ can only be unsealed if the platform is in the agreed state, I
19. A_D: Decrypts $E_{K1_{S,A_D}}(\text{MAC}_{K2_{S,A_D}}(A_C))$.
20. A_D: Verifies $\text{MAC}_{K2_{S,A_D}}(A_C)$.
21.   Once A_C is executing, A_D precludes the potential interference of any other application with A_C.
22. A_D: Deletes A_C, and all other keys, when they are no longer required.
      The encrypted copy of A_C may remain stored for future use, space permitting.

7.4.8   Analysis of the secret key protocol

As before, the analysis uses the threat model described in Section 7.4.6 to examine the threats to the secure delivery of the application to the intended host.

1.   *Confidentiality of the application while in transit.* As was the case in the previous protocol, symmetric cryptography is deployed to protect the confidentiality of the application. However, rather than using the public encryption key of the mobile host to securely deliver the symmetric keys, the Diffie–Hellman key agreement protocol is employed. Since the key agreement is authenticated, the protocol is safe from man in the middle attacks.
2.   *Integrity protection of the application while in transit.* As was the case in the first protocol, a MAC is deployed to protect the integrity of the application in transit.
3.   *Entity authentication.* As this protocol is based on the station-to-station protocol [14] (a type of authenticated Diffie–Hellman protocol) it offers mutual authentication. The software provider can verify the identity of the TM and the state of the protected execution environment which utilises TM security services. This may be accomplished via the platform attestation mechanism, that is, the verification of the TM's signature upon b_M, b_S, Id_S and the integrity metrics representative of the protected execution environment. The mobile device can authenticate the software provider's identity via the verification of the digital signature which has been generated over b_S, b_M and Id_M.
4.   *Origin authentication.* Since S signs b_M and b_S in step 4, and A_C is protected by using keys derived from b_M and b_S, then M is able to verify the origin of A_C. As before, an attacker attempting to deliver a malicious application would require collaboration from S.
5.   *Freshness.* The inclusion of a unique, freshly generated b_S in step 4 prevents an attacker from blocking the message in step 12 and sending an older version captured from a previous protocol run.
      The attacker could replace the message in step 17 with an older message destined for the same mobile host, or with a corresponding message destined for

a different mobile host. However, since a unique K_{S,A_D} is generated for each protocol run, the verification in step 20 would detect this. As an additional measure, if deemed necessary, a timestamp may be included in step 17 to prevent replay.

7.4.9   Concluding remarks

In both protocols, when the broadcast application, A_B, needs to access and execute the conditional access application, A_C, keys must be obtained from the TM to decipher A_C. A_C may be deciphered and executed only if the chosen execution environment is in the appropriate state. Once A_C has been deciphered, A_D prevents the potential interference of any other application with A_C. Once A_C has run, it is deleted. A copy of the encrypted application may, however, remain stored for future use, space permitting.

7.5   Mapping the protocols to trusted computing architectures

Section 7.4 described the two protocols in general terms, without reference to any specific trusted platform architecture. This section considers how the technologies described in Chapter 3 may be utilised in the implementation of the protocols. The major challenge is mapping the concept of the TM, onto each technology, and making use of the specific security mechanisms associated with that technology.

We will initially examine trusted platform components as defined by the Trusted Computing Group (TCG) and Microsoft's Next Generation Secure Computing Base (NGSCB) project. These are major industry initiatives and it is important that the protocols can be supported by these technologies if they are to find practical applications. An open source project is considered in Section 7.5.3 as an alternative to commercial platforms. The order of elements in the protocol steps may differ slightly from the generic protocols due to the order of input and output parameters specified in particular TM specifications.

7.5.1   Building the protocols using TCG specifications

The TCG have specified the components of a Trusted Platform Module (TPM) [15–17] that meets the requirements for the TM in the protocols described above. The TPM is defined as a tamper-resistant module which contains all platform functionality that must be trusted, if the platform itself is to be trusted. The TPM contains both protected capabilities and shielded locations as described in Chapter 3. It is a self-contained processing engine with specialist capabilities such as random number generation, asymmetric key generation, digital signing, encryption capabilities, a SHA-1 engine, a HMAC engine, monotonic counters, as well as volatile and non-volatile memory, power detection and I/O. In conjunction with this, integrity measurement, recording and storage are supported. It is desirable [7], although not compulsory, that the Core Root of Trust for Measurement (CRTM) instructions are also contained within the TPM. The TPM facilitates the storage of integrity metrics in internal registers, that is, the Platform Configuration Registers (PCRs), and the reporting of these metrics. The TPM itself must be inextricably bound to the platform.

The TPM may have an identity, a signature key signature pair, (or multiple identities) associated with it. This identity provides evidence that a target platform contains the capabilities and data that must be trustworthy if reports about the software are to be trusted. The private key is protected within the TPM and the public verification key is available externally.

The TPM is also capable of generating an asymmetric key pair on demand. These keys may be linked cryptographically to the state of the trusted environment at the time of key generation, thereby ensuring that the private key from this pair is securely stored within the TPM and only accessible when the trusted environment is in a specific state. The corresponding public key may then be certified by the TPM, using an identity key as described above.

The TPM also facilitates secure storage or sealing. This feature may be used to encrypt and store any symmetric keys that are generated, and to ensure that access to these symmetric keys is only permissable when the trusted environment is in the specified state.

Finally, in the protocols being defined, the TPM is able to sign external data, for example, b_M, b_S and Id_S, in conjunction with I, providing platform attestation that can be verified by S.

In defining the protocols, use of the version 1.2 TPM command set [17] and data structures [16] is implied. TPM commands used will include TPM$_\text{CreateWrapKey}$, TPM$_\text{CertifyKey}$, TPM$_\text{Quote}$ and TPM$_\text{Seal}$. The data structures used include TPM_Key, and TPM_Certify_Info. The secret key protocol will also use the exclusive transport session mechanism described in the TPM design principles document [15].

7.5.1.1 Public key protocol

This section describes the public key protocol of Section 7.4.5 in terms of the TPM command set, and assumes the presence of a TPM (in conjunction with a CRTM) bound physically or cryptographically to the mobile host M.

An important feature of the TPM in this implementation of the protocol is the TPM$_\text{CreateWrapKey}$ command. This is used in step 3 of the protocol, to instruct the TPM to generate the asymmetric key pair A_D(public) and A_D(private). The input parameters associated with the TPM$_\text{CreateWrapKey}$ command include information about the key to be created, for example, key length, and authorisation data necessary to access the parent wrapping key. Encrypted authorisation data for the newly generated key pair may also be input if required.

For this particular use case we require that the key to be created is non-migratable. This implies that the key cannot be migrated from the TPM in which it is created.

Alternatively, using a new command described in the TPM version 1.2 specifications, a certifiable migratable key may be created using the TPM$_\text{CMKCreateKey}$ command. This creates a migratable key which may be certified by the TPM and migrated but only under strict controls. This prohibits the key protecting the conditional access application from being migrated to any random platform authorised by the TPM owner but facilitates its migration to select devices, for example, other TPMs owned by the same entity. Before key migration, the key owner must authorise the migration transformation. The migration destination must be authorised not only by the TPM owner but also by a migration selection authority. This authority may be the trusted download agent, A_D, for example. We will focus, however, on the case where the key to be created is non-migratable.

In response to the TPM$_{CreateWrapKey}$ command, the TPM returns a TPM_Key data structure. This data structure contains A_D(public), and the encrypted private key, A_D(private). The data structure also identifies the operations permitted with the key, and contains flags to indicate whether or not the key is migratable. The data structure may also identify the PCRs to which A_D(private) is bound, and may include the PCR digests at key creation and the PCR digests required for key release. The PCR data provides the integrity metrics, I, used in the protocols.

In our particular scenario, S may, for example, require that the returned PCR digest at creation reflects a trusted execution environment which consists of correctly functioning broadcast and download applications running on a particular Trusted Operating System (TOS). The required PCR digest at release could be incorporated into the application, A_D, and then inserted as an input parameter to the TPM$_{CreateWrapKey}$ command by A_D. Verification of the returned PCR digest at creation (reflecting correctly functioning broadcast and download applications running on a particular TOS) would ensure that all protocol steps and the value input as the digest at release by the download application could be trusted to be correct. This value input into the digest at release by A_D should be checked by S before A_C is dispatched.

The PCR digest at release could also reflect a state in which a particular Operating System (OS), a particular video player and a particular download application, are running, but nothing more. The PCR values describe the state of the execution environment at key creation and that required for key release. However, if this data is to be communicated to the challenger, S, proof must exist that the data originated from a genuine TPM and that it has not been replayed. This is discussed below.

The final part of the TPM_Key structure to consider is the TPM_Auth_Data_Usage field. This field may take one of three values: TPM_Auth_Never; TPM_Auth_Always or TPM_Auth_Priv_Use_Only. In our scenario, it is A_D that must access the private key to decipher A_C. The first option is to permit A_D to load the private key without the submission of any authorisation data. In this case the TPM_Auth_Data_Usage field is set to TPM_Auth_Never. Alternatively, the TPM_Auth_Data_Usage field could be set to TPM_Auth_Always or TPM_Auth_Priv_Use_Only, where, on key pair generation, 20 bytes of authorisation data are associated with the public/private key pair, or with just the private decryption key, respectively.

To make use of this feature, before a request for key pair generation, A_D could request that the user provides a password, from which the authorisation data for private key use would be derived. Thus, when access to the private decryption key is required, the correct password would have to be re-entered by the user. This option is acceptable provided that user interaction with A_C is feasible.

Once a key pair has been created using the $\text{TPM}_{\text{CreateWrapKey}}$ command, the handle associated with this key can be given to the TPM in a $\text{TPM}_{\text{CertifyKey}}$ command. One hundred and sixty bits of externally supplied data which, in this protocol, is used to submit a one way hash of R_S, and Id_S may also be given as an input parameter to this command. In response, the TPM returns a TPM_Certify_Info data structure. This structure describes the key that was created, including authorisation data requirements, a digest of the public key and a description of how the PCR data is used. In addition to this structure, the TPM also signs and returns a hash of the public key digest, the 160 bits of external data and the PCR data contained in TPM_Certify_Info, respectively.

Having described the commands and the data structures used, the protocol may be defined as follows:

1. $A_D \rightarrow S$: Request for A_C.
2. $S \rightarrow A_D$: R_S.
3. $A_D \rightarrow$ TPM: $\text{TPM}_{\text{CreateWrapKey}}$.
4. TPM: Generates $A_D(\text{public})$ and $A_D(\text{private})$, where $A_D(\text{private})$ is bound to a specified protected environment state.
5. TPM $\rightarrow A_D$: TPM_Key.
6. $A_D \rightarrow$ TPM: $\text{TPM}_{\text{CertifyKey}}$.
7. TPM $\rightarrow A_D$: TPM_Certify_Info$\|$
    $S_{\text{TPM}}(H(A_D(\text{public}))\|H(R_S\|\text{Id}_S)\|I)$.
8. $A_D \rightarrow S$: $R_S\|\text{Id}_S\|$TPM_Key$\|$TPM_Certify_Info$\|$
    $S_{\text{TPM}}(H(A_D(\text{public}))\|H(R_S\|\text{Id}_S)\|I)$.
9. S: Retrieves Cert_{TPM} and verifies it.
    S: Verifies TPM_Certify_Info and $S_{\text{TPM}}(H(A_D(\text{public})\|H(R_S\|\text{Id}_S)\|I))$.
10. S: Verifies R_S to ensure the message is fresh and verifies that the message was intended for S.
11. S: Decides if I represents a sufficiently trustworthy state.
    Given I, S can verify that the A_D is executing as expected, that it has not been tampered with, and that there is also a legitimate broadcast application executing on the mobile host.
12. Assuming the signature, R_S, Id_S and I are acceptable,
    S: Extracts $A_D(\text{public})$ from TPM_{Key}.
13. S: Generates $K1_{S,A_D}$ used for data encryption.
    S: Generates $K2_{S,A_D}$ used for data integrity protection.
14. $S \rightarrow A_D$: $E_{A_D(\text{public})}(K1_{S,A_D}\|K2_{S,A_D})\|$
    $S_S(E_{A_D(\text{public})}(K1_{S,A_D}\|K2_{S,A_D}))\|E_{K1_{S,A_D}}(\text{MAC}_{K2_{S,A_D}}(A_C))$.
15. A_D: Verifies $S_S(E_{A_D(\text{public})}(K1_{S,A_D},K2_{S,A_D}))$.
16. $A_D \rightarrow$ TPM: Request to load $A_D(\text{private})$.
17. TPM: Decrypts $E_{A_D(\text{public})}(K1_{S,A_D}\|K2_{S,A_D})$.
    Use of the corresponding private key and, therefore, decryption of the shared symmetric keys will only be completed if the platform is in the agreed secure state bound to the wrap key. Authorisation data may also be required depending on the value of the TPM_Auth_Data_Usage field set in step 3.

18. A_D: Decrypts $E_{K1_{S,A_\mathrm{D}}}(\mathrm{MAC}_{K2_{S,A_\mathrm{D}}}(A_\mathrm{C}))$.
19. A_D: Verifies $\mathrm{MAC}_{K2_{S,A_\mathrm{D}}}(A_\mathrm{C})$.
    Once verified the application can be executed.
20. Once A_C is executing, A_D precludes the potential interference of any other application with A_C.
21. A_D: Deletes A_C, and all other keys, when they are no longer required.
    The encrypted copy of A_C may remain stored for future use, space permitting.

7.5.1.2 Secret key protocol

Mapping the secret key protocol defined in Section 7.4.7 onto the TCG platform makes use of several TCG specific commands and features. The first of these is the *exclusive transport session*. An application can request the establishment of an exclusive transport session with the TPM. Once an exclusive transport session has been established, any TPM command made from outside the application will result in that exclusive session being terminated. Any changes to the platform configuration automatically raise a $\mathrm{TPM_{Extend}}$ command to update the PCRs. Therefore, once an exclusive transport session has started, any alteration of the platform state will result in a premature termination of the session, which is detected by the application that established it. This feature is used in step 8 in the following protocol to ensure that the platform state cannot be changed after the agreed keys have been sealed.

The $\mathrm{TPM_{Seal}}$ command is used in step 9 to store the keys $K1_{S,A_\mathrm{D}}$ and $K2_{S,A_\mathrm{D}}$ in protected memory. The parameters taken by this command include the data to be sealed, and the authorisation data necessary to unseal the data. The $\mathrm{TPM_{Seal}}$ command is also given information identifying the PCRs whose value is to be bound to the protected data. In response, the TPM returns a TPM_Stored_Data structure. Specifically, this data structure contains a reference to the PCRs that the data is bound to and a TPM_Sealed_Data structure. The latter contains the encrypted data, and the authorisation requirements to access the data.

For our application we require that the key used in the seal operation is non-migratable. This implies that the private key cannot be migrated from the TPM in which it is created.

Alternatively, using a new command described in the TPM version 1.2 specifications, a certifiable migratable key, created with the $\mathrm{TPM_{CMKCreateKey}}$ command, may be used in the seal operation. This migratable key may be certified by the TPM and migrated, but only under strict controls. This prohibits the sealing key, which essentially protects the conditional access application, from being migrated to any random platform authorised by the TPM owner but facilitates its migration to select devices, for example, other TPMs owned by the same entity. We will focus, however, on the case where the sealing key is non-migratable.

Finally, the $\mathrm{TPM_{Quote}}$ command instructs the TPM to attest to the platform configuration. The parameters given to this command include the indices of the PCRs defining the platform integrity metrics, I. The $\mathrm{TPM_{Quote}}$ command may also be given

160 bits of externally supplied data which, in this protocol, is used to submit a one way hash of b_M, b_S and Id_S for attestation.

Using the above TPM commands, the secret key protocol may be mapped onto the TCG platform as follows:

1. A_D: Chooses a Diffie–Hellman private value a_M and calculates b_M based on g and p which are retrieved from the public key certificate of the software provider, Cert$_S$.
2. $A_D \rightarrow S$: Request application $A_C \| b_M$.
3. S: Chooses a Diffie–Hellman private value a_S and calculates b_S using g and p which are contained in Cert$_S$.
4. $S \rightarrow A_D$: $b_S \| S_S(b_S \| b_M \| Id_M)$.
5. A_D: Verifies the signature on the message received.
6. A_D: Calculates the shared key K_{S,A_D}.
7. A_D: Uses K_{S,A_D} to derive:
   $K1_{S,A_D}$ used for data encryption and
   $K2_{S,A_D}$ used for data integrity protection, by an agreed method.
8. $A_D \rightarrow$ TPM: Request for exclusive transport session.
9. $A_D \rightarrow$ TPM: TPM$_{Seal_I}(K1_{S,A_D} \| K2_{S,A_D})$.
10. TPM: Securely stores $K1_{S,A_D}$ and $K2_{S,A_D}$ using the protected storage mechanism such that $K1_{S,A_D}$, $K2_{S,A_D}$ can only be decrypted when the protected environment is in a specified state.
11. $A_D \rightarrow$ TPM: TPM$_{Quote}(H(b_M \| b_S \| Id_S) \| I)$.
12. TPM $\rightarrow A_D$: $S_{TPM}(H(b_M \| b_S \| Id_S) \| I)$.
13. $A_D \rightarrow S$: $S_{TPM}(H(b_M \| b_S \| Id_S) \| I)$.
14. S: Obtains and verifies Cert$_{TPM}$ and then verifies $S_{TPM}(H(b_S \| b_M \| Id_S) \| I)$.
15. S: Verifies $H(b_M \| b_S \| Id_S)$ to ensure the message is fresh and was destined for S.
16. S: Decides if I represents a sufficiently trustworthy state.
    Given I, S can verify that the A_D is executing as expected, that it has not been tampered with and that there is also a legitimate broadcast application executing on the mobile host. Thus, S can be sure that an exclusive transport session has been set up between A_D and the TPM, and be confident that $K1_{S,A_D}$ and $K2_{S,A_D}$ have been sealed to the PCR data defined by I.
17. S: Calculates K_{S,A_D} and derives $K1_{S,A_D}$ and $K2_{S,A_D}$ by an agreed method.
18. $S \rightarrow A_D$: $E_{K1_{S,A_D}}(MAC_{K2_{S,A_D}}(A_C))$.
19. $A_D \rightarrow$ TPM: Request to unseal $K1_{S,A_D}$ and $K2_{S,A_D}$.
    $K1_{S,A_D}$ and $K2_{S,A_D}$ can only be unsealed if the platform is in the agreed state. Furthermore, authorisation data may also be required depending on the value of the TPM_Auth_Data_Usage field set at step 9.
20. A_D: Decrypts $E_{K1_{S,A_D}}(MAC_{K2_{S,A_D}}(A_C))$.
21. A_D: Verifies $MAC_{K2_{S,A_D}}(A_C)$.
    Once verified the application can be executed.
22. Once A_C is executing, A_D precludes the potential interference of any other application with A_C.

23. A_D: Deletes A_C, and all other keys, when they are no longer required. The encrypted copy of A_C may remain stored for future use, space permitting.

7.5.1.3   Analysis

We next consider how security requirements 6 and 7 from Section 7.3 are met by our TCG-based protocols.

6.   *Confidentiality and integrity protection of the application on the host platform and the prevention of unauthorised access to the application while in storage.* The confidentiality and the integrity of the application while in storage on the mobile platform are protected by the same mechanisms used to protect the application in transit: MACing and symmetric encryption.

In the public key protocol, the MACing and encryption keys are encrypted under a public key, where the corresponding private decryption key is securely stored by the TPM and is non-migratable.

If either the encrypted and MACed application or the encrypted MACing and encryption keys are captured, they will remain privacy protected due to their encryption under the public key. The corresponding private key is stored in the TPM. If, on the other hand, either the encrypted and MACed application or the encrypted MACing and encryption keys are modified, the MAC upon the application will fail.

In order to prevent unauthorised access to this private decryption key, two further measures may be taken. The private decryption key may be bound to a specific execution environment state such that this key may not be loaded until the current environment configuration matches that to which the private key is bound.

In conjunction with this, 20 bytes of authorisation data may be stored with the private decryption key. However, a problem arises regarding where this authorisation data may be stored. It may be securely stored by the TPM, that is, encrypted and bound to a specific execution environment but this offers no additional protection than if the first access control mechanism described above is used in isolation. This is an important issue, but one that is not dealt with in the TCG specifications.

Nevertheless, as an alternative option, it may be relatively straightforward for a *user* to provide the necessary password, during key pair generation, from which authorisation data is derived. This option may be acceptable so long as user interaction with A_D is permitted and there is a secure link between the user entering the password and the TPM.

In the secret key protocol, the MACing and encryption keys are directly encrypted by the TPM and bound to a specific execution environment state (sealed). Twenty bytes of authorisation data may also be associated with the sealed MACing and encryption keys for more stringent control against unauthorised access.

No integrity mechanisms are offered by the TPM-protected storage functionality. However, if the encrypted MACing and encryption keys are modified, the MAC on the application will fail to verify.

7. *Confidentiality and integrity protection of the application code and data during execution.* Throughout the above protocol descriptions we refer to a 'protected execution environment', as we did in the abstract protocols. There are, however, no mechanisms described by the TCG with respect to partitioning the system into trusted and untrusted environments, nor is there mention of trusted operation systems or applications which may exist within these environments.

On the face of it, one could take this to imply that the 'protected execution environment' we speak of in relation to the TCG protocol implementation encompasses the entire platform. Consequently, platform use could therefore become very restricted. A software provider/challenger of a platform may potentially require that only an OS and limited application set may be running on the platform, such that the state can be considered trustworthy for a particular purpose. Alternatively, if platform use is to remain open, a challenger may be faced with the task of verifying a large set of potentially complex integrity metrics, making the process of PCR verification an arduous one.

In reality, however, it would appear that the TCG never intended the security mechanisms they describe to be deployed in isolation. Memory management, for example, represents a vital additional trusted platform component, but its implementation is left open. For our particular scenario, therefore, it is preferable that memory protection is deployed in order to partition the system into trusted and untrusted environments. This facilitates simpler PCR verification and enables the execution of untrusted applications in parallel to, but in isolation from, those running in the trusted environment.

We also require functionality so that the conditional access application running within a 'trusted execution environment' may not be manipulated while executing. In this instance, the protected storage mechanism in conjunction with some application layer controls may be used in order to ensure the executing conditional access application is secure, as follows.

A_C may not be unsealed until the 'protected execution environment' is in a trusted state which has been verified by the challenger. Therefore, it is reasonable to assume that a TOS, in conjunction with few trusted applications, for example, A_B and A_D, are present before A_C executes. A_D then precludes the potential interference of any other application with A_C. Thus, the trusted application A_D will prevent the execution of any malicious application.

In order to ensure the confidentiality and integrity protection of application code and data during execution, we must also consider attacks via direct memory access (DMA). In this instance, bona fide software that may be running, and reflected in the integrity metrics, may be overwritten via DMA. If this occurs, integrity measurements would reflect the original application or OS, but the application or OS loaded via DMA may facilitate a security breach. Virtual memory protection mechanisms, which may be deployed in order to partition the system, may also be circumvented by this means.

It becomes clear that in order to implement the above protocols as securely as possible, the entire system needs to be considered, not merely the trusted foundation upon which that platform is built.

Although the functionality described in the TCG specifications provides a solid starting point to implement the protocols, a more complete architecture detailing the entire trusted platform, from the trusted foundation to the application layer, would be advantageous. This complete architecture may be provided using a combination of additional hardware and/or software built around the TCG standard components. Section 7.5.2 describes a proposed commercially available architecture that may provide these additional features, while Section 7.5.3 describes an alternative open source architecture.

7.5.2 Building the protocols on NGSCB

The NGSCB architecture, described in Chapter 3 aims to provide a high assurance run-time environment for trustworthy applications. The architecture consists of a trusted hardware foundation, which may, for example, take the form of a TPM v1.2; a CRTM; and an isolation kernel to facilitate platform partitioning. This allows a trusted OS and trusted applications to run in isolation, free from being observed or compromised by software running in the standard partitions.

Given that a NGSCB may be based on the trusted foundation, for example, the TPM v1.2, as described by the TCG, it is reasonable to assume that the protocols we are proposing will be executed in a way similar to that described in Section 7.5.1. Based on this assumption, we now analyse the difference that the NGSCB architecture would make to the threats to security of the protocols described in Section 7.5.1.

6. *Confidentiality and integrity protection of the application on the host platform and the prevention of unauthorised access to the application while in storage.* Protected storage is essentially provided through the utilisation of mechanisms offered by the trusted crypto chip upon which the NGSCB platform is built. Currently the only example of such a crypto chip is the TPM v1.2.

   The confidentiality and integrity of the application will be protected on the host platform since it is stored in a MACed and encrypted form.

   As was described in Section 7.5.1.3, the NGSCB architecture will protect the confidentiality protection of the keys, $K1_{S,A_D}$ and $K2_{S,A_D}$, through its protected storage functionality. This allows $K1_{S,A_D}$ and $K2_{S,A_D}$ to be encrypted in such a way that they are only accessible to the protected execution environment when it is in a particular state.

   Additional authorisation data may also required for access. No supplementary mechanisms have been introduced to support the storage of this authorisation data. Also no mechanisms have been introduced to provide explicit integrity protection of sealed MACing and encryption keys in the secret key protocol.

7. *Confidentiality and integrity protection of the application code and data during execution.* The NGSCB architecture facilitates system partitioning through the implementation of an isolation kernel which exposes the hardware to one guest

OS. This offers the advantage that legacy operating systems and applications may remain in use, despite the adoption of trusted computing technologies.

As described above, this system partitioning enables simpler PCR verification, as the number of applications running on a TOS in a particular protected execution environment may be strictly controlled.

With respect to memory partitioning, the NGSCB isolation kernel uses an algorithm called Page Table Edit Control (PTEC) to partition physical memory among guests. This is described in further detail in Chapter 4 but from a security perspective, protection is analogous to that of traditional virtual memory protections such as those that use translation lookaside buffers (TLBs) or page tables.

In order to facilitate efficient implementation of parallel environments, a new CPU mode has been introduced such that the isolation kernel may run in a new ring −1, and guest operating systems can still execute in ring 0. This avoids problems in relation to the virtualisability of particular OS instruction sets which may arise if a Virtual Machine Monitor (VMM) were to be deployed in ring 0.

As described in Section 7.5.1.3, memory protection mechanisms, as described above, offer no protection against an attacker attempting to subvert or bypass the OS kernel via DMA. Such an attack could lead to the execution of malicious code that has not been recorded in the PCRs, as described in Section 7.5.1.3, or alternatively bypass virtual memory protections, described above.

In order to prevent this type of attack, NGSCB have encouraged chipset manufacturers to make changes to the hardware such that an access control policy map may be defined by software (e.g., the isolation kernel) and stored in main memory. This policy map then indicates whether a particular subject (DMA device) should be able to access (read or write to) a particular resource (physical address). The enforcement of this policy map is completed by hardware. Further details of this are available in Chapter 4.

7.5.3   *Implementing trusted download using PERSEUS*

The PERSEUS architecture has focused on the construction of a trusted platform that claims to fulfil the needs of the end-user, and the needs of the content provider [18, 19]. This is accomplished through the integration of the hardware components, as described by the TCG and Microsoft, with an open source security kernel that controls all critical hardware resources. Above the security kernel a conventional OS runs in parallel with security critical applications.

The PERSEUS architecture is described in the literature at a high level, focusing on the description of the PERSEUS architectural components, the security requirements fulfilled by the PERSEUS security kernel and a description of the fundamental kernel elements. Specific instruction sets, data structures and specific system functionality will depend on the underlying hardware utilised.

Therefore, as was the case with the NGSCB architecture, it is reasonable to assume that the hardware foundation deployed within the PERSEUS architecture could consist of components specified by the TCG, together with the chipset extensions described in Chapter 3. Thus, it may be assumed that the protocols of Section 7.4 would be implemented in a way similar to that described in Section 7.5.1.

6. *Confidentiality and integrity protection of the application on the host platform and the prevention of unauthorised access to the application while in storage.* As was the case in Section 7.5.2, the confidentiality and integrity of the application will be protected on the host platform as it is stored in a MACed and encrypted form.

   The confidentiality protection of the keys, $K1_{S,A_D}$ and $K2_{S,A_D}$, will be guaranteed through utilisation of the protected storage mechanism provided by the TCG TPM or the NGSCB crypto chip. This allows for $K1_{S,A_D}$ and $K2_{S,A_D}$ to be encrypted in such a way that they are only accessible to the protected execution environment in a particular state.

   Additional authorisation data may also required for access. No additional mechanisms have been introduced with respect to the storage of this authorisation data. No mechanisms have been introduced in order to provide explicit integrity protection of sealed data.

7. *Confidentiality and integrity protection of the application code and data during execution.* In the PERSEUS architecture, memory protection or partitioning is realised through the deployment of traditional memory management methods. PERSEUS uses virtual address spaces and a memory manager to ensure that one process cannot access a memory page of another process. The fact that each application may run in its own trusted domain offers good protection for applications; however the use of virtual machines to achieve this separation may require unacceptable levels of computational power, particularly for a mobile device.

   As was the case with the NGSCB architecture, the PERSEUS architecture supports legacy OSs, which may run as applications on top of the security kernel. However, problems may arise in relation to the virtualisability of the chosen conventional OS.

   Furthermore, in their architectural proposal [19], Stüble and Sadeghi identify the potential security threat that may be posed by DMA-enabled hardware. If, for example, a malicious process is allowed to control DMA-enabled devices, an untrusted component may gain unauthorised access to application code or data. This would circumvent standard memory protection mechanisms by bypassing any policy enforcing mechanisms.

   The proposed solution is to include all critical code, such as all device drivers, in the Trusted Computing Base (TCB). The inclusion of such device drivers in the base layer (the microkernel) of the PERSEUS system may, however, result in a more closed hardware platform. This solution may be possible for closed mobile devices such as phones or PDAs, but could cause problems with mobile PC platforms where users wish to control the installation of such drivers. This contrasts with the NGSCB architecture where DMA device drivers can be excluded from the TCB without violating safety or restricting the openness of the architecture.

   Instead of this, the authors suggest the integration of chipset extensions as described in the NGSCB architecture as a possible alternative.

7.6 Protocols for secure application download using alternative architectures

The computing platforms described in Section 7.5 allow the mobile host to respond to a challenger with a statement which indicates its software environment. A_C can then be delivered to the platform protected by mechanisms that prevent access to (decryption of) A_C unless the host platform is in the demonstrated state, which has been deemed trustworthy by the challenger. An alternative approach to protecting applications is to use tamper-proof security hardened processors, and to bind the application code cryptographically to the individual processor authorised to execute the code. Thus only the security hardened processor need be trusted. This section describes two recently proposed architectures that are based on this principle, and shows how a trusted download protocol might be implemented on each. These architectures were built with code security, Digital Rights Management (DRM) and the prevention of unauthorised software execution or examination in mind. Therefore, as well as describing how the application is securely stored and executed on the host platform, the method by which the application is securely transmitted from the software provider to the mobile host is also described in both architectures.

7.6.1 Model

The model to which these protocols apply is identical to that described in Section 7.4.1, involving the user, who has a mobile receiver, M; the broadcasters, B and the software providers, S. The fundamental component in this model, the TM, is a physically tamper-proof processor chip modified to facilitate the secure delivery and execution of software.

7.6.2 Assumptions

In describing the protocols, we make the following assumptions with respect to our particular protocol application:

1. In this instance we define the TM as a hardened processor, with the following capabilities: secure storage for a unique private TM key, encryption and decryption functionality, integrity verification, security enhanced registers and caches, and a secure context manager.
2. A unique asymmetric key pair is associated with each hardened processor.
3. The private key is securely stored in the hardened processor.
4. The associated public key is certified. The certifying entity generates a certificate in which the properties of the hardened processor and its identity are associated with the public key.
5. The software provider, S, has a private signing key securely stored.
6. The software provider, S, has a certificate, Cert$_S$ issued by the certification authority, CA. This certificate associates the identity of the S with a public key used for the verification of digital signatures. This certificate must be obtainable by M.

7. Every mobile device wishing to receive video broadcast must have a trusted broadcast application, A_B, running in the protected environment.
8. The TM, in this instance, the hardened processor, facilitates the secure execution of the conditional access application.

7.6.3 Initiation of the protocols

As was the case in Section 7.4.4, our abstract public key protocol begins when the user makes a request to the broadcast application, A_B, to view a specific video broadcast. If reception of this broadcast is controlled by a particular conditional access application, A_C, then A_B carries out the following steps:

1. A_B checks to see if the mobile device already has dedicated hardware or software installed to support A_C.
2. If no dedicated hardware exists on the mobile device, for example, a common interface module, then A_B determines whether A_C has previously been downloaded and is still available in secure storage. If so, the download application, A_D, is called to retrieve A_C from secure storage and execute the application.
3. If A_C is not available on the mobile device, then A_D is called to download the application.
4. The download of A_C will be accomplished by deploying the protocol specified in Section 7.6.4.

7.6.4 Alternative protocol

The alternative technologies examined both utilise a secure download protocol which takes the following form:

1. $A_D \rightarrow S$: Request for $A_C \|$ Claimed ID of hardened processor.
2. In the case of XOM: $S \rightarrow A_D$:
   $E_{TM(Public)}$(Symmetric key, k)$\|E_k(A_C)$.
   In the case of AEGIS: $S \rightarrow A_D$:
   $E_{TM(Public)}$(Symmetric key, $k \| h(A_C))\|E_k(A_C)$.
3. If the data bundle received in step 2 can be verified by the TM, in this instance the security hardened processor, A_C is executed in a manner which ensures its integrity and confidentiality. Technology-specific mechanisms used to ensure the security of A_C while executing are examined below.

7.7 Mapping the alternative protocol to specific hardware architectures

7.7.1 The XOM architecture

The Executable Only Memory (XOM) architecture proposed by Lie *et al.* [8,20] attempts to fulfil two fundamental objectives: the prevention of the unauthorised execution of software; and the prevention of any software customer from examining protected executable code. These aims are achieved through the process of marking code to be protected with an 'executable only' tag. Such 'execute only' code is stored in encrypted form and can only be deciphered by a specific XOM processor chip. This prevents any user from examining the actual instructions or anyone other than the specified XOM processor chip from decrypting and gaining access to the code.

In a full XOM machine, the protected execution of 'XOM code' is fully implemented, including support for code interrupts, and external untrusted memory is used for the storage of trusted data.

Lie *et al.* describe two possible XOM architecture implementations, one using a Virtual Memory Machine (VMM) running on a slightly modified CPU and the second using hardware alone. Due to the performance implications associated with the XOM VMM (XVMM) implementation, we will focus our attention and analysis on the hardware implementation. A full description of the XOM abstract machine and an examination of both the XVMM and hardware implementations is given in Chapter 3.

7.7.2   Application of XOM to trusted download

Using the XOM architecture, the protocol begins when A_D requests to download the application, A_C. In conjunction with this request, the claimed identity of the hardened processor upon which A_D is executing is also sent to the software provider.

S chooses a symmetric compartment key. XOM compartments serve to isolate programs from each other on the XOM machine, preventing the unauthorised flow of information between them. S is then able to encrypt this symmetric compartment key under the public encryption key of the XOM processor. Therefore, the compartment key, and consequently A_C, cannot be accessed by any entity other than the intended recipient (the XOM processor with the claimed ID from the request message). The following bundle is representative of the message returned by the software provider:

$$E_{\text{XOMChip(Public)}}(k) \parallel E_k(A_C)$$

where k is the XOM symmetric compartment key.

It is assumed that this XOM encrypted code bundle received by M is preceeded by the enter_xom instruction, where the source address holds the starting memory address of the encrypted symmetric compartment key, $E_{\text{XOMChip(Public)}}(k)$, for the XOM code.

Execution of the enter_xom instruction causes the XOM machine to check whether the symmetric compartment key has been decrypted on a previous occasion by comparing a 128-bit $H(E_{\text{XOMChip(Public)}}(k))$ with the hashes of all decrypted symmetric compartment keys securely stored in an XOM key table.

If no match is found, an XOM key table entry is allocated to the XOM application. An XOM identifier (XOM ID) is assigned to the execute only code. The symmetric compartment key is decrypted and stored with the XOM ID. In conjunction with this, a mutating register key is associated with the XOM ID and used in the protection of register values on interrupts and context switches. In order to prevent replay of registers, this key is updated every time the XOM process is interrupted.

During the execution of the protected application, A_C, there are a number of other commands that may be used to ensure the integrity and confidentiality of the application while executing [20]. A full description of these instructions is given in Chapter 3.

7.7.3   Analysis of XOM trusted download

We now assess the XOM trusted download process performs against the security service requirements specified in Section 7.3.

1. *Confidentiality of the application while in transit.* As stated above, the bundle sent from the software provider to the mobile host is:

    $$E_{\text{XOMChip(Public)}}(k) \parallel E_k(A_C)$$

    By encrypting A_C under a symmetric compartment key, k, which is then in turn encrypted under the public encryption key of a specific 'hardened' tamper-proof XOM processor the software provider protects the confidentiality of A_C while in transit, as only the intended processor can access the static key and therefore the application.

    In their description of the XOM architecture, the authors fail to mention the certification/accreditation infrastructure that must be assumed in order to support the secure use of public key pairs as described above. As was the case with the TCG architecture, if XOM processors were to be deployed, these hardened processors would need to be tested and checked as to their conformance with the definition of a 'hardened processor'. The public encryption key would then have to be associated with a statement regarding the trustworthiness/security of the processor's ability to fulfil specific tasks.

    Assuming the presence of a certificaiton/accreditation infrastructure, the encryption of the static compartment key used to encrypt A_C under the public encryption key of the destination XOM processor provides for the confidentiality of the static key and thus A_C.

2. *Integrity protection of the application while in transit.* According to Reference 8, no mechanisms are deployed to protect the integrity of A_C during its transmission from the software provider to the mobile host. The software distribution model described in the more recent thesis of Lie [20], does not explicitly mention integrity protection either. Such mechanisms are, however, implied by the enter_xom instruction definition, where the author states that the enter_xom instruction must always be followed by an encrypted and MACed application. No mention is made as to how the MAC key is derived. This issue should not be overlooked.

    For our application, it is vital that the integrity of A_C is protected during transmission. We therefore require that, before the application is encrypted under the symmetric compartment key, it is MACed using an independent MACing key. This key must also be communicated to the mobile host encrypted under

$E_{\text{XOMChip(Public)}}$ as follows:

$$E_{\text{XOMChip(Public)}}(k \,\|m)\|E_k(\text{MAC}_m(A_C))$$

where k is the symmetric compartment key, and m is the MAC key.

Once again, this mechanism is only useful if a full certification/accreditation infrastructure is in existence, so that the software provider can be sure that only the intended bone fide XOM processor can access the application.

3. *Entity authentication.* Neither authentication of the XOM processor by the software provider nor the software provider by the XOM processor is facilitated by the XOM download protocol. In order to do this, modifications would have to be made to the XOM download protocol such that either unilateral or mutual authentication protocol passes could be included in the protocol outlined above.

4. *Origin authentication.* In the defined XOM protocol, the origin of A_C cannot be authenticated. In order to make their proposed software distribution model more secure, the software provider should be required to sign the encrypted symmetric compartment key used to encrypt A_C before its transmission. Preferably, an encrypted MACing key used to protect the application's integrity would be signed in conjunction with the encrypted symmetric compartment key used for encrypting the application, as follows:

$$S_S(E_{\text{XOMChip(Public)}}(k\|m))\|E_k(\text{MAC}_m(A_C))$$

In this scenario, it would also be required that this software provider's signature be verified before the application is executed.

5. *Freshness.* The freshness of the application received from the software provider cannot be verified. Assuming we include the signature of the software provider on keys protecting A_C, it may initially appear that if the protected A_C is now replayed the host only learns something he already knows. However, instead of being sent the new application he requested, an old version application may be replayed by an adversary, and accepted by the mobile host. By concatenating a timestamp with the application before it is encrypted, this attack may be prevented.

6. *Confidentiality and integrity protection of the application on the host platform.* By encrypting A_C under a symmetric compartment key, k, the software provider protects its confidentiality. This symmetric key is also protected using the public encryption key of a specific hardened XOM processor, such that only the intended processor can access to the compartment key and therefore the application.

With respect to integrity, issues discussed with respect to the integrity protection of the application while in transit also apply here.

Prevention of unauthorised access to the application while in storage: Through the encryption of the static key under the public encryption key of a particular hardened XOM processor, it can be ensured that A_C will only be decrypted by the instruction loading path on a specific main processor XOM chip.

7. *Confidentiality and integrity protection of the application code and data during execution.* In order to ensure the protected execution of A_C, various security mechanisms are implemented on the XOM hardened processor. Full details of XOM mechanisms are available in Chapter 3.

On-chip caches. While 'execute only' code and data is held in the on-chip caches, XOM ownership tags are associated with cache lines and are used to prevent unauthorised access. By virtue of the fact that on-chip caches are embedded within a tamper-resistant chip, they are also secure from physical attack.

On-chip registers. Registers are also tagged with register ownership tags, such that unauthorised access by malicious software (OSs) may be prevented. By virtue of the fact that on-chip registers are embedded within a tamper-resistant chip, they are also secure from physical attack.

Context switching and interrupt support. Secure interrupts and context switching may be supported via the additional instructions introduced for securely storing and restoring register values. When an interrupt occurs, the register content for a protected program is still in the registers. Thus the tags, as mentioned above, can be used to prevent an untrusted and potentially malicious OS from reading the register values. The OS may then issue an instruction which causes register values to be MACed, encrypted and cleared. Register contents are protected using the current mutating register key associated with the active XOM ID in the XOM key table. This allows an OS to schedule and interrupt XOM processes without violating the security of the XOM application.

A mutating register key is used in order to prevent the replay of register values on interrupts and context switches. If a static register key were used, an adversarial OS could first interrupt a running process and save the register state. The adversarial OS could then restore the process state and restart the process. At a later time, the adversarial OS could interrupt the process again, but instead of restoring the register values from the second interruption, restore the values from the first interruption. When the process restarts, it will be using the replayed register values [20].

To counteract this, the key, labelled the register key, is regenerated every time a particular XOM compartment is interrupted. Therefore, the register key used to protect the register values on the first interrupt will no longer be valid when a register value is being restored after a second interrupt. Trying to restore a replayed state value will therefore result in an exception.

External memory. Application data, when pushed from caches and registers into external off-chip memory, must also be protected. In order to achieve this application data is MACed and encrypted under the symmetric compartment key associated with the active XOM application identity in the XOM key table before it is exported.

An attacker may, however, try to replay data securely stored in external memory. To accomplish this, the attacker waits for the OS to record MACed and encrypted data to memory, and then overwrites the same location at a later time with the old MACed and encrypted data.

To defend against this attack, a hash of the region of memory is made and stored in a secure register. To replay the specified region in memory, the hash in the register must also be replayed, but as a result of the anti-replay mechanism for the protection of register values described above, this memory replay attack can be defeated. The overhead associated with this mechanism may become excessive if the region of memory is large, or if the values in the region change frequently. If, however, hash trees or Merkle trees are deployed for memory authentication, see, for example, Reference 20, the performance impact may be lessened to a degree.

A hash tree is a hierarchical hash structure that allows for the efficient update of a hash value. In this particular instance the lowest level in the tree is composed of segments of memory. On the next level, each node will contain a hash of child values and so on until the secure root is reached. All that is required is that this secure root is integrity-protected.

Lie [20] decided that the most secure, but far from the most efficient, implementation of hash trees was to calculate the hash function every time a user writes to cache and to verify the hash every time a value is read into the cache, from memory and before a new hash is calculated.

In their architecture, Lie *et al.* [8] focus primarily on the protection of code while executing. In order to strengthen their protocol, we emphasise the importance of a certification/accredition infrastructure as reflected in our assumptions: the certifying entity generates a certificate in which the properties of the hardened processor and its identity are associated with the public encryption key.

We also assume that the software provider, S, has a private signing key securely stored, and that the software provider, S, has a certificate, $Cert_S$ issued by the Certification Authority, CA, where this certificate associates the identity of the S with a public key value for the verification of digital signatures and is obtainable by M. This allows us to suggest the addition of software provider signatures on encrypted symmetric keys protecting A_C before they are sent, so that the origin of A_C can be verified.

This software provider signature key pair may also be utilised in the construction of a unilateral authentication protocol such that the mobile receiver could authenticate the software provider. Further modifications to the architecture and protocol are necessary if mutual authentication is required.

In the analysis above, we also suggest the addition of freshness indicators, and raise the security concerns relating to the re-use of the same public key pair for all transactions.

More specifically it would be helpful if it could be made clear whether incoming XOM code is just encrypted or both MACed and encrypted. Current papers [8] and the thesis of Lie [20] are ambiguous.

Use of separate MACing and encryption keys is also advisable.

7.7.4   The AEGIS architecture

The architecture for a single chip AEGIS processor bears a strong resemblance to the XOM architecture described above.

> AEGIS provides users with tamper-evident authenticated environments in which any phys-
> ical or software tampering by an adversary is guaranteed to be detected, and private and
> authenticated tamper-resistant (PTR) environments where additionally the adversary is
> unable to obtain any information about software and data by tampering with, or otherwise
> observing, system operation [9].

In the context of the protection of the conditional access application, our interest is focused on the construction of a PTR environment, as it is required that the conditional access application received by and executed on the mobile host is protected from threats to both its integrity and privacy. To implement such an architecture, the mobile device will require a single AEGIS processor chip which is protected from both software and hardware violations.

As was the case with XOM, the key architectural mechanisms include memory integrity verification; encryption/decryption of off-chip (external) memory; and secure context switching and interrupts.

Two possible implementations of the AEGIS architecture are explored by Suh *et al.* [9]. The first secure computing model assumes a hardened AEGIS processor and an untrusted OS, whereas the alternate model assumes a hardened AEGIS processor and a security kernel which runs at a higher privilege level than the regular OS. The fundamental hardware extensions necessary to support this architecture all relate to the processor chip. A hardened AEGIS processor should provide secure tamper-sensing storage of secret information, for example, a secret key or a physical random function. It should provide secure registers and caches and have a hardware encryption engine. Furthermore, it should have a hardware integrity verification mechanism and a Secure Context Manager (SCM), where a private master key may be held in secure storage for use in encrypting data from the SCM table when it is moved off-chip. While on-chip, the SCM table is stored in a special on-chip cache. In the scenario where the TCB contains a security kernel, the security kernel may supply the context management.

7.7.5   Application of AEGIS to trusted download

As described in Section 7.6.4, a request for A_C is initially sent from A_D to the software provider. In return, the software provider sends a bundle resembling one of the following, either:

$$E_{\text{AEGIS(public)}}(H(\text{program})\,\|\,(k))\,\|\,E_K(\text{program});\ \text{or}$$

$$E_{\text{AEGIS(public)}}(H(\text{securitykernel})\,\|\,H(\text{program})\,\|\,(k))\,\|\,E_K(\text{program}).$$

where k is a static key.

In our particular scenario, the $H(\text{program})$ will be the hash of a correctly func-tioning conditional access application. The software provider would therefore send:

$$E_{\text{AEGIS(public)}}(H(A_{\text{C}})\|(k))\|E_K(A_{\text{C}}); \text{ or}$$

$$E_{\text{AEGIS(public)}}(H(\text{securitykernel})\|H(A_{\text{C}})\|(k))\|E_K(A_{\text{C}}).$$

When this is received by A_{D}, the encrypted bundle is passed to the processor.

$(H(A_{\text{C}})\|(k))$ can only be recovered using the hardened processor's secret decryp-tion key if it has been received by the intended AEGIS processor. In the case of

$$E_{\text{AEGIS(public)}}(H(\text{securitykernel})\|H(A_{\text{C}})\|(k))\|E_K(A_{\text{C}}).$$

$(H(A_{\text{C}})\|(k))$ can only be recovered using the hardened processor's secret decryp-tion key if it has been received by the intended AEGIS processor and if the identity of the security kernel running on the device matches the security kernel hash sent by the software provider.

The static key is then used to decrypt $E_K(A_{\text{C}})$. When decrypted, the hash of A_{C} is calculated, and if and only if this generated hash matches $H(A_{\text{C}})$, the static key is assigned to the A_{C}. This process is facilitated by two AEGIS instructions which are integrated into the protected application, enter_aegis, used to start the execution in a Tamper-Evident (TE) environment and set_aegis_mode, used to enable a Private, Tamper-Resistant (PTR) environment from a TE mode.

During this process, a dynamic register key, described below, is also set for A_{C} such that data generated during the program's execution can be encrypted and decrypted. A_{C} can then be executed in a PTR environment.

7.7.6   Analysis of AEGIS trusted download

We now assess the AEGIS trusted download process against the security service requirements specified in Section 7.3.

7.7.6.1   Confidentiality of the application while in transit

As stated above, the bundle sent from the software provider to the mobile host can be represented by either:

$$E_{\text{AEGIS(public)}}(H(\text{program})\|(k))\|E_K(A_{\text{C}}); \text{ or}$$

$$E_{\text{AEGIS(public)}}(H(\text{securitykernel})\|H(\text{program})\|(k))\|E_K(A_{\text{C}})$$

By encrypting A_{C} under a static symmetric key, k, which in turn is protected using the public encryption key of a specific hardened processor, the software provider guarantees that only the intended processor can gain access to the static key and therefore the application, thereby ensuring its confidentiality while in transit. If the mobile host TCB is composed of a security kernel in addition to the AEGIS chip, its identity may also be included in the encrypted bundle. In this instance, the static key is only decrypted and output when the processor contains the corresponding private decryption key and the identity of the security kernel matches that sent by the software provider.

In their description of the AEGIS architecture, the authors fail to identify the certification/accreditation infrastructure that must be assumed in order to support the secure use of public keys as described above. As was the case with the TCG architecture, if AEGIS processors were to be deployed, these hardened processors would need to be tested and their conformance with the definition of a 'hardened AEGIS processor' checked. The public encryption key would then have to be associated with a statement regarding the trustworthiness/security of the processor to fulfil a specific task, for example, to facilitate the execution of an application in TE or PTR environments. Without this, the software provider cannot prove that his code is only going to be decrypted by a specific hardened AEGIS processor and not someone feigning the identity of an AEGIS processor. This could lead to a violation of the application confidentiality.

Assuming the presence of a certificaiton/accreditation infrastructure, however, the encryption of static application key under the public encryption of the destination AEGIS processor, may provide confidentiality for A_C.

7.7.6.2 Integrity protection of the application while in transit

The integrity of A_C is also protected while in transit. A hash of A_C is encrypted under the public key of the hardened AEGIS processor embedded in the mobile host. When the encrypted bundle is received, the hash of the decrypted application is compared against the hash value received from the software provider. Any discrepancy found indicates that the application may have been maliciously or accidently corrupted in transit.

Once again this mechanism is only useful if a full certification/accreditation infrastructure is in existence such that the software provider can be sure that only the intended bona fide AEGIS processor can gain access to the application.

7.7.6.3 Entity authentication

Neither authentication of the AEGIS processor by the software provider nor the software provider by the AEGIS processor is provided by the AEGIS download protocol. In order to facilitate this, modifications would have to be made to the AEGIS download protocol such that either unilateral or mutual authentication protocol passes could be integrated into the protocol outlined above.

7.7.6.4 Origin authentication

In the defined AEGIS protocol the origin of A_C cannot be authenticated. In order to make their proposed software distribution model more secure, the software provider should be required to sign the encrypted symmetric static key and $H(A_C)$ before its transmission.

In this scenario, it would also be required that this software provider's signature be verified before the application is executed.

7.7.6.5   Freshness

The freshness of the application received from the software provider cannot be verified. Assuming we include the signature of the software provider on the encrypted A_C and $H(A_C)$, it may initially appear that if A_C is replayed the host only learns something he or she already knows. However, instead of being sent the new application he or she requested, an old version of the application may be replayed by an adversary and accepted by the mobile host. By concatenating a timestamp with the application before it is encrypted, this attack may be prevented.

7.7.6.6   Confidentiality and integrity protection of the application on the host platform

By encrypting A_C under a static symmetric key, k, which in turn is protected using the public encryption key of a specific hardened processor, the software provider guarantees that only the intended processor can gain access to the static key and therefore the application. If the mobile host architecture is composed of a trusted kernel, its identity may also be included in the encrypted bundle. In this instance the static key is only decrypted and output as long as the processor contains the corresponding public decryption key and the identity of the security kernel matches that sent by the software provider. If at any stage the encrypted application is tampered with while in storage in external memory, the discrepancy between the application hash and the hash included in the encrypted bundle, which is calculated and compared before the program executes, will lead to its detection.

7.7.6.7   Prevention of unauthorised access to the application while in storage

Through the encryption of the static key, under the public encryption key of a particular hardened AEGIS processor, it can be ensured that only this processor can decrypt and execute A_C. If there is a security kernel running on the machine, its identity (hash) may also be encrypted alongside the static key such that the static key is only decrypted and output as long as the processor contains the corresponding public decryption key and the identity of the security kernel matches that sent by the software provider.

7.7.6.8   Confidentiality and integrity protection of the application code and data during execution

As described in Section 7.7.4, two implementations are explored by Suh *et al.* [9]. The first secure computing model assumes a hardened AEGIS processor and an untrusted OS, whereas the alternate model assumes a hardened AEGIS processor and a security kernel which runs at a higher privilege level than the regular OS. In our analysis of this particular service, we refer to the TCB, which may consist of the processor chip and optionally part of the OS.

When considering the confidentiality and integrity protection of the application code and data during execution, the main issues discussed: include process start-up; the protection of on-chip caches and registers; the protection of register state of the program on interrupts and the protection of off-chip memory (RAM).

Process start-up
The initial instruction, *enter_aegis*, is used to enter a Tamper Evident (TE) mode. The stub region specified by this instruction guarantees that the initial state of program is properly set-up. Either the AEGIS processor, or the security kernel, takes a hash of the program after it has been decrypted, such that this hash can be compared to the hash sent by the software provider. As before, either the AEGIS processor, or the security kernel, checks any other code or data the application relies on. This stub code must also check the environment it is running in, that is, whether its mode is TE or PTR; the position of the stack; and the virtual address of the stub code, for example.

On-chip caches
In terms of physical or hardware attacks, it is assumed by Suh *et al.* [9] that an adversary cannot physically tamper with on-chip caches. With respect to a faulty or malicious software, the protection of on-chip caches is provided using tags. Whenever a process accesses a cache block, the block is tagged with the identity of that process. On future accesses the identity of the active process is compared to the identity the cache block has been tagged with, and access is only granted if a match is found. In the case of a PTR environment, access is only granted if the active ID matches the cache tag and the active process is in PTR mode.

On-chip registers
In the PTR environment, all registers are considered private and protected. In the AEGIS architecture, it is the processor which saves/clears the registers on an interrupt and restores them on a resume. Therefore, there is no need to tag registers as untrusted and potentially malicious OSs will not have access to register values even following an interrupt or when context switching.

Context switching and interrupt support
In order to support context switching and interrupts, register values are securely saved to the TCB by the processor. In the case of a PTR environment values are additionally flushed from the registers before a potentially untrusted interrupt handler starts, in order to protect the integrity and confidentiality of register values.

Externally stored memory values
Both hardware and software attacks on off-chip memory must also be considered. Confidentiality of cache data is protected via the symmetric encryption of cache blocks before their eviction. Off-chip memory integrity protection mechanisms are also implemented between the L2 cache and the encryption engine, and involve the implementation of hash trees.

In their paper, Suh *et al.* [9] criticise the XOM scheme [8] for focusing primarily on the replay of registers and failing to recognise the potential for replay of data in memory. This criticism, however, appears to be unjustified. While Lie *et al.* do not explicitly detail their chosen method to prevent the replay of data in memory, it is briefly mentioned in Reference 8 and thoroughly explored in the Ph.D. thesis of David Lie [20].

In the AEGIS architecture, integrity is protected using hash trees or Merkle trees, which 'are often used to verify the integrity of dynamic data in untrusted storage' [9]. The process deployed to check the integrity of a tree node and update a node is defined as follows.

The process begins by checking the integrity of the node to be updated: the node and its siblings are read from memory and their data concatenated together: a hash of the concatenated data is calculated and checked to verify that the resultant hash matches the parent hash. The node is then modified and the parent hash is then updated to be the hash of the concatenation of the node and its siblings [9]. Since the integrity of the old node is checked before an update can occur, this process prevents the replay of external memory.

As with the XOM architecture Suh *et al.* [9] focus primarily on the protection of code while executing. In order to strengthen their protocol, we emphasise the importance of a certification/accredition infrastructure as reflected in our assumptions: the certifying entity generates a certificate in which the properties of the hardened processor and its identity are associated with the public encryption key.

We also assume that the software provider, S, has a private signing key securely stored and that the software provider, S, has a certificate, $Cert_S$ issued by the Certification Authority, CA, where this certificate associates the identity of the S with a public key value for the verification of digital signatures and is obtainable by M. This allows us to suggest the addition of software provider signatures on the encrypted keys protecting A_C before it is sent so that the origin of A_C can be authenticated.

This software provider's signature key pair may also be utilised in the construction of a unilateral authentication protocol such that the mobile receiver could authenticate the software provider. Further modifications to the architecture and protocol are necessary if mutual authentication is required.

In the analysis above, we also suggest the addition of freshness indicators and raise security concerns relating to the re-use of the same public key pair for all transactions.

In a more recent report by Suh *et al.* [21], which is awaiting publication, they examine the use of Physical Unclonable Functions (PUFs) rather than asymmetric key pairs in order to identify and securely communicate with AEGIS processors. Use of these functions may tackle the security issues associated with the overuse of a single asymmetric key pair.

7.8   Conclusions

The objective of the work described in this chapter was to provide mechanisms for the secure download and execution of security-sensitive applications to mobile devices. Through the careful development of two fundamental secure download protocols, we have met our first major objective in ensuring that the confidentiality and integrity of the application is protected as it is transported from the software provider to the host platform. Our second objective, ensuring the confidentiality and integrity protection of the application on reaching and while executing on the host platform, was also met, by the application of various trusted computing and related technologies.

Through the incorporation of protocol enhancements suggested in Sections 7.7.3 and 7.7.6, the hardware implementations of the XOM and AEGIS architectures could meet our requirements regarding the secure download of the application. These architectures also protect the confidentiality and integrity of the application while executing on the platform against both software and physical (DMA) attacks. This level of protection, however, requires significant hardware modifications and additions to be made to the traditional platform architecture.

While the 'security kernel implementation' of AEGIS also demands CPU modifications, the utilisation of a security kernel for the provision of some of the necessary security services reduces the extent of the hardware modifications required. Through the addition of secure boot functionality and security services loosely-coupled with the sealing and platform attestation mechanisms, as described in Chapter 3, the boundaries of trust may be moved from the trusted hardware core to encompass the security kernel running on the AEGIS hardware. This will have the effect of decreasing the necessary hardware modifications. In order to facilitate this, however, roots of trust similar to those described in the TCG specifications are required.

The trusted computing technologies, described in Section 7.5, meet the majority of our requirements, with minimal modifications to the traditional platform architecture. The TPM chip has become the most common (although by no means the sole) method of implementing the TCG TPM specifications. This stand alone hardware TPM implementation is low-cost and easy to integrate.

Prevention of physical attack (DMA attack) on the code, however, requires additional hardware modifications, such as chipset extensions and CPU enhancements to be made to the platform, as described in Chapter 3 under Intel's LaGrande initiative [22].

Thus, by the adoption of the concept of 'roots of trust' as described in Chapter 3, in conjunction with an AEGIS hardened processor, the 'security kernel implementation' of the AEGIS architecture may meet all of our requirements including protection against DMA. Alternatively, through the adoption of a trusted platform which has some additional hardware extensions as described in Reference 22 a trusted platform would meet all of our requirements including protection against DMA attacks.

Essentially, both implementations require, at a minimum, CPU extensions and trusted roots functionality, to be integrated into the existing platform architecture in order to facilitate the secure download and execution of security-sensitive code.

From a pragmatic view point, the trusted platform technologies discussed at length in Chapter 3 and utilised in protocol implementation and the CPU extensions developed to support these trusted platform technologies are the result of large industry initiatives and a public standardisation process, thereby making their deployment more viable.

Acknowledgement

The work reported in this chapter has formed part of the Core 3 Research Programme of the Virtual Centre of Excellence in Mobile and Personal Communications, Mobile VCE, www.mobilevce.com, whose funding support, including that of EPSRC, is gratefully acknowledged. Fully detailed technical reports on this research are available to Industrial Members of Mobile VCE.

References

1 D. J. Cutts. DVB conditional access. *IEE Electronics and Communications Engineering Journal*, 9(1):21–27, 1997.

2 ETSI. Digital video broadcasting (DVB); head-end implementation of DVB simulcrypt. ETSI Standard TS 103 197 V1.3.1, European Telecommunications Standards Institute (ETSI), Sophia Antipolis, France, January 2003.

3 CENELEC. Common Interface Specification for Conditional Access and other Digital Video Broadcasting Decoder Applications. CENELEC Standard 50221, European Committee for Electrotechnical Standardization (CENELEC), Brussels, Belgium, February 1997.

4 ETSI. Digital video broadcasting (DVB); support for use of scrambling and conditional access (CA) within digital broadcasting systems. ETSI Technical Report ETR 289, European Telecommunications Standards Institute (ETSI), Sophia Antipolis, France, October 1996.

5 A. Menezes, P. van Oorschot, and S. Vanstone. *Handbook of Applied Cryptography, volume 6 of Discrete Mathematics and its Applications*. CRC Press, Boca Raton, Fl, 1997.

6 W. Stallings. *Cryptography and Network Security, Principles and Practices,* 2nd edn. Prentice Hall, Upper Saddle River, NJ, 1999.

7 B. Balacheff, L. Chen, S. Pearson, D. Plaquin, and G. Proudler. *Trusted Computing Platforms: TCPA Technology in Context*. Prentice Hall, PTR, New York, 2003.

8 D. Lie, C. Thekkath, M. Mitchell, P. Lincoln, D. Boneh, J. Mitchell, and M. Horowitz. Architectural support for copy and tamper resistant software. In *Proceedings of the 9th International Conference on Architectural Support for Programming Languages and Operating Systems (ASPLOS-IX)*, pp. 169–177. ACM Press, New York, November 2000.

9 G. E. Suh, D. Clarke, B. Gassend, M. van Dyke, and S. Devadas. The AEGIS processor architecture for tamper–evident and tamper-resistant processing. In *Proceedings of the 17th Annual ACM International Conference on Supercomputing (ICS'03)*, pp. 160 – 171. ACM Press, San Francisco, June 2003.

10 Microsoft. Hardware platform for the next-generation secure computing base. Windows platform design notes, Microsoft Corporation, 2003.

11 Microsoft. NGSCB: trusted computing base and software authentication. Windows platform design notes, Microsoft Corporation, 2003.

12 Microsoft. Security model for the next-generation secure computing base. Windows platform design notes, Microsoft Corporation, 2003.

13 ISO/IEC. Information Technology – Security Techniques – Entity Authentication – Part 3: Mechanisms using Digital Signature Techniques. ISO/IEC Standard 9798-3, International Organisation for Standardisation, Geneva, Switzerland, 1998.

14 A. W. Dent and C. J. Mitchell. *User's Guide to Cryptography and Standards*. Artech House, Boston, MA, 2005.

15 TCG. TPM Main, Part 1 design principles. TCG specification version 1.2 Revision 62, The Trusted Computing Group, Portland, OR, USA, October 2003.

16 TCG. TPM Main, Part 2 TPM data structures. TCG specification version 1.2 Revision 62, The Trusted Computing Group, Portland, OR, USA, October 2003.

17 TCG. TPM Main, Part 3 Commands. TCG specification version 1.2 Revision 62, The Trusted Computing Group, Portland, OR, USA, October 2003.

18 B. Pfitzmann, J. Riordan, C. Stuble, M. Waidner, and A. Weber. The PERSEUS system architecture. Technical Report RZ 3335 (#93381), IBM, IBM Research Division, Zurich Laboratory, April 2001.

19 A.-R. Sadeghi and C. Stuble. Taming 'trusted platforms' by operating system design. In K. Chae and M. Yung, eds, *Proceedings of the 4th International Workshop. Information Security Applications, (WISA 2003), volume 2908 of Lecture Notes in Computer Science.* Springer-Verlag, Berlin, Germany, August 2003.

20 D. Lie. *Architectural Support for Copy and Tamper Resistant Software.* Ph.D. thesis, Department of Electrical Engineering, Stanford University, December 2003.

21 G. E. Suh, C. W. O'Donnell, I. Sachdev, and S. Devadas. Design and implementation of a single-chip secure processor using physical random functions. In *Proceedings of the 34th Annual International Symposium on Computer Architecture (ISCA),* June 2005.

22 Intel. LaGrande technology architectural overview. Technical Report 252491-001, Intel Corporation, September 2003.

Chapter 8

Enhancing user privacy using trusted computing

Anand S. Gajparia and Chris J. Mitchell

8.1 Introduction

User Location Information (LI) has the potential to be the basis of many different services, ranging from route planning to user location in emergency situations. Such services are frequently associated with, but are not limited to, mobile devices. Fixed devices, such as desktop PCs, may also be used to receive such services. As these services become widely available, privacy concerns will also become more significant. Of course, user location is not the only personal attribute which may cause privacy concerns. Medical information and personal bank details are amongst the many other types of personal details a user may not wish to publicise.

In previous work [1], a trusted party, referred to as a Location Information Preference Authority (LIPA), was introduced to help protect the privacy of LI. Here LI simply means any data that may be used to help determine the current or recent location of a subject. A simple model for LI protection was introduced, where LI was distributed within the scope of an LI token. This LI token has the property that only the LIPA entity is able to view the information held within it. Along with the LI, constraints are also included in the LI token. Constraints are simply statements which limit the use, distribution and storage of LI. This is discussed further in Reference 2. In our simple model, a Location-Based Service (LBS) provider wishing to use LI may only view it by making requests to the LIPA. The LIPA makes a decision whether or not to send LI based on the constraints in the LI token. If permitted, the LI will be sent to the requesting LBS provider. The problem remains that a dishonest LBS provider may either use the LI in unauthorised ways or may redistribute it to other

The research presented in this chapter has been supported by sponsorship from Toshiba Telecommunications Research Laboratory, UK.

Service Providers (SPs). Whilst this problem is clearly a very difficult one to deal with, in this chapter we consider ways in which trusted computing facilities might be used to help address it. Rather than look at LI specifically, we look more generally at Personal Information (PI).

First note that SPs will almost inevitably be using a specific application running on one or more servers to manage and use PI. Verifying the integrity and provenance of this application software, as well as of the platform on which the application is running, will potentially give the user additional assurance that their data is managed in the proper manner.

In this chapter we explore how, using the mechanisms found within the Trusted Computing Group (TCG) specifications [3–5], a device wishing to send private data to another device can reliably discover the software state at the destination device. This can then be used to help decide whether or not the data should be sent. Further to this we discuss how an entity is able to ensure that only software which is implicitly trusted by the sending entity is able to use this private data. Finally we show how our LIPA model may be extended to use these mechanisms to enhance the privacy of LI.

8.2   Trusted computing

Physical access to a machine will typically allow the software integrity of that machine to be compromised. If a (secure) computer digitally signs a message, then trust in the message depends on trust in both the computer software that computed the signature, and the physical security of the underlying hardware (and in the correct application of security procedures by administrators). This makes sense in a conventional 'computer centre'. However, PCs are typically not stored in a physically secure environment; even though modern versions of Microsoft Windows (and Linux) have multi-user security features, users and programs often run as the 'administrator' user, and there are many ways that the operating system integrity can be damaged. Thus today, neither the user of a PC nor a communicating party can trust very much about a PC, despite major efforts to improve security of operating systems. Anyone with access to the PC hardware can modify the operating system (e.g., by removing the hard disk and changing files).

Even if the user looks after the physical security of their PC, there are many other threats to system integrity. Modern operating systems and applications are highly complex, and it is almost impossible to remove all vulnerabilities; moreover, users can accidentally run malicious software which can damage system integrity.

However, the user may nevertheless want to trust the integrity of their PC. For example, the PC may be used for managing a bank account, performing e-commerce transactions or managing PI, all of which require user trust in the PC. A third party may also want to trust the integrity of a PC. This could be for a variety of reasons, for example, the third party is a bank and the PC is being used for e-commerce, the third party is a content provider and the PC is performing Digital Rights Management, or the PC is performing other security functions (e.g., authentication, key management) on behalf of a third party, all of which require third party trust in the PC. Trusted computing enables trust in the integrity of a PC based on a combination of software and hardware features. In particular trusted computing enables remote third parties to measure the integrity of the PC software environment.

8.3   The PI model

We next describe a general model for the generation and use of PI. We will use trusted computing to protect PI in the context of this model.

- Personal Information (PI). This is data which provides PI regarding the subject. PI may occur in many forms ranging from telephone numbers to medical records.
- Service Provider (SP). This is an SP which makes use of PI in the provision of services.
- Subject. The subject is the entity about whom PI is gathered and used.
- Trusted Platform (TP). A TP is one that contains a trusted subsystem which is able to both measure the current software state and reliably attest to this state to remote third parties (see Chapter 3). In the context of this chapter, this is the platform owned by the SP.
- Regulator/Legal authority. This is an entity which exerts legal or regulatory control over the management and use of PI. This includes telecommunications regulators, data privacy authorities, law enforcement bodies and auditors.

8.4   Scenarios

Using our model, we look at various scenarios involving the use of PI and identify some of the associated risks.

8.4.1   Registration scenario

Suppose a subject wishes to make a purchase using a website. Payment and delivery information, such as credit card and address details, will typically need to be provided for such a transaction to take place. By using a secure means of transmitting data, the subject can be assured that the confidentiality of data is preserved during transmission. The concern which remains is the nature of the security mechanisms implemented by the SP. That is, even though the subject is assured that data was transmitted over a secure channel, in many cases there is little or no assurance that data will be stored securely once it reaches the SP's server.

One example of an issue arising in this scenario is provided by those websites that require a verified e-mail address in order to gain access to the services they provide. In some cases these e-mail addresses are then sold to advertisers who send unsolicited mail to the subject. It would be desirable if a subject could ensure that e-mail addresses (and any other PI) are handled in a way consistent with the subject's privacy requirements.

8.4.2   *Location-based service scenario*

Consider a subject that wishes to take advantage of a location-based service. The subject must provide its location to the SP (or allow the SP to obtain its LI from a third party) in order to enable the provision of such a service. This LI is clearly just a special type of PI. Once the LI has been provided to the SP the subject has no direct way to control how this PI will be used.

8.4.3   *Medical records*

In our third scenario we consider a clinic where all personal medical records are held on a computer. Precautions should be taken to ensure that, when they are sent to other locations, records are not accessed by people who do not have the necessary access privileges. For example, if a patient is being treated at a specialist clinic at a different location, it is important that only the relevant practitioners have access to that patient's medical records. If some evidence of the conditions in which these records will be kept was available to the holder of the records, then it may aid the holder of the records in deciding whether or not to pass the records to this remote entity. It is also common for medical records to be accessed for research purposes. In such a case it would again be desirable if the clinic could establish the conditions in which medical records would be held by the researchers.

8.5   TCG mechanisms

We now give a brief overview of the TCG mechanisms relevant to this chapter. Many of the mechanisms discussed here are described in detail in Chapter 3.

The TCG specifications [3–5], define a TP as a computing platform which contains a trusted subsystem (TPS). The subsystem contains the parts of the TP which provide fundamental trust and security capabilities. The mechanisms which seal, measure, store and report integrity metrics in a trusted manner are now discussed. Using a combination of these mechanisms we will show how it may be possible to ensure that data is being sent to a trusted machine.

The TPS contains the Trusted Platform Module (TPM), which is the Core Root of Trust for Measurement (CRTM) and the Trusted Platform Support Service (TSS). The TPM is an integrated circuit responsible for various security aspects of the TP. The TSS may exist as software and may not be trusted itself; however, it may be required for the functionality of the TP.

When a subject communicates with a TP, it can decide whether or not to divulge information to it depending on its state. Furthermore, the user may also ensure that the data it provides will only be accessible to the remote platform when that platform is in the same state as it is at the time of the transfer.

To facilitate trusted measurement, storage and reporting of integrity metrics, the TP relies on two roots of trust. These are the Root of Trust for Measuring integrity metrics (RTM), and the root of trust for storing and reporting integrity metrics.

These roots of trust enable entities to trust the TP. The roots of trust are described further below.

8.5.1   TPM identities

A TPM identity is used to attest to aspects of the TP. A TP can use this identity to prove that it is a valid TP.

One example of such an identity is called the TPM identity credential. This credential contains an identity label and a public key certificate, signed by a privacy Certification Authority (CA). The privacy CA attests that the identity label shown in the TPM identity credential belongs to a particular TP. The main role of TPM identity credentials is to protect user privacy by providing anonymity for the TP (see Chapter 3).

For a privacy CA to sign a TPM identity credential, the TPM must first prove that the TP possesses certain properties. This proof is based on three credentials, in the form of certificates. These are the TPM endorsement credential, the platform credential and the conformance credential. These credentials have the following properties.

TPM endorsement credential. This credential attests that a TPM conforms to the TCG specifications. The credential is signed by an appropriately authorized entity, such as the TPM manufacturer or a TPM conformance laboratory. The entity responsible for generating this credential is known as the Trusted Platform Module Endorsement (TPME) entity. By generating this credential, the TPME vouches that the TPM conforms to TCG specifications. The credential contains the public key (PUBEK) of an endorsement key pair. This credential can be used by the privacy CA to generate a TPM Identity Credential and create identities for the TP. The corresponding private key is called PRIVEK, and is kept in a shielded location in the TPM for confidentiality and integrity protection.

Platform credential. This credential attests that the platform as a whole correctly incorporates protected capabilities and shielded locations within the TPS. The entity that generates the Platform Credential, known as the Platform Entity (PE), may be the platform manufacturer or a conformance laboratory. The information found in this credential is used by the privacy CA to generate a TPM Identity Credential. Access to this credential is restricted for privacy reasons.

Conformance credential. The Conformance Credential attests that the design of the TPS and its incorporation into the TP conforms to the TCG specifications. This may be generated by the platform manufacturer or a conformance test laboratory. The information found in this credential is used by the privacy CA to create a TPM Identity Credential. Access to this credential is restricted for privacy reasons.

8.5.2   TCG measuring, reporting and storing processes

As mentioned earlier, the RTM is the point of trust from which all integrity measurements are derived. The CRTM is a component of the RTM, and is the point from which all trust in reporting measured information is derived. When the platform starts up, the CRTM makes an integrity calculation of the first component to be executed on the TP. This is reported to a Platform Configuration Register (PCR). The measured component then becomes the RTM, and is responsible for measuring the integrity of the next component to be executed. This measurement is then stored in the PCR and, again, the measured component is responsible for measuring the next value. This process then continues as the components of the TP execute.

An entity wishing to challenge the TP to determine if it is in a trusted state, receives PCR values together with validation data. Validation data contains values which should result when integrity measurements are made by a TP, and is signed by a trusted third party. For example, validation data may vouch for the integrity of particular software. Using this validation data, the challenger may verify the PCR values sent by a TP in response to a challenge. If the PCR values received from the TP are not the values expected by the challenger, based on the trusted validation data, then the TP may not be in a trusted state.

A TP may choose only to send PCR values in response to a challenge from a remote challenger if it first successfully authenticates this challenger. However, in general, validation data itself is not confidential information. It describes the values which should be produced if the platform is working correctly [6, p. 2].

The PCRs are responsible for storing integrity values from the time that the platform was first booted up. We next describe the mechanisms used to compute and report on the values stored in the PCRs.

The TPM_Extend operation. This operation records new integrity measurement values for the PCRs at boot-up. The method used for this operation is described below.

When the TP boots up, a TCG_PCRVALUE is initialised to zero. PCR_0, the first PCR value, is then set to 0 concatenated with a representation of the first event to be recorded. This representation is known as the 'inDigest' value. The next PCR value, PCR_1, is the message digest of PCR_0 concatenated with the inDigest of the second event. This procedure continues. The TCG specification states that there must be at least 16 PCRs available for use to store these integrity digest values.

The TPM_Quote operation. This operation provides cryptographic reporting of PCR values. The values are signed using the private signing key corresponding to the public verification key found in the TPM Identity Credential. As mentioned earlier, a TP may have many TPM Identity Credentials, corresponding to its collection of identities.

8.5.3   Sealing data

The TCG specification provides mechanisms used to dictate the platform state that must hold in order for encrypted data to be decrypted. We next discuss the use of this feature with regard to the release of personal data. This feature may also be used to encrypt cryptographic keys.

The mechanism relies on three objects, the digestAtCreation, the digestAtRelease and a set of PCR values. The PCR values used are those which correspond to the aspects of the platform which should be considered when data is to be released. This is not necessarily all the PCRs. The digestAtCreation is an integrity value calculated from the set of PCR numbers and their corresponding PCR values when the sealed data item was created. The PCR numbers indicate particular PCRs. The digestAtRelease is an integrity value calculated from a set of PCR numbers and corresponding PCR values indicating the state of the platform that must hold in order for the sealed data to be released (i.e., to be made available in decrypted form). These three objects, together with the plaintext data, are all encrypted using the TPM_Seal function of the TCG specification. The sealed item is then stored on the platform in unprotected form together with the set of PCR numbers found in the digestAtCreation.

When a request is made to unseal this data, the TPM decrypts the sealed item. The data held within this sealed item is only released if, when using the listed PCRs, the recalculation of digestAtRelease corresponds to the values found in the sealed item.

> *TCG_Seal*. This operation is used to encrypt data. Additional information may be provided to ensure that this data is only released if a platform is in a pre-specified state.
>
> *TCG_Unseal*. This operation is used when the release of encrypted data is requested. The release of data using the TCG_Unseal operation may or may not depend on a pre-specified platform state.

8.6   Protecting PI using trusted computing

We now show how the privacy of PI can be protected using the operations given in the TCG specifications.

A user may send PI to an entity for various reasons. It may be necessary for the provision of a service to a user, or it may be a legal requirement, as is the case with E911 in North America [7]. In the E911 example, the user is required to send its LI when making an emergency call.

A secret can be defined as data which has not been subject to unauthorised disclosure. PI can then be regarded as a form of secret data. The exact definition of what constitutes personal data varies from person to person. A personal telephone number can be obtained from a public telephone directory. A person who considers this information to be personal data can typically choose to have it removed from public directories. A personal phone number is often passed between friends and acquaintances of the owner of the number without authorisation from the owner of the number being explicitly obtained. Although the telephone number is no longer strictly secret by our definition, we still regard the telephone number as PI, since it may still not be generally known (as is the case with a personal telephone number listed in a public directory).

When PI is provided over the internet, for example, for access to websites, the user's privacy may be protected by legal requirements on the entity to which this information is passed. The user may also gain assurances about the protection of their PI by only passing information to trusted organisations. For example, when a major e-commerce company stores billing and credit card information, it would not be good business practice to be found passing this information to other parties, even by accident, and so the user gains assurance from this.

Our aim is to reduce this implied method of trust and gain practical assurance when releasing PI.

8.6.1 Overview

Typically, when a subject transmits PI to a remote entity, it is then held in a database belonging to the receiving entity, in our case the SP. It would clearly be desirable that the SP's database stores PI in a manner which assures the subject that the PI is properly protected. Clearly, additional assurance is obtained if the user has guarantees of the platform state when data is used in the future. This ensures that the future use of PI depends on the platform being in a pre-defined trusted state.

This brings us to our first question. How does the subject know that the SP is in a trusted state? To answer this question we refer to the TCG specifications. Assuming the SP is a TP, there are a host of mechanisms at our disposal. Using these mechanisms a subject can establish various properties of the SP platform. This includes identifying the software which has executed since the platform boot. The subject can then ensure that the software used is trustworthy.

This leads us to our next question: how does the subject know which software to trust? Knowledge of which software can be trusted could be established by a laboratory and made available to the subject. This may include checks for the way in which personal data is managed by the software and those security aspects of the software that affect the likelihood of unintended distribution of PI. The user can thus discover if the software used passes tests for trustworthiness. Of course the laboratory making the statements would itself need to be a trusted entity.

At this point we raise a possible objection to these proposals, namely that the software that makes use of PI is likely to be different at every SP. If this is the case, then the practicability of the solution appears questionable, since it would seem to require every SP to have its software checked by a trusted third party laboratory. We make two observations about such a requirement. First, if the SP is a major corporation, then this is probably not such an onerous task. Second, whilst the software that actually uses information derived from the PI to provide a service is likely to be SP-specific, the software that stores and processes the PI does not necessarily need to be. That is, one could imagine cases where the PI is handled by a trusted 'standard' application running on the SP server, the integrity and trustworthiness of which can be externally checked. This trusted application then releases only that part of the PI needed by the SP to provide its service, which might mean that the SP application itself does not need to be trusted.

The process of ascertaining the software state on the target platform is initiated by a request for a proof of the state of the platform to which the PI is being sent. This request is in the form of a challenge. The platform then responds with a signed version of the challenge and PCR values, together with validation data. The private signing key used corresponds to the public key in the TPM identity certificate. The use of this key assures the user that the TP with which they are interacting, has been deemed a valid TP by the TPM certificate provider. The inclusion of the challenge in the signed response prevents replay attacks. The validation data allows the user to recalculate the PCR values found in the signed response. The validation data may be provided by the testing laboratory, specifying the state that the software should be in if it is to be trusted. Trust in software may also be derived from the reputation of the software vendor. When the PCR values are recalculated, they can be compared with those sent by the SP. If they are the same, the user is assured of the target platform state and that of the software executing on it. The user can then determine whether or not to trust the software.

Given that the user now knows exactly which software is being used by the SP, the user can then decide whether or not to send its personal data to this entity. Additionally, the user can specify that the platform must be in a trusted state whenever the PI is used in the future. This is guaranteed by sealing PI as discussed in Section 8.5.3. Simply, the user may state whenever that their private information may only be used if this particular trusted software is executing on the platform.

8.6.2   Using trusting computing with PI

In this section we discuss how a subject acquires reliable information about an SP platform. In particular, we discuss the TCG mechanisms which may be used by a subject to assess software found on the SP platform.

8.6.2.1   Initiating a request for PI

The first stage in our scenario involves an SP making a request to the subject for PI. This is usually the result of a request to the SP for the provision of a service to the subject. Before any information is provided to the SP the subject must establish certain properties of the SP's platform.

8.6.2.2   Verifying SP platform state

When the subject receives a request for PI, it must ensure that the SP is in a suitable state to receive the PI. This will depend on the subject's judgement of the trustworthiness of the software found on the SP platform.

The TCG mechanisms allow the subject to ensure that a TCP is using trusted software. The subject can request information regarding the software found on a TP.

8.6.2.3   Sending PI to the TP

To check the software executing on a target SP platform, the subject must first transmit a random challenge to it. The SP may also require authentication of the subject.

Upon receiving the challenge, the SP performs the TPM_Quote operation described in Section 8.5.2. This provides a signed version of the current PCR values for the SP platform, which is the result of the TPM_Extend operation. This operation is responsible for recording PCR values starting when the platform boots. The random value in the challenge is included within the scope of the signature generated by the TPM_Quote operation, preventing replay attacks.

Information regarding the software executed since platform boot is also sent. This is in the form of the TCG_PCR_EVENT data. Validation data, enabling the integrity of the software found on the platform to be verified, is also sent. The validation data is signed by the entity which created it. This may be a software vendor or a laboratory responsible for ensuring that software used for managing PI is secure and trustworthy. Using the information sent by the SP, the subject can recalculate the values calculated by the TPM_Extend and compare this with the PCR values sent by the SP.

The subject must first validate the signed data and verify the TPM Identity Credential. If the signature and the credentials are valid, the subject can trust that the identity was created by the privacy CA. That is, at some time in the past, the SP has sent its credentials to the privacy CA, the privacy CA verified these credentials, and sent the SP a TPM Identity Credential. This is evidence that the privacy CA attests to the credentials presented by the SP. Of course, the subject must trust that the privacy CA performs its functions correctly.

The subject also re calculates the PCR values. If the result of this re-calculation is as reported by the SP, the subject has assurances about the integrity of the SP platform state. Most importantly, the subject has assurances about the software used to manage PI and its integrity. If this software satisfies the conditions of the subject, it can then send its PI to the SP.

The subject may also request that PI sent to the SP is sealed. This means that the PI must be stored on the platform in encrypted form. Also contained within the encrypted data are objects which specify the conditions which the platform must satisfy in order for the data to be released. This ensures that, when the PI is used in the future by the SP, the SP platform is in a trusted state.

8.6.3   Constraints, LIPA and LI tokens

As discussed in Reference 2, constraints are statements which control the use, storage and distribution of LI. We next show how an LI software constraint can be included within the larger set of constraints. This special type of constraint can then be used to ensure that LI is only sent to LBS providers running trusted software to manage LI. By ensuring that an LBS provider uses specific software, the LI subject has assurance that the platform to which LI is sent will manage LI in a trustworthy manner.

We suppose that constraints are sent within the scope of an LI token, as discussed in Reference 1. We further suppose that an LI token is encrypted in a manner such that only the LIPA is able to view the LI and the associated constraints. The LI token may then be distributed freely without any risk to the subject's privacy. When LI is required by an LBS provider, the LI token is sent to a LIPA. The LIPA decides whether or not the requesting LBS provider is authorised to have access to the LI contained in the token depending on the constraints contained in the LI token. If the LBS provider is a TP the LIPA can check, using the mechanisms described above, that the LBS provider is using trustworthy software. The subject may also state in the constraints that LI must only be sent to LBS providers using trustworthy software. The presence of this software assures the subject that its LI is managed appropriately.

8.7 Concluding remarks

We have discussed how a TP may be used to gain assurance about the integrity of software found on a platform. This may be used by a subject to address concerns about the control of PI. This can be done by verifying the integrity of software found on the platform to which PI is being sent, and by ensuring that this software is trustworthy. The mechanisms described in this chapter rely on SPs being TPs.

This chapter does not discuss how users might find out the uses an SP wishes to make of personal data. For example, it may be possible for an SP to state that they wish to use PI for one particular purpose, whereas they may actually be using it for a different purpose. One possible means of addressing this concern might be to generate a list of SPs and the corresponding services provided. This might, for example, be created by a third party. An entity may thus be able to establish with some degree of confidence that the service which the provider is claiming to provide is actually the service provided.

Another possible concern relates to how a user can establish whether or not the software used to manage PI is trustworthy. Modern applications are constantly being modified and, in many cases, modifications are made by vendors to enhance the performance of software. In such a case, there is no malicious intent in the modification. However, any change in the software will, of course, change the integrity measurement. One possible solution to this problem may be to have independent testing laboratories which are responsible for ensuring that the software performs securely in the interests of the user. Of course this task may also be carried out by the original vendor.

A further problem which arises from this relates to differences in interests. The software vendor is selling its product to the SP, so its primary concern is to keep its customer satisfied. How can the end user trust that the software vendor will act in its interests? Future research may look at possible solutions to this problem.

References

1 Anand S. Gajparia, Chris J. Mitchell, and Chan Y. Yeun. Using constraints to protect personal location information. In *Proceedings of IEEE Semiannual Vehicular Technology Conference (VTC 2003 Fall)*, vol. 3, pp. 2112–2116, IEEE Press, New York, 2003.
2 Anand S. Gajparia, Chris J. Mitchell, and Chan Y. Yeun. The location information preference authority: supporting user privacy in location based services.

In S. Liimatainen and T. Virtanen, eds, *Proceedings of the 9th Nordic Workshop on Secure IT Systems*, pp. 91–96, Helsinki University of Technology, Finland, November 2004.

3 Trusted Computing Group. Main Specification. Trusted Computing Group, 1.1b edn, September 2001.

4 Trusted Computing Group. TPM Main: Part 1 Design Principles. Trusted Computing Group, 1.2 edn, October 2003.

5 Trusted Computing Group. TPM Main: Part 2 TPM Structures. Trusted Computing Group, 1.2 edn, October 2003.

6 Trusted Computing Group. TPM Main: Part 3 Commands. Trusted Computing Group, 1.2 edn, October 2003.

7 Dale N. Hatfield. A report on technical and operational issues impacting the provision of wireless enhanced 911 services. Technical Report, Federal Communications Commission, 2002.

Chapter 9

Certificate management using distributed trusted third parties

Alexander W. Dent and Geraint Price

9.1   Introduction

A Trusted Third Party (TTP) is an entity in a network that is trusted to provide a security service to the other users of that network. Examples of the use of TTPs in secure systems include key generation and distribution, electronic notarisation and digital archiving. Typically, a TTP service is offered by a single (or small number of) dedicated machine(s) that have strong security counter-measures installed to prevent the TTP's service from being compromised. This centralised approach is easy to manage, update and test.

The use of a TTP in a security system is almost always based on a business agreement. The users trust the TTP because they know that any attempt the TTP makes to subvert or make malicious use of the service that it offers will result in a violation of the business agreement. If the TTP service is being offered by a company then this could involve the contract to run the TTP service being cancelled and the business sued. If the TTP service is being offered by some internal entity within a company then the manager of that entity will have to explain the reason for the deviation from the security policy.

There are a couple of problems that are typically associated with traditional TTPs. The first is that, by their very nature, a TTP provides a static, centralised point of attack. For example, an attacker can compromise a whole Public Key Infrastructure (PKI) by compromising the CA that issues certificates for that infrastructure. The second is that, in many cases, the TTP will need to be constantly online and will often have to deal with large volumes of traffic quickly. This may cause a bottleneck in the system and impact system performance. The combination of these two problems makes TTPs a tempting target for attackers wishing to launch a denial of service attack.

Another problem with traditional TTPs is their placement within a network. Once a TTP is placed within a network topology, it may well be infeasible or impossible to change its location. This can be disadvantageous for ad hoc or rapidly changing network topologies, such as wireless or mobile networks, as the TTP can quickly become difficult to reach.

One particular, widely discussed, example of a TTP is a Certification Authority (commonly known as a CA). CAs aid in the deployment of public key cryptography by attesting to the fact that a given public key belongs to the user who claims it. A CA does this by issuing certificates which contain the user's identity, his or her public key, information about the validity period of the public key and information about the situations in which the public key can be used (the 'policy' associated with the public key). These certificates are digitally signed by the CA to prevent unauthorised modification or impersonation. The *Handbook of Applied Cryptography* [1] attributes the concept of a CA to the 1978 thesis of Kohnfelder [2]. More information about PKIs and CAs can be found in Reference 3.

9.1.1   Secure execution environments

For the purposes of this chapter, we will assume the existence of a highly resilient Secure Execution Environment (SEE) within platforms running the distributed elements of a TTP. Furthermore, for the purposes of the chapter, we assume that the SEE has a hardware protection mechanism which differentiates it from other protected execution environments, such as the Java sandbox. This distinction is important as we require an additional level of protection to be afforded to cryptographic secrets which cannot be provided by any other means. It is generally considered good practice to store cryptographic keys within protective hardware [4]. We also assume that, for all practical purposes, the SEE cannot be influenced or impersonated and should never leak any information about the application that it is running.[1] As we can see from previous chapters, this is an idealised assumption, and neither the Microsoft Next Generation Secure Computing Base (NGSCB) nor the Trusted Computing Group's Trusted Computing Platform makes any such strong claim. However, by abstracting the notion of a SEE we can concentrate on the uses of such an environment rather than on technical details.

We therefore define a SEE as a logically separate computing environment with certain security properties, which can be trusted to execute programs securely even when the environment is hosted by an untrusted machine. In particular, we envisage the SEE as having the following four main characteristics:

- It can demonstrate to a third party that it has been initialised correctly and is ready to receive an application. This could be done by various means, such as the SEE

---

[1] We do note that some classes of attacks on certain types of SEEs exist [5–7], but are beyond the scope of this discussion.

providing evidence that a proper boot sequence has been executed or by demonstrating knowledge of some secret that only the properly configured SEE has access to.

- It can, and is able to demonstrate to a third party that it can, download applications in a secure fashion. In particular, it should be able to demonstrate that it can download applications in a manner that protects their confidentiality and integrity.
- It can, and is able to demonstrate to a third party that it can, execute applications supplied to it by a third party in a secure manner, without any other application having access to the downloaded application or the data which it produces, or the downloaded application having access to any other application or data on the host machine.
- It can demonstrate to a third party that an application has been successfully executed by the SEE. This can be done explicitly or implicitly. In the implicit case, the third party is convinced that the SEE has executed the applet simply by observing that the applet has produced a correct output and that, because the applet has been downloaded securely to the SEE, the SEE is the only entity capable of producing such an output. In the explicit case, the SEE engages in some further protocol to, or outputs some extra data that, demonstrate that the SEE has correctly executed the applet.

Essentially a SEE provides an environment in which a third party can install a 'black box' application on a user's machine without compromising the security of that application.

The remainder of the chapter is organised as follows. The next section will discuss the advantages and disadvantages of distributing a central TTP's functionality to an application running on a user's SEE, and suggest a general method by which this could be achieved. The idea of distributing a TTP service onto a SEE under the control of the user is not entirely novel – it is also discussed in Chapter 6 in the context of Single Sign-On Servers – but we believe that this is the first time the general model has been stated. We will then concentrate on the idea of using a distributed CA to aid certificate management (Section 9.3) and discuss the real-world applications of such an approach (Section 9.4). Lastly, we will discuss some new problems that arise from using this technique (Section 9.5).

9.2 Distributed TTPs

Functionally, a TTP service can be thought of as a secure, tamper-proof black box that is trusted to perform a particular function. From this point of view, it is easy to see that it is unnecessary for the TTP service to be hosted on a machine that is physically separated from the user's machine. Two of the reasons why these services have traditionally been hosted on physically separate machines are that:

- Having a distinct physical location may aid the functionality of the TTP. It may, for example, be convenient to have a single point of reference for a network-wide service, or it may be necessary for the service to interact heavily with a resource (such as a backup device) and, hence, be convenient to locate the service near that device.

• It is easier to secure a TTP service as a secure tamper-proof black box when the service is running on a physically separate machine on which the attacker is assumed to have no privileges.

The first of these reasons depends only on the nature of the functionality that the TTP service is offering. The second is becoming less of a requirement with the advent of SEEs.

The central thesis of this chapter is that it is possible to delegate most[2] TTP services to a TTP-applet running in a SEE on a user's machine. Instead of requesting a service directly from a central TTP, a user would request that a TTP-applet be downloaded into the user's machine's SEE, where the applet could be executed and provide the requested service. The advantage of this is that (potentially) the applet could offer the same service multiple times with little or no interaction from the TTP.

Also, we draw attention to the fact that there may be no physical or logical security protection for the link between the TTP and the SEE prior to the downloading of the TTP-applet. In particular, the SEE can be remote from the TTP at the time of download. Thus, in certain scenarios we are using the SEE as a bootstrapping tool for a secure relationship.

Typically, a TTP-applet would be downloaded and executed in a six-stage process:

1. The user authenticates itself to the TTP and requests a service to which it is entitled.
2. The TTP would verify the authenticity of the SEE. If the SEE is not authentic then the TTP will refuse to provide the service.
3. The TTP establishes a shared secret key with the SEE using a key establishment protocol. This key will enable the TTP-applet to be downloaded in a way that protects both its confidentiality and integrity, and also guarantees its origin.
4. The TTP encrypts and uploads the TTP-applet to the SEE. Along with the encrypted TTP-applet, the TTP must provide some means for the SEE to verify that the applet is authentic (i.e., the SEE is provided with data origin authentication and data integrity guarantees).
5. The SEE decrypts the applet and checks that it is authentic.
6. The SEE executes the applet and provides the service to the user, along with a proof that the applet was executed successfully.

The download phase, step 3, of the above protocol bears further examination. The key security services that are required in this phase are data origin authentication and data integrity: the SEE should not execute applet code if it cannot guarantee its

---

[2] Whilst it is always possible to delegate the running of a TTP service to a TTP-applet that interacts with a central TTP, the advantages and disadvantages of doing so depend upon the specific operational requirements of the TTP service. An example of a service that is not suitable for delegation is a notarisation service, which is likely to rely upon a high degree of centralised connectivity and decision-making in order to establish probable causal effects.

origin and integrity, as the user could not trust the output of such an applet. In some scenarios these services will be enough to secure the whole process. This is because the applet will have no access to other data in, or processes running on, the user's machine, and the user will be presented with exactly the same data that it would have been if it were interacting with a remote TTP.[3] In other scenarios, for example, when the applet contains confidential material such as cryptographic keys, it may also be necessary for the applet to be downloaded in a confidential manner.

Further attempts to use the TTP service could be handled directly by the TTP-applet running on the user's machine. The applet would only need to contact the central TTP directly if it was unable to offer the correct service on its own, or if the applet's policy dictated that it should do so.

9.2.1   Advantages and disadvantages

The technique has several potential advantages (which will depend on the nature of the service the TTP is offering). Possibly the most important is the flexibility of placement that the distributed TTP approach offers. Since a distributed TTP can be downloaded and executed on the SEE of any machine in a network, it is possible to dynamically place the TTP service within an evolving network so that it is in the best position to offer its service to that network's users. This is particularly useful for networks whose topology changes rapidly, such as Personal Area Networks (PANs) [8] and Personal Distributed Environments (PDEs) [9].

A second important advantage is the potential for decreased traffic at the central TTP. This should speed up the operation of the system by removing the TTP bottle-neck. As the central TTP is only required to download the initial applet, and possibly, updated versions of the applet, the user is likely to have fewer interactions with the central TTP. Also, if the TTP service has a high computational overhead then dis-tributing the service to the user's machine may ease the computational burden placed on the central TTP.

Additionally, our technique has the potential to increase the availability of the TTP service. Using the TTP-applet architecture to flexibly replicate a service can help increase the number of clients to which the TTP can offer a service at any given time.

Another potential advantage is that, in some scenarios, the decentralised nature of the TTP service might make the service more difficult to attack: an attacker might have to attack many different TTP-applets in order to make a significant impact on the security of the entire system, and this may be detectable or preventable. Alternatively, an attacker may choose to attack the central TTP that distributes the TTP-applets. However, the system could be designed in a manner such that attacking the central TTP may not be enough to compromise the security of TTP-applets already distributed throughout the system. For this to be the case, the TTP-applets would need to be able

---

[3] It should be noted, however, that the ability for the central TTP to download code to be executed on the user's machine may aid the TTP in launching a denial of service attack against the user, by allowing the TTP to use the computational resources of the user's SEE.

to function independently of the central TTP. To clarify our argument we will describe a potential TTP service which provides this property. A confidentiality service could be designed such that the central TTP does not keep copies of any secrets given to each TTP-applet, and TTP-applets do not replicate secrets (beyond the basic replication of any shared secrets needed to provide the service to its clients). Thus, after an applet has been distributed, the central TTP cannot impersonate that applet at any point in the future.

The technique also has several potential disadvantages (again, depending rather heavily on the nature of the service that the TTP is offering) and most of the potential disadvantages mirror the potential advantages. The first arises from the distributed nature of the TTP-applets. By having the applet running on the user's machine, it may become easier for that user to attack the TTP service and compromise the security of the system. However, the impact of compromising a user's TTP-applet can be minimised by using forward and backward secrecy techniques to protect any sensitive data contained in the applet (see, e.g., Diffie *et al.* [10] for details of forward secrecy in key exchange protocols or ISO/IEC 18031 [11] for details of forward and backward secrecy in random number generators).

Also, if the TTP-applet cannot be designed to function independently of the central TTP, then the communication between central TTP and TTP-applets could provide a means of attacking the TTP-applets. If the TTP was to be compromised this could, depending on the nature of the service, lead to the attacker having a base from which they could attack all current TTP-applets. As a result, it would be desirable to design the link between the TTP and the TTP-applet in order to minimise such exposure.

Another potential disadvantage involves the fact that many TTP services need to be continuously offered. It might be important that a user's TTP-applet is always available to the surrounding network, in which case the applet must be hosted on an 'always-on' machine. Of course, if an entity in the network were to find that a user's TTP-applet was unavailable, they may always have the option of querying the central TTP for the service directly, but this can lead to synchronicity problems.

9.3   Distributed CAs

We now describe an application of the distributed TTP concept to CAs. In particular, we introduce the idea of a distributed CA-applet. The CA service is particularly suited to being distributed. Traditionally, the service has to deal with large volumes of traffic at the TTP, and, therefore, the TTP could be a major target for denial of service attacks. Distributing the CA service to user's machines can potentially make denial of service attacks harder, whilst simultaneously reducing traffic at the central TTP. Furthermore, technical advances in the field of digital signatures mean that PKIs are being seriously considered for use in ad hoc networks and PANs [12]. Thus, the ability to dynamically place a CA within a network could be seen as a great advantage.

9.3.1 The CA-applet concept

The basic idea of a CA-applet is that the user's machine hosts the functionality of the CA that certifies that user's own public keys. This CA-applet will actually fulfil two roles: (1) it will certify new public keys that belong to that user, and (2) it will make these certificates available to other network users. The former stops the user from having to communicate with the TTP whenever it wishes to produce a new public key (a user may wish to do this for key separation purposes or if it is responsible for multiple public keys, for example, if the user is an email server). The latter stops the traffic bottleneck at the directory service that hosts the public key certificates.[4]

One unusual advantage of distributed CA-applets is that they may be hosted on a machine which gives an implicit assurance that the correct CA is being used. For example, an email server could host a CA-applet for public encryption keys. If such a system is being used then a user will always know the location of the CA that certifies a certain email address – it is the email server that hosts that address.

9.3.1.1 CA-applets versus sub-CAs

There are many similarities between a user running a CA-applet and a user running a sub-CA that has been certified by the central CA. The main difference between these two situations is in the level of trust that has to be present between the central CA and the user. For a user to run a CA-applet, the central TTP merely has to trust the user's initial authentication and SEE. For a user to run a separate CA certified by the central CA, the central CA has to trust that the user is capable of correctly installing and maintaining a full CA. The central CA also has to trust the user not to abuse the power they have to create certificates. This obviously means that the CA has to extend a much higher level of trust.

It is possible to limit the trust that a central CA needs to place in a sub-CA running on a user's machine by specifying policies in the certificate that the central CA issues for the subordinate's public key. For example, the central CA may specify a policy that states that the subordinate CA's public key can only be used to verify certificates issued to a particular identity. Hence, the subordinate CA can only issue certificates to one entity. This seems, on the surface, to offer the same functionality as a CA-applet without the need for a SEE. However, there are a few subtle differences. Since the subordinate CA is not running in a SEE, the user can extract the CA's private signing key and create a certificate valid in his or her name for any public key without having to prove knowledge of the corresponding private key. This is not possible with CA-applets. Second, the use of policies places the security burden on the verifier, who must recognise the policy and correctly check it before trusting a certificate. The use of CA-applets places the security burden on the issuer who will only provide a CA-applet after checking the policies associated with issuing certificates to the recipient of that applet.

---

[4] Although we note that, in certain circumstances, the directory service at the central TTP can be replicated on several separate machines to reduce this problem without using secure execution environments.

9.3.2   CA-applet functionality

In this section we will describe the various functions that a CA-applet should offer. We consider this to be a minimum set: a CA-applet could conceivably offer significantly more functionality than is listed.

9.3.2.1   Initialisation

The CA-applet is initialised when it is first downloaded. Before the download process begins, the user might need to authenticate itself to the central CA before requesting the applet. Having a separate authentication from user to CA provides an end-to-end authentication channel, which could provide for user roaming if the user were willing to use third party SEEs which it could vouch for in some manner. However, user to CA authentication might not be a necessary requirement if the CA could convince itself of the right of the SEE to download the applet during the SEE validation stage.

The central CA then generates the CA-applet. This applet has the power to produce certificates for public keys that are registered to those identified by the scope of the policy that the CA issues with the applet. In order to do this, the central CA would generate a new key-pair for use within the CA-applet. The public key is included in a certificate signed using the central CA's key-pair for applet issuance. This certificate would be included in the CA-applet and would also indicate the validity period for the CA-applet's key-pair (which can be relatively short).

The CA-applet would be downloaded into the SEE using exactly the same method as any other TTP-applet. The central CA would check the authenticity of the SEE, and the central CA and the SEE would then execute a secure key establishment protocol. Finally, the central CA would deliver the applet to the SEE in a secure manner using this key, that is, with confidentiality, integrity and data origin authentication.

9.3.2.2   Registering a public key with a CA-applet

Only the user to which the CA-applet has been issued should be able to register a key with the CA-applet. To do this the user must authenticate itself to the CA-applet in some way. This could be done either explicitly, through the use of some authentication protocol, or implicitly if the SEE authenticates users before allowing them to access processes which they own.

Whenever a user wishes to register a public key with a CA-applet, the user must provide the applet with the public key to be registered and proof that the user possesses the corresponding private key (along with any other supplementary information). If this proof is deemed to be valid then the applet creates a certificate that certifies that the given public key belongs to the user. Optionally, the CA-applet may also register that public key with the central CA, either for backup purposes or to provide an additional distribution method.

Note that the need for the CA-applet to produce a proof that it has been executed correctly has been removed. This proof is provided implicitly by the production of a signed certificate. This is because we trust the central CA to provide a trustworthy applet, and only that applet can produce a signature using the key-pair authorised by the central CA – hence, the presence of a valid signature is proof that the applet has been successfully executed.

If a third party requires further evidence that the applet was executed by a suitably secure SEE, it may be possible for the central CA to include information about the state of the SEE when the applet was first downloaded in the certificate it produces to certify the CA-applet's key-pair. For example, if the SEE was a trusted computing platform following the TCG's standards, then the central CA may wish to include the PCR values of the TCP (see Chapter 3) within the CA-applet's certificate, to demonstrate to a third party that the applet was downloaded into a properly secure SEE.

9.3.2.3 Requesting a public key certificate from a CA-applet

One of the functions the CA-applet could provide is to make the CA-applet-signed certificates available to other users within the network. In this case, the service must then be publicly available. If the SEE only allows users to access processes which the user owns, then it will be necessary for a separate, publicly available process (outside the SEE but belonging to the user) to provide access to this service to other users.

On request, the CA-applet will output the certificate for a public key that it has certified. It will also, on request, output the certificate for its own public verification key that was certified by the central CA.

Hence, whenever a network user wishes to find a certificate for a user's public key, the network user only needs to contact the user's host machine to receive the certificate from the CA-applet. If the CA-applet is unavailable then the network user may (optionally) request the certificate from the central CA or wait for the CA-applet to come online again before completing the task.

9.3.3 Potential problems with CA-applets

There are a range of problems associated with the use of PKIs and CA-applets. In this section we discuss the main problems and suggest some solutions for our distributed CA architecture.

9.3.3.1 The revocation problem

One of the ways in which a CA-applet may also be useful would be in easing the traffic problems associated with certificate revocation. The two main approaches to certificate revocation are the use of certificate revocation lists (CRLs) [13] and online checking methods such as Online Certificate Status Protocol (OCSP) [14, 15]. Both of these approaches have problems [3].

One of the main problems associated with online approaches such as OCSP are that they require highly available TTPs to verify the status of a certificate. The status of a certificate is likely to be checked on a regular basis, and some policies might dictate that a check is required every time a signature is verified. Thus, the TTP which answers certificate queries must be capable of dealing with a heavy traffic load. This problem could be significantly eased if CA-applets were also able to verify the status of certificates they had issued. Each CA-applet would then only be responsible for verifying the (relatively small number of) certificates it had issued.

Similarly, if CRLs are used, a CA-applet could also be responsible for storing them. It would be an easy job for the CA-applet to keep accurate CRLs for the (again, relatively small number of) certificates for which it is directly responsible.

However, for either of these solutions to work effectively we have to assume that the CA-applet is going to be highly available. If the CA-applet is ever unavailable to the network then it could be necessary for a network user to wait until the applet came online again before completing their task.

We believe that there are several ways in which we can overcome this potential problem. It may be possible to allow the central CA to mirror the CA-applet's revocation responsibilities, although this approach may not always be practical because of synchronicity problems.

Another solution would be to have peer-to-peer replicated distribution of the revocation information. The source CA-applet could nominate a set of other CA-applets to which it periodically sends revocation updates. The client could then poll the broader set of CA-applets should the source be unavailable.

It may also be possible for the client requesting the revocation information to continue processing while waiting for the CA-applet to come back online. However, this solution would only work in support of applications which could effectively roll-back the transaction should the client eventually receive confirmation that the certificate had been revoked.

9.3.3.2   The renewal problem

The private certification key issued to a CA-applet by a central CA must have a limited lifespan – indeed, it might be better for security reasons if this lifespan was quite short. The shorter the lifespan of a private key-pair in a CA-applet, the less time an attacker has to attempt to compromise the CA-applet's private key or to abuse the system if the CA-applet is compromised. After this time, or if it is suspected that the private key has been compromised, the private signing key of the CA-applet will need to be renewed.

The simplest method to cope with the expiry of the private signing key would be for the CA-applet to simply delete itself. After this time, should the CA service still be required, the user can re-install a CA-applet by contacting the central CA and downloading a new version complete with a new private signing key. Of course, if this approach is used naively then there is a problem: certificates issued using the old signing key will no longer be valid and the user will need to re-certify all of his public keys.

This problem can be avoided if the CA-applet informs the central CA that its private key is about to expire. The CA-applet (with the user's permission) could then download a new CA-applet to be run in a separate area of the user's SEE. This new CA-applet could re-certify all the public keys that the old CA-applet has certified.

Of course, there is no need for a new CA-applet to be downloaded at all if the CA-applet contains a mechanism for updating its own key-pair and requesting a new certificate from the central CA. However, such an approach has the disadvantage of allowing a single CA-applet to continue running indefinitely. In this case, if that

CA-applet is compromised, and that compromise is not detected, then the entire security of the part of the system which relies on the CA-applet could be indefinitely compromised.[5]

9.3.3.3 Compromise of a CA-applet

The most disastrous event that can occur whilst using a CA-applet, apart from the compromise of the central CA, is the compromise of a CA-applet. This would allow an attacker to extract the private signing keys and forge certificates for any combination of public key and identity. It is important to limit an attacker's advantage in this case.

An easy first step is to only certify the CA-applet's private signing key for relatively short periods of time. This means that if an applet is compromised then the attacker will only have a limited amount of time in which to forge certificates.

If the CA-applet was to be certified for a longer period of time, the CA may want to maintain a CRL of possibly compromised applets. Therefore, in the case of suspected CA-applet compromise, the CA could issue a revocation of the CA-applet key, and all keys signed with the CA-applet key would have to be considered suspect. In this case, it would be prudent to have some notification channel from the CA to the CA-applet owner suggesting that they re-initialise the SEE and download a new applet.

Another solution would be to use multiple CA-applets. Here, every public key that is submitted to one CA-applet would automatically be submitted to a second applet (running in distinct execution environments, either on the same machine or on a physically separate machine). If a single CA-applet is compromised then it will be easy to isolate those certificates that have been forged as they will not have a corresponding second certificate issued by the second applet.[6] Of course, as with any system that involves multiple CAs, the problem with this approach is one of synchronicity between the applets – both applets must be 'up-to-date' with each other or the system would be open to abuse.

Another option to limit the effects of CA-applet compromise is for the central CA to only certify the applet to carry out tasks conforming to a given policy. For example, the applet could be limited to creating certificates for a named individual. If this applet is later compromised then the keys contained within the applet can only be (mis)used within the scope of the policy statements identified within the applet's certificate.

9.4 Applications

It is clear that there are risks associated with using a distributed CA over a traditional, static, central CA, and the distributed approach may not be appropriate in all situations.

---

[5] We note that if the inability to detect compromise was an issue, then periodic forced recovery could be used to re-issue an uncompromised applet.

[6] We make an assumption here that the separate applets are controlled independently and that, in addition, the second applet has not been compromised.

In this section we aim to highlight a few situations where we believe a distributed CA may be useful.

9.4.1   Personal CAs

A personal CA [12,16] supports the distribution and use of public keys in a PAN [8] or a PDE [9]. Mitchell and Schaffelhofer [12] list the following functional requirements for a personal CA:

1.   The personal CA key-pair can be securely generated within the device, or securely generated and transferred to the device, and (in both cases) the private key is securely stored when in the device.
2.   The root public key of the personal CA can be securely transferred to those devices that will have to verify certificates issued by the personal CA.
3.   The personal CA can generate public key certificates for mobile devices.
4.   Mobile devices can verify certificates issued by the personal CA, and can check the certificate validity and revocation status where appropriate.
5.   No third party passive interceptor of communications can learn any secret information.
6.   No third party active interceptor of communications can manipulate the exchanges between the mobile device and the personal CA so that a public key certificate is created for an incorrect device or that contains incorrect data.
7.   When securing the transfer of the personal CA root certificate from the personal CA device to another mobile device, the interaction between the mobile device and the personal CA is secured by at least a 'weak' shared secret and the method of this use should be capable of resisting 'brute force' attacks on the shared secret.

It is easy to imagine a distributed CA architecture that satisfies or exceeds all of these requirements: consider a situation where a manufacturer or distributor implants a public verification key into each device. This would allow that manufacturer (or their representative) to offer authenticated software to these devices. In particular, the manufacturer could offer a CA-applet for which it has vouched – in other words the manufacturer could act as a central CA by making a CA-applet available. This would allow the mobile device to act as a verifiably secure CA. The manufacturer would, of course, need to generate the certificate that certifies the CA-applet's master key. Also, manufacturers could cross-certify each other's public verification keys to ensure that the CA-applet could be used with a range of different devices.

This distributed CA-applet would even offer the optional and desirable functionality described in Reference 12, in that the security-critical CA functionality would be removable, personal, transferable and verifiable.

Indeed, this service not only meets all of the above requirements, it offers some attractive additional features. For example, the transfer of the CA service from one CA-applet to another could be done in a fully secure manner without needing to resort to the use of user interaction or 'weak' secrets. A CA-applet would merely need to be executed on a second machine and that applet would need to certify all the existing certificates.

Furthermore, a CA-applet has the advantage of being configured by security experts (i.e., the manufacturer) rather than by the user, and would allow a user to demonstrate to a third party that two devices belong to the same PAN or PDE. A user can prove this to a third party because the user does not know the private signing keys that the CA-applet is using and is therefore unable to abuse them. This contrasts with the way that personal CAs have previously been envisaged, where the personal CA's private keys would potentially be accessible to the user.

9.4.2 Ad hoc networks

We believe that ad hoc networks could provide a suitable environment in which to make use of CA-applets. Proposals for providing distributed certification services within ad hoc networks already exist [17–20]. CA-applets could be used to complement, enhance or provide an alternative solution to previous work. In existing designs, the mobility of the CA signing functionality is seen as important. The CA-applet could provide this mobility by offering a useful means of handing-off CA functionality between different SEEs.

The applicability of CA-applets to ad hoc networks will, by necessity, depend on the environment in which the ad hoc network is being used. CA-applets would appear to be more suited to situations in which ad hoc networks exist within, or in conjunction with, a more permanent security infrastructure. This is not an onerous assumption to make; see, for example, Varadharajan *et al.* [18].

We now outline some of the existing proposals for certificate management architectures for ad hoc networks. In the process, we briefly discuss the significance of their designs in light of our proposals:

1. Varadharajan *et al.* [18] propose a security service for cluster-based Near-Term Digital Radio (NTDR) [21] ad hoc networks:
   - Their work makes use of a permanent CA for setup that would be off-line most of the time. In their discussion, they note that not all ad hoc networks are completely without infrastructure. They use examples where the nodes in the network will have prior access to longer-term certification services before forming the ad hoc network.
   - They highlight that, within NTDR, moves between clusters (localised groups of nodes within the network) are rare, but that changes within the cluster can happen more often. They make use of this fact to develop a two-tier key hierarchy, one within a cluster and one between clusters. This results in a more efficient key management architecture.
   - In their design the hand-off of security state between clusterheads (the leader responsible for administration within a cluster) can occur with notification (where the existing clusterhead hands over the security state to the new cluster) or without notification (where the outgoing clusterhead does not hand over the security state and a new state needs to be configured). In the case where notification is used, we believe that CA-applets and the secure download protocols provide an ideal mechanism for securing the transportation of this security state from the old to the new clusterhead.

2. Zhou and Haas [19] propose a distributed means of generating signatures on certificates.

   - They replicate their key management service by using threshold cryptography. In their scheme, a number of special nodes within the network generate partial shares of a signature. These partial signatures are then combined to generate a valid signature. This allows for a proportion of servers to be unreachable or corrupt, while still allowing for the generation of secure signatures.

   - If nodes in the network are progressively compromised, then an attacker could feasibly collect enough secret key shares over a long period of time to enable certificates to be forged. To defend against this possibility they employ a share refreshing technique. This reduces the time frame within which an adversary must compromise the required threshold number of servers.

3. Luo and Lu [17] propose a similar mechanism to the Zhou–Haas scheme for distributed certificate management within ad hoc networks. Their proposal differs in that all nodes are equal and there are no special server nodes.

   - In a similar manner to that proposed by Zhou and Haas, Luo and Lu employ threshold sharing of a certificate signing key and use proactive share refreshing to guard against the cumulative long-term compromise of nodes.

   - Their scheme employs a local trust model where any k nodes in the ad hoc network can form a coalition to perform certificate management operations.[7] While this allows the infrastructure to be more flexible, it does make it more difficult to enforce a global policy across the ad hoc network. This may or may not pose a problem depending on the environment in which the network is being used.

   - Their share update mechanism uses a randomised algorithm to start the share update process. We believe that this could potentially create problems if the ad hoc network was subject to partitioning.

   - Their design principle is based on the assumption that the network provides no support to the security architecture.[8] This differs from Varadharajan *et al.*'s [18] assumption that some ad hoc networks can rely upon long-term infrastructure intermittently.

   - They identify several problems that a globally trusted centralised CA would present within an ad hoc network. Two of the problems they highlight with centralised CAs are the fact that centralised CAs are not scalable and that they are single points of compromise which makes them targets for denial of service attacks; high mobility makes it more difficult to contact a centralised CA in a timely fashion. We believe that a CA-applet mechanism could counter these particular problems in some scenarios.

---

[7] The value for k is set to be one greater than the anticipated number of nodes which might be compromised at any one time. This means that corrupt nodes cannot form a group large enough to perform valid operations.

[8] Their standard bootstrapping protocol does rely upon a trusted *dealer* to issue shares to the first k nodes. However, they have an enhanced protocol which can do without this dealer by performing distributed generation of an RSA key-pair.

We now review what we believe to be some of the potential benefits of using CA-applets for certificate management within ad hoc networks:

- When compared to other certificate management mechanisms CA-applets could provide a stricter form of centralised policy enforcement when compared to current designs. In some of the current designs [17–20] the decision to issue a new certificate is based on the consensus of a certain threshold of nodes in the network. While this adds robustness to the overall scheme, it makes it more difficult to issue policies that should be globally adhered to. A CA-applet version of this, while possibly having less resilience, could enforce certain policies dictated by a global CA through the protection of the SEE.
- The use of CA-applets could augment the security of current schemes which use pre-emptive share refreshing for threshold cryptography. The use of specialised protective hardware should reduce the chance of compromise. Thus, we can extend the time period required between runs of the share refreshing protocols, hence reducing the communication overheads.
- Short-lived and/or local certificates could offer an important advantage in certain types of ad hoc networks. A CA-applet which managed certificates that were *local* to a subset of the ad hoc network would allow for a more decentralised security management architecture. Cluster-based ad hoc networks (such as NTDR [21]) are examples of an ad hoc network technology which could benefit from such local certificates.

9.4.3 Distributed registration/certificate data preparation

User registration is an important element in most PKI architectures. In many PKIs the registration of users (where an individual has to verify their identity, usually in person) is commonly carried out by a Registration Authority (RA), which is a separate entity to the CA. The two main reasons for separating the functionality into a CA and RA are: running a CA often involves specialist technical and security expertise; the decision to register an individual within a PKI, and hence the corporate security infrastructure, is usually a business decision, not a technical decision. This separation of duties often leads to the CA being hosted by a specialist security service provider, with the registration being carried out at the client organisation's site.

We believe that CA-applets can deliver extra functionality to the resulting link between the CA and RA. By using an SEE, we are making use of hardware protection for what is an important link in the certification process. In addition, the security of this link is under the direct control of the technical specialists, that is, the CA. For example, the confirmation of a registration could be signed locally by the CA-applet, before the certification request is transmitted to the CA for the generation of a new certificate. Assuming that the client trusts the SEE and download protocol, a CA-applet potentially allows the CA to have more control over the security setup of the CA–RA link. This would allow the RA to concentrate on the actual registration process.

As well as helping secure the link between the CA and RA, we believe that the use of CA-applets could help with certificate data preparation. In the case where signature generation at the CA becomes a performance bottleneck, it is always possible to purchase more signature generation hardware. However, we are aware of scenarios where data preparation for the certificate content was the bottleneck in certificate generation. In such cases, the nature and location of the data prior to certification can sometimes be a factor in reducing this bottleneck. We believe that using a CA-applet could allow for a partial certificate to be prepared at the RA before final transmission to the CA to complete the process. By using a CA-applet we are still making use of a protected environment for certificate generation. This could potentially alleviate some forms of throughput problems by utilising the distributed nature of many registration infrastructures.

Also, the CA-applet could, if need be, provide a subset of CA functionality in order to reduce some of the central CA's certificate maintenance tasks. For example, any changes to certificate content could primarily be handled at the RA before being transmitted to the CA for final validation. Such techniques could allow a system to be designed such that the CA would be off-line for longer periods of time, hence reducing the exposure to attack.

9.4.4   Short-lived certificates

Short-lived certificates are (unsurprisingly) certificates whose validity period is very short – sometimes measured in hours or minutes. These certificates are supplied without any kind of framework in place to tell the user if a certificate has been revoked. Instead, the relying party accepts the risk that a certificate may be issued for a public key which has been revoked. However, the relying party is assured that the public key can only be used in an unauthorised manner for a very short period of time.

The main problem associated with traditional implementations of short-lived certificates is that they require the CA to continually re-certify public keys – the shorter the window available to an attacker to abuse a revoked public key, the more frequently the CA is forced to re-certify public keys.

A distributed CA could help mitigate some of the problems associated with using short-lived certificates without severely compromising security. The use of a CA-applet would remove the need for the central CA to continually re-certify public keys, allowing the user's own machine to perform the re-certification calculations. As the CA-applet would only be issuing certificates that are valid for short periods of time, the central CA is given the option of only certifying the private signing keys held by the CA-applet for a short period of time too, thus minimising the dangers involved with a compromised CA-applet.

9.4.5   Lightweight PKI

The cost of building a PKI is one of the factors contributing to the relatively small uptake of PKI within industry. Installing the hardware required to meet the demands of running a fast and consistently online service only adds to the costs. We believe that, in certain scenarios, use of CA-applets could provide a more lightweight PKI which reduces the cost of implementing an infrastructure. In addition, this could allow PKIs to be deployed in environments where traditional PKIs are ineffective.

We believe that making use of CA-applets to distribute CA functionality can provide the benefits of asymmetric cryptography without having to build the heavyweight infrastructure traditionally associated with PKI. We have seen examples where more lightweight infrastructures are used in practice for security services such as key distribution. In some examples this has been used effectively to replace physical couriers. Such infrastructures often use hardware security modules to provide a secure environment. It is our belief that extending such practices to SEEs, as they become more common in the future, could widen the areas in which a PKI is considered to be a solution.

We believe that services which do not relate to the security of a user within a system are best placed to make use of a lightweight PKI. A large part of providing the 'bells and whistles' in a PKI can be attributed to user registration and maintenance within the PKI. If, for example, the PKI was used to support end-to-end key setup for link encryption, we believe that using a CA-applet could significantly reduce the cost of implementation.

As SEEs become more prevalent, this would allow us to use the SEE to provide a distributed means of bootstrapping a PKI that was tailored to a very specific task.

9.4.6 Supporting web services

Secure web services [22,23] are reliant on the use of a PKI. For Internet applications, there is unlikely to be the support of a wide-scale PKI. Certificate usage in the Internet is primarily limited to server-side SSL certificates. The lack of a PKI from which a client can make use of an identity certificate is likely to hamper the deployment of secure web services.

We believe that delivering CA-applets to the client's SEE can allow a limited extension of the server's security domain to the client's machine. This technique would allow the server to calculate the risk associated with the transaction supported by the web services and tailor the CA-applet's functionality accordingly.[9] This effectively allows the client to self-certify within the server's security domain, albeit with a very limited scope. Thus, the CA-applet furnishes us with a simple means of supporting secure services from the server's end.

This provides us with a more closed security model, where the service accepting the risk is acting as CA and relying party in the same transaction model. This method of closing the loop by reducing the number of players in a transaction can be seen in the new BACSTEL-IP system [24]. Similar methods to this are also discussed in Gutmann's assessment of PKIs [25].

---

[9] However, we do realise that we are replacing one assumption with another, namely, we are replacing a requirement for a wide-scale PKI with the verification of the client's SEE. We believe that, in the long run, the means by which SEEs are verified will be more generic and should provide a simple baseline security service based on the functionality of the platform. This would then allow the security services specific to clients and web services to be bootstrapped with increased assurance.

9.4.7 Multiple CAs

The use of multiple CAs has been proposed to solve certain problems in dynamically evolving networks [12]. In particular, their use has been proposed to solve problems related to the compromise of a CA and to ensure that a CA service is 'always-on'. However, the dynamic nature of the network may mean that it is difficult to install a CA in the most convenient position, or that it would be most advantageous to install a CA on an untrustworthy machine.

The use of a distributed CA would allow the central CA to place one or more CA-applets in the best positions within the network in an ad hoc fashion. Furthermore, the central CA could install such an applet on any machine with a suitable SEE.

9.5 Future directions

There are several ways in which the ideas in this chapter can be extended. The obvious option is to examine other types of TTP service in order to see if they could be effectively deployed as distributed TTPs. For example, it might be interesting to investigate the possibility of distributing a timestamping service to a SEE with a tamper-proof clock. One other way in which the ideas in this chapter can be extended is to examine how to deal with the inherent problems in the distributed TTP architecture. Of these, the biggest problem is probably the synchronicity problem associated with using multiple TTPs.

9.5.1 Multiple TTPs

At several points in this chapter we have suggested that using multiple TTPs or TTP-applets might be useful. Indeed, the idea of two or more CA-applets on different machines offering the same service is particularly attractive. It helps solve the 'always-on' problem (which is especially useful when the machines in question have limited connectivity, such as mobile phones or PDAs). It is useful when dealing with the compromise of a CA-applet and allows the ad hoc distribution of the CA service in a dynamically changing network (assuming that a CA-applet has the ability to distribute further CA-applets).

However, the use of multiple TTPs, and multiple CAs in particular, has a problem with synchronicity. In many situations the TTP-applets and the central TTP should have access to the same data (certificates, revocation lists, etc.) or the system could (potentially) be abused. Obviously, the use of a central storage facility would solve this problem but would also re-introduce many of the problems that TTP-applets are designed to avoid! Hence, for a network to effectively use multiple TTP-applets, it seems that some kind of point-to-point update protocol would have to be designed.

9.6 Conclusion

We have proposed a novel way of delegating a TTP service from a central TTP to a SEE running on a user's machine. We have shown that this may have significant advantages for some types of TTP service and, in particular, have shown that it may be a useful technique for solving some of the problems traditionally associated with CAs.

Acknowledgements

The authors would like to thank Keith Martin, Liqun Chen and Chris Mitchell for their valuable conversations and comments. Alex Dent gratefully acknowledges the funding of the EPSRC.

References

1 A. J. Menezes, P. van Oorschot, and S. Vanstone. *Handbook of Applied Cryptography*. CRC Press, Boca Raton, FL, 1997.

2 L. M. Kohnfelder. Towards a practical public-key cryptosystem, B.Sc. thesis, Department of Electrical Engineering, MIT, 1978.

3 C. Adams and S. Lloyd. *Understanding PKI: Concepts, Standards and Deployment Considerations*, 2nd edn. Addison-Wesley, Reading, MA, 2003.

4 American Bankers Association. *ANSI X9.24–2002, Retail Financial Services – Symmetric Key Management – Part 1: Using Symmetric Techniques*, 2002.

5 R. J. Anderson and M. G. Kuhn. Low cost attacks on tamper resistant devices. In B. Christianson, B. Crispo, M. Lomas, and M. Roe, eds, *Proceedings of the 5th International Workshop on Security Protocols*, *LNCS 1361*, pp. 125–136. Springer-Verlag, Berlin, April 1997.

6 M. Bond and R. J. Anderson. API level attacks on embedded systems. *IEEE Computer Magazine*, 34(10):67–75, October 2001.

7 J. S. Clulow. The design and analysis of cryptographic APIs for security devices, M.Sc. dissertation, University of Natal, Durban, South Africa, 2003.

8 The SHAMAN Project. D13: Final technical report – results, specifications and conclusions, 2002. Available from http://www.ist-shaman.org/.

9 J. Dunlop, R. Atkinson, J. Irvine, and D. Pearce. A personal distributed environment for future mobile systems. In *Proceedings of IST Mobile and Wireless Communications Summit 2003*, 2003.

10 W. Diffie, P. van Oorschot, and M. Wiener. Authentication and authenticated key exchange. *Designs, Codes and Cryptography*, 2:107–125, 1992.

11 International Organisation for Standardisation. *ISO/IEC 4th CD 18031, Information technology – Security techniques – Random bit generation*, Geneva, Switzerland, 2004.

12 C. J. Mitchell and R. Schaffelhofer. The personal PKI. In C. J. Mitchell, ed., *Security for Mobility*, pp. 35–61. The Institute of Electrical Engineers, London, 2004.

13 International Telecommunication Union. *ITU-T Recommendation X.509 (03/2000), The Directory – Public-Key and Attribute Certificate Frameworks*, 4th edn. Geneva, Switzerland, 2000.

14 International Organization for Standardization. *ISO/IEC 15945, Information technology – Security techniques – Specification of TTP services to support the application of digital signatures*, 2002.

15 M. Myers, R. Ankney, A. Malpani, S. Galperin, and C. Adams. *RFC 2560, X.509 Internet Public Key Infrastructure: Online Certificate Status Protocol – OCSP*. Internet Engineering Task Force, June 1999.

16 C. Gehrmann, K. Nyberg, and C. J. Mitchell. The personal CA – PKI for a Personal Area Network. In *Proceedings of the IST Mobile and Wireless Communication Summit 2002*, pp. 31–35, 2002.

17 H. Luo and S. Lu. Ubiquitous and robust authentication services for ad hoc wireless networks. Technical Report UCLA-CSD-TR-200030, Computer Science Department, University of California, Los Angeles, October 2000.

18 V. Varadharajan, R. Shankaran, and M. Hitchens. Security for cluster based ad hoc networks. *Computer Communications*, 27(5):488–501, 2004.

19 L. Zhou and Z. J. Haas. Securing ad hoc networks. *IEEE Network*, 13(6):24–30, 1999.

20 C. Zouridaki, B. L. Mark, K. Gaj, and R. K. Thomas. Distributed CA-based PKI for mobile ad hoc networks using elliptic curve cryptography. In S. K. Katsikas, S. Gritzalis, and J. Lopez, eds, *Proceeding of Public Key Infrastructure, First European PKI Workshop: Research and Application, EuroPKI 2004, Samos Island, Greece, June 25–26, Volume 3093 of Lecture Notes in Computer Science*, pp. 232–245. Springer-Verlag, Berlin, 2004.

21 J. Zavgren. NTDR mobility management protocols and procedures. In *Proceedings of the IEEE Military Communications Conference (MILCOM'97)*, November 1997.

22 E. Maler, P. Mishra, and R. Philpott (eds). Assertions and protocols for the oasis security assertion markup language. Available from `http://www.oasis-open.org/committees/security/`, OASIS Committee Specification, 2003.

23 Web Services Security X.509 Certificate Token Profile. OASIS Standard 200401, March 2004. `http://docs.oasis-open.org/wss/2004/01/oasis-200401-wss-x509-token-profile-1.0`.

24 `http://www.bacstel-ip.com/`.

25 P. Gutmann. PKI: it's not dead, just resting. *IEEE Computer*, 35(8):41–49, 2002.

Chapter 10

Securing peer-to-peer networks using trusted computing

Shane Balfe, Amit D. Lakhani and Kenneth G. Paterson

10.1 Introduction

It seems likely that TCG-compliant computing platforms will become widespread over the next few years. Once one accepts that the trusted computing paradigm offers an interesting and powerful set of security features, the natural question arises: for what purposes can this technology be exploited? In this chapter, we examine the application of trusted computing to securing Peer-to-Peer (P2P) networks.

The concept of P2P networking covers a diverse set of network types, supporting a wide variety of applications. The common feature shared by almost all P2P networks is the lack of any centralised control. In this respect, P2P networks are the antithesis of the traditional client–server model. They have most famously become popular in the form of P2P file-sharing networks, providing a means of distributing (often copyrighted) material, such as music and video. Commercially oriented P2P networks are now coming to the fore. Useful introductions to P2P networking can be found in References 1 and 2.

Besides availability, security issues for P2P networks have not yet been widely addressed. A major conflict arises from the perceived requirement to provide anonymity for users of P2P networks and an increasing need to provide robust access control, data integrity, confidentiality and accountability services. These services are increasingly important as P2P e-commerce emerges and as industry moves towards using P2P technology in applications. The security situation for P2P networks is made worse because, by definition, they lack any centralised authority who can vouch for identities or security parameters. Without the foundation of stable, verifiable identities, it is difficult to build any of the desired security services. In particular, pseudospoofing attacks, in which malicious parties claim multiple identities and disrupt the operation of P2P networks, are difficult to prevent. We provide an overview of the main security issues for P2P networks in Section 10.2.

In this chapter, we demonstrate how features of the TCG specification [3,4] can be employed to enhance the security of P2P networks. In particular, we show how the TCG protocols for Direct Anonymous Attestation (DAA) can be used to enforce the use of stable, platform-dependent pseudonyms and reduce pseudospoofing in P2P networks. Further, our use of DAA provides a means of building entity authentication and simple access control mechanisms. Taking this a step further, we show how runs of the DAA protocol, providing authentication of pseudonyms, can be securely linked to the establishment of secure channels with known endpoints. Such channels allow the protection of data in transit in P2P networks. We show how the cryptographic mechanisms we provide can be integrated with standard SSL and IPSec protocols. An important feature of our work emerges here: while earlier authors [5–7] have posited the potential application of trusted computing in P2P networks, we do not halt at that point. Rather, we go as far as describing the specific TCG mechanisms and commands which enable us to establish security in P2P networks.

After establishing how the basic security features can be provided by using TCG mechanisms, we go on to discuss two distinct approaches to using these mechanisms to enhance the security of P2P networks. The distinction arises from the nature of the 'root of trust' for DAA in each version.

In the first version, the root of trust for DAA is assumed to be provided by a credential issued in a controlled manner at the time of manufacture of the platform by one of a small number of platform manufacturers. This model is matched to the widespread deployment of TCG technology on end-user platforms and is most interesting when it is exploited to secure traditional P2P networks. In this context, our research has a quite unusual implication. TCG is often portrayed as a technology which has the potential to provide mechanisms to control the spread of digital content. But in our architecture, it becomes a mechanism that can be used to enhance the security of, for example, a P2P file-sharing network distributing content, some of which may be copyrighted. The security provided does not prevent a copyright owner from purchasing a TCG-compliant platform and joining the network, but it does prevent casual eavesdropping on network communications, and gives a degree of anonymity (strictly, pseudonymity) for the users. While it is still possible for copyright owners or their agents to flood the network with poor quality or bogus material through pseudospoofing, the cost of doing so quickly becomes prohibitive as this would require the use of multiple TCG-compliant platforms in order to claim multiple identities. As we shall report in Section 10.2, such attacks have been well documented as a mechanism by which the value of P2P file-sharing networks can be reduced. In addition, the originators of such material can be pseudonymously identified and barred from the network, using, for example, a reputation mechanism founded on the stable pseudonyms assured by the use of TCG mechanisms. Going further, our DAA-based access control mechanism can be used to add strict controls on who can access the network. In the limit, completely private P2P networks can be constructed, with peers restricting access to a closed group of pseudonyms.

At this point it becomes clear that there is something of a moral dimension to our work. Since the advent of Napster, the distribution of copyrighted materials via P2P networks has soared. Organisations like the RIAA have attempted to prosecute individuals alleged to be infringing their members' copyrights. If implemented, the work presented here might make this endeavour more difficult. It might even force copyright holders to engage more quickly with new business models for content distribution, an outcome that we see as being inevitable in the longer term. We do not wish to become embroiled in the debate over the rights and wrongs of copyright enforcement and copyright abuse in P2P networks. Nor do we wish to provide tools allowing paedophiles and other similarly unsavoury groups even easier access to private networking capabilities than they already have. Yet, it must be recognised that the technology exists and may soon be widespread. It seems better to examine the full range of ways in which it might be used (and abused) than just to ignore these possibilities.

The second version of our security architecture is more commercially oriented. Here, the root of trust for DAA is a company offering content or information services to customers who are willing to pay for the service. Now DAA can be used to register customers, authenticate registered customers and prevent customers sharing registrations. The accesses made by a particular customer (or rather platform) to different service providers are unlinkable because of the properties of DAA. This kind of usage of DAA has already been anticipated in a presentation given by Camenisch [8]. Our work can thus be seen as filling out the details of this approach by specifying which TCG commands need to be issued in order to register and authenticate customers. But, in addition, we present a P2P twist on this fairly routine application of TCG. We propose that registered customers can act as nodes in a P2P network for distributing the content owned by the service provider. Because of the trust properties of a TCG-compliant platform, the service provider can allow this to happen without fear of losing control of its content. At the same time, the service provider can reduce its requirements for storage and bandwidth, instead relying on peers to do this work. One potential incentive for peers to become content distributors could be a reduction in access fees; further possible incentives are discussed in Section 10.6.2. We also discuss mechanisms by which the service provider can continue to collect revenue from customers who obtain their content from network nodes rather than the service provider itself.

We close this chapter with a discussion of some of the issues and open problems raised by our work. We also point to areas which are opened up by our work and which seem ripe for further exploration.

10.2   Overview of security issues for P2P networks

10.2.1   Introduction

Before discussing the security issues, we provide a short overview of P2P networks.

There is a multitude of definitions for the concept of P2P networks in the literature. The one we prefer here is taken from [1]:

> A peer-to-peer network is a class of systems and applications that employ distributed resources to perform a critical function (usually in a decentralised manner).

Resources here could be computational power, data or network bandwidth, while critical functions could include data or information sharing, distributed computing, communications or collaborative working. Within this broad definition of P2P networks, one can include systems, such as Napster and Gnutella as well as systems less traditionally thought of as being P2P, such as eBay. While eBay itself is very much a centralised architecture, the reputation system within eBay exhibits P2P aspects, with peers contributing to the reputation of other peers.

Despite the initial and still main use for content sharing, P2P networks have come a long way in a short time and are gradually being adopted in commercial and corporate applications, such as network storage [9], content distribution, web caching [10] and application level multicast [11]. P2P networks represent something of a paradigm shift from the traditional client–server model. The P2P approach can bring many benefits: scalability, efficiency, fault resilience and, of course, reduced reliance on central servers. It is through the entities in these networks, called *peers*, that resources are replicated and shared.

10.2.2   Security issues

Whilst many aspects of P2P networks have been thoroughly researched, security within these networks still remains a challenge. It is not our intention to exhaustively review security issues for P2P networks here. Indeed, good overviews of this topic can be found in References 12 and 13. Rather, we focus on identifying some key security issues in P2P networks and pointing towards some of the approaches to solving them that have been identified in the literature.

The security architecture [14] associated with the ISO/ITU Open Systems Interconnection (OSI) reference model serves as a useful framework for assessing security issues in networks. According to Reference 14, a secure system is governed by the set of security services it provides, and the mechanisms put in place to cater for these services. The set of potential security services in Reference 14 are divided into five main classes:

- Confidentiality,
- Integrity,
- Authentication – including data origin authentication and entity authentication,
- Access Control, and
- Non-repudiation.

Additional services not explicitly included in Reference 14 could be added to this list. Accountability is an important service in networks where users are to be charged for their use of resources. Anonymity in various forms is often cited as being desirable, especially in the context of P2P networks. Anonymity can refer to obscuring all identifying information of an individual, or it can refer to making the actions of a particular individual unlinkable. Availability is sometimes considered separately from security. Since many malicious attacks on networks are directed at reducing availability for legitimate users, we explicitly include it here as a security service. However, we do not consider it in any further detail – a good summary of the issues can be found in Reference 12. Any particular network may require a combination of all, some or even none of these services.

In traditional client–server systems, users are typically identified with a user account, and platform- or system-specific controls can be applied to these accounts to provide security mechanisms. Security services, such as access control and account-ability can be implemented in this manner, with the accounts providing a form of stable identity. Other services, such as authentication and non-repudiation clearly also rely on the establishment and preservation of stable identities. Moreover, if we want to establish cryptographic keys for confidentiality and integrity of data in transit, then entity authentication of one or more of the communicating endpoints is usually necessary for security. Often, entity authentication is enabled using Trusted Third Parties (TTPs). For example, one might rely on a Public Key Infrastructure (PKI) and the certificates issued by a certificate authority, or one might use the services of a dedicated TTP as in Kerberos. Thus most (though not all) of the generic security services we might wish to provide are reliant on the provision of stable identities.

In a P2P environment, there are by definition no centrally administered accounts or TTPs who can provide assurances as to the identities of entities in the network. Instead, each peer is typically identified based on a *handle* or *pseudonym* that is selected by the peer for itself. In most P2P networks, there exists no standard registration procedures for these pseudonyms, and indeed entities can claim multiple pseudonyms, including those of other entities in the network. The use of pseudonyms provides a degree of anonymity for peers and eases discovery and routing of resource queries in P2P networks, but is clearly in conflict with the stable identities that are needed, as noted above, to provide many other security services. This problem of providing entity authentication in the face of untrusted networks of peers seems to us to be a central challenge in providing wider security services for P2P networks. Having identified this challenge, we now go on to make a more detailed examination of the security issues in P2P networks, and their relationship to the identity/authentication issue.

10.2.2.1 Authentication and pseudospoofing

Pseudospoofing, a term coined by Detweiler [15], refers to a peer creating and handling more than one pseudonym at once. Potentially, an attacker might manipu-late tens or even hundreds of pseudonyms to his advantage. An attacker might also make use of the pseudonym of an existing peer, preferably one with a good rep-utation. This type of attack has been named '*ID stealth*' in the literature [16], but we prefer the term '*pseudotheft*'. An attacker who engages in pseudospoofing or pseudotheft in a P2P network may do so in order to manipulate a reputation mecha-nism in place in that network. A peer, having gained a bad reputation, can discard the corresponding pseudonym and re-join the network with a fresh pseudonym. In on-line auction systems, a peer can use a pseudonym to generate false bids, an attack known as '*shilling*'. In general, a peer can create a number of pseudonyms, build up the reputation of one or all of the pseudonyms using the others and then make use of the now reputable pseudonyms to persuade other peers to trust him. Clearly any P2P network attempting to rely on a reputation system for building trust in peers would need to address the problems of pseudospoofing and pseudotheft. It is evident that pseudotheft can also lead to loss of confidentiality. It has been argued [17] that in any P2P system without a centralised point of trust, such attacks on identity are endemic and can never be effectively combatted.

Lest these attacks seem theoretical, let us note that there are many concrete cases citing the issue of pseudospoofing as a potential problem. We briefly discuss two examples. The reputation system used in eBay, essentially a P2P system, has constantly been under pseudospoofing attack. A particularly well-documented case is that of the philatelic frauds perpetrated by the Saratoga gang on eBay.[1] The Recording Industry Association of America (RIAA) and their agents have been accused of setting up bogus identities in order to spread poor quality music files in certain P2P file-sharing networks, notably Kazaa and networks based on Gnutella, with the alleged aim of disrupting these networks to prevent sharing of copyrighted materials.[2] These activities amount to attacks on the authenticity of resources on the networks.

The key aspect to note in the above examples is the relative ease with which peers can create, use and abuse identities. In the absence of strong registration and entity authentication procedures, it becomes hard, if not impossible, to enforce stable identities or pseudonyms. While the problem is widely recognised, research directed towards preventing pseudospoofing has been sparse, perhaps reflecting the truly decentralised nature of P2P networks. For example, the problem is discussed in Reference 16, but it is simply assumed there that identifiers are tamper-resistant. A statistical, quorum-based approach to building a PKI suitable for supporting P2P security services, including entity authentication, was proposed in Reference 18. Another important contribution to a potential solution to this problem is given by Advogato[3] where trust relationships are modelled as a directed flow graph. Trust between peers is modelled as the presence/absence of an edge in the graph and the amount of weight assigned to this edge determines how much one peer trusts another. How trustworthy a peer is in relation to the graph as a whole is calculated as the maximum flow that can be pushed from a source (trusted) peer to another peer. When a peer joins the graph it is isolated from other peers and so there is little reason to trust it.

10.2.2.2 Accountability and reputation mechanisms

In the P2P context, accountability means the ability to hold peers responsible for their actions and the resources that they share. This aids in achieving efficient utilisation of resources, discourages peers from consuming resources whilst only providing nominal resources in return (a practice widely known as free-riding) and gives peers protection against fraud.

---

[1] An interesting account of this case, 'The Saratoga Fakes', has been compiled by the Stamp Collectors Against Dodgy Sellers (SCADS) institute, http://www.scads.org/alterations/Saratoga.htm

[2] See, for example, the website http://www.riaamix.com, which jokingly hails the 'music' in these corrupted files as a new art form. Patents owned by Overpeer (http://www.overpeer.com) specifically refer to this kind of disruptive activity

[3] http://www.advogato.org

Despite these known benefits, it is hard to ensure accountability due to the inherently autonomous and transient nature of P2P networks. A peer can join and leave the network at any time. Network topologies are dynamic and it is uncommon to have a known history of all peers, nor are there any contractual obligations between peers. Most obviously, anonymity and accountability requirements are in clear opposition. Moreover, these problems are exacerbated by the lack of stable identities in P2P networks.

There are various schemes in the literature aimed at addressing the issue of accountability in P2P networks. A common approach is to use some kind of reputation mechanism to build trust in P2P entities and the resources they hold. The rationale for this approach is that knowledge that peers will consider each other's past interactions while pursuing present and future transactions constrains peer behaviour in the present, thus imposing accountability in the form of non-abuse of resources [19].

A classic example of such a reputation mechanism is the web-of-trust approach adopted in PGP [20]. Here, a user can calculate a trust level associated with another user's public key, where the calculation depends on a number of factors, including which other users are prepared to trust that key, and how well they themselves are known to the relying party. The scalability and applicability of this kind of approach for large and widely distributed P2P networks have been questioned in Reference 18, where an alternative approach based on distributed PKI was suggested. Another interesting approach, based on micropayments, was proposed in Reference 21: users are made accountable for their use of resources via micropayments. The micropayment tokens are generated through work performed by the users. The P2P network Mojo Nation[4] uses its own currency called 'mojo' to handle micropayments between peers. On the other hand, Free Haven [22] requires participants to provide storage space for other peers to use, a form of payment in kind for accessing the network.

However, we have already seen that these reputation mechanisms are open to manipulation through pseudospoofing and other attacks.

10.2.2.3 Anonymity

Anonymity in a P2P context, in its strongest sense, means that there should be no mechanisms that link peer identities, aliases, actions or responses within a network. Anonymity greatly appeals to the P2P user base because it not only offers them privacy protection, enabling facilities, such as censorship resistance and freedom of speech, but also the ability to break copyright laws or publish libellous material without fear of retribution.

Anonymity for P2P networks has been classified into four distinct categories [22] – *author anonymity* (which user created which resource), *server anonymity* (which peers store a particular resource), *reader anonymity* (which peers access which resources) and *document anonymity* (which resources or documents are stored at a given peer node). As we have already noted, the provision of these forms of anonymity conflicts with other security goals and hampers the design of strong

---

[4] http://sourceforge.net/projects/mojonation

reputation mechanisms. Moreover, providing complete anonymity usually impacts on network performance and routing [23,24]. As examples, the P2P networks Freenet[5] and Publius[6] have made efforts to provide anonymity. Freenet, in particular, encrypts data between its nodes and routes messages through other nodes. In the process, it is made difficult to determine which node is requesting data and what the data contents are. Also, peers have to contribute a portion of their disk space to the network, but peers do not know what is stored in their local data stores. These techniques are, in general, adapted from existing anonymity techniques, such as MIX networks [25,26], crowds [27] and onion routing [28].

An absence of anonymity implies a loss of privacy. Therefore present systems typically employ a middle ground whereby each peer within the network is recognised by a pseudonym. Here, the actions associated with a particular pseudonym can be linked, but there is not a strong binding between the pseudonym and an underlying peer identity.

10.2.2.4   Access control

Another security problem faced by peers within a P2P network is access control. Within a P2P environment, this would mean restricting access to authorised peers, for example, peers who have paid for the queried resources. This would certainly be desired by companies managing intellectual property and digital rights, but may also be of interest in more traditional P2P networks. The (deliberate) absence of such controls has led to widespread abuse of copyright laws and a consequent fusillade of litigation against companies making P2P-based software and individuals operating on P2P file-sharing networks. However, it is certainly not the case that access control is needed in every P2P network. A careful analysis would be required to evaluate what impact an access control mechanism would have on peer reputations. For example, a peer restricting access to queried resources may get a bad reputation with other peers. Moreover, building robust access control mechanisms once again depends on authentication: without stable identities, traditional access controls cannot be implemented. One piece of relevant research can be found in Reference 29, which proposes the distribution of the access control problem within communities of peers. These communities, in turn, are governed by a set of L1 (level 1) peers who maintain the security architecture. They authorise L2 (level 2) peers and protect access to resources within that community. However, this notion of a hierarchial P2P network runs counter to the decentralised nature of numerous P2P networks in current use.

10.2.2.5   Confidentiality and integrity

Confidentiality and integrity can be classified broadly as applying to storage (data at rest) or communications (data in transit). In the context of P2P networks, the former refers mainly to resources stored at peers, while the latter refers to transactions that occur between peers, for example, resource queries and replies, distribution of

---

[5] http://freenet.sourceforge.org
[6] http://cs1.cs.nyu.edu/waldman/publius/

reputation information and so on. Attacks on confidentiality and integrity can be achieved by a variety of means. For example, it may be possible to manipulate the routing protocols used in a P2P network so that data of interest to an attacking peer is routed via that peer.

A common method for ensuring integrity of resources in transit and at rest in P2P networks is to calculate and append MAC values or digital signatures to the resources. While an integrity service guarantees that a resource has not been altered (either in transit or while at rest), it may say little about the original source of that data. Questions of that nature can be settled using a data origin authentication service in combination with, for example, a time-stamping service. This is referred to as file authenticity in Reference 12, but we prefer the terminology of Reference 14.

Confidentiality and integrity are not often discussed in the context of P2P security. Some research and implementation has already taken place in certain networks like Groove[7] but these services are optional there. If one regards PGP as providing a secure P2P messaging system, then it provides a good example of the careful implementation of confidentiality and integrity services in a P2P context. Confidentiality and integrity are clearly fundamental to security, and we believe they are set to become more important with the emergence of commercial P2P networks. The requirement to protect valuable resources at rest and in transit is likely to outweigh the processing and management overheads associated with these services, and will be a key enabler for P2P e-commerce.

Once again, a barrier to the development and deployment of these security services for data in transit in P2P networks is the lack of stable identities. The problem is not that one cannot implement the services using well-established encryption and MAC mechanisms, but that there is little point in doing so if peers do not know with whom they are establishing communications. Otherwise, a peer may fall victim to man-in-the-middle attacks or send sensitive data to unintended recipients. Once again, authentication of peers is a vital precursor to providing security services in P2P networks.

10.2.3 Summary of security issues

Research on P2P security has covered a variety of problems and is summarised here and elsewhere [12,13]. We have identified what we believe to be a fundamental issue which must be addressed if better than trivial security is to be added to P2P networks: the lack of stable identities and the inability to provide strong authentication services, which in turn underpin the security of reputation systems, accountability, access control, confidentiality and integrity services in P2P networks. We have also seen that full anonymity in P2P networks clashes with other security services. A reasonable compromise is to work with pseudonyms, shielding the binding between on-line and 'real-world' identities, and to find methods to prevent pseudospoofing and pseudotheft attacks.

---

[7] http://www.groove.net/home/

10.3   Overview of trusted computing

10.3.1   Background

Before we move on to the main focus of this chapter, it is necessary to re-introduce certain core aspects of TCG technology. In particular, we review the mechanisms involved in integrity measurement and storage as well as that of DAA (see also Chapters 3 and 5). In the context of the TCG specification, integrity measurement and storage fall under the remit of the Root of Trust for Measurement (RTM) and the Root of Trust for Storage (RTS), respectively. These two roots of trust form the basis for the trustworthiness of a platform and are responsible for the acquisition and storage of integrity metrics within a platform. The rationale behind measuring and storing integrity-altering events is that it allows a platform to transition into any number of possible states which can be made visible to interested external parties, but the platform is unable to falsely adduce its current state.

10.3.2   TCG integrity mechanisms

Examining the TCG integrity measurement and storage mechanisms at a high level, we note two structures of particular relevance to this chapter, namely Platform Configuration Registers (PCRs) and the Stored Measurement Log (SML), alternatively referred to as the event log. In the context of a TCG-enabled platform, it is the SML that is responsible for maintaining an ordered database of integrity changing events. Each PCR has the responsibility for the maintenance of a cumulative digest of one or more of these events. The data held in a PCR, in conjunction with the relevant portion of the SML, is used as evidence to attest to a current platform state.

Each PCR is a 20-byte storage area held within a Trusted Platform Module (TPM). A PCR contains a representative digest of a number of measured values, typically consisting of embedded data or program code. The basic mechanisms of PCR usage have already been covered elsewhere in this book so we shall not dwell on them here. However, for clarity we will briefly review one aspect, as it is integral to our discussion – that of PCR updates.

PCR updates occur by appending the new event being measured to the existing value contained in the register, and then taking a SHA-1 hash of this value. This can be expressed programatically as follows:

$$PCR[n] \leftarrow \text{SHA-1}(PCR[n] \parallel \text{measured data})$$

Here n is the number of the PCR being updated. This operation is commonly referred to as extending the digest. The use of this approach guarantees that related measured values will not be discarded as the previous register value is incorporated into the new register value. It also ensures that updates to a PCR are not commulative: the order in which events occur and the measured values they contain both affect the value of the stored digest. As it is necessary to preserve the complete event histories for a particular PCR, and the specification mandates that there be at least 16 PCRs within a TPM, there is the potential for the SML to grow quite large. For this reason the SML may be stored outside the TPM in non-shielded memory.

The PCRs and the SML are intimately related. Without the representative digests contained in PCRs, the events maintained by the SML are meaningless (as there is nothing to stop someone from generating false events in the log). Without the relevant portion of the SML, a PCR digest is devoid of any meaning (as the context from which the digest was generated would be lost). Consistency between the two structures is preserved by the fact that PCRs are maintained internally to the TPM and that PCR extension operations are only permitted via TPM protected capabilities. These PCRs provide evidence of attempted tampering of the log, since the sequence of events tied to a specific PCR can be extracted from the SML, rehashed and compared to the actual value contained in the PCR. Thus, the ability to securely update PCR registers is integral to the trustworthiness of a platform.

Now that we have a better understanding of the basics of how integrity measurements are taken and stored within a trusted platform, we can move on to examine the topics of integrity reporting and attestation.

10.3.3   Platform attestation

When a verifier wishes to inspect a host platform's configuration, it may request a specific set of PCR values which, as discussed above, contain a representative digest of a sequence of events within a platform. Assurance as to the validity of a PCR value is provided by means of a signature on the register value produced by the TPM. The TPM uses the private component of a key pair called an Attestation Identity Key (AIK) to perform the signing operation. Within a TCG-conformant platform, AIK pairs are used as aliases for another key pair called the Endorsement Key (EK). There is no prescribed limit on the number of AIKs that can be used within a platform. This provides an anonymity mechanism, whereby the TPM can use different AIKs each time it signs a PCR value, making those attestations unlinkable. The reason for introducing this anonymity mechanism is that the EK uniquely identifies the platform, and possibly the owner of the platform.

The actual TCG attestation protocol is illustrated in Figure 10.1 and outlined below.

1.   A Challenger wishes to inspect one or more PCR values on a platform.
2.   A Platform agent gathers the relevant SML entries corresponding to the PCR values requested.
3.   The TPM sends the Platform agent the requested PCR values.
4.   The TPM attests to the values contained in the requested PCRs by producing a signature using a private AIK.
5.   The Platform agent assembles credentials that vouch for the TPM. The signed PCR values with their corresponding SML entries and relevant credentials are returned to the Challenger.
6.   The Challenger verifies the supplied data. The measurement digest is computed from the returned SML entries and compared with the signed PCR values. The platform credentials are evaluated and signatures checked.

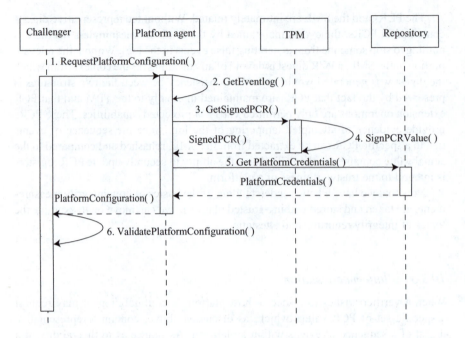

Figure 10.1   TCG attestation protocol [4, p. 9]

As shown in Figure 10.1, a Challenger obtains a portion of the SML (possibly all of it) and one or more PCR values, allowing it to confirm that the platform is indeed in a specific state by examining event sequences. The way in which a platform proves that it is in possession of the relevant credentials differs in versions 1.1 and 1.2 of the TCG specification. In version 1.1, it was envisaged that the platform would obtain a credential from a TTP known as a privacy CA. The credential would come in the form of digital certificate issued by the privacy CA on a specific AIK, with the privacy CA being aware of the binding between AIK and EK. Thus the privacy properties of the scheme would depend on the trustworthiness of the privacy CA, and, to an extent, the commercial success of trusted computing would depend on the emergence of suitable organisations offering privacy CA services. Version 1.2 still supports this privacy CA mechanism, but also introduces a new approach called DAA. DAA, the subject of the following section, uses more sophisticated cryptographic techniques to ensure the privacy of users, without introducing the requirement for special TTPS.

10.3.4   Direct anonymous attestation

We provide here a brief overview of the key features of DAA that we will use in building security for P2P networks. The full cryptographic details can be found in Reference 30, while the TCG specification [4] contains implementation specifics. We also refer the reader to Chapters 3 and 5.

Before a platform can provide attestations to a Challenger (called a *'verifier'* in Reference 30) concerning its current configuration state, it is necessary for the platform to go through a *'join phase'* where it obtains a credential from a TTP called an *'issuer'*. In practice, the part of the issuer might be played by the platform manufacturer or by a third party who wishes to offer services exploiting TCG features.

During the join phase the platform asks to become a member of the group of platforms to which credentials have been issued by that issuer. During this process, the platform proves that it has knowledge of a specific TPM-controlled, non-migratable secret value f and is authenticated to the issuer via its EK. If the issuer accepts in this step, then it provides the platform with a credential in the form of a *'Camenisch-Lysyanskaya (CL) signature'* [31] on the secret value f. It is this CL signature that will later enable the platform to convince a verifier that it has previously successfully completed the join phase with a particular issuer. Note that the issuer does not actually learn f in this process. Nor does the TPM actually store the value f – due to the limited resources available within a TPM, f is generated by the TPM every time it is needed from a seed value in conjunction with some information supplied by the issuer.

In order for a platform to obtain a credential for its secret value f, the platform must reveal a pseudonym N_I of the form ζ_I^f, where ζ_I is derived from the issuer's name and is an element of some suitable group. By maintaining a history of pseudonyms that it has seen, the issuer can check if credentials have already been issued to this TPM. The issuer can also check for rogue platforms at this stage, by testing if $N_I = \zeta_I^f$ corresponds to an f appearing on a blacklist.

Once the join phase is complete, the TPM (with the help of the platform) can use the DAA-Signing algorithm to prove to any verifier that it has an appropriate issuer credential (in the form of a CL signature), and at the same time, sign a message m using the secret value f. Here, m is typically the public component of an AIK pair, but, according to Reference 30, Section 10.4.6, it can also be an arbitrary external 160-bit string. In the former case, the output of the DAA-Signing algorithm amounts to an attestation that the TPM is in possession of a valid issuer credential and has a particular AIK. This gives the verifier a similar assurance concerning that AIK's linkage to a particular platform to that gained using the Privacy CA approach described in the previous section. In turn, this allows any PCR value signed by the particular AIK to be checked as being genuine by the verifier. Corresponding to the DAA-Signing algorithm is a DAA-Verify procedure that is executed by the verifier.

In the DAA-Signing algorithm, the platform is only identified by a pseudonym. As in the join phase, this pseudonym is of the form $N_V = \zeta^f$, where now the selection of ζ determines the anonymity properties of the attestation process. The value of the base ζ will typically be chosen by the verifier. In this case, if the verifier fixes on a choice of ζ (deriving ζ from its name, e.g.), then this will also fix the value of the pseudonym N_V used by a particular platform. This will allow all the transactions involving a particular TPM to be linked. It is worth pointing out here that the secret value f is non-migratable, so an f value should not be able to leave the confines of a TPM, and hence only the TPM that generated that value should be capable of using it. If a value of f should escape the TPM, then the blacklisting approach used during the join phase can be used, provided verifiers have access to the list of rogue f values. The value of ζ might also be selected at random by the platform for each transaction with the verifier – this would allow the platform's transactions to become completely unlinkable.

10.4   P2P pseudonymous authentication using trusted computing

In this section, we consider how the use of stable pseudonyms can be enforced in any P2P network in which each peer is TCG-enabled and has appropriate DAA credentials. In subsequent sections, we will examine how this basic property can be leveraged to provide security services in P2P networks.

The mechanism for enforcing stable pseudonyms is simple. We assume only that the P2P network has a particular name, that is, a unique identifier. The pseudonyms used in our network are strings of the form $N_P = \zeta^{f_P}$, where ζ is derived from the network name by applying a suitable hash function to produce a group element, and f_P is the secret associated with the TPM located on the peer P claiming the pseudonym.

Whenever a peer claims a particular pseudonym, the peer verifying that claim can challenge the claimant to supply a DAA signature on, say, a random message M. Later, we will see how to enable other security services by selecting M to include additional values. The verifying peer can check, using the DAA-Verify algorithm, that the claimant has a valid credential supplied by a particular issuer and can be convinced that the value f_P used in forming the claimed pseudonym N_P is the same as the one claimed at the time of credential issuance. The use of a random message M prevents replay attacks in which a rogue peer captures and replays credentials. Through these checks, the pseudonym N_P that can be claimed by peer P is fixed, and is determined as a function of the network name and the particular f_P certified during the joining phase. In summary, we have built a *pseudonymous authentication mechanism* from the DAA algorithms. Through this mechanism, peers can be authenticated by other peers, but platform identities are not revealed in the process.

To make this a workable method for enforcing stable pseudonyms, we need to ensure that a particular platform will only ever obtain one credential from one of a set of authorised issuers that are recognised by the verifying peer. Otherwise, it may be difficult to prevent a peer obtaining multiple credentials for different f values, from one or more issuers, and using these to produce multiple pseudonyms. One mechanism for ensuring that a platform can only ever obtain a single credential is to assume that an initial credential is issued to the platform in a controlled fashion at the time of manufacture. The set of authorised issuers is then the set of platform manufacturers, and the peer software can be configured to insist on seeing a credential issued by one of these manufacturers. Here, then, the manufacturers become the root of trust for DAA. This is a likely scenario in the deployment of trusted computing. We explore this situation further in Section 10.6.1. We relax the assumption about issuance of single credentials in our second model for the use of DAA in P2P networks, described in Section 10.6.2.

We now examine the extent to which our approach prevents pseudospoofing and pseudotheft attacks. We note that, if our condition on credential issuance is met, then a peer cannot claim multiple pseudonyms. Nor can a peer claim the pseudonym of another peer. Thus these attacks, so destructive in P2P networks, are prevented. The usual blacklisting mechanisms can be used by peers to detect the use of a rogue TPM, provided the relevant information can be distributed and kept up-to-date. Of course, nothing in our approach prevents an attacker from purchasing multiple TCG-compliant platforms and using these to create multiple pseudonyms. However, this kind of attack has an economic cost for the attacker.

It is clear that, by enforcing the use of pesudonyms, a given peer's actions on the network become linkable, so our approach does not offer a full level of anonymity. We have already established that this is necessary if other security services are required. Moreover, the use of DAA never reveals the platform identity (in the form of the EK) to verifying parties, so the peer's actions cannot be linked to a particular TPM. Notice too that the pseudonym used during the join phase is different from that revealed during DAA-Signing (because $\zeta_I \neq \zeta$ in general). Thus the pseudonyms do shield the actions of a peer effectively. We also note that the pseudonyms we propose for use do not relate to particular individuals; rather they are linked to particular platforms (more precisely, TPMs).

A given peer may wish to operate in more than one P2P network. Because of the use of the network name in determining the value of ζ used to form pseudonyms, we obtain the nice feature that a peer's actions in different networks will remain unlinkable.

Finally, we note that a somewhat less attractive authentication mechanism can be built using the legacy privacy CA approach. The idea is to extend PCRs using nonces exchanged between peers as measured data. The PCRs can be signed using AIKs, which are in turn signed by the privacy CA. The signed nonces can be exchanged by interleaving two runs of the TCG attestation protocol. We omit the details since they are closely related to the techniques introduced in the next section.

10.5   Securing P2P networks using trusted computing

In this section we will demonstrate how a range of security services can be built from our DAA-enabled authentication mechanism and the stable pseudonyms which it enforces.

10.5.1   Access control and accountability

As outlined in Section 10.2.2.2, access control is particularly problematic in large unrestricted P2P networks. Given the above authentication mechanism built from TCG mechanisms, it would be trivial to implement a simple access control mechanism based on access control lists. In this case, an access decision could be made based on the peer pseudonym presented to (and verified by) the peer granting access to resources. Clearly a more sophisticated and application-dependent access control system could be implemented on top of the stable pseudonyms.

As we have reported in Section 10.2.2.2, accountability and robust reputation models are hard to build in the presence of pseudospoofing and pseudotheft. Now that we have the ability to enforce stable pseudonyms in a P2P network, it becomes possible to build robust reputation systems that will not be undermined by pseudospoofing and pseudotheft attacks. Such a reputation system provides a means to hold each peer accountable for its actions. We note that the deployment of reputation systems seems to be a necessary precursor for the development of P2P e-commerce as envisioned in Reference 18. The description of specific reputation systems is beyond the scope of this chapter.

10.5.2   *Authenticated key establishment and secure channels*

Whilst authentication (even at the level of pseudonyms) is a very useful service to provide in a P2P network, its usefulness is limited if it cannot be extended to provide protection for an entire communication session between peers. We address this next, showing how our authentication mechanism can be extended to an authenticated key establishment protocol. From there, it is a short step to integrating our DAA-based mechanisms with SSL and IPSec, these being two widely used existing methods for providing secure channels for communicating entities.

10.5.2.1   Two generic approaches

Suppose we have two peers P and Q, with pseudonyms N_P and N_Q, in a particular P2P network. We assume these peers wish to authenticate one another[8] and establish keying material for protecting further communications.

In the simplest form of our approach, the peers exchange random nonces R_P, R_Q, ephemeral Diffie–Hellman values g^{x_P}, g^{x_Q} (where g is a generator of a suitable group negotiated in advance or by peer software configuration) and signatures on the 160-bit hash[9] of the message

$$M = N_P \| N_Q \| R_P \| R_Q \| g^{x_P} \| g^{x_Q}$$

The signatures are obtained by each peer using their TPM and platform to execute the DAA-Signing algorithm on the hash of M. Using the DAA-Verify algorithm, each peer can check that the other has a valid credential supplied by a particular issuer and can be convinced that the values f_P, f_Q used in forming the claimed pseudonyms N_P, N_Q are the same as those claimed at the time of credential issuance. Here, we are essentially re-using the pseudonymous authentication mechanism from Section 10.4, but with M made up of a longer string including pseudonyms, nonces and Diffie–Hellman values. If both signatures are confirmed by DAA-Verify, then the parties can safely compute common secret keying material $K = g^{x_P x_Q}$, and then derive keys for MAC and symmetric encryption algorithms from K.

---

[8] The authentication need not be mutual, and the alterations to our methods needed in this case are trivial.

[9] The TCG specification limits externally generated messages that are to be DAA signed to be at most 160 bits in length.

Here, we have used the facility that a platform can ask the TPM for the DAA signature on any message M. However the TPM may be configured to only execute DAA-Signing on AIKs. If this is the case, we can use an alternative (but slightly less efficient) approach involving PCRs and AIKs. Each peer can use the string $M = N_P \| N_Q \| R_P \| R_Q \| g^{x_P} \| g^{x_Q}$ as measured data to extend a PCR, using the process outlined in Section 10.3.2. Then each peer can request its TPM to produce an attestation to the PCR value, which takes the form of a signature on the PCR value produced using the private component of the peer's AIK. Next, at each peer, the DAA-Signing algorithm can be used to sign the peer's AIK. Finally, the peers can exchange the DAA signatures on their AIKs and the AIK signatures on the string M. Checking these signatures provides the necessary authentication for the Diffie–Hellman key exchange. This approach can be realised in practice by first extending the PCRs and then interleaving two runs of the TCG attestation protocol outlined in Section 10.3.3.

We now go on to investigate a third approach, better suited to integration with existing secure protocol suites, in Section 10.5.2.2. After that, we examine which specific TCG commands are needed to implement our ideas.

10.5.2.2 Integration with SSL/TLS and IPSec

We have outlined two mechanisms by which DAA can be bootstrapped to build secure communications between pseudonymously authenticated endpoints. Our motivation here is to build on existing protocols to achieve the same aim, still using DAA and attestation of PCRs as a basis for authentication, but re-using protocol components where possible. We focus on SSL/TLS and IPSec as starting points.

SSL/TLS [32] is a protocol suite running on top of TCP and providing a reliable, end-to-end secure communications service. Traditionally, entities engage in the SSL/TLS Handshake Protocol to establish keying material and authenticate. This keying material is then used in the SSL/TLS Record Layer Protocol for data integrity protection and encryption. SSL/TLS supports a wide variety of key exchange methods, including both anonymous and ephemeral Diffie–Hellman exchanges, supported by digital signatures, as well as key establishment based on RSA public key encryption. Both unilateral (server to client) and mutual authentication are allowed.

Either one or both parties in SSL/TLS will have a key pair that is used in the Handshake Protocol. Validity of these public keys is ensured through the verification of X.509 certificate chains back to a trusted root. We show how to replace this process with pseudonymous authentication in a TCG-enabled P2P architecture. The main idea, once again, is to extend a PCR, this time using the public key(s) as measured data. By signing the extended PCR using an AIK, and then signing the AIK using the DAA-Signing algorithm, a chain of signatures extending from the SSL/TLS public key(s) to the DAA issuer's public key can be constructed. Thus, in this approach, the SSL/TLS root CA would be represented by the issuer of DAA credentials.

One complexity here is that at least one of the signatures in this chain is not of the type traditionally seen in SSL/TLS, namely the Camenisch–Lysyanskaya signature representing the issuer credential. Another complexity is that the chain of signatures is not arranged in a neat X.509 certificate chain. For this reason, it may be simpler to just use self-signed X.509 certificates in the SSL/TLS Handshake Protocol and follow this protocol run with a second phase comprising an exchange of DAA credentials and PCR attestations using two runs of the TCG attestation protocol. Ciphersuite negotiation in SSL/TLS would determine which keys needed to be incorporated into PCRs in the TCG attestation protocol. Nonces exchanged in the SSL/TLS Handshake Protocol should be included as part of the measured data in the PCR extension step to bind the SSL/TLS key exchange and pseudonymous authentication steps.

This approach is sufficiently flexible to support any of the SSL/TLS standard key exchange methods. As options, the issuer names in the self-signed certificates could be the peer pseudonyms N_P, N_Q and the subject name field could be a meaningful handle that the peer (user) wished to be known as on the network. This last option would help to address the issue of associating a meaningful name with a platform's pseudonym, an issue we will return to in Section 10.7.1.2. All of this could be made transparent to the users in the same way that SSL/TLS hides the intricacies of its protocol in web browsers today.

Using similar ideas, we can also build on the IKE protocols within IPSec, as specified in Reference 33, to establish secure channels between peers. Further traffic between peers can then be protected using IPSec's AH and ESP protocols in appropriate combinations. In the simplest version, we can use either of the generic key exchange mechanisms from Section 10.5.2.1 to establish a shared key, then use the shared key version of IKE Phase 1 to establish a secure ISAKMP channel over which further Security Associations can be exchanged. Alternatively, any of the IKE Phase 1 versions using public key techniques can also be supported. We can use the technique of extending PCRs, with measured data being replaced by the relevant public keys, followed by TCG attestations, to establish authenticated public keys at the communicating endpoints. This can then be followed by the appropriate version of IKE Phase 1, again using self-signed certificates to simplify certificate processing, and using DAA pseudonyms N_P and N_Q as initiator and responder identities. After this, IKE Phase 2 can be used to establish multiple further SAs containing keys for use in AH and ESP protocols between the peers.

Some care needs to be taken with these approaches to ensure that the IKE and TCG attestation protocol runs are bound in an appropriate cryptographic manner. We also have not sought to optimise the protocols to any great degree. Much scope remains for developing these ideas further.

10.5.2.3   Implementation

In order to make our proposals for TCG-based authentication, access control and secure channel establishment mechanisms as concrete as possible, we give here an indication of the specific TCG commands that are needed to implement our ideas.

In order to understand the mechanisms for extending a PCR register we need to examine the event-logging mechanism for trusted computing in greater detail.

We will base our discussions on the assumption that our P2P application is running on a TCG-conformant platform. The general principles and commands discussed here are transferable to any TCG-enabled device. As we mentioned previously, the SML is not really a log. It is better to envisage it as an array of events in which each entry is in the form of a TSS_PCR_EVENT structure [3, p. 3]. In a TCG-enabled device it is a TSS_PCR_EVENT that provides information regarding individual PCR extension events. The rgbEvent parameter in a TSS_PCR_EVENT is the one we are interested in, as it is a pointer to event information data, in our case a string formed from cryptographic parameters. It is the TCS (TCG Core Services) Event Log services that are responsible for maintaining the SML. These services are responsible for allowing PCR extension events to be logged and allowing challengers interested in these events access to them.

To incorporate an event into a PCR two things must happen. A call to the TPM_Extend command [34, p. 114] is needed. This is the command that is responsible for extending the PCR. Then an additional call to a function, such as Tcsi_LogPcrEvent is needed. This function is responsible for adding the new event to the end of the array associated with a named PCR [3, p. 230]. When a challenger wishes to verify a system by examining one or more PCRs (as indicated in step 1 of the TCG attestation protocol) the platform must perform a number of operations to satisfy this request. A call to Tcsi_GetPcrEventsByPcr returns an event log of all events in the SML that are bound to a single PCR [3, p. 234]; this can be called multiple times depending on the number of requested PCR values. The event log is returned as an ordered sequence of TSS_PCR_EVENT structures. Attestation of the chosen PCR values occurs after a call to TPM_Quote [34, p. 116]. This operation is responsible for providing cryptographic reporting of PCR values, using an AIK to sign the current value of a chosen PCR.

The TPM_DAA_JOIN command [35, p. 129] is responsible for obtaining the issuer's CL signature on the DAA secret f, while the TPM_DAA_SIGN command [35, p. 131] is responsible for running the DAA-Signing algorithm and, through this, proving that the TPM in question does indeed possess valid credentials. By performing the TPM_DAA_SIGN command upon the AIK used in the TPM_Quote command, a TPM can prove to the verifier that it is in possession of the private component of the AIK that was used to sign a requested PCR value.

10.6 Two approaches to securing P2P networks using trusted computing

In this section, we investigate further the application of TCG functionality (particularly DAA) to securing P2P networks. We consider two distinct approaches here. In the first, we consider augmenting the security of today's 'anarchic' P2P networks by exploiting the presence of manufacturer-issued DAA credentials. The second is more tuned to existing commercial services for distributing content, but we sketch how secure P2P features can be added to these networks, giving potentially significant benefits to service providers.

10.6.1   Securing anarchic P2P networks using trusted computing

As we have seen in the previous sections, DAA can form the basis for a number of security services in P2P networks in which peers are equipped with TCG-compliant platforms. Foremost amongst these services is pseudonymous authentication, from which other useful services (access control, reputation mechanisms, secure communications) can be built.

To achieve this, we have made the single, but vital, assumption that, in any given P2P network, the TPMs embedded in peers are guaranteed to only possess a DAA credential from one of a set of isuers that will be recognised and accepted by other peers. We stress that there can be many issuers of DAA credentials for the platforms in our P2P network, but we need to be sure that each platform has only one credential from one of these issuers, and not multiple credentials from a single issuer or single credentials from each of multiple issuers. Otherwise, misbehaving peers will be able to create and prove possession of multiple pseudonyms.

As discussed above, one way of ensuring this assumption holds is to assume that manufacturers will provide DAA issuer functionality for the platforms that they produce. This seems to be an attractive supposition, since, in reality, customers would gain a privacy advantage if they were to obtain their credentials from their original equipment manufacturer. Either the DAA credential could be embedded into the platform at the time it is shipped to the customer, or it could be obtained at a later stage through a run of the join protocol. A manufacturer can keep track of which EKs it has injected into the TPMs that it has produced and which EKs it has already issued credentials to. Since during the join protocol a TPM is authenticated with respect to its EK, the issuer can be sure that it is dealing with a given TPM that it has manufactured and not previously issued a credential to.

If this situation holds, then we can configure our P2P software with a list of manufacturers' public keys used for issuing credentials (much in the same way that SSL is usually configured with a list of root public keys). Alternatively, manufacturers may choose to obtain certificates for their public keys from other certification authorities, in which case some form of PKI would be involved. Here we are assuming that the number of manufacturers of TCG-enabled platforms would be a small and relatively static group. This would allow an owner of a platform created by one manufacturer to transparently verify a DAA signature from a platform assembled by a different manufacturer while maintaining a high level of confidence in the authenticity of the end platform.

The obvious question is what does this mean for P2P computing? The traditional view of P2P networking is that it is an all-you-can-eat buffet of file sharing, where content flows as fast as connection bandwidth permits. At the same time, it is a commonly held belief that trusted computing represents a threat to this free-for-all as a tool for enabling Digital Rights Management (DRM). However, our analysis shows that the opposite may be the case. If TCG-compliant platforms become prevalent on end-user systems, then the techniques developed here will make it expensive for copyright holders or their agents to engage in pseudospoofing and the flooding of networks with poor-quality content. With the development of suitable reputation mechanisms, the reputations of the offending peers would rapidly decline and they could be barred altogether. Our techniques will also enable users of P2P networks to maintain secure end-to-end communications, immune from monitoring by Internet Service Providers or other entities. This could significantly hamper the prosecution of individuals operating illegally on P2P networks. Using simple access control lists based on pseudonyms, small groups could set up completely private, access-controlled subgroups within a given P2P network. Users could form their own groups based on content of choice or personal preferences, and so an existing P2P network could be utilised to bootstrap multiple private P2P networks. There is naturally the danger of such a feature being abused by certain groups. It would be difficult to prevent the formation of such groups, given that any platform can act as an issuer (and not just manufacturers).

10.6.2   Securing commercial P2P networks using trusted computing

There is an alternative model to the one presented above which is more commercially orientated in application. In this model we reposition the root of trust from the platform manufacturer to a service/content provider. The security measures that we present here are not intended to provide a solution to all the possible problems that may be potentially encountered in a real-world setting, but they do address some of these issues, such as discouraging bad behaviour by peers.

We will begin by sketching a relatively simple example using a fictional application herein referred to as TrustedPeer. In this example we also make use of a fictional TTP named ContentCorp. In our scenario ContentCorp provides both the TrustedPeer application as well as acting as an issuer of DAA credentials.

Peers download the application from a ContentCorp server and install it on their TCG-enabled device. In order for a peer to become a member of the network, it must register with ContentCorp. DAA can be used for the registration. A successful run of the join phase provides a peer with a credential in the form of a CL signature on its secret value f (as in Section 10.3.4). This credential can later be used by the peer to authenticate itself to the service provider and to other peers through the DAA-Signing protocol. Thus this credential effectively becomes proof of registration.

During this registration procedure the platform must reveal a pseudonym $N_I = \zeta_I^f$. Here the quantity ζ_I is set by ContentCorp and allows them to associate a 'handle' with a peer as well as to check for rogue platforms. The handle may be used later by ContentCorp, for example, at the stage of collecting payment for access (in which case, it may be necessary to collect additional payment details at the time of registration). Once this stage is complete a peer can gain access to the TrustedPeer network.

So far, the approach we have described is broadly similar to a TCG application scenario described in Reference 8: we have a centralised infrastructure, making content available to subscribing peers. The benefits this approach offers are twofold. The benefit to service providers is that only platforms that have a credential issued by them, that is, that are registered, will be permitted access to the network and its content. It benefits registered participants insofar as other platforms will not be able to impersonate them and gain access to content that they have paid for.

This type of content distribution application could start to evolve into a more decentralised P2P architecture by allowing peers to obtain content from other peers as the content spreads out from ContentCorp to subscribing peers. In this scenario a peer looking for specific content sends out a query onto the network, receives a list of matching hits, examines them for relevance and then decides which peer to use to download the required content. In order that peers can distinguish genuine ContentCorp content from rogue content, ContentCorp could digitally sign their content and embed their public key in the TrustedPeer application. As more and more content becomes distributed, query results for content could start to be returned by other peers on the network, thus reducing the load at ContentCorp servers.

The TrustedPeer application could be configured to demand that the requesting peer provide a proof (in the form of a CL signature) that it is a peer registered with ContentCorp before supplying the requested content. It could be further configured to supply the requesting peer with the content in an encrypted form, with the session key used for encryption further encrypted under ContentCorp's public key, perhaps along with the responding peer's pseudonym and some metadata describing the content. It would then be incumbent on the requesting peer to contact the ContentCorp server to obtain the session key, at which point ContentCorp could collect payment for the content. Here, the communication with ContentCorp would involve only short messages and low bandwidth rather than the high bandwidth required for content distribution. Further, ContentCorp would have visibility of which peers were supplying content, and those peers could perhaps be rewarded appropriately (perhaps with reduced fees for subsequent downloads). Thus ContentCorp could generate revenue from its content without being directly involved in its distribution.

This approach could be further enhanced by adding a reputation system, enabling peers to search out peers with fast connections or rich content. Building on the stable pseudonyms that are enforced by the DAA protocols, such a mechanism would naturally resist pseudospoofing and pseudotheft attacks. ContentCorp could also keep state regarding which EKs have already been registered in order to prevent multi-credentialised platforms joining the network.

One important issue that remains to be addressed is the prevention of 'leakage' of content from the ContentCorp network. There is nothing in our system as described so far that prevents a peer registering, obtaining content and then re-distributing it on traditional, anarchic P2P networks. There is a form of economic incentive to prevent this activity: a peer, having paid for the content, may be less likely to distribute it freely to others. Moreover, a peer who knows that ContentCorp will give him credit of some kind if other peers download content from him is more likely to conform and use the encrypted session key mechanism that we have described above. In turn, this forces peers wishing to obtain content to pay ContentCorp for it.

A technical measure that could further discourage unrestricted re-distribution of content would be to use watermarking, marking content with the requesting user's DAA pseudonym before distribution. In the event that a peer offers content from the TrustedPeer network on another network, then the peer could be identified via the watermark and potentially permanently banned from the TrustedPeer network. Of course, there is the problem of 'watermark handoff' in the case where peers themselves become responsible for distributing content: if peer A sends content X to peer B then the watermark on content X would need to be changed from ζ^{f_A} to ζ^{f_B}.

A far stronger mechanism would be to rely on the ability of a TCG-enabled platform to lock availability of content to particular software configurations: with this in place, ContentCorp could be assured that the correctly behaving TrustedPeer application is in operation before content is available at a peer. This would limit a rogue peer's ability to re-distribute content. However, this kind of mechanism would depend on the extension of the domain of control of TCG from the OS level to applications themselves. This is certainly something we expect to see in the years ahead. (We emphasise that none of the other security techniques built from TCG that we have outlined in this chapter require that kind of control.)

10.7 Issues and open problems

We briefly summarise some issues with our approach to securing P2P networks using trusted computing. We also highlight some open problems and areas suitable for further development.

10.7.1 Issues

10.7.1.1 Credential replacement

Replacement of credentials is a non-trivial task in DAA. If it is necessary to issue replacement credentials then the previous DAA history of the platform gets erased, at least as far as the DAA credentials from that issuer are concerned. This potentially allows a rogue to rejoin a system from which it has previously been barred. However decisions on credential replacement are a matter of policy for a given issuer. For example, an issuer can consult a black list before issuing a credential to a platform.

10.7.1.2 Data representation

Another issue in our approach to securing P2P networks is that of data representation. There is something of a semantic gap between dealing with a DAA pseudonym (a sequence of ones and zeros) and working with the more traditional 'handles' to which users of P2P networks are accustomed. One possible solution to this problem is to link a local name space with a network name. If a peer on a particular network maintains a list of pairs (ζ, ζ^f) then with each of these pairs it can associate a particular name or handle. In this scenario ζ represents the network and ζ^f a particular pseudonym on that network. This mapping would be akin to that used in SPKI/SDSI[10] but instead of using a public key for identification as in SPKI/SDSI, we would use (ζ, ζ^f). In SPKI/SDSI every principal maintains a name space where names are bound

---

[10] See, for example, http://www.ietf.org/html.charters/spki-charter.html

to values, possibly in other principal's name spaces. This kind of mechanism is suitable for use in a P2P network as it is not necessary for peers to know every other peer on a network. Instead, they need only know those peers with whom they have previously interacted or are intending to interact.

10.7.2   Open problems

10.7.2.1   Reputation

One area of our work where further development is possible is that of reputation systems for TCG-enabled P2P networks. For example, it may be possible to set up a recommendation system whereby peers pass on their experiences to other peers by sending a subset of their named handles to other peers following a SDSI naming convention. In this case peers could provide DAA-signed reference subsets based on successful interactions with other peers. It would be interesting to see various established rating schemes examined in the context of TCG-based P2P networks: it would seem that they could be far more robust than is currently the case in standard P2P networks. Given the network-based unlinkability property established in Section 10.4, developing the ability to securely transfer a peer's pre-existing reputation in one network to another seems like an interesting challenge.

10.7.2.2   Confidentiality and integrity of stored data

We have mainly concentrated on confidentiality and integrity of data *in transit* in P2P networks. A TCG-enabled platform provides *sealing* mechanisms which, in combination with attestation, can provide confidentiality and integrity for stored data. Such secure storage mechanisms could be exploited to further enhance the security of P2P networks, and it would be interesting to see further research in this area.

10.7.2.3   Anonymity

Anonymity challenges other security goals within P2P networks, such as accountability and reputation. DAA provides a certain degree of anonymity in the form of unlinkability of transactions arising from a user, but by fixing the name base (ζ) in our approach we have restricted the provision of such anonymity. However, anonymity within multiple networks is still present as long as different name bases (ζ) are used. Providing complete anonymity would bring with it problems relating to routing and discovery of resources, but it would be worthwhile continuing research in this area.

Research into P2P-based architectures has given rise to various mechanisms to achieve anonymity, for example, onion routing and MIX networks. It would be interesting to see the extent to which these mechanisms could be combined with our ideas to enhance the anonymity properties of our approach without compromising its other security properties.

10.7.2.4   Authenticity

Another issue within anarchic P2P networks is the question of how to guarantee the authenticity of resources. There has been considerable work done within the research community to establish certain measures of authenticity. In the P2P context, Daswani *et al.* [36] have proposed evaluating authenticity based on expert opinion, polls or first-serve basis. In our work, we have not identified authenticity as an important security issue in P2P networks, though we briefly touched on it in Section 10.2.2.1. Our work in Section 10.6.2 does provide an explicit authenticity mechanism, in the form of digital signatures on resources by the content provider. By preventing pseudospoofing attacks in anarchic P2P networks, our methods also go some way to ensuring resource authenticity in that less-restricted world. It would be interesting to explore further how resource authenticity could be enhanced using TCG in such networks.

10.8   Conclusions

In this chapter, we have outlined the security issues faced in P2P networks and discussed the extent to which features of the TCG specifications can be used to enhance security. All but one of our proposals for enhancing security use only those TCG features which are in place and available on platforms today. We have applied our ideas in two distinct types of P2P network: one anarchic and modelling today's file-sharing networks, and the other more commercially oriented. One perhaps counter-intuitive implication of our work is that TCG-enabled P2P networks can make P2P networks harder to effectively police. Our work also points the way forward to using TCG to enable secure P2P commerce, through the development of secured commercial P2P networks and P2P networks free from pseudospoofing and pseudotheft.

Acknowledgements

We wish to convey our thanks to Liqun Chen and Graeme Proudler of Hewlett-Packard Laboratories Bristol for answering many questions on the TCG specifications and their applications.

References

1 D. S. Milojicic, V. Kalogeraki, R. Lukose, K. Nagaraja, J. Pruyne, B. Richard, S. Rollins, and Z. Xu. Peer-to-peer computing. Technical Report HPL-2002-57, HP Labs, March 2002. Available at http://www.hpl.hp.com/techreports/2002/HPL-2002-57.html

2 A. Oram, ed. *Peer-to-Peer: Harnessing the Power of Disruptive Technologies.* O'Reilly & Associates, Inc., 2001.

3 Trusted Computing Group. TCG software stack specificiation version 1.1, 2003. Available at https://www.trustedcomputinggroup.org/downloads/specifications

4 Trusted Computing Group. TCG specification architecture overview revision 1.2, 2004. Available at `https://www.trustedcomputinggroup.org/downloads/specifications`

5 T. Garfinkel, M. Rosenblum, and D. Boneh. Flexible OS support and applications for trusted computing. In *Proceedings of the 9th USENIX Workshop on Hot Topics in Operating Systems (HOTOS-IX)*, pp. 145–150, 2003.

6 M. Kinateder and S. Pearson. A privacy-enhanced peer-to-peer reputation system. In K. Bauknecht, A. M. Tjoa, and G. Quirchmayr, eds, *Proceedings of EC-Web 2003, volume 2738 of Lecture Notes in Computer Science*, pp. 206–216, Springer-Verlag, Berlin, 2003.

7 S. E. Schechter, R. A. Greenstadt, and M. D. Smith. Trusted computing, peer-to-peer distribution and the economics of pirated entertainment. In *Proceedings of the Second Workshop on Economics and Information Security*, May 2003.

8 J. Camenisch. Direct anonymous attestation: achieving privacy in remote authentication. Talk given at Zurich Information Security Colloquium. Available at `http://www.zisc.ethz.ch/events/infseccolloquium2004`

9 J. Kubiatowicz, D. Bindel, Y. Chen, S. Czerwinski, P. Eaton, D. Geels, R. Gummadi, S. Rhea, H. Weatherspoon, W. Weimer, C. Wells, and B. Zhao. Oceanstore: an architecture for global-scale persistent storage. In *Proceedings of the 9th international Conference on Architectural Support for Programming Languages and Operating Systems (ASPLOS 2000)*, pp. 190–201, ACM Press, New York, November 2000.

10 S. Iyer, A. Rowstron, and P. Druschel. Squirrel: a decentralized peer-to-peer web cache. In *Proceedings of the 21st Annual Symposium on Principles of Distributed Computing*, pp. 213–222, ACM Press, New York, 2002.

11 M. Castro, P. Druschel, A. M. Kermarrec, and A. Rowstron. Scribe: a large-scale and decentralised application-level multicast infrastructure. *IEEE Journal on Selected Areas in Communications*, 20(8):1489–1499, 2002.

12 N. Daswani, H. Garcia-Molina, and B. Yang. Open problems in data-sharing peer-to-peer systems. In D. Calvanese, M. Lenzerini, and R. Motwani, eds, *Proceedings of the 9th International Conference on Database Theory (ICDT'03), volume 2572 of Lecture Notes in Computer Science*, pp. 1–15, Springer-Verlag, Berlin, 2003.

13 D. S. Wallach. A survey of peer-to-peer security issues. In M. Okada, B. C. Pierce, A. Scedrov, H. Tokuda, and A. Yonezawa, eds, *Proceeding of the International Symposium on Software Security – Theories and Systems (ISSS 2002), volume 2609 of Lecture Notes in Computer Science*, pp. 42–57, Springer-Verlag, Berlin, 2003.

14 *International Organisation for Standardization. Information processing systems – Open Systems Interconnection – Basic Reference Model – part 2: Security Architecture. ISO 7498–2*, ISO, Geneva, 1989.

15 L. Detweiler. The snakes of medusa – internet identity subversion, 1993. Available at `http://www.interesting-people.org/archives/interesting-people/199311/ms%g00054.html`

16 E. Damiani, S. De Capitani di Vimercati, S. Paraboschi, P. Samarati, and F. Violante. A reputation-based approach for choosing reliable resources in peer-to-peer networks. In V. Atluri, ed., *Proceedings of the 9th ACM conference on Computer and Communications Security*, pp. 207–216. ACM Press, New York, 2002.

17 J. R. Douceur. The Sybil attack. In P. Druschel, M. F. Kaashoek, and A. I. T. Rowstron, eds, *Proceedings of the 1st International Workshop on Peer-to-Peer systems, (IPTPS 2002), volume 2429 of Lecture Notes in Computer Science*, pp. 251–256, Springer-Verlag, Berlin, 2002.

18 A. Datta, M. Hauswirth, and K. Aberer. Beyond 'web of trust': enabling P2P e-commerce. In *Proceedings of the IEEE Conference on Electronic Commerce (CEC'03)*, pp. 303–312, IEEE Computer Society Press, Los Alamites, CA, June 2003.

19 P. Resnick, K. Kuwabara, R. Zeckhauser, and E. Friedman. Reputation systems. *Communications of the ACM*, 43(12):45–48, 2000.

20 P. Zimmermann. *PGP Source Code and Internals*. MIT Press, Cambridge, MA, 1995.

21 R. Dingledine, M. J. Freedman, and D. Molnar. Accountability. In A Oram, ed., *Peer-to-peer: Harnessing the Power of Disruptive Technologies* In [2], pp. 171–213, O. Relly & Associates, Inc., 2001.

22 D. Molnar, R. Dingledine, and M. J. Freedman. Free haven. In Oram ed., *Peer-to-peer: Harnessing the Power of Disruptive Technologies*, pp. 102–120, O. Reilly & Associates, Inc., 2001.

23 I. Clarke, O. Sandberg, B. Wiley, and T. W. Hong. Freenet: a distributed anonymous information storage and retrieval system. In H. Federrath, ed., *Proceedings of the International Workshop on Design Issues in Anonymity and Unobservability, volume 2009 of Lecture Notes in Computer Science*, pp. 46–66, Springer-Verlag, Berlin, 2001.

24 S. Marti and H. Garcia-Molina. Identity crisis: anonymity vs. reputation in P2P systems. In *Proceedings of the 3rd International Conference on Peer-to-Peer Computing*, pp. 134–141, IEEE Computer Society Press, Los Alamitos, CA, September 2003.

25 D. L. Chaum. Untraceable electronic mail, return addresses, and digital pseudonyms. *Communications of the ACM*, 24(2):84–88, 1981.

26 M. Rennhard and B. Plattner. Practical anonymity for the masses with Mix-networks. In *Proceedings of the IEEE 8th International Workshop on Enterprise Security (WETICE'03)*, pp. 255–260, IEEE Computer Society Press, Los Alamitos, CA, June 2003.

27 M. K. Reiter and A. D. Rubin. Crowds: anonymity for web transactions. *ACM Transactions on Information and System Security*, 1(1):66–92, 1998.

28 P. F. Syverson, D. M. Goldschlag, and M. G. Reed. Anonymous connections and onion routing. In *Proceedings of IEEE Symposium on Security and Privacy*, pp. 44–54, IEEE Press, New York, 1997.

29 P. Fenkam, S. Dustdar, E. Kirda, H. Gall, and G. Reif. Towards an access control system for mobile peer-to-peer collaborative environments. In *Proceedings of the*

IEEE 11th International Workshops on Enabling Technologies: Infrastructure for Collaborative Enterprises (*WETICE 2002*), pp. 95–101, IEEE Computer Society Press, Los Alamitos, CA, June 2002.

30 L. Chen, E. Brickell, and J. Camenisch. Direct anonymous attestation. In V. Atluri, B. Pfitzmann, and P. McDaniel, eds, *Proceedings of the 11th ACM Conference on Computer and Communications Security,* (*CCS 2004*), October 2004.

31 J. Camenisch and A. Lysyanskaya. A signature scheme with efficient protocols. In S. Cimato, C. Galdi, and G. Persiano, eds, *Proceedings of the 3rd International Conference on Security in Communication Networks,* (*SCN 2002*), *volume 2576 of Lecture Notes in Computer Science*, pp. 268–289. Springer-Verlag, Berlin, 2003.

32 T. Dierks and C. Allen. Request for Comments 2246 – The TLS Protocol Version 1.0, January 1999.

33 D. Harkins and D. Carrel. Request for Comments 2409 – The Internet Key Exchange (IKE), November 1998.

34 Trusted Computing Group. TPM main: part 3 commands, 2003. Available at `https://www.trustedcomputinggroup.org/downloads/specifications`

35 Trusted Computing Group. TPM main: part 1 design principles, 2003. Available at `https://www.trustedcomputinggroup.org/downloads/specifications`

36 N. Daswani, P. Golle, S. Marti, H. Garcia-Molina, and D. Boneh. Evaluating reputation systems for document authenticity. Technical Report, Computer Science Department, Stanford University, 2003.

Chapter 11

The future of trusted computing: an outlook

Klaus Kursawe

11.1 Applications

At the current time, the number of applications that use trusted computing (TC) is quite limited, both in volume and in scope. For now – and probably the near future as well – these applications focus on the business world, and are mainly part of large scale, integrated security solutions, such as virtual private networks (VPNs). One can expect a number of new applications that support the management of large networks, for example, to automatically verify that all machines have a proper patch level or only contain company authorised software, to maintain control over signature and encryption keys, etc. As TC technology exists on the lowest hardware level of the computer, it has to be further supported by higher-level functionality – such as the operating system – before mainstream applications can fully profit from the concept.[1] Thus, outside of such applications and those that use cryptography anyway, little use will be made of TC in the near future.

The candidate application that always did (and still does) most commonly appear in the press and various Internet discussions is the use of TC for Digital Rights Management (DRM), that is, the option to attach a policy to a piece of data and remotely enforce this policy. While research in this area is becoming rather active, the author is not aware of any attempts to use Trusted Computing Group (TCG) technology to this end on a Personal Computer (PC) platform. It is debatable if the TC concepts can significantly assist a DRM system on a PC platform without massive changes to the underlying operating system. Without some significant innovation, a DRM system using the Trusted Platform Module (TPM – see Chapter 3) will probably not be much

---

[1] In spite of the early rejection of the technology, a number of Linux variants, such as the Bear System [1], Trusted-Grub [2] and the Gentoo Linux distribution are now implementing a good level of support for TC. Nevertheless, it may take several years until full utilisation is possible.

more secure than one without (which does not mean, however, that it will not be tried).

The use of TC for the purposes of DRM may look different in consumer devices, which are significantly easier to secure than the all-purpose PC platform burdened with legacy applications. DRM will be implemented in those devices in one form or another (and already is, as for example in the CSS system for DVDs and Macromedia), and the role of TPMs in such devices is currently being discussed. For now, however, it remains open how these two issues will be connected.

11.2   Infrastructure

The specification for the TCG Software Stack (TSS) is already an order of magnitude larger than the specification for the hardware itself, and some major functionality is not even specified. Similarly, some of the TC concepts require quite significant external infrastructure, which will not be provided by the TCG itself.

For example, the concept of remote authentication (in theory) allows an entity to trust that a remote party possesses certain properties. In practice, it is not that easy – if a service provider (e.g., an online bookstore) provides the user with a log-file of the booting sequence of their server, the user still has no idea if that means they will adhere to their privacy policy. What is required is an entity who looks at the code, certifies the privacy properties and then publishes the corresponding boot sequences. Similar issues hold for private PCs. Even for a relatively homogeneous operating system such as Windows, the number of possible versions, patches or other perfectly reasonable modifications is much too large for anyone but specialised companies to manage.

It is not yet clear if the software and infrastructure needed to fully utilise the TPMs not only within organisations, but on a large scale, will ever appear. Support from the operating system vendors is limited – Microsoft is following the Next Generation Secure Computing Base (NGSCB) agenda (see Chapter 4), and thus may not be interested in supporting any features that are not directly related to NGSCB. The open source community is still slow to embrace the concept (due mostly to some early misrepresentations, but partially to some genuine possibilities of abuse). This reluctance may well slow down the development of the infrastructure as well, up to the point that one may doubt it will ever be available outside of closed networks and specialised applications.

11.3   Trusted operating systems

As long as the operating system does not provide sufficient security, both security hardware and building secure applications are only of limited use. An important aspect of TC – and one of the main goals – is to allow for secure operating systems. In the short term, TC will be used to harden the currently used operating systems. However, as this approach will reach its limits rather quickly, in the longer term we can expect to see rather fundamental changes in the operating system world.

11.3.1   Hardening existing operating systems

There are various ways in which a TPM can be used to harden a given operating system. The easiest is to use the TPM's key management facilities; any part of the operating system that relies on a secret key (e.g., the login, encrypted disk drives, etc.) can be modified to store the key in a more secure way. This is done, for example, by IBM's Embedded Security Subsystem (ESS). With the increasing availability of TC-enabled computers, those concepts will be more deeply integrated, although they will play a minor role in achieving a significantly higher level of security.

One of the real strengths of the TC concept lies in the possibility of monitoring the boot process, that is, to detect any unauthorised changes in the boot sequence. This does not help much to prevent an attack from happening, but – if properly implemented – can prevent an attacker from maintaining control over the attacked machine beyond the next reboot.

The main activity in this area is within the Linux world. For the most commonly used Linux boot-loaders, LILO and GRUB, versions that utilise the TPM are now available, and complete packages that build on top of those are nearing completion [1,3]. It can be expected that some large Linux distributors will soon include this option in their packages – for political reasons potentially only in the enterprise versions, but the consumer versions may follow eventually. So far, there is no public activity to utilise this concept for the Windows operating system (outside of NGSCB, which follows a different path). However, as the Linux boot-loaders can be used to boot Windows as well, it is possible that third-party vendors may develop a trusted boot system that verifies the integrity of a Windows computer before Windows is booted.

11.3.2   Secure operating systems

Unfortunately, even by using secure hardware, there are fundamental limits to the degree to which the commonly used operating systems can be made secure. These limits are set by design issues that are deeply embedded into the systems – for example, the presence of a large, monolithic kernel which allows third-party code to be executed in kernel mode. The Linux 2.4 Kernel has about 1.5 million lines of code; according to some estimates, average code contains approximately 1 security critical bug in 1000 lines of code. Numbers for Windows operating systems are not available, but can be assumed to be comparable.

To generate real trustworthiness, it is necessary to completely redesign the operating systems to be based on a small microkernel, such that the code base that needs to be trusted consists of only a few thousand lines of code. There are several ways to implement such a concept; in the early proposals for the NGSCB architecture, for example, it was planned to run a small microkernel-based system in parallel to the main operating system. As most research is either too far away from a mainstream product or kept confidential, it is hard to predict how the winning system will look in detail. One may argue that, independently of TC, it would have been a good idea to design operating systems that way. Unfortunately, when the basic structure of today's common PC operating systems was designed, other issues – such as performance – were considered more important. The challenge now is to design a secure operating system that is compatible with existing applications, which probably means a microkernel on top of which one or more applications, or even instances of Windows/Linux, can run. Today, several research groups at universities (e.g., Perseus [2], Xen [4] and Terra [5]) and in industry (mainly IBM and Microsoft) are putting significant effort into developing such a system on the basis of trusted hardware. It will still be several years (optimistically two, realistically more) until the first such systems will be mature enough to be actually used, but they may be one of the largest changes the PC world will see in the coming years.

11.4   Pervasive TC

11.4.1   PCs and servers

The current TCG Model assumes that all parts of a platform are located within the same physical device. While this is still mostly the case, one can – especially within large enterprise networks, but also increasingly in the area of privately used PCs – expect platforms to be increasingly broken up into independent parts. Many peripherals such as printers, storage, I/O devices or (assuming GRID computing or similar concepts also become useful for smaller-scale systems) even part of the computing power are likely to become decentralised and accessed via some sort of network. Furthermore, peripherals are becoming increasingly complex, connected and thus security critical – directly hacking a printer to access confidential documents may at some point be easier than attacking the computer that stores the documents. With respect to TC, this raises two new trust issues.

First, there will be a trust relationship between the various devices – it is not enough for the platform to be trusted to handle a document; the document owner will also need to authenticate the printer (to ensure that the printout ends up at the correct device), establish a secure channel and even attest to its correctness (as the printer could well store documents or send them out using its network connection). One can thus expect TPMs to appear in more and more peripherals, and in the long run no device may want to communicate with any other device (at least within the same organisation) that does not demonstrate its correctness.

The other aspect of the increasing distribution of computing platforms is that the concept of remote authentication may need to be extended. It may no longer be enough to attest to properties of the operating system of the platform. There is little point in trusting one platform if, for example, its screen can be attacked directly from the outside to access or manipulate its content. Depending on the scenario, it may therefore become necessary to remote-authenticate an entire network of platforms simultaneously to allow a remote entity to fully trust a system.

These issues will also raise a new management problem. While it is already quite hard to determine the security properties of an operating system by logging the boot sequence, evaluating the log-files of ten TPMs from various devices may well prove impossible unless they are all under the control of the same entity.

The most probable solution – creating a virtual TPM that authenticates not one physical platform, but a virtual entity – is already an issue, though for a different reason: each virtual machine running on a server may need a separate (virtual) TPM, which cannot be supplied by the hardware. Similarly, a virtual TPM may want to combine several physical TPMs. Given that TPMs are – by their very nature – close to the hardware of the platform, it is not entirely clear how this might be achieved.

An orthogonal approach is to let a TPM attest to abstract properties of a platform (rather than its exact configuration) [6,7]. Thus, it may be possible to abstract the remote attestation from the actual hardware to allow virtualisation of TPMs as well as transitive attestation without compromising the security gained from the hardware mechanisms.

11.4.2 Embedded trust

The current TCG Specification is largely dominated by the needs of the PC industry – currently, it is not specified how to put a TPM in any other kind of platform, even though prototypes of other devices – such as the IBM e-LAP reference design for a Linux PDA – do exist. In the near future, one can expect this to change dramatically. The above-mentioned peripherals and the TCG working groups on mobile devices are only a first step towards broadening the scope of the specification. With the increasing openness and connectivity of embedded systems, trust issues are already occurring in consumer devices (such as DVD players and TVs), the automotive industry and even household devices such as fridges.[2]

As an example, several large car manufacturers are working on systems in which cars exchange information with service providers (e.g., to feed traffic information into the navigation system and thus find the fastest route, or to pay road tax) and with each other (a car could, for example, notify following cars that it is about to brake, automatically causing them to lower their speed as well). The safety-critical nature of this data, and the absence of any human who could intervene in time, raises trust issues far larger than those we see in a PC today – one really wants to be sure it is the (unaltered) car in front that has sent the signal to slow down, and not some kids with a home-made device playing 'Traffic Jam'.

As these environments come with their own special demands and applications, they may well be the driver for future TCG specifications.

References

1 J. Marchesini, S. Smith, O. Wild, A. Barsamian, and J. Stabinerr. Open-source applications of tcpa hardware. In *Proceedings of the ACSA/ACM Annual Computer Security Applications Conference (ACSAC 2004)*, Tuscon, AZ, December 6–10, IEEE Computer Society Press, Los Alamites, CA, pp. 294–303, 2004.

[2] Although promises about smart household devices have been looming since the very start of the Internet bubble, the set of players involved and the money spent now suggests that this time it could be for real.

2   A.-R. Sadeghi, C. Stüble, and N. Pohlmann. European multilateral secure computing base – open trusted computing for you and me. *Datenschutz und Datensicherheit (DUD)*, 2004(9):548–554, 2004.

3   R. Sailer, X. Zhang, T. Jaeger, and L. van Doorn. Design and implementation of a tcg-based integrity measurement architecture. In *Proceedings of the 13th Usenix Security Symposium*, p. 223, USENIX Association, Berkely, CA, 2004.

4   P. T. Barham, B. Dragovic, K. Fraser, S. Hand, T. L. Harris, A. Ho, R. Neugebauer, I. Pratt, and A. Warfield. Xen and the art of virtualization. In *Proceedings of the 19th ACM Symposium on Operating Systems Principles*, Bolton Landing, New York, October 19–22, ACM Press, New York, 2003. In *Proceedings of the SOSP*, pp. 164–177, 2003.

5   T. Garfinkel, B. Pfaff, J. Chow, M. Rosenblum, and D. Boneh. Terra: a virtual machine-based platform for trusted computing. In *Proceedings of the SOSP*, pp. 193–206, In *Proceedings of the 19th ACM Symposium on Operating Systems Principles*, Bolton Landing, New York, October 19–22, ACM Press, New York, 2003.

6   J. Poritz, M. Schunter, E. V. Herreweghen, and M. Waidner. Property attestation – scalable and privacy-friendly security assessment of peer computers. Technical Report RZ3548, IBM, 2004.

7   A.-R. Sadeghi and C. Stüble. Property-based attestation for computing platforms: caring about policies, not mechanisms. In *Proceedings of the New Security Paradigms Workshop*, ACM Press, New York, 2004.

Index